Contents

Word Events

Word Events

Perspectives on Verbal Notation

John Lely and James Saunders

continuum

The Continuum International Publishing Group
80 Maiden Lane, New York, NY 10038
The Tower Building, 11 York Road, London SE1 7NX

www.continuumbooks.com

Library of Congress Cataloging-in-Publication Data
A catalog record for this book is available from the Library of Congress.

ISBN: PB: 978-1-4411-7310-2

Typeset by Fakenham Prepress Solutions, Fakenham, Norfolk NR21 8NN

Illustrations

Introduction

The focus of this book is verbal notation, an approach to scoring that uses the written word, as opposed to symbols, to convey information to whoever chooses to interpret it. Verbal notation has been adopted and developed in the field commonly referred to as experimental music, as well as related areas of arts practice involving performance or object making. Practitioners point to a number of advantages to this form of notation: written words are accessible to a wide range of people, including those who cannot read traditional Western music stave notation; verbal notation can express temporal relationships between elements of a composition in a flexible way; it makes associations with other writing genres, such as poetry, rule books, instructions, recipes and koans; it can express ideas with great precision; it can express generalities; it can suggest many different types of relationships between the author and reader; it can express ideas and concepts, as well as providing prescriptions for action.

The aim of this book is to present a broad range of perspectives on how and why people use verbal notation. As practitioners ourselves, our priority has been to engage at first hand with as many scores as possible, and to have dialogue with other practitioners about their experiences with this kind of notation. In general, we use 'verbal notation' and 'verbal scores' as broad terms to include what have also been called 'text scores', 'prose scores', 'word scores' and 'event scores', among other things. From Lawrence Halprin we borrow the word 'scorer', an inclusive term for anyone who makes scores, be they, for example, a composer or visual artist. Some scorers refer to their works as 'scores' or 'notations', but others may refer to 'instructions' or 'plans', and while some scorers may talk about 'performance', others may use the terms 'realisation' or 'actualisation'. In this book, our use of all these terms is dependent on the immediate context of the work at hand.

The book is in two parts. Part 1 examines the use of grammar in verbal notation, employing the model of Systemic Functional Grammar to explore how and why scorers choose to adopt particular grammatical structures in their work. The study presents some of the resources that are available to scorers who choose the English language as a notation medium. Different grammatical domains are explained in terms of their potential roles, with examples demonstrating how these domains have been used in scores. This part includes many verbal scores and refers to other works, many of which may be found in the second part of the book.

Part 2 presents a variety of perspectives on verbal notation. It is organised by scorer, with most entries comprising one or more scores, together with a statement by the scorer and/or a reflection on the work in the form of either a commentary or an interview. We have chosen these particular scores in order to exemplify some of the main characteristics of verbal notation as outlined in Part 1. Scores are presented mostly as facsimiles of the original editions, although in some cases scorers have asked for texts to be reset for this book. Some scorers have also taken the opportunity to make corrections and small changes to previously published scores. The facsimiles reveal some of the range of approaches that individual scorers have taken to design and typography.

Many of the scorers' statements focus on the role of verbal notation and their use of it as a medium. Additionally, we have chosen to include other previously published texts relating directly to verbal notation (by Brecht, Cardew, Halprin, LeWitt, Maue, Neuhaus, Ono, Satie and Young). Together, these texts represent a wide variety of attitudes and examine various issues of scoring, including the articulation of aesthetic priorities, arguments surrounding dissemination, practical considerations and compositional technique, as well as the explanation of historical and other contexts.

The commentaries and interviews provide detailed examinations of the approaches that selected scorers have taken and how the notations might be realised. We look at a scorer's choice of language and its relation to the activity of realising the score in question. We draw on comments from the scorers themselves and on observations from those who have realised the works, in order to document any preferences that a scorer may have for how a score is performed or realised, or any performance tendencies that may have arisen since the work was created.

Since many of these scores have been informed by notions of indeterminacy, their focus is not necessarily on musical ideas with a high degree of reproducibility, but rather on processes that produce potentially very different results each time they are realised. Our aim, therefore, cannot be to prescribe how these scores should be realised. Rather, we attempt to expose and describe the diversity of options and outcomes that the notations make possible.

In the commentaries we do occasionally offer our own interpretation of what appears to have been intended by the scorer. These interpretations are based on our readings of the notation, our experiences of performance and on what we have learned through dialogue with others. That said, interpretations of these notations will inevitably differ and, along with several of the practitioners in this book, we recognise the fact that there will also always be the potential for 'perverse readings', as illustrated in Alice's exchange with Humpty Dumpty:

> 'There's glory for you!'
> 'I don't know what you mean by "glory",' Alice said.
> Humpty Dumpty smiled contemptuously. 'Of course you don't – till I tell you. I meant "there's a nice knock-down argument for you!"'
> 'But "glory" doesn't mean "a nice knock-down argument",' Alice objected.
> 'When *I* use a word,' Humpty Dumpty said in rather a scornful tone, 'it means just what I choose it to mean – neither more nor less.'

'The question is,' said Alice, 'whether you *can* make words mean so many different things.'

'The question is,' said Humpty Dumpty, 'which is to be master – that's all.'[1]

---

[1] Carroll, *Through the Looking Glass*, 1992, p. 254.

Acknowledgements

The two-year research project that enabled the completion of this book was funded by the Arts and Humanities Research Council as part of their Research Grant programme. It ran from October 2008 to September 2010, based at Bath Spa University, UK.

The book would not have been possible without the help of the many contributors and we are grateful for the generous support they have given through allowing their works to be reprinted and, in many cases, creating new pieces or statements especially for this volume. There are many other people who have offered us invaluable support and advice in the course of the research, whether this has been through extended discussions and correspondence, by providing research materials, translating, advising on the work of particular scorers, or helping in negotiations with composers and artists, so we would like to thank: G. Douglas Barrett, Antoine Beuger, William Brooks, Alastair Brotchie, Gavin Bryars, Michael Budmani, Carolina Carrasco, Stephen Chase, Philip Corner, Eric km Clark, Laurence Crane, Ben Curry, Angharad Davies, Rhodri Davies, Mari Dumett, Kara Feely, Alfred M. Fischer, Ken Friedman, Harry Gilonis, Richard Glover, Kenneth Goldsmith, Pedro Gomez-Egaña, Jennie Gottshalk, Jeremy Grimshaw, Anna Halprin, Jon Hendricks, Travis Just, Matthias Kassel, Amanda Keeley, Seth Kim-Cohen, Alison Knowles, Joseph Kudirka, Laura Kuhn, Aygün Lausch, Sofia LeWitt, Sebastian Lexer, Anton Lukoszevieze, Kenneth Maue, Nicholas Melia, Antony Melville, Tim Parkinson, Tom Perchard, Michael Pisaro, Keith Potter, Lauren Pratt, Eddie Prévost, Matt Robertson, Martin Rogers, Dave Smith, Mark So, Suzanne Stephens, Harry Stendal, Ian Stonehouse, Taylan Susam, Chiyoko Szlavnics, Colin Theobald, Philip Thomas, Stefan Thut, David Toop, Markus Trunk, Carolina di Vonzo, Alex Waterman, Ulrich Wehner, Manfred Werder, John White, Michael Winter, Daniel James Wolf, Matthew Wright, Seymour Wright, Barnabas Yianni and Martin Zingsheim.

The authors and publishers would also like to thank the following for permission to reproduce additional copyright material: Artists Rights Society/VG Bild-Kunst for George Brecht's 'The Origin of "Events"', (©Artists Rights Society (ARS), New York/VG Bild-Kunst, Bonn), page 111; C. F. Peters Corporation for Cornelius Cardew's 'On the Role of the Instructions in the Interpretation of Indeterminate Music', (Copyright © 1970 by Hinrichsen Edition, Ltd. Used by permission of C. F. Peters Corporation. All rights reserved), pages 150–4; Anna Halprin for Lawrence Halprin's 'A Summary of the Characteristics of Scores', pages 200–6; Sofia LeWitt for 'Wall Drawings' and 'Doing Wall Drawings', pages 246–7; Kenneth Maue for extracts from 'Ideas Around the

Experiences', pages 279–83; The Estate of Max Neuhaus for 'LISTEN' (www.max-neuhaus.info for further information) pages 286–7; Yoko Ono for 'Record of 13 Concert Piece Performances', (© Yoko Ono 1964, 1970, Renewed 1992, 1998), pages 296–301; Antony Melville and Ornella Volta for Erik Satie's 'Performance Indications' (originally published in *A Mammal's Notebook: Collected Writings of Erik Satie*, Atlas Press) pages 330–3; La Monte Young for 'Why I Withdrew from Fluxus', pages 436–7. The authors and publishers have made every effort to trace the copyright holders for all the works reprinted, but in a few cases this has not been possible.

We are also very grateful to colleagues and students in the Music Department and Graduate School of Bath Spa University for their under-standing and advice. In particular we would like to thank the members of Material, the University's experimental music group, for trying out many of the pieces in the book.

We would like to thank David Barker at Continuum for his consistent enthusiasm for the project and acceptance of the gradually escalating scale of the book, and to Joanne Murphy, Kim Storry and Richard Crane for their patience and expertise in its production. We are grateful to Geoff Thompson for his generous assistance with the finer points of grammar, Ross Parfitt and Michael Parsons for their continued encouragement and for casting a critical eye over the manuscript, and Bridget Lely for her valued assistance with editing.

James would like to thank Becky, Florence and William for letting him close the study door on occasions and work late into the night. John would like to thank Bridget, Peter, Polly, Paul, Charlotte Webb, Mark Jackson, Jen Allum, Claire Singer, Stefan Abela, Nik Sopwith, the Millers, the archers, and especially little Elsie and Connie, fellow students of language.

Part 1: Grammar

Part I: Grammar

On the Use of Grammar in Verbal Notation

John Lely

Introduction

Grammatical choices can create very different perspectives on the world; for instance, through a change in one element of grammar, a description of an activity can be transformed into a command. Such choices have considerable implications, both for the processes that may feature in a verbal score and for how that score might be interpreted. They can also reveal a great deal about the writer's own attitude to a score, and this too may inform how a performer engages with the notation. As landscape architect Lawrence Halprin remarks:

> Nuances in scoring have great importance – often the scorer himself is not completely aware of how he is projecting himself and his own biases and preconceptions into the score.[1]

This part of the book introduces some of the grammatical resources that are available to the writer of English language verbal scores and demonstrates how various writers have employed these resources in their work. The inherent flexibility of the English language means that different grammatical structures can be used to refer to an activity in a variety of ways. The central question to consider therefore is what motivates a scorer to privilege one grammatical structure over another.

Grammars

A description of the grammar of a particular language is likely to provide an account of the rules that govern the structure of sentences in that language. This is usually achieved by identifying smaller units such as *words*, *phrases* and *clauses*, and explaining the rules for how these smaller units can

---

[1] Halprin, 1969, p. 190; and p. 200 of this book.

combine to make sentences. As well as traditional formal grammar, there are a number of other grammars available to the student of language, each with its own analytic aims and principles. For our purposes it is useful to distinguish between *prescriptive* and *descriptive* grammars.

Prescriptive grammars, such as that outlined in Gowers' *Complete Plain Words*[2] (written for civil servants), are practical writing guides, which promote what their authors consider to be 'correct' usage. They often take the form of rules or guidelines to clarify meaning and tighten up sentence structure. For example, the following are chapter titles from Wydick's *Plain English for Lawyers*,[3] a book commonly recommended as the standard guide for effective legal writing:

Omit Surplus Words.
Use Base Verbs, Not Nominalizations.
Prefer the Active Voice.
Use Short Sentences.
Arrange Your Words with Care.
Choose Your Words with Care.
Avoid Language Quirks.
Punctuate Carefully.[4]

Such grammars can raise awareness of the importance of precision in written language, but they also have their limits. Most importantly, there is disagreement over what actually constitutes 'correct' grammar and, since language use is undergoing constant adaptation, such guides may need constant revision in the light of changes.

Descriptive grammars adopt a different approach. Rather than prescribing usage, they examine and document actual patterns of usage. Central to this approach is the use of a *corpus*, a large collection of texts that supplies real-world examples. This corpus is analysed to reveal patterns of usage and provide illustrations. An example of a descriptive corpus-based approach is the *Longman Grammar of Spoken and Written English*,[5] which is based on a 40-million-word corpus made up of a wide variety of texts, and is arranged along the lines of traditional formal grammar, with detailed descriptions of how, and with what frequency, elements like nouns, verbs and adverbs occur.

There are various other descriptive grammars, including generative grammar (which is concerned with what is possible in a language, rather than what occurs) and emergent grammar (which sees grammar as emerging out of human interaction). Systemic Functional Grammar (SFG) focuses on how language is used to interpret reality, make choices and enact social relationships. SFG recognises a language as a vast network of systems, which

---

[2] Gowers, 1987.
[3] Wydick, 2005.
[4] Ibid., pp. vii–viii.
[5] Biber *et al.*, 2007.

are collectively referred to as 'the system of language', and any text created with that system is regarded as an 'instance' of the system. As Halliday and Mathiessen explain:

> A language is a resource for making meaning, and meaning resides in systemic patterns of choice [...] Structural operations – inserting elements, ordering elements and so on – are explained as *realizing* systemic choices. So when we analyse a text, we show the functional organization of its structure; and we show what meaningful choices have been made, each one seen in the context of what might have been meant but was not.[6]

The basic unit dealt with by SFG is the *clause*, with one or more clauses making up a sentence. SFG analysis is founded on 'system networks', which explain all the possibilities within a particular grammatical domain. For instance, here is a typical system network describing the primary grammatical tenses:

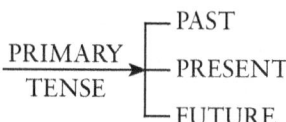

Different grammars will provide different insights into the possibilities afforded by verbal notation. As the name suggests, Systemic Functional Grammar engages with the *function* of grammatical choices, and, like language itself, it remains in constant development. Because SFG is concerned with actual usage, it is an effective tool for looking at the function of grammatical choices in verbal notation. This study therefore takes a descriptive approach, informed by elements of SFG.[7] It begins by considering the role that *context* can play in how verbal scores may be written and interpreted. There follow sections exploring the grammatical domains of *register*, *processes*, *tense*, *modality*, *mood*, *voice* and *circumstances*. Where appropriate, examples are provided from a corpus of approximately 2,500 verbal scores collected during the research.

Context

Context provides a frame within which a particular text may be understood. A lack of context can make a text confusing or ambiguous, as demonstrated by a psychological experiment carried out in the early 1970s by Bransford and Johnson. Participants in the experiment were read the following passage

---

[6] Halliday and Matthiessen, 2004, pp. 23–4.
[7] The study makes reference to SFG terminology throughout. For more detailed information about the structure of SFG, and descriptions of grammatical domains, see Halliday and Matthiessen, 2004.

and then asked to recall as much information as possible about what they had just heard:

> If the balloons popped the sound wouldn't be able to carry since everything would be too far away from the correct floor. A closed window would also prevent the sound from carrying, since most buildings tend to be well insulated. Since the whole operation depends on a steady flow of electricity, a break in the middle of the wire would also cause problems. Of course, the fellow could shout, but the human voice is not loud enough to carry that far. An additional problem is that a string could break on the instrument. Then there could be no accompaniment to the message. It is clear that the best situation would involve less distance. Then there would be fewer potential problems. With face to face contact, the least number of things could go wrong.[8]

The passage was purposely designed to be quite abstract and hard for a listener to comprehend. The participants were divided into groups: 'No Context', 'Context Before' and 'Context After'. The 'Context' took the form of a picture of the situation to which the passage referred (see Fig. 2 overleaf). This picture was only found to be useful when presented to participants before the passage was read out. From the maximum 14 'ideas' in the passage, the 'No Context' group recalled an average of 3.6 ideas, the 'Context After' group also recalled an average of 3.6 ideas, but the 'Context Before' group recalled an average of 8.0 ideas. So, we may conclude that context aids our understanding of a text, and this in turn contributes to our ability to recall information about that text more accurately.

A reason why the balloon text might be hard to understand is that it features very little *connectivity*. In interpreting a text, it is likely that a reader or listener will attempt to connect different elements to forge some kind of meaning. There are many bits of information in the balloon text, and none is introduced explicitly in connection with the others. There is a great deal of what linguists call *New* information, and very little reference to *Given* information, i.e. information provided previously within the text. Indeed, most of the New information ('the balloons', 'the sound', 'the correct floor', and so on) is first mentioned as though it has *already* been introduced, as Given information. Although the simple juxtaposition of arbitrary sentences may be enough to imply some kind of connection between them, connectivity between New and Given information is an important tool for conveying context.

Some scorers exploit this feature of language to encourage creative thinking on the part of the reader. Cornelius Cardew's *Making A* from *Schooltime Compositions* (1967) is a playful example of a verbal score in which there may not be quite enough information (see Fig. 1). By remaining somewhat aloof, and withholding contextual information, Cardew poses a

---

[8] Bransford, J. D. and Johnson, M. K., 'Considerations of Some Problems of Comprehension' in Chase, 1973, pp. 392–3.

Making A

When A in the A-gauge glass
becomes level with white line,
make more A as follows:
1. Place WET B in glass bamer.
2. Empty one pack of A into
the wet B.
3. Draw off two full measures
of hot boiling C and pour
them over the dry A in the B
(using circular motion).
4. Draw off one FULL measure
of A and repour it into B.
5. Close B between pours.
6. Never make more A if the A
in A-gauge glass is above
white line.

1 *Cornelius Cardew,* Making A, *from* Schooltime Compositions *(1967).*

challenge to the reader to deduce what properties will be required to realise the piece.[9]

There are many other things that contribute to context, including the wider social and cultural conditions surrounding the production and dissemination of a score. On the linguistic level, grammar makes an important contribution to the shaping of context, particularly in relation to the style or *register* of a text.

---

[9] For the curious, in an 'Appendix' to *Schooltime Compositions* Cardew includes a list of 'Properties required for Making A' (not printed here), which provides a would-be performer with some more clues.

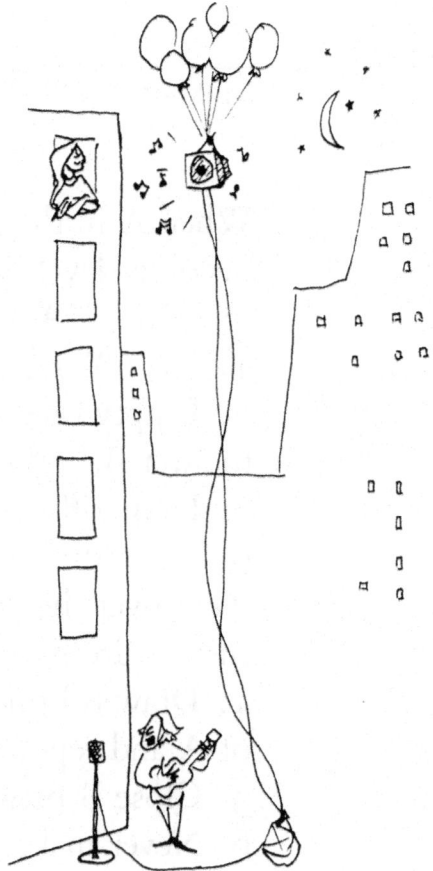

2 *The 'Context' for the balloon passage.*

Register

Register may be defined as the configuration of linguistic choices that make up a distinctive 'style' that is used in a particular context. For example, recurring fields of discourse such as scientific scholarship and newspaper journalism have developed their own quite different registers. Patterns of grammatical choices 'construe' the register, meaning that there is a two-way relationship. On the one hand, the patterns are determined by the register, e.g. a writer adopts certain patterns to conform to the register of a particular community. On the other, registers employ distinctive configurations of linguistic choices, and therefore we recognise registers by the language chosen by an individual for a particular purpose. The register of a verbal score is realised, even if unconsciously, by the scorer's choice of grammar, and as may be seen throughout this book, scorers can and do draw freely from the registers of such fields as academic writing, gastronomy, folklore, rule books, spoken conversation, and so on, each with its own distinct set of recurring grammatical features.

Michael Halliday, the developer of SFG, outlines three dimensions within the domain of register; *field* refers to the setting and purpose of the interaction (for example, instructions from composer to performer), *tenor* refers to the relationship between participants involved in the interaction (includes aspects of status, formality and emotional involvement), and *mode* refers to the medium of communication (for example, whether the text is written or spoken). Various other grammatical domains contribute to the register of a text. For instance, *mood* can affect whether the utterance is presented as an order, a statement of fact or belief, or a question; and the difference between these choices may contribute to creating a different register. The *voice* is important in clarifying who is responsible for carrying out a particular action. *Modality* realises areas such as possibility and obligation. The register is also realised by the types of *process* that feature in the text.

Prior awareness of the register of a particular text will affect how someone reads that text. The kind of knowledge that a reader brings to a text from his or her experience of other texts is often referred to as *intertextuality*. For example, aside from its references to scientific terminology, Cardew's *Making A* will likely be construed as a set of instructions because, as with some of the instructions for experiments found in scientific textbooks in schools, it is presented as a numbered list of stages and conforms to the grammatical patterns expected of such information (i.e. featuring *material* processes and being marked for the *imperative* mood).

Register enables verbal scores to function within the traditions of different *genres*. For example, some scores, such as those made by artists associated with Fluxus, adopt the registers of genres such as epigrams, aphorisms, idioms and koans. Such scores are often short enough to be passed on through word of mouth and may even be paraphrased as a result. Scandinavian folklorist and Fluxus artist Bengt af Klintberg comments on the capacity that these scores have to become part of an oral tradition:

> Examples of folklore genres are: fairy-tale, joke, riddle, singing game. We all recognize them when we meet them. This is because they conform to a set of rules or conventions, governing their form, contents and perfor-mance. The folklorists describe genre as a cognitive matrix or grammar, shared by the performer and the audience. Creations which do not conform – at least to some degree – with the matrix will fall outside the genres and never become part of an oral tradition.[10]

A scorer's choice of register may also set a precedent for how a performer approaches realising a score. The following excerpt from *Hannah Im Winter B* (1997) by Alison Knowles suggests an attitude of 'quiet scientific perusal', while the text itself is descriptive and speculative, and seems to embody something of that attitude:

> The most important aspect of this piece is the attitude of the performer, his focus on the tools and on the score. This attitude is one of quiet scien-tific perusal rather than a poetic or musicianly stance. It is as if, with the

---

[10] Klintberg, 1993, p. 120.

indulgence of the audience, the performer is uncovering the true nature of the objects or tools.[11]

Processes

The grammar of a clause gives order to the way events are articulated. In SFG, each distinct event is modelled as a type of *process*. These processes represent events like sensing, saying and doing. Each event is represented as being located in, and unfolding through, time. By systematically identifying these grammatical processes it becomes possible to observe the different ways in which events can be represented.

SFG recognises six types of process, which have evolved their own distinctive grammatical properties. The three main types are: *material* processes, which represent doings and happenings; *mental* processes, which represent our internal sensory experiences; and *relational* processes, which deal with identification and classification. On the boundaries of these main categories are three additional process types. Between material and mental processes are *behavioural* processes, representing physiological and psychological behaviour. On the border between mental and relational processes are *verbal* processes, which are clauses of saying. Finally, between relational and material processes lie *existential* processes, which are concerned with being.

It is important to note that these process types have not been imposed 'from above', but have been found through differences in the structures of the clauses that express them. However, the boundaries of these processes are somewhat indeterminate. For instance, some behavioural processes that feature verbs such as 'look', 'watch' and 'listen' may exhibit characteristics of mental processes. A verb may also take on different meanings when used to express different types of process. For instance, the verb 'read' may be used in a mental process, as in 'I read that the government has collapsed', or a behavioural process, as in 'What are you doing?' 'I'm reading.'

Material Processes

Material clauses represent processes of doing-and-happening, which bring about changes in the physical world, and can feature such verbs as 'play', 'draw', 'build' and 'pour'. They are often used for descriptions of procedures or instruction manuals. There is always an outcome to a material process, and texts that describe material procedures are typically concerned with expressing how that outcome is achieved. An example of a short instruction that represents a material process is an untitled event made by Milan Knížák in 1965,[12] consisting solely of the material clause: 'Get a cat' (see Fig. 3).

---

[11] Knowles, A. (1997) *Hannah Im Winter B*, fragment of score, in Jean Brown Archive, The Getty Research Institute.

[12] According to the artist, this untitled event is incorrectly referred to as *Cat* in some publications. This event, along with the untitled event described on p. 54, is from a series of game

3 *Milan Knížák, untitled (1965).* ▶

Get a cat.

In contrast to the Subject–Verb–Object structure of traditional formal grammar, SFG distinguishes between different types of *participants*, depending on the process. In material processes the Subject is known as the *Actor* (which may or may not be a conscious being), and the Object is known as the *Goal* (that is the person or thing to which the process is extended).

Clauses may be either *transitive* or *intransitive*. In intransitive material clauses there is only one participant, the Actor, involved in the process, e.g. 'the violinist plays', where 'the violinist' is the Actor and the only participant in the process. In transitive material clauses there is another participant, the Goal, to which the process is extended, e.g. 'the violinist plays football', where there are two participants in the process, 'the violinist' being the Actor and 'football' being the Goal.

There are two main types of material clause: *creative* and *transformative*. With a creative material clause either the Actor or the Goal comes into existence. Creative clauses may be realised with such verbs as 'create', 'prepare', 'compose', 'write', 'draw' and 'build'. In a transformative clause, either the Actor or Goal exists prior to the onset of the process, and then either the Actor or the Goal undergoes some kind of change. Transformative creative clauses can be realised with such verbs as 'adapt', 'adjust' and 'retune'.

Material clauses are very common in verbal notation and can express an enormous range of actions and events. A score may describe a process in a very simple way, but the actual realisation of that process will likely involve the performer in a complex set of interactions with other events and things in the world. La Monte Young takes this to a logical extreme in *Composition 1960 #13 to Richard Huelsenbeck* (1960): 'The performer should prepare any composition and then perform it as well as he can' (see Fig. 153, page 425). In this score the material processes are 'prepare' and 'perform', and these are supplemented with a *circumstantial* of *manner*, 'as well as he can' (see *Circumstances* section, pages 48–74). Other scores may require the performer to commit time, energy and resources to building or adapting an instrument, as with Alvin Lucier's *Music on a Long Thin Wire* (1977) (see Fig. 103, page 252) and Seth Kim-Cohen's *Forever Got Shorter* (2010) (see Fig. 91, page 212). A score may even call for a new score to be made, as with Christopher Hobbs' *125 Questions for Pianists* (1969) (see Fig. 26, page 38), Daniel James Wolf's *The Long March* (2009) (see Fig. 148, page 400) and *Danger Music #12* (1962) by Dick Higgins, which consists solely of the creative imperative, 'Write a thousand symphonies.'

A verbal score might specify only the Actor and the Goal of a material process, thus leaving significant details of how to realise that process up to the performer. One such example is Alison Knowles' *Proposition* (1962), the score of which features the single creative material clause, 'Make a salad'

pieces that Knížák wrote 'on sidewalks and walls' all over Prague in 1965. The artist explains: 'They were also printed (typed or hand written) on paper gliders [that] were used during a few actions, and also for a publication called *Paper bird book*, which in reality was just a shoebox containing about twenty paper gliders with the texts.' (Milan Knížák, in correspondence with James Saunders, October 2010.)

(see Fig. 4). In this clause 'you' are the understood Actor (see *Mood* section, pages 28–47), and 'a salad' is the Goal. The materials and circumstances of realisation remain unspecified, and this seems to be in keeping with the scorer's intentions; Knowles herself has realised *Proposition* both as a publicly staged event, leading to the creation of a salad large enough for the whole audience, and as a private activity recognised simply as 'the making of a salad', though she acknowledges that there are other potential interpretations.[13] (For a variation on this piece, see Bengt af Klintberg's *Orange Event Number 25* ('Proposition') (1963–6) (see Fig. 93, page 225), which notably features one additional material process.) Alternatively, a scorer may wish to use circumstantials to specify in more detail how a process is to be realised (see *Circumstances* section, pages 48–74).

#2 —

Proposition (October, 1962)

Make a salad.

Premiered October 21st, 1962 at Institute for Contemporary Arts in London.

4 *Alison Knowles,* Proposition *(1962).*

Mental Processes

Mental clauses represent our internal sensory experiences, which do not directly bring about changes in materials. Mental processes are very common in spoken conversation and are construed as either emerging from a person's consciousness or impinging on it. There are four types of mental processes: *perception*, *cognition*, *desire* and *emotion*. The person who does the perceiving, thinking, wanting or feeling is called the *Senser*. The *Phenomenon* is that which is perceived, thought, wanted or felt. The Phenomenon may not only be a thing but may also be an act or a fact.

Again, there are many instances of mental clauses in verbal notation. A score may ask performers to draw on their own perceptions of their surroundings in order to influence the course of a performance. Christian Wolff's *Looking North* (c. 1968–71) features processes of perception and cognition (see Fig. 5). The score uses verbs expressing cognitive mental processes, e.g. 'think', 'imagine', 'devise' and 'forget', in relation to the performer's own privately arrived at pulse, and verbs expressing perceptive mental processes when referring to the performer's awareness of external

---

[13] Alison Knowles, in interview with the author, Cambridge, MA, 27 September 2009.

Looking North

Think of, imagine, devise, a pulse, any you choose, of any design.

When you hear a sound or see a movement or smell a smell or feel any sensation not seeming to emanate from yourself, whose location in time you can sense, and its occurrence coincides, at some point, with your pulse, make your pulse evident:

in some degree; for any duration.

(a) Express all coincidences.

(b) Express only every tenth one.

(c) Forget your pulse and play as closely as you can to every second, fifth, twentieth and single expression of pulse of one other player (this can be repeated as in a loop).

(d) Play a very long, generally low pitched and quiet melody without particular reference to a pulse (once only).

(e) At any point stop.

(f) At any point stop, think of another pulse, and proceed as above.

Or: think of, imagine, devise, any number of pulses. . . and so on, as above.

5 *Christian Wolff,* Looking North *(c. 1968–71).*

phenomena, e.g. 'hear a sound', 'see a movement', 'smell a smell', 'feel any sensation', as a cue for when to make that pulse evident.

In other scores performers may be asked to learn, invent, remember or conjecture about something. For instance, in Jennifer Walshe's *THIS IS WHY PEOPLE O.D. ON PILLS/AND JUMP FROM THE GOLDEN GATE BRIDGE* (2004) the performer must 'learn to skateboard, however primitively', 'Re-learn your body's weight', 'Meditate on pressure', and so on (see Fig. 6). A performer's own desires may be brought into play, as in Cardew's *Desire* (1967) (see Fig. 7), or a score may draw on a performer's emotional response to what is occurring, as in Cardew's *Schooltime Special* (1968) (see Fig. 27, pages 39–41).

6 *Jennifer Walshe,* THIS IS WHY PEOPLE O.D. ON PILLS/AND JUMP FROM ▶
THE GOLDEN GATE BRIDGE *(2004).*

THIS IS WHY PEOPLE O.D. ON PILLS /AND JUMP FROM THE GOLDEN GATE BRIDGE

This piece is performed by 1-10 performers performing on any instruments (including voice). Each performer prepares and practices their own individual "path" according to the directions given below. The piece consists of the performance of this/these "path(s)."

If the piece is performed by a soloist, it should be a minimum duration of 5 minutes long, and is called "THIS IS WHY PEOPLE O.D. ON PILLS."

If the piece is performed by a group, the group should agree on a performance duration (minimum 10 minutes). Each member of the group's path should be a minimum duration of 5 minutes long, and a performer can begin/end their path anywhere within the chosen performance duration. A performance by a group is called "/AND JUMP FROM THE GOLDEN GATE BRIDGE."

Directions:

1. Learn to skateboard, however primitively. Re-learn your body's weight, muscles, bones, geometry, abilities, flash-points afresh. Meditate on pressure, torque, weight, movement, air, light, space, lines. Focus minutely on surface, micro-surface, bumps, cracks, debris, concrete, asphalt, granite, marble, plastic, wood; gradients, slopes, verticals, the architectural qualities of what you skate on, the "wallness of wall." See, smell, hear, feel, how your body relates to the board and through it to space. Try to learn or at least attempt a few tricks. Even if you cannot do the tricks, analyse and understand them in your head and body, the basic concepts, movements, weightings, shifts and throw involved in ollies, grinds, kickflips, aerials, backslides, boardslides, rock'n'rolls, varials (or other tricks, and combinations of any of them). Feel time compress and expand as you move in and out of these tricks, launch, rise, catch stillness, fall; spin, slide, pivot, leap.

2. Augment this experience by watching skaters, visiting skateparks, viewing skateboard photos, videos, looking at skating magazines, books, films, websites. Try to understand and absorb what you see with your body, internalizing these ways of achieving speed, height, weightlessness, skating the paths virtually with full attention.

3. Examine and meditate on optimum skating environments, either real or imagined, taking in the macro- and micro-structure of these environments. Go for a walk and imagine being able to skate everything you see – streets, roads, walls, trees, curbs, planters, slopes, gardens, bins, lamp-posts, footpaths, bushes, cars, signs, window-sills, ramps, shopping trolleys, pools, slides, bollards, roofs, benches, cows, hand-rails, fences, edges, lips, steps, drains, ditches, rims, gutters. Contemplate the ability of skate-boarding to articulate space, find new paths through architecture, fresh uses for it, notice and exploit visible/invisible relationships.

4. Compose an imaginary path you would like to skate. This path should push and force you to limits, be rich, beautiful, complicated and stylish, and incorporate some tricks. The path is limited only by your imagination. Internalise this path, skate and inhabit it in terms of body, space and time. Feel space moving around you as you articulate your lines, intersecting, crossing, glancing, spinning away, grabbing at movements and air, smells and sounds.

5. Choose a pitch on your instrument. Skate your imagined path on this pitch. (You may choose to skate the path in slow-motion.) Every micro-detail of the pitch (tuning, timbre, dynamic, envelope, consistency, colour, texture, weight, feel, pressure, clarity, strength) should correspond absolutely to the experience of skating the path in your head. Pay attention to every minute detail, the micro-cartography of the path you are skating, the tiny shifts in muscle, weight, speed, direction. Carve through air in long, sweeping paths with the sound you produce. Reveal and inhabit new spaces, smooth new lines.

MILKER
Corp. 2004

Pictures from upper left, clockwise: "skateboarding" by David Chief; "untitled" by nugunslinger; "skatepark" by Flor Hartigan; "IMG_2150 by rednuht. All used under Creative Commons Attribution Licence 2.0.

Title taken from "Weightless Again" from *Through the Trees* (1998) by The Handsome Family.

Desire

Want to do something; Do it

Do something without wanting to

Do something wanting not to

Be done to

Be done

note 1: Perform all or none of the instructions
note 2: Instructions are to be followed only by
qualified person

7 *Cornelius Cardew,* Desire, *from* Schooltime Compositions *(1967).*

Mandatory Happening

A card printed:

"You will decide to read
this score or not to read it".

When you have made your decision,
the happening is over.

1966

8 *Ken Friedman,* Mandatory Happening *(1966).*

Various scores take advantage of the fact that by reading a score the reader is actually carrying out a mental process, as in Eric Andersen's Opus 55 (1963) (see page 81) and Ken Friedman's *Mandatory Happening* (1966) (see Fig. 8). Friedman explains the occasion of the first performance:

> This event was first scored at midnight on May 1, 1966. It was first performed at the same time. For the first performance, the text was typed on a sheet of paper. I went around Shimer College, knocking my way from door to door. When someone answered, I handed him or her the paper.[14]

In each piece in his *Reading* series (2008), Francesco Gagliardi gives an instruction to read a found book in a particular way. These scores are presented on cards, with text printed on both sides. In some of these pieces, the reading process is mirrored by the way the text is presented on the card, as in *Reading 5* and *Reading 6* (see Fig. 9).

In *Music for Solo Performer* (1965) by Alvin Lucier the performer's alpha brainwaves are amplified through loudspeakers (see Fig. 10). In turn, the loudspeakers activate a number of stationary percussion instruments. As the score explains:

> The alpha rhythm of the brain has a range of from eight to twelve hertz, and, if amplified enormously and channelled through an appropriate transducer, can be made audible. It can be blocked by visual attention with the eyes open or mental activity with the eyes closed. No part of the motor system is involved in any way. Control of the alpha consists simply of alteration of thought content – for example, a shifting back and forth from a state of visual imagery to one of relaxed resting.

Perhaps surprisingly, even though this work relies on the mental activity of the performer for its realisation, the score itself does not feature any mental processes. Rather, the performer's mental activity is described in terms of material processes. This grammatical choice seems to be in keeping with the observational philosophy of Lucier's work, as linguist Geoff Thompson explains:

> The mental aspect comes in because the participants are 'mental' ones (especially the alpha rhythm); but they are being talked about as participants in material processes. There is a kind of tension here, but it is in the subject matter itself: we aren't being told about the thoughts or feelings of the performer, but about the interface between mental and physical activity, with mental activity as an Actor bringing about material actions (literally, in that the result is the production of sound). This is a (presumably deliberate) 'scientific' perspective on the brain, seeing it as a matter of electrical impulses generated by the brain or being passed from one synapse to another (i.e. material processes) rather than as 'thoughts' being thought by the mind. You would lose that if you tried to force the processes into a mental model.[15]

---

[14] Friedman, 2002, p. 111.

[15] Geoff Thompson, in correspondence with the author, August 2010.

5 Reading

Backwards book a from read (silently).

2008 October, NYC   Gagliardi Francesco

Reading Reading 66

(silently) (silently) Read read every every word
word twice twice. Keep keep track track of of
the the meaning meaning.

Note Note: really really read read each each word
word twice; twice; don't don't just just repeat repeat
it it in in your your head head.

Francesco Gagliardi   NYC, October 2008

9 *Francesco Gagliardi,* Reading 5 *and* Reading 6 *(both 2008).*

Music for Solo Performer

for enormously amplified brain waves and percussion

The alpha rhythm of the brain has a range of from eight to twelve hertz, and, if amplified enormously and channeled through an appropriate transducer, can be made audible. It can be blocked by visual attention with the eyes open or mental activity with the eyes closed. No part of the motor system is involved in any way. Control of the alpha consists simply of alteration of thought content – for example, a shifting back and forth from a state of visual imagery to one of relaxed resting.

Place an EEG scalp electrode on each hemisphere of the occipital, frontal, or other appropriate region of the performer's head. Attach a reference electrode to an ear, finger, or other location suitable for cutting down electrical noise. Route the signal through an appropriate amplifier and mixer to any number of amplifiers and loudspeakers directly coupled to percussion instruments, including large gongs, cymbals, timpani, metal ashcans, cardboard boxes, bass and snare drums (small loudspeakers face down on them), and to switches, sensitive to alpha, which activate one or more tape recorders upon which are stored pre-recorded, sped-up alpha.

Set free and block alpha in bursts and phrases of any length, the sounds of which, as they emanate from the loudspeakers, cause the percussion instruments to vibrate sympathetically. An assistant may channel the signal to any or all of the loudspeakers in any combination at any volume, and, from time to time, engage the switches to the tape recorders. Performances may be of any length. Experiment with electrodes on other parts of the head in an attempt to pick up other waves of different frequencies and to create stereo effects. Use alpha to activate radios, television sets, lights, alarms, and other audio-visual devices.

Design automated systems, with or without coded relays, with which the performer may perform the piece without the aid of an assistant.

Alvin Lucier, 1965

10 *Alvin Lucier,* Music for Solo Performer *(1965).*

Relational Processes

Relational processes deal with identifying and classifying, allowing us to relate and generalise about different elements of experience. They can describe both inner and outer experience, but unlike material and mental processes the focus is on *being* rather than doing or sensing. While material clauses emphasise dynamic motion, relational clauses emphasise a more static perspective.

There are three main types of relational clause. *Intensive* clauses take the form '*x* is *a*', as seen in La Monte Young's *Composition 1960 #15 to Richard*

Huelsenbeck (1960), 'This piece is little whirlpools out in the middle of the ocean' (see Fig. 153, page 425) and Tony Conrad's *This Piece is its Name* (1961) (see Fig. 81, page 161). *Possessive* relational clauses take the form '*x* has *a*'. The first sentence of Lucier's *Music for Solo Performer* contains a possessive relational clause, 'The alpha rhythm of the brain has a range of from eight to twelve hertz'. *Circumstantial* relational clauses take the form '*x* is at *a*'. For example, the first procedural step of Robert Ashley's logistically intricate solo for organ, *The Entrance* (1965–6), features the circumstantial relational clause, 'the most recently placed "heads" stack (or "tails" stack) is on the opposite manual' (see Fig. 54, page 84).

Behavioural Processes

Behavioural processes settle on the border between material and mental processes. They represent physiological and psychological behaviour, through use of such verbs as 'smile', 'hiccup', 'dream' or 'read'. They are similar to mental processes in that, like the Senser in mental clauses, there is a conscious being, the *Behaver*, doing the 'behaving'. However, the process is more like a material process of 'doing'. You can usually perceive someone else's behavioural process, but that process does not affect the grammatical Object, which is usually referred to as the *Scope* or *Behaviour*.

Yoko Ono's instruction score *Cough Piece* (1961) consists solely of the clause, 'Keep coughing a year' (see Fig. 11). As with other works by Ono, such as *Laugh Piece* (1961), there is a semantic tension here: the behavioural verb 'cough' is very close to the boundary of material processes, and Ono's phrasing seems to make it even more 'material-like': normally coughing is an instinctive physiological process, but in this case it could be a deliberate (and repeated) action. Alternatively the text could be interpreted as an example of designating an existing condition (a 'found process'), rather than as an instruction.

COUGH PIECE	LAUGH PIECE
Keep coughing a year.	Keep laughing a week.
1961 winter	1961 winter

11 *Yoko Ono,* Cough Piece *and* Laugh Piece *(both 1961).*

Verbal Processes

Verbal processes are clauses of saying, as in 'she said', and may be accompanied by quotes. They are often used to shape narratives in fiction, and to give accounts of dialogue. The main participant in a verbal process is the *Sayer*. The recipient of the process is the *Receiver*. The content of what is said is the *Verbiage*. Verbs that can serve as processes in verbal clauses include 'say', 'speak', 'talk', 'command', 'announce' and 'ask'. A score may require a performer to say something specific, as in Ken Friedman's *Long Ships Event* (1989) (see Fig. 12).

Long Ships Event

Performers enter from stage left and stage right. Each stands at the far edge of the stage.
One shouts, "Hail, Einar!"
The other replies, "Hail, Ragnar!"

Ken Friedman, 1989

12 *Ken Friedman,* Long Ships Event *(1989).*

Other scores make use of the conjunction 'that' to indicate what must be said, as with La Monte Young's *Composition 1960 #3* (1960) (see Fig. 153, page 424):

Announce to the audience when the piece will begin and end if there is a limit on duration. It may be of any duration.
Then announce that everyone may do whatever he wishes for the duration of the composition.

In the first sentence, 'when the piece will begin and end' is an *embedded clause* in SFG (a *noun clause* in traditional grammar), whereas in the third sentence, 'that everyone may do whatever he wishes for the duration of the composition' is a *projected clause* (a *reported clause* in traditional terms). The latter is complete, and the announcer need not add anything. However, the former is incomplete, with the specific details of the WH-element, 'when the piece will begin and end', needing to be filled in.

Existential Processes

Between relational and material processes lie *existential* processes, which are concerned with being. Existential clauses are often used to conjure a thing into being by beginning, for instance, 'there are'. Existential clauses are useful in presenting New information; most limericks start with an existential clause.

Smokers Die Younger
for Ben Patterson

there is a quiet humming in the background

Joseph Kudirka
2009

13 *Joseph Kudirka,* Smokers Die Younger *(2009).*

The thing that is brought into existence is called the *Existent*. The score for Joseph Kudirka's *Smokers Die Younger* (2009) features an existential clause (see Fig. 13), and in Craig Shepard's *Lines (1)* (1999), 'Between the drawing of lines, there is silence' (see Fig. 129, page 335).

Tense

The *past*, *present* and *future* tenses are used to represent when processes occur in time. Tense marks two positions in time, the *utterance* time, which is the time that the utterance is understood to have been made, and the *reference* time, which is the time that is talked about. Though there are exceptions, past and present tenses are generally used to talk about past and present time. Because English verbs do not have an inflected future form, prediction of and hypothesising about future processes, as well as the expression of intentions, can be achieved through use of *modal auxiliaries* such as 'will' and *semi-modals* such as 'going to'.

The past tense is commonly used to give an account of something that happened some time before the utterance time. The *simple past* is used to describe a process that occurred in the past, as in 'Tim played the piano'. The *past continuous* is used to talk about continued states or repeated actions that occurred prior to the utterance time, as in 'Tim was playing the piano'.

Perhaps because the majority of verbal scores appear to conform to the registers of instructions or descriptions of procedures, which represent processes happening either during or after the utterance time, there seem to be very few scores that are wholly in the past tense. However, occasionally there may be a past tense account of a performance included in a score, as in the instruction page for John Cage's *4'33"* (1952) (see Fig. 14), and Stuart Marshall's *A Sagging and Reading Room* (1972) (see Fig. 47, page 65).

14 *John Cage, instruction page for 4'33" (1952).* ▶

NOTE: THE TITLE OF THIS WORK IS THE TOTAL LENGTH IN MINUTES AND
SECONDS OF ITS PERFORMANCE. AT WOODSTOCK, N.Y., AUGUST 29. 1952,
THE TITLE WAS 4'33" AND THE THREE PARTS WERE 33", 2'40", AND
1'20". IT WAS PERFORMED BY DAVID TUDOR, PIANIST, WHO INDI-
CATED THE BEGINNINGS OF PARTS BY CLOSING, THE ENDINGS BY OPEN-
ING, THE KEYBOARD LID. AFTER THE WOODSTOCK PERFORMANCE, A
COPY IN PROPORTIONAL NOTATION WAS MADE FOR IRWIN KREMEN.
IN IT THE TIMELENGTHS OF THE MOVEMENTS WERE 30", 2'23", AND 1'
40". HOWEVER, THE WORK MAY BE PERFORMED BY ANY INSTRUMEN-
TALIST(S) AND THE MOVEMENTS MAY LAST ANY LENGTHS OF TIME.

FOR IRWIN KREMEN

Other scores may also make use of the past tense, but in less literal ways. La Monte Young's *Piano Piece for David Tudor #3* (1960), is wholly in the past continuous (see also Fig. 153, page 425):

most of them
were very old grasshoppers

The *simple present* is usually employed to describe processes taking place at the time of the utterance. It can be used to describe general truths, as in Davi Det Hompson's *Calculations* (1970) (see Fig. 15). Cardew's *Song of Pleasure* (1967) uses both the simple present and *present continuous* tenses to evoke a proposed or imagined situation (see Fig. 16).

In the score for Alvin Lucier's *'I am sitting in a room'* (1969) the performer is provided with a text to read aloud (see Fig. 17). This text is written in a variety of tenses, including the future tense, and describes the process of performance. It begins in the present continuous, 'I am sitting...', 'I am recording...'. It then moves to the future tense, with

Calculations

Sixty two and sixty two and sixty two is one hundred eighty six.

15 *Davi Det Hompson,* Calculations *(1970).*

Song of Pleasure

I am rowing a boat on a lake.
The sounds – the regular
breathing, the small creaking
and thudding sounds of the
oars in the rowlocks, the
water lapping and sucking at
the belly of the boat, the
occasional passing bird–
all combine to make a song
of pleasure.

16 *Cornelius Cardew,* Song of Pleasure, *from* Schooltime Compositions *(1967).*

intention modality, '… I am going to play it…' (see *Modality* section, pages 26–8). Then there is a prediction, again in the future tense, 'What you will hear then…'. The text ends with a declaration of an ongoing fact in the simple present tense, 'I regard this activity…'.

'I am sitting in a room'
for voice and electromagnetic tape

Necessary Equipment:
  one microphone, two tape recorders, amplifier and one loudspeaker.

Choose a room the musical qualities of which you would like to evoke.
  Attach the microphone to the input of tape recorder #1.
  To the output of tape recorder #2 attach the amplifier and loudspeaker.
  Use the following text or any other text of any length:

"I am sitting in a room different from the one you are in now.
  I am recording the sound of my speaking voice and I am going to play it back into the room again and again until the resonant frequencies of the room reinforce themselves so that any semblance of my speech, with perhaps the exception of rhythm, is destroyed.
  What you will hear, then, are the natural resonant frequencies of the room articulated by speech.
  I regard this activity not so much as a demonstration of a physical fact, but more as a way to smooth out any irregularities my speech might have."

Record your voice on tape through the microphone attached to tape recorder #1.
  Rewind the tape to its beginning, transfer it to tape recorder #2, play it back into the room through the loudspeaker and record a second generation of the original recorded statement through the microphone attached to tape recorder #1.
  Rewind the second generation to its beginning and splice it onto the end of the original recorded statement on tape recorder #2.
  Play the second generation only back into the room through the loudspeaker and record a third generation of the original recorded statement through the microphone attached to tape recorder #1.
  Continue this process through many generations.
  All the generations spliced together in chronological order make a tape composition the length of which is determined by the length of the original statement and the number of generations recorded.
  Make versions in which one recorded statement is recycled through many rooms.
  Make versions using one or more speakers of different languages in different rooms.
  Make versions in which, for each generation, the microphone is moved to different parts of the room or rooms.
  Make versions that can be performed in real time.

Alvin Lucier, 1969

17 *Alvin Lucier,* 'I am sitting in a room' *(1969).*

Primary tense is past, present or future relative to the utterance time. However, since tense is a recursive system, there are more complex forms possible, which use secondary tenses to describe, say, what was planned but did not occur. In *Far Away and Dimly Pealing* (1972) Gavin Bryars provides an enigmatic account of his first failed attempt at performing the piece (see also Fig. 70, page 123):

(the only attempt I ever made at this was thwarted by an express train severing the means whereby the sound was to be made)

At the time in the past that Bryars is writing about, when the express train intervened, the 'making of the sound' was still to take place in the future. The primary tense is past, and the secondary tense is future, so this tense is called 'future in past' (with this tense it is a common implication that the planned event did not take place).[16]

Modality

A group of words centred around a verb is called a *verbal group*. Verbal groups are marked for either tense or modality. Since English has no future form of the verb, we make use of modals to predict and hypothesise about the future. Modality occupies the area between 'yes' and 'no', and can realise permission, possibility or ability, as with the modals 'can', 'could', 'may' and 'might'. It can also describe the necessity for something to occur, or the level of personal obligation an *agent* (the person who carries out the action) need have, as with the modals 'must', 'should', 'need to'. It may also mark volition and prediction, as with 'will', 'shall' and 'would'. Modals are often used for hedging bets, and enable a writer to give different levels of commitment to a proposition. *Modalisation* of a clause therefore provides a subtle way to refine the function of a command, statement, or question and it contributes to the tenor of the relationship between the participants.

Modality is often realised by *modal auxiliaries* such as 'can', 'might', 'should' and 'must', as well as *semi-modals* like 'need to' and 'dare to', and essentially these constitute the traditional view of modality as taken by formal grammar. SFG presents a wider view, and includes a range of other grammatical resources, such as *modal adjuncts* like 'probably', 'possibly' and 'perhaps', *modal adjectives* like 'possible' and 'probable', and *modal nouns* such as 'the possibility'. Some processes are also used for modalisation, such as the mental process verbs 'think' and 'believe', and the material process verbs 'allow' and 'guarantee'.

---

[16] This is a relatively tame example of nested tenses, and things can get far more involved. Michael Halliday cites one of the longest tense forms he has recorded in use as 'it'll've been going to've been being tested', the tense of which is 'present in past in future in past in future' (Halliday and Matthiessen, 2004, p. 339).

Philip Corner makes extensive use of modality as a tool to promote a multiplicity of realisations: 'I write generalized scores because I always glimpse many more valid possibilities than any written version could contain.'[17] Corner's GAMEL'OONY (2004) is a summary of the 'structural essences' of his other gamelan scores, and the copious use of the modal auxiliaries 'will', 'can', 'would', 'might', 'may' and 'could', as well as other modal elements such as 'possible', contributes perhaps to a tenor of collaboration between writer and reader (see Fig. 82, page 166).

Modals can either be *intrinsic*, referring to actions and events that agents control directly (permission, obligation, volition), or *extrinsic*, referring to the logical status of events or states, usually assessment of likelihood (possibility, necessity, prediction). Modals also operate differently depending on context. For instance, with the modal 'should', if an agent is mentioned explicitly, then we consider this as an obligation. If there is no agent mentioned explicitly, then we consider this a necessity. Paul Whitty's *ricercare or where the f*** are we?* (2008) features both these uses: 'each performer should select a different edition' (obligation); 'the volume should be at a domestic level' (necessity) (see Fig. 18).

ricercare or **where the f*** are we?**   paul whitty **SEPT-2008**
for tim parkinson & james saunders

to be played by any number of performers with found scores; recordings; turntables; cassette players; CD players; and any other appropriate sound reproduction devices.

materials
1. select a pre-existing score or scores – they can be of the same work in which case each performer should select a different edition – or of different pieces.
2. search out as many alternative recorded interpretations of the work or works as possible on a diverse range of formats.
3. procure the means to play the recordings.

activity
1. select a single event from each page of your score – use a systematic method of your own choice. in this context an event is considered to be a single action – it could be a chord or a single note – the event or action ends when the next event or action is performed.
2. search out the chosen events on the recordings of the work – in performance you should be seeking out the events for the first time. searches should not be pre-prepared
3. do not seek to minimise the sounds resulting from your search – for example do not use headphones or turn the volume down to a level lower than the level at which you will finally play the selected event.
4. when the event has been found - play it once. as far as possible seek to isolate the event from the other events surrounding it.
5. once the event has been played begin to search for the next event on the same or an alternative recording and format.

amplification
Where possible use internal amplification – where external amplification is required the volume should be at a domestic level.

18 *Paul Whitty,* ricercare or where the f*** are we? *(2008).*

---

[17] Philip Corner, in correspondence with the author, July 2010.

Like tenses, modals can also be nested. Returning to Bryars' *Far Away and Dimly Pealing*, the score has two nested modal expressions in the clause 'The sound should be able to be heard by the performer', which features necessity ('should' with no agent), and ability ('be able to'). It is therefore necessary for the performer to be able to hear the sound. This formulation has a very different meaning to, say, 'The sound should be heard by the performer', which locates the necessity with the actual hearing of the sound, rather than the performer's ability to hear it (see Fig. 70, page 123).

Mood

English clauses can be divided into two main mood types: *imperative* and *indicative*. The imperative mood is commonly used to give commands, as in 'Shake this book'. The indicative is normally used to exchange information, and is made up of two further sub-types: *declarative* and *interrogative*. The declarative mood is commonly employed to make statements of fact or belief, such as 'These boots are made for walking'. The interrogative mood is generally used for questions such as 'Who wants to dance?'

In his book *Language and Power*, linguist Norman Fairclough suggests that, in general, the written imperative, declarative and interrogative moods may be seen as setting up different role relations between the writer and reader. In the case of the imperative, the writer is the person giving the order, and the reader is the person who carries out that order (assuming, of course, that the reader complies); with the declarative it is the writer who is giving the information, and the reader who is receiving the information; with the interrogative, the writer requests information, and the reader is expected to provide that information.[18]

These role relations are made more complex by the fact that the mood does not wholly determine whether a clause expresses a command, statement or question. For example, declarative clauses can be used to express the speech function of a command or injunction, e.g. 'There is no smoking on this station', as can interrogatives, e.g. 'Would you take a seat, please?' However, within this study's corpus of verbal scores, the structure and the function are, for the most part, congruent, i.e. imperatives realise commands, declaratives realise statements, interrogatives realise questions. Therefore, unless otherwise stated, in this study (and in the commentaries in Part 2) mood choices are taken to realise these congruent functions.

Mood contributes to the register of a text in significant ways. For instance, a predominant or exclusive use of declaratives may promote a rather detached tenor and is commonly used in texts that require some degree of formality, such as scientific papers and official documents. The imperative, on the other hand, is commonly used in more interactive settings such as instruction manuals, recipe books and spoken conversation.

---

[18] Fairclough, 2001, pp. 104–5.

Imperative

This study found the majority of scores in the corpus to be marked, at least to some extent, for the imperative. Often scores feature straightforward imperatives, such as in the English version of *RIGHT DURATIONS* (1968) by Stockhausen, which begins 'play a sound' (see Fig. 138, page 361). A more unusual example is Tom Johnson's *Chain II* (1976), which consists of a network of short imperative clauses in the form of a flow diagram, which the pianist can negotiate at will (see Fig. 19). Imperatives can be marked for either *positive* or *negative* polarity. Christian Wolff's *Stones* (1968) begins with an imperative marked for positive polarity, 'Make sounds with stones', and ends with an imperative marked for negative polarity, 'Do not break anything' (see Fig. 151, page 411).

An example of a single-sentence imperative score is La Monte Young's *Composition 1960 #10 to Bob Morris* (1960), 'Draw a straight line and follow it' (see Fig. 153, page 425). Imperative clauses are notable for their lack of a stated agent. For instance, in the first clause 'Draw a straight line', the unstated agent is 'you'. While in spoken English the imperative is most often addressed at a specific agent, for the writer of an imperative clause the agent need not be known. The implied 'you' remains indeterminate, since it may refer to male or female, singular or plural. The written imperative instruction therefore announces itself as available for anyone to read and interpret, and this may account for why so many scores are marked for this mood.

By using an intransitive verb in the imperative mood, it is possible to make a complete one-word clause. Some composers have used this aspect of grammar to create highly economical scores. In his 'Lecture 1960' La Monte Young describes a piece 'discovered' by Dennis Johnson, which 'was entirely indeterminacy, and left the composer out of it'.[19] The score consisted of the single intransitive verb 'LISTEN'. Here the language is concentrated purely on the process of listening itself, with that which is listened *to* remaining indeterminate. Max Neuhaus later organised a series of events in which audience members would have the word 'LISTEN' stamped on their hands and then be taken on a walk (see Fig. 113, page 285):

> After a while I began to do these works as 'Lecture Demonstrations'; the rubber stamp was the lecture and the walk the demonstration. I would ask the audience at a concert or lecture to collect outside the hall, stamp their hands and lead them through their everyday environment. Saying nothing, I would simply concentrate on listening, and start walking. At first, they would be a little embarrassed, of course, but the focus was generally contagious. The group would proceed silently, and by the time we returned to the hall many had found a new way to listen for themselves.[20]

---

[19] Young, 1965, p. 77.
[20] Neuhaus, 2004. See p. 286 of this book.

Chain II

Begin at the upper right and stop whenever the piece seems to you to be finished.

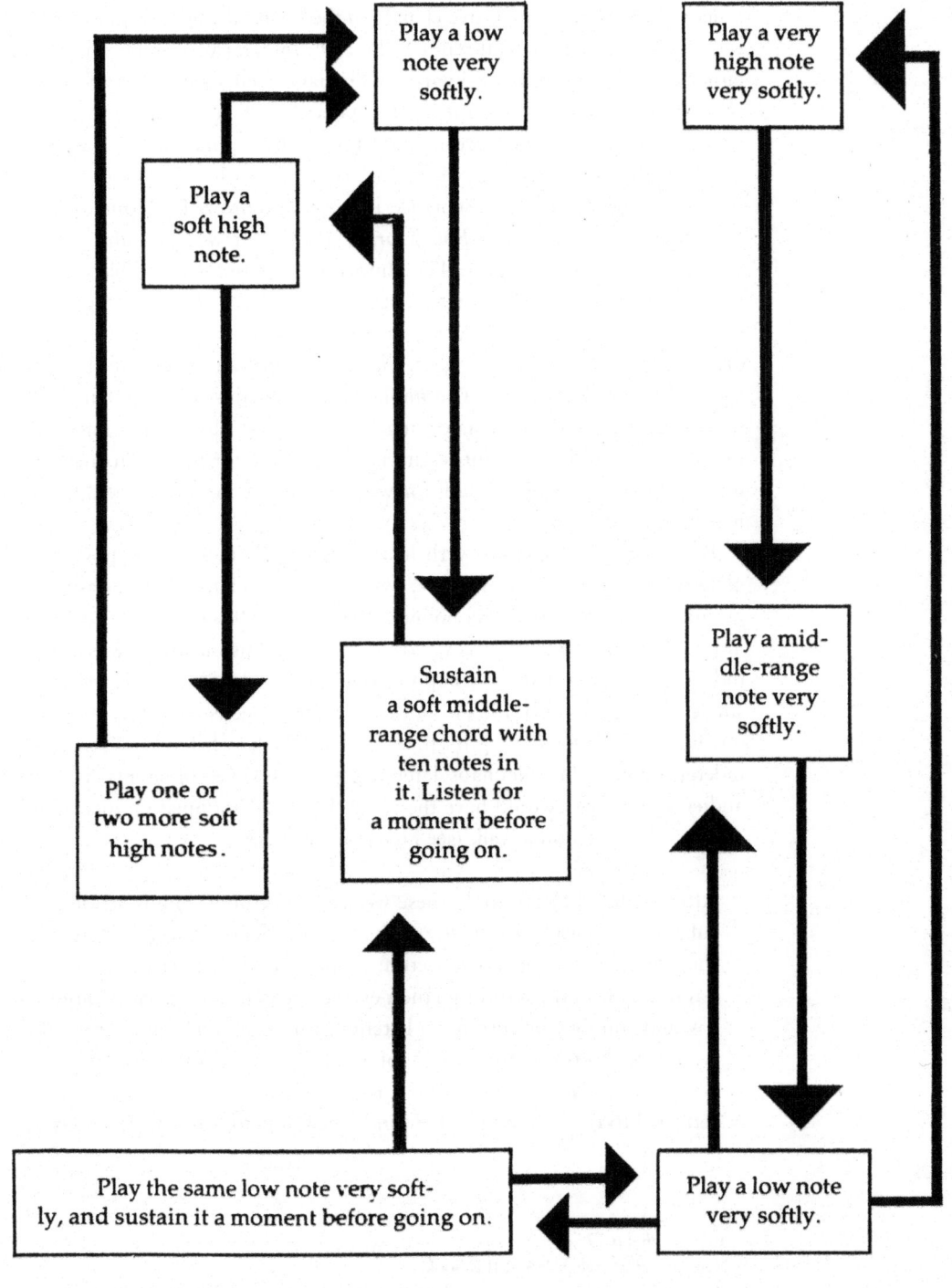

◀ 19 *Tom Johnson,*
Chain II, *from*
Private Pieces
(1976).

As part of her ongoing investigations into human attention processes and strategies, Pauline Oliveros has composed various training exercises and pieces that explore her practice of Deep Listening. She explains:

> The central concern in all my prose or oral instructions is to provide attention strategies for the participants. Attention strategies are nothing more than ways of listening and responding in consideration of oneself, others and the environment.[21]

In scores such as *The New Sound Meditation* (1989) the composer's use of the imperative mood seems to reinforce the experiential urgency of her practice. Given this context, the instructions have a fitting immediacy. The score begins with the instruction 'Listen', and then guides the reader through a series of related activities that call for an ongoing meditative awareness of the situation. The use of the imperative mood here gives priority to the performer's perceptions and actions (see Fig. 20).

The New Sound Meditation (1989)

Listen

During any one breath

Make a sound

Breathe

Listen outwardly for a sound

Breathe

Make exactly the sound that someone else has made

Breathe

Listen inwardly

Breathe

Make a new sound that no one else has made

Breathe

Continue this cycle until there are no more new sounds.

20 *Pauline
Oliveros,* The New
Sound Meditation
(1989).

[21] Oliveros, 2005, p. 29.

Since imperative clauses are often used in spoken conversation, scores written in the imperative can evoke an informal register, which might seem more immediate and accessible to a reader than the potentially more remote declarative mood (see below). On the other hand, because with an imperative there is always someone understood to be delivering the command, some may regard the use of this mood as too assertive, perhaps even dictatorial.

Declarative

Unlike clauses in the imperative mood, those in the declarative mood need not be addressed to an agent, and so are useful when a scorer wants to describe a procedure rather than give a command. However, declaratives may still be used to realise commands or injunctions, through use of the '[be] to' form, e.g. 'the pianist is to begin', and sometimes clauses can be ambiguous between declaratives and imperatives, as in Michael Parsons' *Walk* (1969), which features the ambiguous clause 'All begin together' (see Fig. 116, page 305). The field of scientific discourse is often characterised by declarative statements.[22] Depending on how they are used, clauses marked for the declarative tend to play down the role of any agents, with the emphasis on what happens rather than who makes it happen.

The procedural characteristics of Steve Reich's *Pendulum Music* (1968, rev. 1978) are reflected in the register of the score, which is wholly in the declarative mood (see Fig. 21). As with descriptions of scientific experiments, this score begins by explaining the technical set-up while making no mention of any agents. Here the language emphasises the arrangements of materials rather than actions carried out by agents. The score only explicitly refers to agents in the description of the actual performance, 'The performance begins with the performers taking each microphone...'.[23] The score

---

[22] The scientific register may be traced back to a conscious decision made by the Royal Society in an attempt to make scientific communication as effective as possible, as described by Thomas Sprat, Bishop of Rochester, in his *History of the Royal Society* (1667):

> They have therefore been more rigorous in putting in Execution the only Remedy, that can be found for this *Extravagance*; and that has been a constant Resolution, to reject all the Amplifications, Digressions, and Swellings of Style; to return back to the primitive Purity and Shortness, when Men deliver'd so many *Things*, almost in an equal Number of *Words*. They have exacted from all their Members, a close, naked, natural way of Speaking; positive Expressions, clear Senses; a native Easiness; bringing all Things as near the mathematicall Plainness as they can; and preferring the Language of Artizans, Countrymen, and Merchants, before that of Wits, or Scholars (Scollon and Scollon, 1995, p. 111).

[23] In the course of research, five different versions of the score for *Pendulum Music* were found: the 1968 version, two versions from 1973 (with very slight differences between them), the 1978 version printed here, and another typeset version from 1980, which is the 'official' score as currently distributed by Universal Edition. Each version features slight revisions, additions and deletions, which fortuitously document how the performance practice of the piece has developed since its conception, and which reveal much about how the composer has chosen to express those developments in written form. There are also some quite fundamental compositional changes. The 1968 version specifies that, after releasing their microphones, 'Performers then carefully turn up each amplifier to the point where feedback occurs.' However, the 1973 revisions specify that another performer should be responsible for raising volume levels on the

PENDULUM MUSIC

FOR MICROPHONES, AMPLIFIERS SPEAKERS AND PERFORMERS

Three, four, or more microphones are suspended from microphone boom stands, or some other 3 to 6 foot high support, by their cables so that all hang the same distance from the floor and are all free to swing with a pendular motion. Each microphone's cable is plugged into an amplifier which is connected to a loudspeaker. Each microphone hangs a few inches directly above or next to its loudspeaker.

Before the performance each amplifier is turned up just to the point where feedback occurs when a microphone swings directly over or next to its speaker, but no feedback occurs as the mike swings to either side. This level on each amplifier is then marked for future reference and all amplifiers are turned down.

The performance begins with performers taking each microphone, pulling it back like a swing, and then holding them while another performer turns up the amplifiers to their pre-marked levels. Performers then count off "one, two, three, four, release" and release all the microphones in unison. Thus, a series of feedback pulses are heard which will either be all in unison or not depending on the gradually changing phase relations of the different microphone pendulums.

Performers then sit down to watch and listen to the process along with the rest of the audience.

The piece is ended sometime shortly after all microphones have come to rest and are feeding back a continuous tone by a performer pulling out all the power cords of the amplifiers.

Steve Reich 8/68
revised 5/73 + 1/78

21 *Steve Reich,* Pendulum Music *(1978 revision, not published version).*

amplifiers *prior* to the release of the microphones. This has a considerable effect on the sounding result, since in this version the process will be audible from the moment the microphones are released, a revision that seems in keeping with the composer's preoccupation with the clean delivery of an audible process. The 1978 version is the first to feature the instruction about performers counting in, and the first not to mention the microphones being suspended from the ceiling. In terms of process, the 1980 version is broadly similar to the 1978 version, although it also features another section, 'Directions for Performance', which contains a great deal more information about the technical set-up and performance technique, including what kind of loudspeakers will produce 'musically attractive results'. Whether the performers are counted in is now optional ('the performer adjusting the amplifiers may give a simple signal to the three or more other performers to release their microphones in unison by simply counting rhythmically, "One – two – three – four – release"'), and this instruction is also relegated from the main score to the 'Directions'. The 1980 version also features French and German translations.

also states that: 'Performers then sit down to watch and listen to the process along with the rest of the audience', a sentence which exemplifies Reich's 'observational' ethos of that time, as described in his 1968 essay 'Music as a Gradual Process':[24]

> Performing and listening to a gradual musical process resembles:
> pulling back a swing, releasing it, and observing it gradually come to rest;
> turning over an hour glass and watching the sand slowly run through the bottom;
> placing your feet in the sand by the ocean's edge and watching, feeling, and listening to the waves gradually bury them.

Hugh Davies takes the notion of performer absence to an extreme in *Music for Strings No. 2* (1971) (see Fig. 22). Not only is the text marked for the declarative with no agents specified, but it explicitly states that no performers are required and that those responsible for setting up the work should not be 'available' to the audience. Note that the last two clauses of the score, while marked for the declarative, are injunctions with obligation modality.

MUSIC FOR STRINGS No. 2

During the first half of a concert, string instruments (violins, violas, cellos, double basses) are piled up in a reasonably ordered fashion in a large heap outside the hall; this could be indoors or - preferably - outdoors, in a place where they can be best observed from a distance, such as in the middle of an outdoor grass area near or around which the audience can walk during the interval. No performers are required, and none of the people responsible should be available to "explain" the meaning of this event. The instruments must be removed during the second half of the concert.

---

22 *Hugh Davies*, Music for Strings No. 2 *(1971)*.

Markus Trunk's *slightly ajar* (1993) also makes use of the declarative mood to describe a general situation, without making explicit mention of preparation or agency (see Fig. 23). The composer avoids using imperatives such as 'At various times open and close doors to an enclosed space', or 'Keep the space dark'. Instead he uses the declarative mood to fold the limits of the composition into a general description of the performance, by writing 'Doors to an enclosed space are opened and closed at various times' and – again an example of the declarative mood realising an injunction using the '[be] to' form – 'The space is to be kept dark'.

[24] Reich, 2002, p. 34.

23 *Markus Trunk,* slightly ajar *(1993)*. ▶

Markus Trunk

slightly ajar

for any number of doors, sound and light sources

Doors to an enclosed space are opened and closed at various times, allowing sounds from outside to enter for certain periods of time.

Invisible from inside the hall, the sound sources are located outside in rooms that are separate from each other. Continuous drones or sustained sounds are produced by any kind of musical instruments, voices, or machines, at a volume that makes them virtually inaudible as soon as the door is closed.

The position of each door is changed at certain points in time that have been determined by chance. Swiftly, the doors may be opened, closed, or brought to a characteristic state in between, with as little noise as possible.

The space is to be kept dark so that light enters through an opened door along with sound.

I-III'93
Middletown, CT
© Markus Trunk

Interrogative

Less commonly used in verbal notation is the interrogative mood, which often appears in the dialogues found in spoken conversation and in fiction. It is also found in questionnaires, exam papers, surveys and quizzes. The corpus contains relatively few examples of scores that use this mood. There are three main types of interrogative clauses: *WH*-questions requesting missing information, *yes/no* questions asking the addressee whether something is true or not, and *alternative* questions offering the addressee a choice of answers.

Questions are a way of encouraging critical reflection on the part of the reader. Such reflection can then feed back into a performance. In another of her Deep Listening pieces, *Rhythms* (1996), Pauline Oliveros asks a series of (mostly) *WH*-questions, the answers to which will be entirely personal and specific to each performer (see Fig. 24). Oliveros has employed questions in many of her scores, including *Ear Piece* (1998) (see Fig. 114, page 289).

Rhythms (1996)

What is the meter/tempo of your normal walk?
How often do you blink?
What is the current tempo of your breathing?
What is the current tempo of your heart rate?
What other rhythms do you hear if you listen?
What is your relationship to all of the rhythms that you can perceive at once?

24 *Pauline Oliveros,* Rhythms *(1996).*

Asking questions with several possible answers can be an effective way of delegating responsibility for some decisions to the performers, and can perhaps contribute to a sense of collaborative problem solving between the scorer and whoever is realising the score. For instance, Robert Ashley's *The Entrance* features a number of thought-provoking questions regarding the identity of the work, including 'Is it to be performed?', 'For whom is it to be performed?', and 'Is the work more important than the sounds, or vice versa, or neither?' (see Fig. 54, page 85). The score for Philip Corner's *Amplified Audience* (2008) ends with three questions concerning the piece's presentation in time, and it is up to whoever presents the piece to answer these questions. In their fragmentary nature the questions mirror the speculative openness of the rest of the score; a general situation is proposed, the specifics of which will no doubt be resolved (somehow) by all those taking part (see Fig. 25).

Questions in scores can also compel a performer to refer back to the score for prompts for how to progress. Networks of interrelated questions can create the textual equivalent of flow diagrams, as in *125 Questions for Pianists* by Christopher Hobbs (see Fig. 26). The score consists of questions regarding five different categories of sound production: *A* striking the key, *B* plucking the string, *C* muting the string, *D* producing harmonics and *E* preparing the

25 *Philip Corner,* Amplified Audience *(2008).* ▶

Amplified Audience

The stage is to be set-up with an electronic amplification system

The whole place is wired!

contact microphones under seats

directional microphones overhead

a starting-state of empty expectations

selected volumes turned-up

sites of sensitive sounding

unsuspecting perpetrators

their speech (whispers out-loud)

squirmings (uncomfortable seats)

played by ear   for everyone's ear

(for humour too)

whatever the audience happens to do

———————————————————

going on the whole evening? through other performances? on and off?

Philip Corner

2008

```
A      (key struck)

1.     Is the key depressed 1. gently  2. with moderate force  3. forcefully?

2.     Is the pedal depressed?  If not, answer 7, then end.

3.     Is the pedal depressed 1. before or 2.  after the key has been depressed?

4.     Is the pedal depressed 1.  slowly  2. with moderate speed 3.  quickly?

5.     Is the pedal released 1. before or 2.  after the key has been released,

       or 3. is the note damped manually before the pedal is released?  If

       1 or 2, proceed to 7.

6.     Is the note damped 1. before or 2. after the key has been released?

       If 1, proceed to 8.

7.     Is the key released 1. slowly 2. with moderate speed 3. quickly?

8.     Is the pedal released 1. slowly 2. with moderate speed  3. quickly?
                                                                (series ends)
```

26 *Christopher Hobbs, excerpt from* 125 Questions for Pianists *(1969).*

string. Answers to questions in a particular category are to be obtained by random means, using dice or number tables. One or more pianists use these answers to create their own performance parts. For each category, the random answers gradually contribute to a detailed description of the structure of a single sounding event, one possibility among many. For instance, one set of random answers will produce the following event in category *A*:

1. (answer = 3) The key is depressed forcefully.
2. (yes) The sustaining pedal is depressed.
3. (2) The pedal is depressed after the key is depressed.
4. (1) The pedal is depressed slowly.
5. (2) The pedal is released after the key has been released.
6. (2) The note is damped (finger on the string) after the key has been released.
7. (1) The key is released slowly.
8. (2) The pedal is released with moderate speed.

In summary: The key is depressed forcefully. The sustaining pedal is depressed slowly. The key is released slowly. The note is damped. The pedal is released with moderate speed.

Cardew uses the yes/no interrogative form exclusively in *Schooltime Special*, a kind of open-form examination paper, in which performers are continually encouraged to assess and respond to their own perceptions and desires (see Fig. 27). As in *The Great Learning*, Paragraph 6 (see Fig. 80, page 149), Cardew chooses to focus the player's attention on a very localised form

27 *Cornelius Cardew,* Schooltime Special *(1968).* ▶

Schooltime Special

Read the questions of A in sequence until you make a Yes
or reach the end (silence)

If you make a Yes in A move to B
and answer questions at random

Spend plenty of time on A and B before tackling C and D

Read the questions of C in sequence (possibly continuing B
the while) until you make a Yes or reach the end (silence)

If you make a yes in C move to D
and answer questions at random

Take breaks for consideration as required

Silent participants may recommence with A at any time

© 1968 Cornelius Cardew

A

(1) Do you want to sing a note? Yes? Sing one.

(2) No? Do you want to sing a noise? Yes? Sing one.

(3) No? Do you want to play a note? Yes? Play one.

(4) No? Do you want to play a noise? Yes? Play one.

(5) No? Do you want to make a note? Yes? Make one.

(6) No? Do you want to make a noise? Yes? Make one.

(7) No? Do you want to hear a note? Yes? Hear one.

(8) No? Do you want to hear a noise? Yes? Hear one.

(9) No? Do you want to leave the room? Yes? Leave it.

(10) No? Stay, silent.

B

Can the note or noise rise? Yes? Raise it.

No? Hold it constant.

Can it get louder? Yes? Get louder.

No? Cut it off.

Can it vibrate? Yes? Vibrate it.

No? Reiterate it.

Can you hold it long? Yes? Hold it long.

No? Hold it as long as possible.

Can it change colour? Yes? Change its colour.

No? Let it change in any way of its own accord.

C

Does the music set you in motion? Yes? Move around (dance).

No? Does it hurt your ears? Yes? Duplicate a sound close to you.

No? Does it let your mind wander? Yes? Duplicate a sound far away (real or imaginary).

No? Does it accelerate or retard your heartbeat? Yes? Trace the tempo audibly.

No? Does it fray your nerves? Yes? Gyrate and wail.

No? Does it make you feel ridiculous? Yes? Laugh and recommence as from A(2).

No? Does it remind you of something? Yes? Pursue and substantiate the memory.

No? Does it suggest an impression (a picture)? Yes? Add touches to the picture.

No? Does it affect you at all (in an unspecified way)? Yes? Define it verbally. and enhance the affect.

No? Be silent.

D

Do you want the music to go on for ever? Yes? Listen.

*No? Exert yourself to the **maximum**.*

Do you want someone to tell you what to do? Yes? Tell your neighbour what to do.

No? Move out of range.

Do you want the music to stop now? Yes? Block your ears.

No? Breathe on it to keep it glowing.

Do you notice gaps in the total sound spectrum? Yes? Trickle into them.

No? Create some.

Do you need more questions? Yes? Make them up.

No? Close your eyes and follow your inclination.

of decision-making, with the overall sounding result being outside the direct control of individual players. Note that there is no opportunity to answer the questions with any degree of uncertainty, for example 'perhaps'. Rather it is up to each performer to provide a truth value in the form 'yes' or 'no'. In sections A and C the questions are read in order, with a 'yes' then requiring an action, a 'no' directing the performer to another question. In sections B and D the performer selects questions at random, with each possible answer requiring a specific action. Two of these answers in particular are striking in the way they engage the performer in the act of thinking about music in words:

Does [the music] affect you at all (in an unspecified way)?
    Yes? Define it verbally, and enhance the affect.
    No? Be silent.
[...] Do you want to tell someone what to do?
    Yes? Tell your neighbour what to do.
    No? Move out of range.

'No Mood'

Whilst most written or spoken clauses are marked for the imperative, declarative or interrogative moods, in many verbal scores there is the (apparently) deliberate use of a kind of 'no mood', which remains ambiguous. There are various ways that this can be achieved, and one of the most conspicuous may be characterised as follows. A collection of words centred around a noun is a *nominal group*. Nominal groups do not qualify as clauses because they do not centre around verbs, and therefore cannot be marked for mood. Thus a nominal group may be simultaneously suggestive of more than one mood, in which case it is up to the reader to determine what meaning to privilege. There are various instances of scorers employing 'moodless' nominal groups to achieve a kind of 'strategic indeterminacy'.

To illustrate, it will be useful to discuss the work of Lawrence Weiner, a visual artist who writes texts that could, but need not, be regarded as scores. He produces 'statements' describing materials, process and structure. In his *Statement of Intent* (1968),[25] Weiner writes:

1. The artist may construct the piece.
2. The piece may be fabricated.
3. The piece need not be built.
Each being equal and consistent with the intent of the artist the decision as to condition rests with the receiver upon the occasion of receivership.

The notion that the piece need not be built is expressed in Weiner's work through his use of nominal groups that describe objects, without referring

---

[25] Fietzek and Stemmrich, 2004, p. 21.

explicitly to agents or involving the objects in a time-based representation. For instance, his work *MANY COLORED OBJECTS PLACED SIDE BY SIDE TO FORM A ROW OF MANY COLORED OBJECTS* (1979) may be realised by the receiver, but need not (see Fig. 28).

28 *Lawrence Weiner,* MANY COLORED OBJECTS PLACED SIDE BY SIDE TO FORM A ROW OF MANY COLORED OBJECTS *(1979).*

Why Weiner should privilege this type of structure over others becomes clear when attempting to turn his text into a clause. For instance, by rewriting it as a declarative clause centred around the material verb 'to place', i.e. 'MANY COLORED OBJECTS ARE PLACED...', the clause remains temporally ambiguous, but there is now a suggestion of an agent affecting a change. Rewriting the text as an imperative clause, i.e. 'PLACE MANY COLORED OBJECTS...' again limits possible interpretations by locating the event in the future, and it also alters the register significantly. Indeed, Weiner himself has expressed antipathy towards the use of the imperative mood: 'To use the imperative would be for me fascistic... The tone of command is the tone of tyranny'.[26]

Alternatively, one could consider the text as the title of a work. In this case, if the nominal group were to be expanded into a relational identifying clause it might most plausibly take the form 'THIS IS (OR WOULD BE) MANY COLORED OBJECTS...'. Nevertheless, that clause still involves the objects in a time-based representation, something that Weiner's original nominal group sidesteps completely. This work is one example of the many of Weiner's statements that occupy a similar grammatical territory, in what Dieter Schwarz has called 'an abstract formulation that allows unlimited

[26] Alberro and Zimmerman, 1998, p. 49.

realizations'.[27] It is important to note that, for this type of formulation to be effective, Weiner insists that it must at least be possible for such works to be realised, since 'if they were not possible to be built, they would negate the choice of the receiver as to whether to build them or not'.[28]

Nominal groups of this sort are to be found in many verbal scores, and may be regarded as a source of strategic indeterminacy. In Cardew's *The Great Learning*, Paragraph 6, nominal groups are nested between verbal clauses that are (by necessity) marked for mood (see Fig. 80, page 149). In such a case, the immediate grammatical context might provide a clue as to how a performer decides to interpret a particular nominal group. However, other scores may offer no such context and remain ambiguous.

On a related note, non-finite clauses also provide an effective way to create grammatical indeterminacy. Non-finite forms of the verb do not require a Subject or agent. Non-finite clauses are not marked for mood, but unlike nominal groups they do feature a process. In the original 1968 version of Reich's *Pendulum Music,* for example, there are three non-finite clauses in quick succession, all headed by non-finite verbs: 'taking each mike, pulling it back like a swing, [...] releasing all of them together'. This type of clause is also found in titles, e.g. *Saving Private Ryan.*

There are many examples of non-finite clauses in the performance indications above traditional Western stave notation; see, for example, Erik Satie's indications above his piano pieces: 'Broadening your head', 'Looking at yourself from afar', etc. (see pages 330–3). A very early use of an isolated non-finite clause in a wholly verbal score can be found in George Brecht's *Incidental Music* (1961), which features the single non-finite clause, 'Photographing the piano situation' (see Fig. 29). It is apparent from Brecht's notebooks that he arrived at this formulation after a few attempts (see Fig. 30).[29]

It seems likely that the first attempt was 'a photograph of the piano is taken', which conforms to the declarative mood of the rest of the score. The second attempt was probably 'Taking a photograph of the piano', now a non-finite clause, but one that, like the first attempt, limits the number of photographs to one, and does not necessarily include the photographing of anything other than the piano (e.g. the piano seat). Brecht's final solution is 'Photographing the piano situation', a formulation that is now suggestive of ongoing activity. This new version does not limit the number of photographs (or indeed cameras), and it broadens the area available to be photographed (the seat, the blocks, the peas, the performance area, etc.).

Brecht's wording also exhibits a semantic instability that is a common characteristic of non-finite clauses. In such clauses the '-ing' form of the verb is often ambiguous between verbal and nominal, meaning 'photographing'

[27] Schwarz, D. (1989) 'Learn to Read Art: Lawrence Weiner's Books' in *Lawrence Weiner Books, 1968–1989: Catalogue Raisonné*, Cologne: Walther Koenig, p. 131, referenced in Kotz, 2007, p. 205.

[28] Weiner, L., quoted in Kotz, 2007, p. 300, note 32.

[29] Brecht, 2005b, p. 58.

INCIDENTAL MUSIC

Five Piano Pieces,
any number playable successively or simultaneously, in any
order and combination, with one another and with other pieces.

1.
The piano seat is tilted on its base and brought to rest against
a part of the piano.

2.
Wooden blocks.
A single block is placed inside the piano. A block is placed
upon this block, then a third upon the second, and so forth,
singly, until at least one block falls from the column.

3.
Photographing the piano situation.

4.
Three dried peas or beans are dropped, one after another, onto
the keyboard. Each such seed remaining on the keyboard is
attached to the key or keys nearest it with a single piece of
pressure-sensitive tape.

5.
The piano seat is suitable arranged, and the performer seats
himself.

Summer, 1961. G. Brecht

29 *George Brecht,* Incidental Music *(1961).*

may be considered as a verb or a noun (a *gerund*); the verbal form would
be along the lines of 'George is photographing the piano situation', and the
nominal form would probably be 'the photographing of the piano situation'.
Since it doesn't require a Subject, a non-finite clause is almost as condensed
as a nominal group. However, a non-finite clause is centred around a verb, so
it does express a process.

It is clear this kind of grammatical indeterminacy was important to
Brecht, who around this time began writing 'event scores' such as *Word Event*
(1961), which consists solely of the bullet-pointed word 'EXIT' (see Fig. 31).

→ Writing ~~for score~~ *all artists have the greatest simplicity.*

photo

~~I.~~ ~~II.~~ ~~III.~~ A photograph of the piano is taken

③ *Photographing*

1 Taking a photograph of the piano situation.

includes (not fallen bench.

~~I.~~ ~~II.~~ ~~III.~~ ~~VII.~~ The piano bench, or stool, is suitably ~~placed, and adjusted~~ *arranged,*

⑤ and the performer seats himself.

1 2 3 4 5
1 2 3 5 4
1 2 4 5 4
1 3
1 4
1 5

to the second
*are peas
beans?*

① Separate pgf? yes
② in any order?
③ in any combo?

in time or space and

~~Any number of~~

~~when~~ *practicable,*

These pieces may be ~~performed separately or together~~ *separately or simultaneously performed,* ~~by~~ in any order or combination ~~with~~ *with one another and* ~~or~~ with other pieces.

3 4 5 2 1

→ Five Piano Pieces
any number of which may be separately, or ...

◀ 30 *George Brecht, sketches for* Incidental Music *(Brecht, 2005b, p. 58).*

These sparse and precisely worded scores celebrate semantic instabilities (for instance, is 'EXIT' a verb or a noun?), and the potentially limitless range of interpretations that such instabilities can promote. And it is an approach that still has relevance for scorers working now. For instance, Michael Pisaro, who readily acknowledges Brecht's influence, employs a mixture of nominal groups and non-finite clauses in his score *Only* (2005–6) (see Fig. 120, page 316).

Voice

Voice is used for indicating who is responsible for carrying out a process. Clauses may be in either the *active* or the *passive* voice, depending on who or what assumes the role of the subject. When the subject of a verbal group is the agent of the verb, the clause is in the active voice, for example La Monte Young's 'Draw a straight line' (see Fig. 153, page 425). When the subject is the patient, target or undergoer of the process, it is passive, for example Sol LeWitt's 'A straight line [...] is drawn' (see Fig. 99, page 244). In the former, it is clear that 'you' are the agent. In the latter, the agent remains indeterminate.

Mood and voice may be combined in different ways. The passive voice is often used in conjunction with the declarative mood, as demonstrated by this sentence. The passive voice tends to contribute to an impersonal and perhaps less interactive register than the active voice, and is often used in academic, technical and legal writing. For instance, a patent application is concerned with all potential future users, and so it may be more effective with no mention of a specific agent.

Voice can be a subtle tool for reinforcing a scorer's intentions. In Bryars' *Far Away and Dimly Pealing* (see Fig. 70, page 123), the use of the passive voice in 'The sound should be able to be heard by the performer' may seem less straightforward than when expressed in the active voice, 'The performer should be able to hear the sound'. However, Bryars' grammatical choice focuses attention on the sound (as the subject of the sentence), rather than the performer.

Returning to Steve Reich's *Pendulum Music* (see Fig. 21, page 33), the focus of the first paragraph is on the technical set-up, and the text is in the passive voice, i.e., 'microphones are suspended from microphone boom stands...'. In the third paragraph agents are introduced, the performance begins, and the voice changes to the active, 'the performers taking each mike, pulling it back like a swing...'. At the end of this paragraph the voice changes back to the passive, as the focus of the text moves from what the performers do to what is heard by the audience, i.e. 'Thus, a series of feedback pulses are heard...'. There is an intriguing

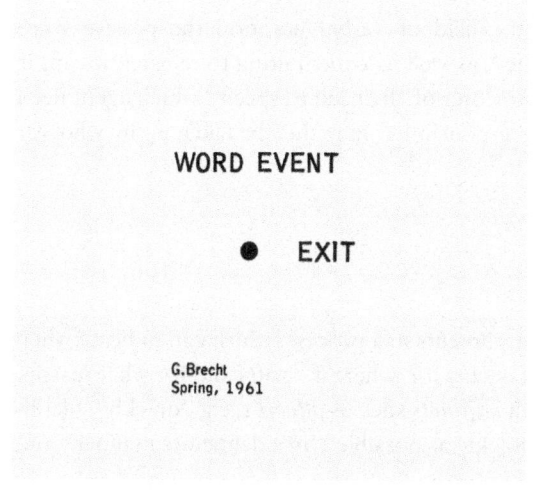

WORD EVENT

● **EXIT**

G. Brecht
Spring, 1961

31 *George Brecht,* Word Event *(1961).*

congruence between what happens in a performance and the way voice is used in the score to express what happens.

However, the passive voice can be used to obfuscate, and it has its critics. Good-writing guides such as Wydick's *Plain English for Lawyers* warn the writer to be cautious of over-using the passive because of its potential ambiguity in terms of agency:

> With the active voice, you can usually tell who is doing what to whom. With the passive voice, however, the writer can hide the identity of the actor. That construction is called the "truncated passive". For example: "The ball was kicked." Who kicked the ball? We have no way to know; the actor is hidden in the fog of the truncated passive. Bureaucrats love to write in the truncated passive because it lets them hide in the fog; the reader cannot discover who is responsible for the action (or lack of it) [...] A writer who wants to befog the matter totally will couple the truncated passive with a nominalization, like this: "A kicking action was accomplished," thus hiding both the kicker and the kickee.[30]

Statistician Edward Tufte also regards the passive voice as a tool of evasion, and he emphasises the need for a clear sense of causality in texts:

> Although often a useful writing technique, passive verbs also advance *effects without causes*, an immaculate conception. To speak of ends without means, agency without agents, actions without actors is contrary to clear thinking. If the issues at hand involve responsibilities or decisions or plans, causal thinking is necessary. The logic of decisions is "If we do such-and-such [cause], then we hope this-and-that will happen [desired effect]." And the logic of responsibility is the logic of the active voice: *someone did* or *did not do* something. Alert audiences should watch out for causality from nowhere and its sometime assistant, the passive voice.[31]

Despite such concerns, in the field of verbal notation the passive voice remains a useful resource since, as well as contributing to register, it can, if used carefully, also relieve the scorer of the need to specify which agent need carry out a process, and this responsibility may then be taken up by whoever decides to realise the piece.

Circumstances

Circumstances are optional arguments in a process, which can indicate when a process occurs, how long it occurs for, where it occurs and for what reason. They are often expressed with *adjuncts* such as *adverbs*, e.g. 'quickly', 'deliberately', *adverbials*, e.g. 'as quickly as possible', 'in a deliberate manner', and

---

[30] Wydick, 2005, p. 30.
[31] Tufte, 2006, p. 142.

subordinate clauses, e.g. 'as if from a great distance'. It is with circumstances that a scorer can provide more detail about a process. Circumstances are not directly involved in the process but are attendant on it, and the types of circumstantial elements are not directly dependent on the process. This final section outlines five prominent types of circumstantials, which indicate *Extent*, *Location*, *Manner*, *Cause* and *Contingency*.

Extent

Circumstantials of Extent indicate the extent to which a process unfolds in either space or time. In terms of space, they indicate the *distance* in space over which the process unfolds e.g. 'for three metres'. For time, there are the two categories of *duration*, indicating the time during which the process unfolds e.g. 'for four minutes', and *frequency*, indicating the extent of repetition of a given process, e.g. 'bang five times'. Usefully, circumstantials have corresponding questions, or *WH*-interrogative forms, which can help the reader to clarify their functions. The interrogative forms for Extent are 'how far?', 'how long?', 'how many [units of measurement]?' and 'how many times?'

Extent: Distance

Spatial distance can be represented with prepositions, most usually 'for', and may be *definite*, e.g. 'for 12 metres', or *indefinite*, e.g. 'a long way'. Note that this describes the distance 'over' which something occurs, not 'at' which it occurs (that is Location).

In *Echo Piece at Muddusjarvi* (1976) by Michael Parsons, two players navigate their ways across the surface of a frozen lake in Finland, using woodblocks to create echoes off a cliff face (see Fig. 32). The natural speed of sound is harnessed to create different rhythmic relationships. Because of the great distances involved, the resultant rhythms will be heard differently depending on where a listener is located in space, and at various stages in the performance the players' actions must be informed by their own perceptions of the sounds and their reflections. The composer takes full advantage of the verbal notation to describe the performance process and the complex set of relationships that arise, in particular how players' perceptions are likely to vary at different stages.

The piece begins, however, with a very controlled activity for each player, which does not immediately rely on the players' perceptions. Each player begins by walking and playing a stroke on the woodblock 'every four steps'. This is a circumstantial of Extent, describing the spatial distance over which each stroke is made. Later in the score this is halved to 'every two steps'. Assuming that the player maintains a constant walking speed, this constraint creates a constant frequency, but it is expressed in the score in terms of space, not time.

32 *Michael Parsons*, Echo Piece at Muddusjarvi *(1976)*. *Overleaf*

Echo Piece at Muddusjarvi
for 2 players with woodblocks

1. Starting at the foot of the cliff the first player [Michael Parsons] begins walking, playing a regular pulse on the woodblock (one stroke every four steps), so that as he moves away the echo from the cliff gradually becomes audible. He continues until he reaches a predetermined point at which the echo is heard one second after each stroke is played. Here he stands still, plays a few more strokes and then stops playing (position 1).

   The distance from the source of the echo at which it is heard after one second is here taken as c. 560 feet (this may vary with atmospheric conditions).

2. After a short pause the second player [Howard Skempton] begins walking away from the foot of the cliff, at a slightly different angle from the first player, playing a stroke on the woodblock every four steps. On hearing the regular pulse of the second player, the first player, standing still at the point he has reached, begins playing a pulse in alternation, fitting in his strokes exactly halfway between Players 2's strokes as he hears them.

   As the second player moves closer, because of the decreasing distance between them, the pulse as heard by Player 1 appears to accelerate, so that he has to accelerate his alternating pulse to keep in time with it.

   For Player 2, a further acceleration in Player 1's pulse (over and above the actual acceleration played) is apparent as he approaches; he does not respond to this, but keeps his own pulse and walking speed as constant as possible, while observing the changing relationship between his own and Player 1's pulse as he hears it.

   Player 2 stops walking at a point half as far out from the cliff (position 2) as the point reached by player 1. Four pulses are now audible: the one played by each player and the two echoes. The rhythmic relationship between them is heard differently by each player, and would of course be heard differently again by listeners in other parts of the space.

(pause)

3. Player 1 walks to a position halfway back to the cliff (position 3). During this movement he plays one stroke on the woodblock every two steps (double tempo). Player 2, standing still, plays in alternation to player 1's pulse as he hears it. Player 1 maintains a constant pulse and walking pace, while the rhythmic relationships which he hears change as he moves back towards the cliff. He stops at the halfway point, parallel with where Player 2 stands. Both continue playing for a short while, then stop.

4. After another short pause, Player 2 walks outwards to a point corresponding with Player 1's previous position (i.e. also about 560 feet from the cliff) (position 4). During this movement he plays a stroke on the woodblock every two steps. Player 1, standing still (position 3), again responds by playing in alternation with Player 2's pulse as he hears it. This time Player 2's pulse appears to him to decelerate as the distance between them increases, so he has to slow down his alternating pulse to keep in time. Player 2

maintains a constant pulse and walking speed, while observing the changing rhythmic relationships with Player 1's pulse and with the two echoes as he moves further away.

(pause)

5. Player 1 walks back from position 3 to the foot of the cliff, playing a stroke every two steps. Player 2, standing still at position 4, plays in alternation, fitting in his strokes exactly halfway between Player 1's strokes as he hears them. When Player 1 reaches the foot of the cliff, both players continue playing for a short while, then stop.

6. After another short pause, Player 2 walks back from position 4 to the foot of the cliff, playing a stroke every two steps. Player 1 remains silent during this final movement.

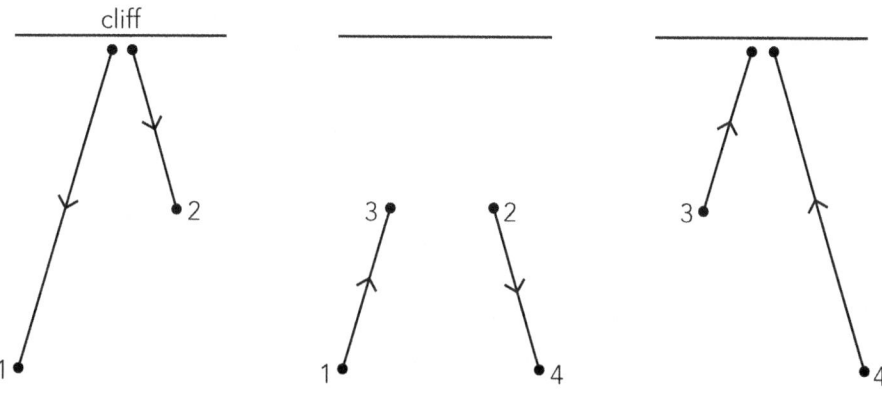

Note: This is a description of a performance which took place in Finland in April 1976.

The general principles may be adapted for performances in other situations. The essential features of the piece are that the players explore changing relationships between outgoing and reflected sounds as they move in relation to the source of the echo, and that they observe the changing rhythmic relationships between sounds played and heard at different distances as they move in relation to each other. The piece may also be adapted for performance by more than two players, and in situations where there are multiple echoes from more than one sound-reflecting source.

Michael Parsons, 1976

Extent: Time: Duration

In terms of duration, the preposition 'for' may be used to describe for how long a process is to continue. *Micro 1* (1961) by Takehisa Kosugi may be considered as a protracted study in the micro-sounds of a large piece of paper gradually unfolding by itself (see Fig. 33). In this score the circumstantial adjunct 'for another 5 minutes' offers a decisive ending to the amplification of a phenomenon with an otherwise unpredictable duration.

MICRO 1

Wrap a live microphone with a very large
sheet of paper. Make a tight bundle.
Keep the microphone live for another 5 minutes

T. Kosugi

33 *Takehisa Kosugi,* Micro 1 *(1961).*

Clock durations in verbal scores can also be reliant on external factors, such as found information. For example, as it continues to expand at a constant rate, the duration of Eric Andersen's Opus 62 (1961) is dependent on the year of performance (see Fig. 34).[32] According to Andersen: 'It has been played at least once a year ever since to reach a duration of 245 sec. this year [2010].'[33]

the frequency a'''' is played as a violinfrequency for
30 sec. - intensity : pp. - each year which passes after
the first of april 1962 involves that the frequency is
lengthened with 5 sec.

34 *Eric Andersen, Opus 62 (1961).*

[32] In the Western musical tradition, there are various accepted systems for denoting note names. One of the most commonly used is the Helmholtz system, as seen in Andersen's Opus 62. This system uses a mixture of italic upper- and lower-case letters with prime symbols (') e.g. C", c', c''''. In the case of Opus 62, the note a'''' corresponds to the top A of the standard piano.
[33] Eric Andersen, in correspondence with James Saunders, November 2010.

Michael Parsons' *Improvisation Rite* (1969), published in *Nature Study Notes* (edited by Cardew), describes a way to determine fixed durations for individual players, based on found information (see Fig. 35).

MPR 109 The time available is divided by the number of people taking part. Each person then plays for this fraction of the total time. He can split it up any way he wishes.

35 *Michael Parsons,* Improvisation Rite, *from* Nature Study Notes *(1969).*

Adjuncts can provide broader descriptions of duration. The vague adjunct 'for a long time' (or variations of it) appears in many scores. La Monte Young's *Composition 1960 #7* (1960) (see Fig. 153, page 425) consists of the notes B_3 and $F\#_4$ written on a musical stave, with the words 'to be held for a long time' handwritten below the stave.[34] Michael Pisaro's *Only* (see Fig. 120, page 316) contains the nominal group 'For a long time'. This is an example of a process-less nominal group, but it may still function like a circumstance, and expanded to a full clause it would perhaps most plausibly take the form, 'This lasts (or would last) for a long time'.

Other scores take into account aspects of the physical situation in order to determine performance duration. A performance of Christian Wolff's *X for Peace Marches* (c. 1986) takes 'as long as it takes' (see Fig. 36), and in another of Milan Knížák's events (1965) the performer must walk in a circle 'as long as possible without stopping' (see Fig. 37).[35]

Extent: Time: Frequency

Frequency represents the extent of the repetition of the occurrence of a process, often within a given period of time. Adjuncts such as 'continuously', 'intermittently', 'constantly' and 'a few times' indicate different types of frequency. Christian Wolff's *Prose Collection* contains many examples of adjuncts describing approximate frequency: in *Sticks* (c. 1968) the performers may 'hum continuously on a low note', in *Stones* they make sounds with stones, 'sometimes in rapid sequences' (see Fig. 151, page 411), and in *Groundspace or Large Groundspace* (1969), 'Movement and making sounds may coincide but neither should make the other obviously awkward or difficult, except very occasionally' (see Fig. 38).

Events occurring with regular frequency may be expressed using adjuncts such as 'every [unit of measurement]' and 'at regular intervals'. In Wolff's *Looking North* a player may decide to obtain a new pulse by listening to and subdividing another player's pulse (see Fig. 5, page 14).

---

[34] The other most commonly accepted system for denoting note names is the American Standard system, which employs roman upper-case letters and subscript Arabic numerals, e.g. C_0, C_4, C_8. In the case of this verbal description of Young's *Composition 1960 #7*, B_3 refers to the B immediately below middle C on the piano, and $F\#_4$ refers to the F# above middle C.

[35] According to the artist, this untitled event is incorrectly referred to elsewhere as *Walking Event* (Milan Knížák, in correspondence with James Saunders, October 2010).

X for Peace Marches

Any number can take part, for as long as it takes, thinking not so much of filling the space and time as indicating a purposeful presence (consider ways of conveying presence sometimes by doing less, even nothing, while maintaining alertness), whistling (a) and clapping hands (b): (a) with exactly two pitches (repeatable); one; four; five; three, not exactly in that order only, (b) with exactly two sounds (claps); three; five; four; one, not necessarily in that order only, any of the above collaboratively or cumulatively, that is, shared out (one pitch yours, the other two—if working with three—another's; one of you whistling, another clapping, etc.), or adding up or on (to another's playing, say, of five, you add two, for a new playing of seven; or play three with another's three; whistling and clapping at the same time by one or more persons, etc.), including, as possible or suitable, material relating to the title of this piece (posters, leaflets, information, slides, videos, etc.), and consider movement, for instance, to, from or between high, very high for a while, soft, low, very low, strong, and so on.

36 *Christian Wolff,* X for Peace Marches *(c. 1986).*

On a busy city avenue, draw a circle about 3m in diameter with chalk on the sidewalk. Walk around the circle as long as possible without stopping.

37 *Milan Knížák, untitled (1965).*

38 *Christian Wolff,* Groundspace or Large Groundspace *(1969).* ▶

Groundspace or Large Groundspace

1. Make single sounds, occasionally very long; very soft to mf.
Play melodies or flourishes of about 4 notes or changes of
sound (or changes of aspects of a sound), of about 3, 8, 25
notes or changes. Allow spaces between playing, at least
so that you may every now and again get a sense of the space
in which you are playing, and at least once so that there
is a point when no one appears to be playing.

2. Instruments or sound sources that carry well start in a
middle distance of the space and then move off and away.

3. Instruments or sound sources that must be immobile can also
use amplification and loudspeakers apart from themselves
and possibly movable.

4. Instruments or sound sources that do not carry far start in
the middle distance and approach potential listeners.

5. At some time a player may seek out another player and play
a duet with him.

(Examples of (2): brass instruments, motors (at no more than medium
loudness; if greater loudness inevitable, start at a remoter place
and move still further away); of (3): piano, if there is no vehicle
to move it or the terrain is bad; of (4): doublebass, electrically
powered sound source with a weak battery.)

For various instruments and sound sources one will have to determine
how well, in the circumstances, they carry, at no more than medium
loudness. Borderline cases could move in directions other than those
indicated for (2) and (4), e.g. on the pattern of a fan, for the most
part away from the center (several centers are possible).

Movement and making sounds may coincide but neither should make the
other obviously awkward or difficult, except very occasionally.

Each player should take the limits of the space to be wherever he is
sometimes audible, at whatever loudness, to one other person and
where he can sometimes hear one other person. If these limits are
passed, he may consider the piece finished.

/Examples of (1) and (5) and additions may follow./

THE HEAT OF THE BEAT   Gavin Bryars

For percussion, brass, and auxiliary performers.

Percussion instruments should be skin-headed drums capable of being
tuned to defined pitches : bass-drums, timpani, tom-toms, bongoes etc.
Brass instruments are tubas, trombones, horns, euphoniums, trumpets,
flugelhorns, cornets.

   The percussion instruments play a constant pulse of eighth notes in
which quarter note = 112, accenting slightly the first eighth-note of a
$\frac{4}{4}$ bar. They are tuned in perfect 5ths and 4ths of D flat, A flat, D flat,
A flat, D flat such that there are more D flats than A flats.   The brass
instruments play the repeated eighth notes in rhythmic unison with the
percussion instruments except that they emphasis slightly the 8th eighth
note of the $\frac{4}{4}$ bar.   They play a common chord of D flat arranged such that
the lowest instrument available plays D flat, the highest plays high A flat,
and a maximum of 2 insturments play the F below the highest A flat played.
There should be at least one D flat and one A flat between the lowest D flat
and the F - still with an A flat above (Thus for there to be any Fs at all,
there must be a minimum of 5 brass instruments).   The instruments play
constantly attempting to maintain consonance throughout; this includes the
percussion instruments.   The piece should start homogeneously, say, with a
footcount.   During the performance auxiliary performers subject the various
instruments to a wide range of temperature treatments (ice, fire, heating
and cooling appliances, fans etc) directly and indirectly applied, such as
will not damage the instruments.   Throughout the instruments maintain
their consonance, re-tuning if necessary, and the piece may be terminated
when the instrumentalist or the auxilliary performers decide that consonance
occurs constantly.   The piece may also terminate following illnes, severe
discomfort, or excessive perspiration odour from any performer.

◀ 39 *Gavin Bryars,* The Heat of the Beat *(1972).*

Forget your pulse and play as closely as you can to every second, fifth, twentieth and single expression of pulse of one other player (this can be repeated as in a loop).

A typescript of what purports to be the earliest handwritten draft of La Monte Young's *Arabic Numeral (any integer) to H.F.* (1960), also known as *X for Henry Flynt*, instructs the player to repeat a piano cluster 'at evenly spaced intervals'. The typescript goes on to qualify that the performer may determine a tempo of 'between one cluster per second and one cluster per two seconds', and that once determined, the tempo 'must remain constant'.[36]

It should be noted that adjuncts of frequency are not the only way to express frequency in verbal notation. Frequency of events is often expressed in scores through the use of a tempo marking, e.g. 'tempo = 120', which may be regarded as a recommendation; it remains arguable whether this is to be regarded as an instruction or part of the composer's definition of the piece. A scorer may need to treat frequency with an even finer degree of precision, to the extent that a particular frequency might be expressed in terms of cycles per second (Hertz), e.g. '261.626 Hertz', or its short-hand nominalised form, e.g. 'middle C'.[37]

Note names are used copiously in Gavin Bryars' *The Heat of the Beat* (1972) (see Fig. 39), in which, while being played, an unspecified number of percussion and brass instruments are subjected to 'a wide range of temperature treatments (ice, fire, heating and cooling appliances, fans, etc) directly and indirectly applied, such as will not damage the instruments'. In the section describing what notes should be played, the composer makes use of a mixture of material and existential processes, with note names functioning as either Goals, e.g. 'the lowest instrument available plays a D flat', or Existents, e.g. 'There should be at least one D flat'. The adjuncts of frequency in this score include 'constant', 'constantly' and 'throughout'.

Location

Circumstantials of Location indicate the location of a process, either the time when it occurs or the place where it occurs, for instance 'at three o'clock', 'after the signal', 'on the stage' or 'in the library'. Interrogatives for circumstances of Location include 'when?' and 'where?'.

Location: Time

Circumstantials of Location in time describe the temporal location of a process. Included in this category are things like clock time, calendar time, the seasons, and the timing of processes in relation to each other, for instance through use of the adjuncts 'before', 'during' and 'after'.

---

[36] These three quotations from *Arabic Numeral (any integer)* are Copyright © 2011 by La Monte Young. Please see the complete copyright notice and performance licensing information for this work on p. 427.

[37] The frequency of a repeated event becomes an audible pitch above c. 20 Hertz.

Sit down during Dec. 11, 1963 fr om 7 PM to 8.03 PM (Danishti me) and think about the people over the whole world, who may be performing this composition.

40 *Eric Andersen, Opus 14 (1962).*

A score may stipulate a particular clock time for performance. Eric Andersen specifies an exact time and date (now long past) for performance of his Opus 14 (1962) (see Fig. 40). According to Andersen: 'the piece is from Dec. 11th (in folklore named The Devil's Day) 1962. It was mailed out during the following days as postcards in many versions.'[38]

Mieko (Chieko) Shiomi's set of nine pieces collectively entitled *Spatial Poem* was produced between 1965 and 1975. Each is a global event, to be carried out within specific dates or at particular times, with instructions sent to potential participants around the world. In *Spatial Poem No. 2* any potential realisations were scheduled to occur at the same moment irrespective of their time zones. In order to minimize confusion, Shiomi provided the participants with a comprehensive list of equivalent times and dates for major cities and countries around the world, beginning with: 'New York – 5:00 pm, Oct. 15, 1965' (see Fig. 41).

A performance may need to occur at a particular time of day. George Brecht's *Motor Vehicle Sundown (Event)* (1960) is to be performed 'At sundown (relatively dark/open area incident light 2-foot candles or less)'. A number of Mark So's scores specify that a performance take place around sunrise or sunset, for instance *The world becomes the world goes on* (2008) is to be realised 'outdoors at dusk' (see Fig. 42). This is an approach that the composer has since reassessed:

> while all those changes constantly underway in the environment are indeterminate and chaotic, essentially unpredictable (even while of the greatest importance) in how they will impact a piece, at certain times – for instance, the transition from day to night – those changes become highly formulaic, definite in their movement from one big concept (day) to another (night). [...] So it seemed perfectly reasonable to deal with this formulaic quality of the environment by indicating it in my scores. [...] Interestingly, the performances of my work in which the imprint of nightfall has been the most compelling have been pieces in which this aspect has not been scored, but simply transpired. This has led me to reconsider the actual indication of a 'daylight function' let's call it – I hardly write it anymore, even as it's become a central consideration in thinking about when to realize certain pieces. It remains in the process, amplified even, but I'd say there's a strange precariousness to its place in the text of the score.[39]

Scores may bring into play other naturally occurring phenomena that are likely to appear at particular times of the day. Two scores by Arthur Bull engage with things that only appear 'in the evening' and 'on a clear night' (see Fig. 77, pages 136–7).

[38] Eric Andersen, in correspondence with James Saunders, November 2010.
[39] Mark So, in correspondence with the author, March 2010.

41 *Mieko (Chieko) Shiomi, Spatial Poem No. 2 (1965).* ▶

SPATIAL POEM No.2

Around the time listed below
what kind of direction are you moving
or facing toward ?
— either performance or spontaneous —
please send me a report about it
which will be edited on a world map

New York ·········· 5:00 pm, Oct. 15, 1965
Amsterdam ········· 11:00 pm, Oct. 15, 1965
Copenhagen ········· 11:00 pm, Oct. 15, 1965
Paris ··············· 11:00 pm, Oct. 15, 1965
Japan ··············· 7:00 am, Oct. 16, 1965
Stockholm ··········· 11:00 pm, Oct. 15, 1965
London ············· 10:00 pm, Oct. 15, 1965
Scotland ············ 10:00 pm, Oct. 15, 1965
Vienna ············· 11:00 pm, Oct. 15, 1965
Nice ··············· 11:00 pm, Oct. 15, 1965
Rome ··············· 11:00 pm, Oct. 15, 1965
Moscow ············· 1:00 am, Oct. 16, 1965
Berlin ·············· 11:00 pm, Oct. 15, 1965
Los Angeles ········· 2:00 pm, Oct. 15, 1965
Montreal ············ 5:00 pm, Oct. 15, 1965
India ·············· 3:30 am, Oct. 16, 1965
Barcelona ·········· 11:00 pm, Oct. 15, 1965
Cologne ············ 11:00 pm, Oct. 15, 1965
Prague ············· 11:00 pm, Oct. 15, 1965
Chicago ············ 4:00 pm, Oct. 15, 1965
Mexico city ········· 4:00 pm, Oct. 15, 1965
Brazil ············· 7:00 pm, Oct. 15, 1965
Iran ··············· 1:30 am, Oct. 16, 1965
Sydney ············· 8:00 am, Oct. 16, 1965
Hawaii ············· 0:00 pm, Oct. 15, 1965
Greenland ·········· 7:00 pm, Oct. 15, 1965

etc.   simultaneous

Chieko Shiomi
7-1 Mizuho-juza
Kitanagase, Okayama
Japan

• Please write in print hand or use typewriter

The world becomes the world goes on

mark so

> *earth*
> *air*
> *fire*
> *water.*

> *The world becomes the world goes on*
>> – John Wieners, from *A book of PROPHECIES*

—for a few musicians, working together

earth

environmental; or as a substance—stone, dirt, sand, etc.—acted upon

air

environmental; or as breath, blown across/into/out of...; or as song, a simple melody

fire

environmental; or as brought to burn; or igniting...

water

environmental; or as a substance—ice, liquid water, steam—acted upon

an open place
outdoors at dusk

(in the world and part of it—simple)

9 may – 26 june 2008
los angeles

42 *Mark So,*
The world
becomes the
world goes on
(2008).

Sounds or activities may need to be synchronised with other players or environmental events. These kinds of correspondences are often achieved in verbal notation through adjuncts such as 'simultaneously', 'at the same time' and 'all at once'. Many of Christian Wolff's scores focus on players cueing each other, whether knowingly or otherwise (see, for instance, *Looking North*, Fig. 5, page 14), and in Cornelius Cardew's *The Great Learning*, Paragraph 6, '"Synchronised sound" means make a sound simultaneously with another player' (see Fig. 80, page 149). In Bengt af Klintberg's *Orange Event Number 17* (1963–6) a performer waits for two environmental sounds to coincide before peeling an orange and letting the peel fall into the Stockholm Stream (see Fig. 93, page 225).

Adjuncts like 'until' and 'when' might suggest a culmination of some sort, allowing a process to be seen through to its natural conclusion. Michael Parsons' *Walk* ends simply when the last person finishes: 'Continue until all have completed an agreed number of journeys' (see Fig. 116, page 305). Steve Reich's *Pendulum Music* is ended 'sometime shortly after all microphones have come to rest and are feeding back a continuous tone',[40] and Karlheinz Stockhausen's *RIGHT DURATIONS* puts the duration in the hands of the performer: 'stop when you feel that you should stop' (see Fig. 138, page 361).

A naturally occurring phenomenon such as a change in temperature could also provide an ending, as in Lee Heflin's *Ice Trick* (1963), which ends 'when the block of ice has melted' (see Fig. 43). Pushing the performer to extremes of personal ability may also induce an end. Physical exhaustion is one way, as in La Monte Young's *Piano Piece for Terry Riley #1* (1960), in which the performer attempts to push a piano through a wall: 'The piece is over when you are too exhausted to push any longer' (see Fig. 153, page 424). George Brecht's *Exercise* and *Exercise* (both 1963) are studies in finite measurement: 'Repeat, until further accuracy is impossible' and 'Repeat, until further precision is impossible' (see Fig. 44).[41] Hugh Shrapnel's *Vodka Rite* (1969) offers a highly effective route to indeterminacy, and ends as you might reasonably expect (see Fig. 45).

43 *Lee Heflin,*
Ice Trick *(1963),*
version from
Fluxus
Performance
Workbook.

Ice Trick

Pass a one pound piece of ice among members of the audience while playing a recording of fire sounds or while having a real fire on stage. The piece ends when the block of ice has melted.

Lee Heflin, 1963

[40] A problematic idea, as anyone realising the work will discover. In the 'Directions for Performance' in the 1980 version of *Pendulum Music*, 'A duration of about 10 minutes is suggested'.

[41] A complete list of Brecht's event scores is available in Robinson and Fischer, 2005, pp. 300–2. The list, complied by Hermann Braun, includes the month and year that each score was written. According to Braun, both *Exercise* (centre) and *Exercise* (limits) were made in April 1963.

EXERCISE

Determine the center of an object or event.

Determine the center more accurately.

Repeat, until further accuracy is impossible.

EXERCISE

Determine the limits of an object or event.

Determine the limits more precisely.

Repeat, until further precision is impossible.

44 *George Brecht,* Exercise *and* Exercise *(both 1963).*

HMSVR48 Members of the group each to perform some action while intermittently consuming a large bottle of Vodka. Actions made should preferably necessitate communication with other members of the group Performance ends for each player when he has consumed the Vodka &/or is completely incapacitated.

45 *Hugh Shrapnel,* Vodka Rite, *from* Nature Study Notes *(1969).*

In *MAXIMUSIC* (1965) by James Tenney, three distinct sections are to be timed in relation to each other (see Fig. 46). The first section is 'very long'. In the second section, the percussionist must 'continue until nearly exhausted from the physical effort'. However, the duration of the second section must not be as long as the first section, so the percussionist would have to judge his or her efforts accordingly. The duration of the third section is in turn determined by the durations of the previous two sections.

46 *James Tenney,* MAXIMUSIC (1965), *from* Postal Pieces (1954–71). ▶

MAXIMUSIC

for Max Neuhaus

(1) Soft roll on large cymbal; constant,
resonant, very long.

(2) Sudden loud, fast improvisation on
all the other (percussion) instruments
except the tam—tam(s)—especially
(but not only) non-sustaining ones;
constant texture; continue until
nearly exhausted from the physical
effort, but not as long as (1); end
with tam—tam(s) (not used until now)—
just one blow, as loud as possible.

(3) Same as (1), but now inaudible until
all the other sounds have faded;
continue ad lib but not as long as
(1) or (2), then let the cymbal fade
out by itself.

James Tenney
6/16/65

Adjuncts of location in time can also provide ways to structure events in pitch space over periods of time. Taking his cue from Sol LeWitt's plans for wall drawings, which describe the relative location of, for instance, lines on a wall (see Fig. 99, page 244), Michael Winter's *for Sol LeWitt* (2009) is an example of what the composer calls 'total scalable relativity' (see Fig. 147, page 396). In this work the durations of elements are described in relation to the overall duration and the temporal positions of other elements, rather than by fixed clock-timings, through the use of adjuncts of location such as 'at the midpoints in time of two sustained tones with the same duration'. This means that the work is scalable to any given duration, similar to the way in which LeWitt's wall drawings are scalable to any given wall space. As the reader may discover, there are many different ways of 'rendering' this set of relationships, and, as the composer points out, to include any graphic representations of these relationships in the score might be to limit potential interpretations of the verbal notation.[42]

Location: Place

Adjuncts of place deal with where in space the process unfolds, and include prepositions such as 'towards', 'on', 'off', 'through', and adverbs such as 'downstairs', 'behind', 'inside' and 'overseas'. Again, they may be definite, e.g. 'at a distance of three metres', or indefinite, e.g. 'near'.

Stuart Marshall's *A Sagging and Reading Room* involves four performers using portable cassette recorders to play back pre-recorded statements, and changing their locations (and therefore the cassettes' locations) depending on what information they hear (see Fig. 47). The cassettes give information to the performers about where to move in relation to the other performers and to two microphones. As Marshall observes, the performers' movements depend on their own individual interpretations of the indefinite adjuncts 'further from' and 'nearer to'. As a result, unpredictable groupings emerge; as Alvin Lucier recounts: 'In one performance all four performers ended up clumped around one microphone.'[43] The 'score' consists of an account of the actions required to create a tape which is, according to Marshall, 'the final work', along with four 'parts' for the performers, each consisting of 14 declarative statements about the location of the different cassettes in relation to one another (see Fig. 48).

Although the account of the required actions is a past tense description of the first realisation, this text has been used as a cue for subsequent realisations in which the performers' movements are carried out live in front of an audience, and the tape recording is then played back in its entirety.[44] The

---

[42] See pp. 397–8.

[43] Lucier, A, 'On Stuart Marshall', in Collins, 2001, p. 51.

[44] In the playback section, the physical location of the sounds is re-presented in the performance space over two loudspeakers, revealing the volume and spatial placement of the original recorded sounds as picked up by the microphones. As well as picking up the sounds of the recorded statements, the microphones also gather other sounds from the environment; during a 2005 performance at Tate Modern in London, the audience's reactions to the first section were clearly audible on the tape.

47 *Stuart Marshall*, A Sagging and Reading Room *(1972)*. ▶

SAGGING AND READING ROOM

The notation was made on an IBM 3600 computer at Wesleyan University
Connecticut, the final work consisting of a tape recording of the live
realisation of this notation.
Parts are provided for four performers, two female and two male, consisting
of a number of statements of the general form:

At the time of the next statement this cassette will be further from/nearer
to microphone 1/2 than A/B/C/D's cassette and further from/nearer to
microphone 1/2 than A/B/C/D's cassette.

Performer A's part specifies locations relative to those of B,C and D.
Performer B's part specifies locations relative to those of A,C and D etc.
These notations were read onto cassette tape recorders as a series of statements separated by two second gaps. The live performance stage consisted of
each performer playing a statement on his/her machine, turning off the
machine, attempting to position himself/herself at the specified location
and then playing the next statement on the cassett.
In order to locate his/her position in space 'at the time of the next statement' each performer had to perform at least two triangulations.
ie further from/nearer to microphone 1/2 than A/B/C/D and
     further from/nearer to microphone 1/2 than A/B/C/D

The programme specifies locations which correlate the performers' movements
so that they describe complex figures in the recording space.
The recording was made on a stereo tape machine, the microphone of the left
channel being designated as microphone 1 and the microphone of the right
channel as microphone 2.
The microphones were positioned 35' apart which was the distance between the
two loudspeakers used for playback (pseudo stereo recording and playback).
Each performer's interpretation of 'further from' and 'nearer to' necessarily
affected the other performers' positions in space and gave rise to great
distortions of the programme's figures in the form of 'bunching' near microphones and 'spreading' to the farthest parts of the space. Distortions were
also caused by the shape of the space and the obstacles within it.

Alvin's cassette

at the time of the next statement this cassette will be nearer to microphone 1 than Roland's cassette and further from microphone 2 than Anthony's cassette

at the time of the next statement this cassette will be further from microphone 2 than Roland's cassette and nearer to microphone 1 than Roland's cassette

at the time of the next statement this cassette will be further from microphone 2 than Roland's cassette and further from microphone 2 than Hildegard's cassette

at the time of the next statement this cassette will be nearer to microphone 1 than Hildegard's cassette and nearer to microphone 1 than Alvin's cassette

at the time of the next statement this cassette will be nearer to microphone 1 than Hildegard's cassette and further from microphone 2 than Anthony's cassette

at the time of the next statement this cassette will be further from microphone 2 than Hildegard's cassette and nearer to microphone 1 than Roland's cassette

at the time of the next statement this cassette will be further from microphone 2 than Hildegard's cassette and further from microphone 2 than Hildegard's cassette

at the time of the next statement this cassette will be nearer to microphone 1 than Alvin's cassette and nearer to microphone 1 than Alvin's cassette

at the time of the next statement this cassette will be nearer to microphone 1 than Alvin's cassette and further from microphone 2 than Anthony's cassette

at the time of the next statement this cassette will be further from microphone 2 than Alvin's cassette and nearer to microphone 1 than Roland's cassette

at the time of the next statement this cassette will be further from microphone 2 than Alvin's cassette and further from microphone 2 than Hildegard's cassette

at the time of the next statement this cassette will be nearer to microphone 1 than Anthony's cassette and nearer to microphone 1 than Alvin's cassette

at the time of the next statement this cassette will be nearer to microphone 1 than Anthony's cassette and further from microphone 2 than Anthony's cassette

at the time of the next statement this cassette will be further from microphone 2 than Anthony's cassette and nearer to microphone 1 than Roland's cassette

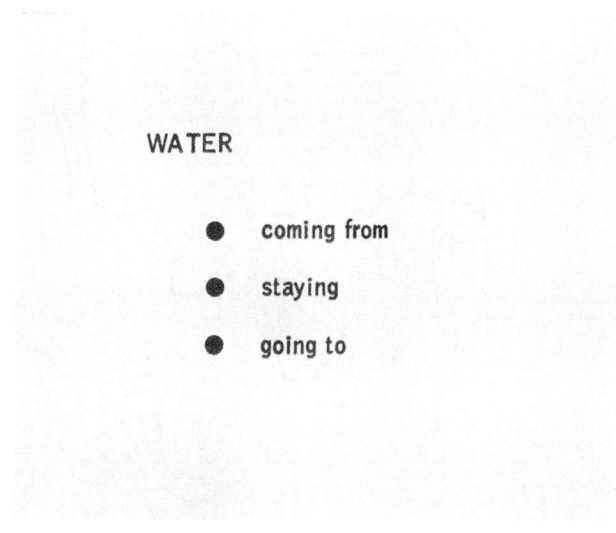

49 *George Brecht,* Water *(1963).*

changes in location must occur sequentially, one at a time, with the performers taking turns to listen to their own cassette and then move to a new location. Each sounding statement thus serves both to confirm that the last statement was true, and to provide information about where to move so that the current statement will be true at the time of the following statement. Some of these statements even suggest spatial conundrums, a result of the impeccable logic of the IBM 3600 computer that was used to create the permutations:

at the time of the next statement this cassette will be nearer to microphone 1 than Alvin's cassette and nearer to microphone 1 than Alvin's cassette.

As well as indicating static location in space, adjuncts may also indicate the source, path or destination of movement. George Brecht's event score *Water* (1963) consists of three non-finite processes that express movement and location: 'coming from', 'staying' and 'going to' (see Fig. 49). In each case an adjunct is implied – 'staying [in a place]' – or partly expressed by prepositions without the expected nominal group that should follow – 'from [a place]', 'to [a place]'. These non-finite processes may suggest many concurrent meanings, and if a performer determines that one particular meaning is to be adopted in order to realise the score, it is not necessarily to the exclusion of other meanings, which remain as potentialities. In the case of *Water*, the adjuncts that are implied by the processes remain unexpressed, waiting for a performer to realise them.

In Mieko (Chieko) Shiomi's *Spatial Poem No. 2*, the score asks 'At the time listed below, what kind of direction are you moving or facing toward?' (see Fig. 41, page 59). Shiomi requested written reports from performers, which she then distributed across a map (see Fig. 50). The reports reveal some inventive interpretations of Shiomi's question. For instance, George Maciunas sent back this report:

George Maciunas was spinning himself on a spinning chair in a freight elevator which was going up in N.Y.

In an undated letter to Maciunas, evidently written after the event but before the final map piece had been completed, Shiomi reveals her own intention behind the use of the word 'direction':

48 *Alvin Lucier's part for realisations of Stuart Marshall's* A Sagging and Reading Room.

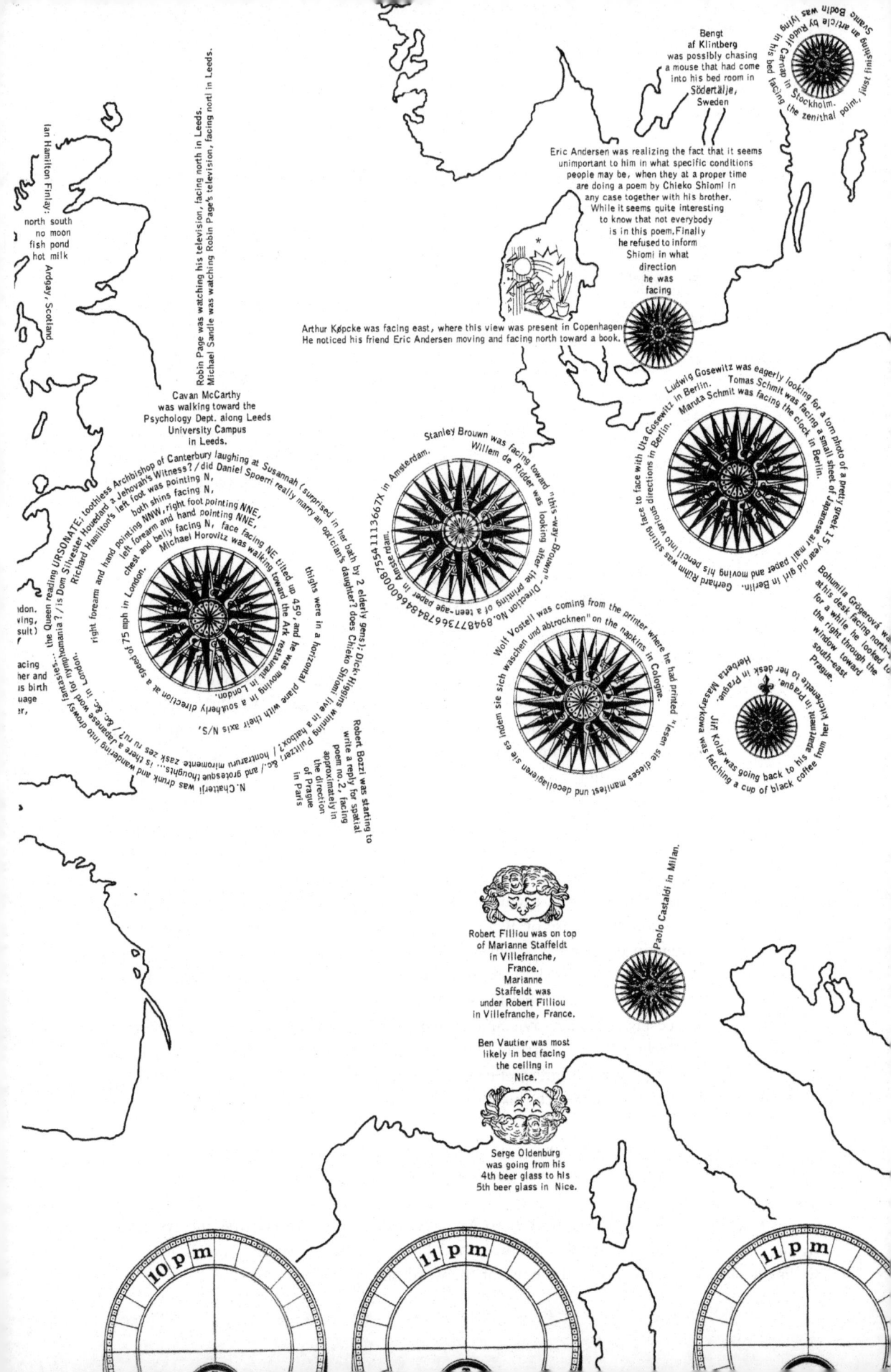

Ian Hamilton Finlay:

north south
no moon
fish pond
hot milk

Ardgay, Scotland

Robin Page was watching his television, facing north in Leeds.
Michael Sandle was watching Robin Page's television, facing north in Leeds.

Cavan McCarthy was walking toward the Psychology Dept. along Leeds University Campus in Leeds.

Bengt af Klintberg was possibly chasing a mouse that had come into his bed room in *Södertälje*, Sweden

Svante Bodin was lying in his bed, facing the zenithal point, just finishing an article by Rudolf Carnap in Stockholm.

Eric Andersen was realizing the fact that it seems unimportant to him in what specific conditions people may be, when they at a proper time are doing a poem by Chieko Shiomi in any case together with his brother. While it seems quite interesting to know that not everybody is in this poem. Finally he refused to inform Shiomi in what direction he was facing

Arthur Køpcke was facing east, where this view was present in Copenhagen. He noticed his friend Eric Andersen moving and facing north toward a book.

Ludwig Gosewitz was eagerly looking for a torn photo of a pretty greek 1.5 year old girl in Berlin.
Tomas Schmit was facing Uta Gosewitz in Berlin.
Maruta Schmit was facing the clock in Berlin.

Gerhard Rühm was sitting face to face with Uta Gosewitz into mysterious directions in Berlin.

Bohumila Grögerová was at his desk facing north for a while he looked for the right through the window toward southeast Prague.

Heribert Masaryk in Prague.

Jiří Kolář was going back to his apartment was fetching a cup of black coffee from her kitchenette to her desk in Prague.

Stanley Brouwn was facing toward "this-way-Brown"
Willem de Ridder was looking after the printing of a teen-age paper in Amsterdam. Direction No. 894877336784860008755411113 7X in Amsterdam.

Wolf Vostell was coming from the printer where he had printed "lesen sie dieses manifest und decollagieren sie es indem sie sich waschen und abtrocknen" on the napkins in Cologne.

...the Queen reading URSONATE; toothless Archbishop of Canterbury laughing at Susannah (surprised in her bath by 2 elderly gens); Dick Higgins; Did Silvester Houédard a Jehovah's Witness? / did Daniel Spoerri really marry an optician's daughter? does Chieko Shiomi live in a hatbox? / Richard Hamilton's left foot was pointing N, both shins facing N, left forearm and hand pointing NNW, right foot pointing NNE, chest and belly facing N, face facing NE tilted up 45°, right forearm and hand pointing NNE, Michael Horovitz was walking toward the Ark restaurant at a speed of 75 mph in London.

N.Chatterji was drunk and wandering into drowsy and grotesque thoughts... 'is there a Japanese word for nymphomania? / is Dom Silvester fantastissimus?...' &c./ and grotesque thoughts... 'is there a Japanese word zask zes ru?/ &c. &c.' for London.

thighs were in a horizontal plane with their axis N/S, he was moving in a southerly direction of Prague in Paris

Robert Bozzi was starting to write a reply for spatial poem no.2, facing approximately in the direction of Prague in Paris

Robert Filliou was on top of Marianne Staffeldt in Villefranche, France.
Marianne Staffeldt was under Robert Filliou in Villefranche, France.

Paolo Castaldi in Milan.

Ben Vautier was most likely in bed facing the ceiling in Nice.

Serge Oldenburg was going from his 4th beer glass to his 5th beer glass in Nice.

10 pm   11 pm   11 pm

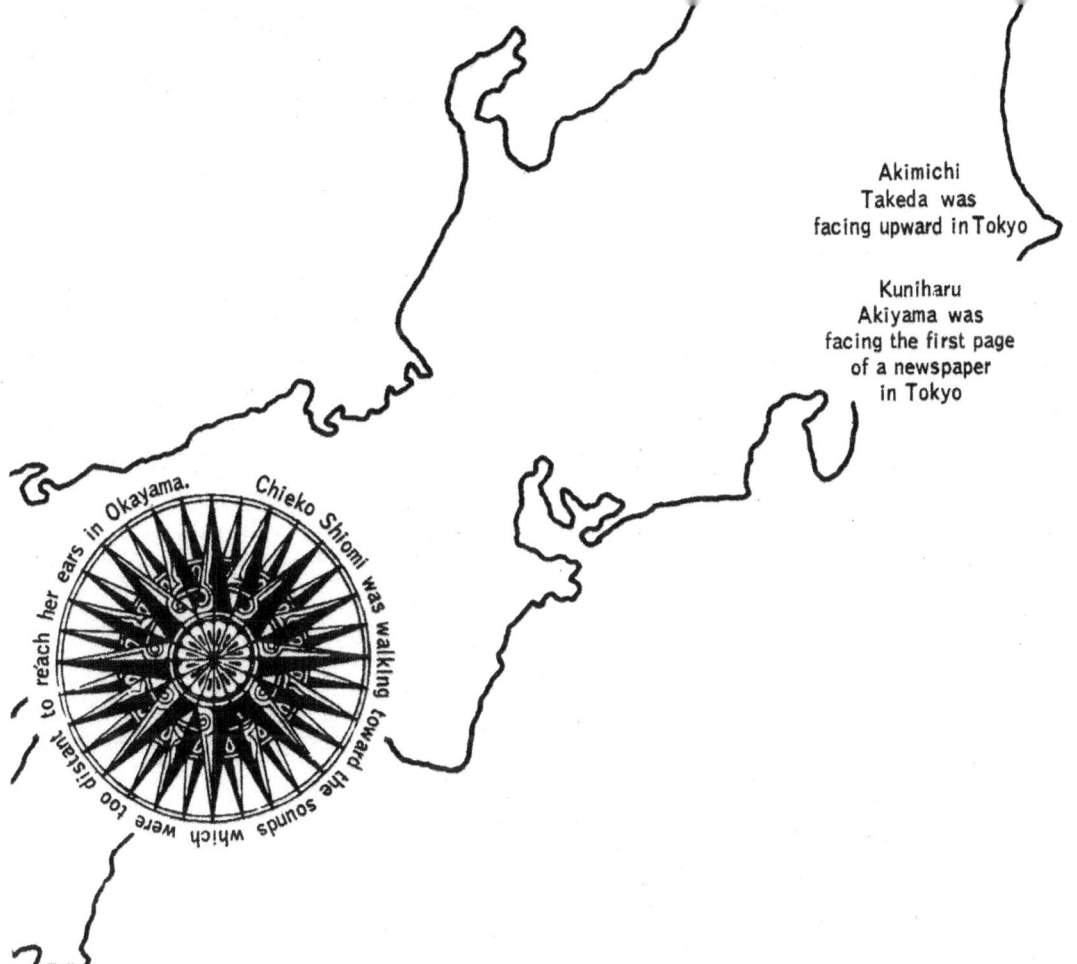

Akimichi Takeda was facing upward in Tokyo

Kuniharu Akiyama was facing the first page of a newspaper in Tokyo

Chieko Shiomi was walking toward the sounds which were too distant to reach her ears in Okayama.

50 *Mieko (Chieko) Shiomi, extracts from* Spatial Poem No. 2.

I liked your performance of *Spatial Poem No. 2* very much. That was [marvellous]. I was walking towards the sounds which were out of distance to reach my ears. I meant "direction" not only direction on compass, in this poem it is rather the state of [consciousness] of the relation between yourself and the outside world. [I've] got about 40 reports so far, and found that most people took it the direction on compass, though some are very interesting.[45]

Adjuncts of place need not solely refer to physical space, but can also refer to abstract space, for instance the distance between frequencies. In Bryars' *The Heat of the Beat* (see Fig. 39, page 56) the notes are discussed in spatial relation to each other, using the Location adjuncts 'below', 'between' and 'above'. Alvin Lucier has made extensive use of Hertz notation to describe the location of frequencies in pitch space. *Still and Moving Lines of Silence in Families of Hyperbolas* (1973–4/1984) is a collection of works for singers, players, dancers, unattended percussion and pure wave (sine tone) oscillators. These works focus on the interference patterns that result when two tones are very close in frequency. The 1973–4 version outlines quite a broad area for exploration, beginning with the general instruction, 'Create standing

[45] Chieko Shiomi, letter to George Maciunas (no date), Jean Brown Archive, The Getty Research Institute.

waves in space caused by constructive and destructive interference patterns among sine waves from loudspeakers'. However, the 1984 version is more specific. In each of the 12 'numbers', mostly for soloist and loudspeaker, the composer employs adjuncts of Location, e.g. 'above', 'below' and 'equidistant', to describe the placement of sung or played long tones within a very narrow frequency range, relative to the pure continuous reference pitch produced by an electronic oscillator. In each number Lucier uses note names and frequencies in Hertz when specifying oscillator tuning. That frequency is then referred to in the description of what the voice or instrument must do. Here, for example, is Part III, Number 9, for viola and oscillator, in which the viola player and the loudspeaker are located on opposite sides of the stage:

Viola
Oscillator tuning and placement: G at 196 hertz, left channel.
Start in unison with the pure wave and, with each alternate tone, move slightly above, then below, in an outward wedge pattern, stopping a few cycles above the 196 hertz tone. Alternate pairs of notes should be equidistant from the 196 hertz tone.

Manner

Adjuncts of Manner can be used to describe the way in which a process takes place. Typical interrogatives for Manner are 'how?', 'with what?' and 'what ... like?'. There are four main types of Manner adjunct: *means*, *quality*, *comparison* and *degree*.

Means refers to the means by which a process occurs, and is often expressed with the prepositions 'by', 'using' and 'with'. The interrogative forms are typically 'with what?' and 'how?'. A score may use an adjunct of means to specify what instrument is required for a particular process, as in Arthur Bull's score, 'using rapid labial, frontal and dental mouth sounds' (see Fig. 77, page 137). Or it may describe a constraint, as in *Walk* by Michael Parsons, which instructs the performers to walk from one point to the next 'by the most direct route' (see Fig. 116, page 305).

Quality is usually expressed by adverbs such as 'slightly', 'quietly' and 'swiftly', and the interrogative forms are 'how?' or 'how... ?' with the appropriate adverb. Manner is a central focus in *FROM HERE TO YOU* (2006) (see Fig. 51), in which Adam Overton provides a collection of adjuncts that could be used to augment Yoko Ono's *Touch Piece* (see page 301). Elsewhere, in Francesco Gagliardi's *Reading 5* the performer must read 'silently' (see Fig. 9, page 18), and in John Cage's *Solo for Voice 6* (1970) the actor should for certain sections 'perform impassively' (see Fig. 78, page 140).

Comparison expresses similarity, and uses prepositions such as 'like' and 'unlike', or adverbial groups such as 'in the manner of'. The interrogative is typically 'what... like?'. In *Relaxing at the Piano* (1977) by Daniel Goode, the instruction is: 'Approach the keyboard of the piano as you would a bed, couch, a chair, or the floor' (see Fig. 89, page 196). In *Orange Event Number 8* (1963–6),

51 *Adam Overton,* FROM HERE TO YOU *(2006).* ▶

FROM HERE TO YOU
Adverbs for Yoko Ono's *Touch Piece*
  or
I'M [NOT] TOUCHING YOU, I'M [NOT] TOUCHING YOU, I'M [NOT] TOUCHING YOU, ...
Adam Overton, June 2006

. . . . .

publicly, privately
appropriately
in any combination, all, some, or [n]one

. . . . .

secretly
suddenly
slightly
almost
barely
breathily
breathingly
blinkingly
unflinchingly
without notice
without fanfare
unnoticeably
unknowingly
invisibly
from afar
from here
grazingly
gazingly
repeatedly
randomly
believingly
unbelievably
hopefully
faithfully
fancifully
fearfully
fearlessly
unmistakably
without hands
without fail
before it is too late

touch someone

Bengt af Klintberg uses a subordinate clause when instructing the reader to eat an orange 'as if it were an apple', and then explains what that entails (see Fig. 93, page 225).

Degree is often expressed using adverbial groups like 'as much' or 'as little'. The interrogative form is typically 'how much?'. Degree adjuncts are often used in verbal scores in order to provide an ideal or target for a performer to aim for. For instance, in G. Douglas Barrett's *A Few Silence* (2008) performers create sounds 'to the best of their ability' (see Fig. 56, page 93). Christian Wolff's *Looking North* also deals with player ability: 'Forget your pulse and play as closely as you can to every second, fifth, twentieth and single expression of pulse of one other player' (see Fig. 5, page 14). In Markus Trunk's *slightly ajar*, the score specifies that doors may be opened and closed 'with as little noise as possible' (see Fig. 23, page 35). The composer explains that this instruction was included in the score as a response to the first performance:

> To be honest, I don't feel very strongly about the quietness of the opening and closing, I just want to prevent it from becoming a feature of the performance which is supposed to focus attention on the sounds rather than the mechanics. I suppose this cautionary note ended up in the score as a reaction against the theatricality and carnival atmosphere of the first performance.[46]

Cause and Contingency

Finally in this section, circumstantials of Cause express why a process occurs. They include the *reason* why a process occurs, and also for what *purpose* it occurs. Adjuncts of reason can give a clear sense of causality. They are typically expressed by phrases such as 'because of', 'as a result of' and 'thanks to'. Adjuncts of purpose convey the intended purpose of a process, and are expressed with phrases like 'for the purpose of', 'so that' and 'in order to'.

Alvin Lucier's *Music on a Long Thin Wire* is an example of a fairly technical score, which describes the construction of a very long powered monochord (see Fig. 103, page 252). Because the instrument needs to be constructed so that it works effectively, there seems to be a clear sense of purpose in Lucier's choice of language. For instance, during the building stage the height of the wire is adjusted, 'so that it passes directly between the poles of the magnet'. There is also a sense of purpose during the performance stage, where the performer should, at the end of each phrase, 'reduce the volume to zero in order to silently retune the oscillator frequency for the next phrase'.[47]

---

[46] Markus Trunk, in correspondence with the author, September 2010.
[47] Although a performance is described in the score for *Music on a Long Thin Wire*, the work is generally now only presented as an installation (see pp. 255–64).

52 *Francesco Gagliardi,* Public/Private 1. *(2009).* ▶

Public/Private 1.

While exercising in public, work yourself up to
the point of crying uncontrollably.

Note:

Aerobic exercise is particularly indicated for this
performance.
Ideal circumstances include, but are not limited to:
jogging on the street; running on a treadmill in a
public gym; aerobics, spinning, and step classes; etc.
Cycling is allowed only if performed as a physical
exercise; the piece should not be performed when
riding the bicycle as a means of transportation.
Aquatics sports; combat sports; gymnastics; team
sports; skiing; weightlifting; etc. are less apt, but may
be attempted nonetheless, as long as they are
performed in public and in circumstances which
allow the crying to be manifest.
Insofar as it is compatible with a natural performance
of the physical activity, listening to music, looking at
pictures, reading, etc. in order to induce the crying is
allowed. The music, image or text used, however,
should not be revealed under any circumstance.

Note:

I performed this piece on a number of occasions in January
2009 while running on a treadmill at the Coles Sport Center
on Mercer St. in New York, NY.

Circumstantials of Contingency specify what it is a process may depend on. They express necessary conditions with phrases like 'if', 'in case of' and 'in the event of'. In *Public/Private 1.* (2009) by Francesco Gagliardi, the performer must, while exercising in public, work him or her self up to the point of crying uncontrollably (see Fig. 52). The score features detailed notes on ways to achieve this, and the ideal circumstances for performance. Using the Contingency circumstantial 'only if', the composer places a particular constraint on the activity of cycling, which is allowed 'only if performed as a physical exercise; the piece should not be performed when riding the bicycle as a means of transportation'.

Postscript

Since, according to Systemic Functional Grammar, language is considered as a system that creates meaning, a survey like this can only ever provide a partial view of the potential inherent in that system. With SFG the language system as a whole is regarded not as a collection of fixed meanings, but rather as a 'structured meaning potential' which is sensitive to context. Any verbal score may be regarded as an 'instantiation' of that system. In terms of the practical realisation of these scores, it therefore seems a natural extension to regard a verbal score as itself a structured meaning potential which is sensitive to context. Any realisation of that score may be considered not merely as 'one of a limited number of possible outcomes', but rather as an instantiation of the structured meaning potential of the score. George Brecht appears to have been exploring similar territory in the summer of 1959, while he was studying with John Cage. A fragment in one of Brecht's diligently kept notebooks reads:

> The performer behaves in a situation partly determined by the composer, partly by himself, partly by ambient conditions. There is an elegant consistency to the viewpoint which allows each of these elements to manifest its own nature, without imbalance, without imposition. Ambient sound penetrates the intended, is "included" in the music. It is relevant to the situation in which the music arises/relevant to the music, which is ever situational.[48]

---

[48] Brecht, 1991c, p. 125.

Part 2: Scores, Writings and Commentaries

Eric Andersen

Opus 18 (1961)

in Mezzo a Quattro Tempi

OPUS 18

ANNOUNCE X
PRESENT Y
DECLARE Z

in Mezzo a Quattro Tempi

§1

A Score can become a notch cut or line, an account kept, number of points made, set of twenty, a topic, piece of good fortune, worst in repartee and much more.

And not to forget a Partitura from the Latin Pars indicating both partial, direction and task. It sounds like music but really isn't.

Following the great industrial wars the human mind started to wander to find other ways of representation than the stereotyped arts framed in categories of production.

It soon became obvious that another understanding of what art could be would rely on change and time.

In the mid-'50s the institutional art world was still traumatized in pompous attitudes and fantasies about the transcendental. An alternative situation opened however in the most abstract of the time based arts; - music. A paradoxical situation since music had for centuries become the most bourgeois of all the arts.

Due to economical and institutional rationales this couldn't last. But for a little more than a decade a remarkable time bracket had opened for intensive experimentation. From the mid-'50s to the mid-'60s InterMedia, Fluxus and Scores surfaced on our planet.

§2

It is quite a myth that concert halls and the streets were chosen and museums and art centers rejected as performance spaces. On the contrary. It was the visual art world that rejected us and we had to find places where we weren't likely to be arrested.

Similarly myths claim that we preferred to work with very inexpensive and fragile matter, were avoiding any kind of colors and abundances; - aiming at the eternal ephemeral. That was absolutely not the case. Any of us would have been most happy to be invited for a major show in any prestigious museum, utilizing extremely advanced and expensive techniques and materials. And the ones of us who got the chance later on did so. There is only one reason why some scores look conceptual or minimal. Because we were poor. For the first time in history the daughters and sons of non-wealthy families could exercise experimental art.

What occupied our bodies and minds in the late-'50s and early-'60s were phenomena such as InterMedia (though coined some years later), Globalism, Simultaneity, Audience Participation, Interactive, Occurrences. All terms that became axiomatic during the '80s when the fast processor-86 was introduced and eventually gave rise to the Internet.

In contrast to the adaption of the following Minimalism and Conceptual Art to the academic practices Scoring seems to have kept clear of most abysses of confinement. It is an essential but mostly ignored fact that most scores were written after their performances. As a report from a sensuous occurrence to be distributed among friends through the mail.

§3

Certain scores are called Event Scores. When George Brecht, who was the first to use the notion, was asked whether Event was identical to the scientific use of the term he confirmed the intent. An Event is defined as an entity that is both an object and an activity. When the other George (Maciunas) came back to New York from Europe and the first Fluxus Performance Festivals he announced that he would publish the collected Scores of all artists presented there. He was rather pissed off when the first George insisted on a very particular way of publishing. Not just printing texts, notes or instruction but turning each Score into an artifact as well as a reflection and initiation of a process. The second George complained numerous times to me that he had to reprint large parts of the edition Water Yam, because the color of the cardboard had been wrong or it had been cut in the wrong size. Or a black dot was missing in the right place or the spacing had been inaccurate or the left margin didn't correspond to the right margin in the right proportion etc. etc. The score itself had to be scrupulous right. As well as the process when performed by the first George himself. It was quite another story when performed by the second. Around the same time Maciunas asked my permission to publish my collected scores. Asking what he meant by collected; - could it be 50 or 100 or 150, he answered 50 because that would fit into the nice plastic boxes he could get from Canal Street. Naturally I gave him the same score to be printed 50 times for each box. He hated the piece and told me that I had wasted a fantastic opportunity that would never recur. Anyway, he designed a beautiful edition that became Opus 50, although he had also here to reprint part of it because he had misspelled unus multurum as unus pulturum. Likewise he hated that I had announced in The Village Voice that I would pay each member of the audience 25 cents if they would attend my performance at the Bridge Theater in the Summer of 1965. Inexpensive art was important to him, - probably even free art. But to bribe the audience to participate was too much. Again he designed a great poster.

§4

Somewhat roughly you can divide Scores into 3 sets. The ones that instruct you to do something, Event Scores that are both an object and an activity and the ones that carry a maximum of implications. The first ones are pretty conventional relying on established notation, interpretation and perception. The Event Scores still to some extent carry the orthodox apprehension of the oeuvre while the third set rather tells you nothing. A fine point of departure. Some of these Scores are:

OPUS 11
To call my pieces by Opus and a number

OPUS 22
do and/or don't do something universally

OPUS 33
I have no copyright to any of my pieces

(whether this applies to more than this piece is questionable)

OPUS 44
The audience could be moved from **A** to **Z** to **A** in ever changing constellations of 10% until less than 10 persons remain

OPUS 55
This sentence should not be read by more than one person at the same time

OPUS 66
Make a remark (i.e. explanation, analysis etc.) to an object using for the reason of documentation and communication abstracts from the object in a way relevant to the method

OPUS 77

```
I have confidence in you :
abcdefghijklmnopqrstuvwxyz
```

(this piece was performed the first time by The Danish National Radio Symphony Orchestra in 1964. Since then it has been performed innumerable times by all kinds of orchestras and non-orchestras, such as shops, actors, shipyards, curators etc. The reason for its tremendous success is probably that the first sentence has the same number of characters (including spaces) as the alphabet)

OPUS 88

```
cdflatdeflatefgflatgaflatabflatb
```

(the piece could consist only of scales. A simple one, reflecting the history of European music, could be to play all c's simultaneously, then all dflat's, d's, eflat's, e's, f's and finally all b's. Or to play the highest c, then the deepest c, then next highest c, next deepest etc. until middle c is reached. Then the deepest dflat, then the highest dflat etc. Or vice versa. All imaginable scales, among others mathematical, statistical and aleatoric, can be utilized or construed)

(or simply) **OPUS 99**

```
The audience leave the space. The doors are sealed. A
tone is played that in frequency corresponds to the
cubic meters of the space and in seconds to the
number of persons left.
```

Eric Andersen   Friday, February 29th, 2008

Robert Ashley

The Entrance **(1965–6)**

Some Notes on a Performance of *The Entrance*

Commentary: *The Entrance*

The Entrance
Robert Ashley

for two-manual electric organ

<u>for Larry Leitch</u>

Make thirty-six equal stacks of pennies; the number of pennies per stack is that minimum number that will cause any key on either manual to be activated. Eighteen stacks should be heads-up; the remaining eighteen, tails-up.

Procedure

Begin by placing one 'heads' stack on any key; then, place a 'tails' stack on the corresponding key of the other manual.

... thereafter:

1. Place a stack, of either denomination, immediately next to (chromatically), or among, the stack(s) of the opposite denomination; thus, producing a display in which all of the 'heads', but one – the most recently placed stack – (or all of the 'tails', but one) are on one manual, while the most recently placed 'heads' stack (or, 'tails' stack) is on the opposite manual.

2. Then, one at a time, move the stacks that were previously on the keyboard to their respective opposite manuals; thus, producing a display in which all of the 'heads' are on the one manual, while all of the 'tails' are on the other manual.

3. Continue in this manner (repeating items 1 and 2 alternately) until all of the stacks are on the keyboard.

   ... when all of the stacks are on the keyboard in a uniform display, and thereafter:

4. Remove any single stack, taking from that stack one penny, which will represent that stack thereafter. Invert that penny so that its denomination is opposite to that of the stack it represents and place it on the key from which the stack was removed; thus, producing a display in which all of the 'heads', but one (or all of the 'tails', but one) are on one manual, while all of the stacks or pennies of the opposite denomination are on the other manual.

5. Then, one at a time, move all of the stacks or pennies, except the most recently placed one, to their respective opposite manuals; thus, producing a display in which all of the 'heads' are on one manual, while all of the 'tails' are on the other manual.

6. Continue in this manner (repeating items 4 and 5 alternately) until all of the stacks have been replaced, on the keyboard, by single pennies.

Conditions

For some instruments, the standard stack of pennies will fully depress some keys, while other keys will be only partially or intermittently activated. In the process of placing the stacks on the keys, the point, of course, is to allow the weight of the stack to activate the key. Thus, it is contrary to the idea of the composition to depress a key before placing a stack on it.

In the process of moving stacks from one manual to the other (items 2 and 5) the 'intervals' described by the moves are irrelevant. The objective is always to 'fill' the displays chromatically.

The performance should be considered as one continuous action at a natural pace – a pace that may vary with the physical complexity of the situation; that is, caution should be exercised to avoid spilling the stacks. If a stack is spilled, it should be reassembled before proceeding.

Voicing is optional, except that added-octave distinctions between the two manuals should be avoided.

The dynamic level is optional, except that it should be unchanging for any one performance.

Postscript

What form should that work take?

Is it to be performed?

For whom is it to be performed?

Is the notion of presenting the work in a continuous span of time implicit in the idea of the composition?

What is the relationship between the work of producing the sounds and the sound world created by the composition?

Is the work more important than the sounds, or vice versa, or neither?

Can the sound world created by the composition be discovered without carrying out the work of producing the sounds?

How shall we prepare for a production of *The Entrance*?

What is the attitude of the person doing the work?

What is the relationship between the composition (sound and work) and persons who might hear the sound or observe the work and who may or may not be performing the work?

How shall we proceed?

Eight Solutions Out of a Numberless Variety

1. Assemble an audience and perform the work as though the idea of the composition and the audience's expectations were identical.
2. Eliminate the audience, but retain the notion of a performance.
3. Allow the audience (a body of people not directing the performance) to determine its own relationship to the performance, and retain the notion of a performance (David Tudor).

4. Eliminate the notion of a performance, but allow for the possibility of a body of observers who may or may not consider themselves to be an audience.

5. Retain the notion of the composition as work performed, but eliminate the notion of performance:

   a) record the composition without regard to the possibility of its reproduction;

   b) record the composition under the strict limitations imposed by the require-ments of reproduction (for example, having defined that the reproduction will last twenty-two minutes, train yourself to accomplish the work of performing the composition within that time).

Item 5 suggests that neither performance nor audience need be retained as a convention in order to satisfy the requirements of the composition.

6. Eliminate the notion of a performance, and eliminate the audience: music as imagi-nation (George Brecht).

7. Allow for observers whose role is undefined, as in item 4, and retain the notion of a performance, but eliminate the act of performing:

   a) perform the composition in a place remote from the place where observers might assemble and without regard for the possibility of reproduction for those observers;

   b) perform the composition in a place remote from possible observers, but allow for the possibility of immediate reproduction in a place that is open to observers.

8. Allow for observers whose role is undefined, as in item 4, and retain the notion of the composition as work performed, but eliminate the notion of a performance and eliminate the act of performing.

Some Notes on a Performance of *The Entrance*

Alex Waterman, July 2011

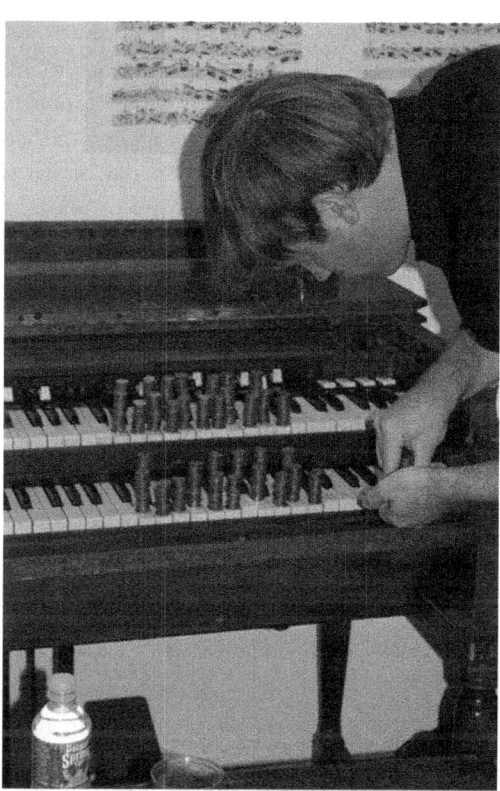

55 *Anthony Coleman (L) and Alex Waterman (R) realising Robert Ashley's* The Entrance *at the Miguel Abreu Gallery, New York, Summer 2007.*

The question at the bottom of page 2, 'How shall we proceed?' has been the question that I've probably asked most when working on the music of Robert Ashley. In all cases the emphasis has been on the 'we'. I've never attempted to produce or understand Ashley's music on my own.

I decided to present Robert Ashley's *The Entrance* as part of *Agape*, an exhibition and series of concerts I had organized at Miguel Abreu Gallery in the summer of 2007. *Agape* was a show displaying works that were concerned with a poetics of notation which questioned how we read together and how we construct/re-construct our readings in front of an audience or for each other. It featured graphic and verbal scores and poetry. Reading out loud, or reading as a 'social act', was the show's theme.

Robert Ashley's piece is full of instructions and imperatives as to its construction; these are to be interpreted and embodied (if it is to be performed at all). As confident in tone as these instructions may read, the latter half of the piece is a careful deconstruction of most everything that precedes it. Its double nature is mirrored in the double-manuals of the Hammond organ.

The performer(s) (in this performance, Anthony Coleman and myself) prepares for the work by reading and re-reading the material. I read the score many times and copied the questions out by hand. I wanted to internalize them, and copying (a kind of sung reading) is the best way I know of putting things in my hands.

I rented the organ from a place in mid-town and put out a notice to friends to gather pennies from their change drawers. (Everyone has a jar of pennies somewhere in their house.) I had amassed more than enough pennies when, on the day of the performance, Anthony Coleman showed up with a duffel bag full of plastic bags stuffed with pennies. The treasury was now overflowing.

Anthony and I divided the labor of the piece between us. The performance lasted around three-and-a-half hours. This meant we each stacked pennies for around an hour and 45 minutes. It was the middle of July and it was hot. We had programmed the piece for the afternoon as a kind of matinee before the evening's concert (Chris Mann performing Ashley and Mann, Ashley's *WHITE ON WHITE*, and a piece by Anthony Coleman). The door was open to the street so that passers-by could see the performance, but there were not many people out on the street that muggy midday. Robert Ashley got stuck in traffic and showed up when the performance was already finished. The pennies were all stacked and the organ was droning when he arrived.

When the audience showed up for the evening's performance, the organ had finally fallen silent. Whether we had intended to or not, we had performed the piece without an audience and retained the notion of performance.

Commentary: *The Entrance*

James Saunders

The Entrance (1965–6) was first published in the Experimental Music Catalogue's *Verbal Anthology*, and is one of a number of verbal scores that Robert Ashley has made since the early 1960s.[1] Some of these scores are conceptual, deriving from his work with the ONCE Group, which he directed from 1964 to 1969; many are instruction scores.[2] Ashley explains the significance of text as a notational medium, noting that: 'Instruction became important because it was no longer possible to symbolise what you were supposed to do. If you symbolise it, you had to explain the symbols, so you might as well just explain what you want people to do.'[3]

The instructions in *The Entrance* generally adopt a measured, bureaucratic register, through the use of somewhat archaic language ('thus', 'thereafter'), and provide thorough alternatives (often in parentheses) to take into account many possible configurations of the performer's actions. This creates a very precise explanation of the activity, but one that is complex, resembling a legal document in its concern with covering all possible eventualities. It is somewhat absurd as a result, as Ashley alludes to in an explanation of the origin of the piece:

> *The Entrance* was dedicated to my friend Larry Leitch, a wonderful piano player whose hands would sometimes tremble during a performance. The charm of this suggested the piece, which is, in a practical sense, unplayable.[4]

The Entrance is unusual in that it contains both instructions for preparing a realisation and philosophical reflections on ways to present the piece and on its status as a work. In this respect it demonstrates a degree of self-reflexivity which is unusual in scores, and this is only made possible through the composer's choice of verbal notation as a medium. This self-reflexivity is suggested in Ashley's comments about the title of the work:

> I have never understood what "The Entrance" means. It was "inspired". I would guess that it means something like the way to get into another,

---

[1] Bryars *et al.*, 1972, pp. 1–5. The score was reprinted in Ashley, 2009, pp. 434–8.
[2] For examples of Ashley's verbal scores, see Ashley, 2009, pp. 368–495.
[3] Robert Ashley, in conversation with John Lely and the author, New York, 28 September 2009.
[4] Ashley, 2009, p. 434, footnote 2. In the Experimental Music Catalogue version, Ashley advises that a performance of the piece should take about 3 hours, although this observation is missing in the version reprinted in Ashley, 2009. In solution 5b in the score's 'Postscript', there is reference to the possibility of a much quicker realisation, but this highlights the need to train oneself 'to accomplish the work of performing' in the suggested 22 minutes. This implies that Ashley did consider the work playable.

different frame of mind – that makes the performance of the piece possible.[5]

The score has three sections, each of which has a particular role in explaining aspects of the piece's operation and presentation. Following instructions for preparing the materials for performance, the first main section, 'Procedure', takes the form of a numbered list of imperative clauses, which explain the actions that should be carried out in a realisation. This is followed by a section called 'Conditions', written wholly in the declarative mood, which explains in more detail how to perform the piece. The final 'Postscript' is in two sections.[6] The first, written wholly in the interrogative, consists of a list of questions about the work and its performance, and the second section, written again in the imperative mood, supplies a number of possible solutions to these questions.

It is in the first section of the Postscript that fundamental questions are posed about the identity of the work and its performance, and this section may be regarded as a kind of treatise on how to read and realise verbal scores in general. Through use of interrogative clauses, the form of the work and the necessity of its physical presentation are brought into question. It becomes clear through these questions that it should not be assumed that the piece is to be performed. A characteristic of some verbal scores is the way they invite a reader to imagine a realisation, and the intricacy and physical complexity of *The Entrance* suggests that possibility here, emphasised by these additional questions. By reading the score, including the Postscript, it is possible for a reader to develop an impression of what a performance might entail, how it might feel to undertake the activity, and what it might be like to witness a performance, but this imagining will be a very different experience to a physical realisation.

This first section of the Postscript ends by asking the reader to consider the relationship between the actions undertaken and the possible sounds produced in a realisation. The questions focus on the relative importance of these two outcomes of the score, suggesting that the reader consider this when working on the piece. No solutions are provided, encouraging the reader to find a personally acceptable response. The section ends with more detailed questions concerning the performer–audience relationship, concentrating on developing strategies for preparing a realisation of the piece.

These questions are partially answered in the second section of the Postscript by the 'Eight Solutions Out of a Numberless Variety', although these in turn may raise further questions. The 'solutions' discuss a range of permutations of the audience (variously defined), the performance, the composition, the act of performing and location, in order to construct various scenarios in which the work might be experienced. Although each solution proposes a distinct configuration of these components, as a whole

---

[5] *Ibid.*, footnote 1.
[6] The title is missing from the EMC version, but appears immediately above the line 'What form should that work take?' in the reprint in Ashley, 2009.

they do not offer practical advice for preparing the realisation. For example, the second solution suggests that a realisation might 'Eliminate the audience, but retain the notion of a performance'. It is not stated how this solution could be realised, and each clause presents a further problem to be solved: how do you eliminate the audience, and how do you retain the notion of a performance?

By presenting these solutions in addition to the instructions for the activity itself, the score also encourages the reader to determine a strategy for engaging with the work as a performer (where relevant) or observer. The list opens up the possibility of a wide range of presentations, and serves as a starting point for countless others. The score perhaps emphasises this need to determine the context for a realisation by asking the questions 'Is the work more important than the sounds, or vice versa, or neither?' and 'Can the sound world created by the composition be discovered without carrying out the work of producing the sounds?' These questions are not answered in the score, and all possibilities are given credence by the suggested solutions. The Postscript destabilises what is otherwise a fairly straightforward instruction score. It is a model which might usefully be considered when preparing realisations of other pieces.

G. Douglas Barrett

A *Few Silence* (location, date, time of performance) (2008)

A Text Score Manifesto

Commentary: *A Few Silence*

A Few Silence (*location, date, time of performance*)

for any number of performers

Preparation

Each performer provides a battery of instruments/objects with a range of sound-producing abilities including but not limited to: sustained noises, sustained tones, pitched or non-pitched percussive sounds, metallic sounds, wood sounds, plant sounds, brief tones or noises. A stopwatch is required for each performer.

I

The piece starts with a duration of five minutes in which the performers listen to the "silence" of the performance space while creating written scores based on their observations of sounds that occur within this time span. A list of timings should be created, each timing to correspond to a textual description of a sound occurring at the given moment. Included in each description should be features such as the overall shape or contour of the sound, dynamic level, duration, etc. An occasional reference to a sound's source is ok but should not predominate. Examples: "low sustaining tone"; "soft sustaining noise"; "quick percussive sound"; "noisy descending glissando". [*See also the included example score.*]

II

At the end of the five minutes the performers reset their stopwatches and perform their respective scores, creating the indicated sounds to the best of their ability using the instruments at hand. The piece ends at the end of this, the second five-minute duration.

G. Douglas Barrett, 2008

Big Orbit 11.09.07, 9 PM

:04 Creaking
:11 creak wood sound
:19 ascending noisy [?]
:30 creaking wood sound
:38 woody creaking
:50 creaking wood sound
1:02 humming sound
1:09 whispering speech
1:20 creak
1:24 noisy constant
1:31 percussive humming sound
1:47 creaky wood sound
1:52 knocking percussive sound
2:06 creak
2:11 repeating low percussive sound
2:24 whispering sound very soft
2:27 noise soft short
2:51 shuffling
2:57 lots of creaking wood sounds
3:10 more wood sounds
3:19
3:22 speech loud
3:30 loud quick successive percussive
3:34 sounds
3:54 percussive metal sound
percussive noisy explosive
4:11 louder percussive sound

4:24 lowered (bodily force)
4:38 speech distant

A Text Score Manifesto

G. Douglas Barrett, 2010

To follow 'Listening to Language: Text Scores, Recording Technology, and Experimental Music', a lecture I presented at the Universität der Künste Berlin on 18 January 2010, as part of the Sound Studies Lecture series.

We can consider a category of mediation with respect to performance which encompasses, outlines, fulfills, works in and around works of experimental music and related performance practices. Mediation might exist as memory, notated scores, recordings, documentation (text, video, photographs) or discourse surrounding a work. Intuitively, we might define the score as falling on the prescriptive side of the equation: ontologically preceding a performance, the score sets up what is to be done, indicates how a performer realizes a work. Indeterminacy plays a special role here, shifting the function of the score from a descriptive (and normative/normalizing) role to a promptive one. Indeterminacy: a wait-and-see attitude, an embracing of the unforeseeable, an openness to the unscriptable, incalculable string of moments that constitute a listening experience.

Between the epigraph and the order-word. Scores can exist in any medium (the score in the age of the post-medium condition). Language presents a special case. Language, as it is sometimes used in text scores, bleeds into poetics and, in other ways, discourse. In the sense of the former – the way in which the specific calling for action contains its own kind of poetics – the performer is given both more and less than a blueprint for what to do with a piece. Less because indeterminacy fills in the details. More because the language used to invoke action carries with it its own aesthetics. The score as its own aesthetic object, constituting, containing, exploding the possibilities of a work's interpretation. In the sense of the latter, the musical score, no longer confined to the workings of a 'secret language' (pace music as universal language), might now address the problematic of its own existence – text scores as inherently meta-textual.

In my *A Few Silence* (location, date, time of performance) (2008), the work records its own history. The piece leaves a messy paper trail documenting each performer's acoustico-textually mediated experience of silence, which comes mediated by the concert situation itself. Prompting a performer-driven recording process of listening, marking and replaying, *A Few Silence* produces a kind of repetition which is always more than what lies 'between repeat bars'. It points to a space between the text of its score (the one I wrote originally), the texts of the scores produced during a performance, the social audience-performer text and texts such as this one. An anthropology of listening and its discursive-situatedness.

In certain cases, text scores work by virtue of a kind of silent, hidden discursivity, stating or saying while pre-empting rebuttal as mere argumentation; a kind of mute statement functioning as a meta-commentary on the status of the work itself. A process which then actually turns the focus of the work away from statement and towards the immanent activity of listening. As the score functions sub-textually (*below/behind* a performance, be it real or virtual), however, contra Phelan,[1] the location of the work cannot be said to exist autonomously in performance. Nor does the score have absolute authority over a performance (cf. indeterminacy, subversive or against the grain readings, 'unauthorized' performances, etc.). The score paradigm is one that demands negotiation, requires a working out of a specific relationality: between author and performer, between performing and listening bodies; further, the nexus of social relations that emerges from the work's animation within the concert/performance situation.

De-essentialization. This relationality need not be confined to the text score. On one hand, we can consider a general relation between language and action: the backgrounding or premising function of language, which may also be at work in timetables, recipes, to-do lists, and so on. On the other hand we can consider statements of various kinds as similarly conditioning aesthetic experience; there's nothing new about manifestos, artist statements, curatorial statements, criticism in general. However, there is perhaps something unique that characterizes the emerging practices of experimental text score creation – the kinds of organizing that occur around practices of listening and writing, these special collective performative–perceptual situations backgrounded by an unspoken discourse, underlined by a hidden poetics.

---

[1] Performance art critic Peggy Phelan writes, 'Performance cannot be saved, recorded, documented, or otherwise participate in the representations *of* representations: once it does so, it becomes something other than performance' (Phelan, P. (1993) *Unmarked: The Politics of Performance*, New York: Routledge, p. 146, [original emphasis]).

Commentary: *A Few Silence*

James Saunders

A Few Silence (location, date, time of performance)[1] (2008) is one of a series of pieces by G. Douglas Barrett which focus on the notion of transcription, exploring how information about events, sonic or otherwise, is encoded and decoded by people and/or through automated processes. This piece in particular brings the act of verbal notation into the realm of performance. In an artist's statement, Barrett contextualises his work:

> In my current work I concentrate on setting up processes that have to do with documenting, replicating, recording and repeating: experiences of space (the gallery, the concert hall, the urban landscape), action (performance works, 'unintended' performances, video documents), and existing music and performance. These processes have involved ordinary recording technologies, algorithmic or automatic interpretation, and what I refer to as performative listening and 'live' notation. In general, I do these things not for any particular desired result, but to allow each to uncover something unforeseen, to follow through with a process the result of which is unknown. I have begun to conceive of this body of work as falling under the umbrella I (and others) have defined loosely as 'transcription' – invoking the specifically music-related practice though in my usage it tends to bleed into other disciplines. Arising out of the context of experimental music, my work is also presented in contexts ranging from performance art to new media, sound art, and experimental theater.[2]

Barrett has used various techniques to explore transcription, including using computer software to make automated transcriptions of recordings of sonic environments in some instances of his ongoing *Derivations* series (2006–). In *A Few Silence* the transcription process takes advantage of players' perceptions and decision-making skills. In a realisation, performers are required to notate the sonic environment using verbal descriptions, marking sounds heard and indicating the timing of their occurrence during an initial five-minute period. This notation is then used as a score for a performance using pre-selected sound-producing objects, with performers individually reading their notation and responding to their earlier observations during a further five-minute period. In the score for *A Few Silence*, the order of events takes the reader through the stages of the piece in sequence. This is explicit in the layout, with sections marked 'Preparation', 'I', and 'II'. As such, it is reminiscent of a recipe or instructions for an experiment: ingredients/apparatus, sequential method.

---

[1] The full title of a performed version of the piece makes reference to its location, date and time of performance. Barrett suggests that the date format to be used in the title is the one native to the performance location e.g. dd.mm.yy in the UK, mm.dd.yy in the USA.

[2] Barrett, 2009.

The activities specified in the score are complex. In the first phase of the piece, the performer hears a sound and formulates a verbal description, acknowledges the time, and writes the description on the score. There is a tension for the performer between the need simultaneously to listen and translate perceived sounds into a verbal description and write this down in relation to a time point. It is hard to undertake these complex tasks continuously for an extended period, given their repetitive nature. Barrett observes that this act of notation is 'something that happens in time, so maybe that complicates things somehow, and you're dealing with all these subjective experiences of that time'.[3] As a result, it is likely that some events will be missed or ignored as performers try to undertake different activities at the same time.

Based on data collected from a recent performance, the average number of events notated by a single performer was 29, averaging out at about 10 seconds per event.[4] While some events might be closer together, especially where they are linked in some way (such as a series of coughs), there seems to be a sustainable pace at which performers can comfortably notate events. This is perhaps harder with text, as opposed to graphic notations, which may be more immediate or intuitive to produce. This pressure to an extent defines the pacing and density in the second phase of a realisation. The score also states that the performers should use a stopwatch as a way of measuring duration throughout. While measurements of time may be altered slightly by the performers' processing of events and notating sounds, the use of a stopwatch provides a reference point, reducing the possibility of a subjective response to time in performance.

Barrett does however admit to some flexibility in his requirement that sounds are notated using only text. In his own performances he says it is 'common for me to include the occasional arrow, or even traditional music notation can crop up sometimes. The emphasis for me is on using text... a version which did explicitly call for graphic symbols only would be a different piece.'[5] Using text can be problematic when trying to notate continuous sounds, such as environmental sounds, that will be present throughout the first five minutes. For example, they could be notated once when they begin or end, or referred to repeatedly whenever such sounds are apparent to the performer. It is a feature of the piece that a performer must make choices about what to notate, and these choices are determined by his or her own attentiveness to the situation.

So, for example, a drone that changes may be notated as a constant event, perhaps using time brackets, or may come and go in the performer's consciousness as more distinct changes become apparent:

What's interesting is that people normally find a way to deal with that notationally. So I've done things where I notice something happening

---

[3] G. Douglas Barrett, in interview with the author, Huddersfield, 22 November 2009.

[4] *A Few Silence (Huddersfield, 23.11.09, 14.20)* had eight performers who notated 22, 24, 25, 27, 29, 35, and 39 events (only seven performance scores were collected), at an average of 28.7 at a density of 10.44 seconds per event.

[5] G. Douglas Barrett, in interview with the author, Huddersfield, 22 November 2009.

during the beginning of the first five minutes and it sounds like it's droning or continuing to sound, then I'll use some kind of graphic notation and just put an arrow, and if I ever notice it stop then I'll mark the time.[6]

The means to describe the sounds themselves using text might take a variety of forms, and the score suggests both morphological descriptors ('contour', 'dynamic level', 'duration') and adjectives which are dependent on context ('quick', 'noisy', 'descending', 'low', 'soft'). While, as the score states, 'an occasional reference to a sound's source is ok but should not predominate', a description which privileges the source or context of a sound will impact on the subsequent performance. However, Barrett feels that describing sound sources directly:

allows the process of transcribing to be a free flowing activity, so I don't want people to be transcribing and something comes right through [and not write] 'glass sound' because a bottle drops. I don't want performers to go back and think, 'Oh no, how do I describe that in acoustic terms?' So in that sense it's OK to have the occasional reference to the source, just to get into this mode where the process is more or less automatic. I think generally it happens because you really have to concentrate in order to do this kind of continual description.[7]

This might, conversely, throw up descriptions that create a more distant relationship with the original sound. A performer may regard his or her description of a sound to be successful and repeatable. However, ambiguities may slip in, and the performer may have problems recalling what the notation was intended to mean. This could create the possibility of radical difference between the source and resultant sounds, mediated by the created score and choice of instruments. Barrett observes that Pierre Schaeffer's notion of acousmatic listening was an important point of reference for A Few Silence,[8] in that it refers to 'a noise one hears without seeing what causes it... [and that it] marks the perceptive reality of sound as such, as distinguished from the modes of its production and transmission.'[9] In relation to the event notated at 1:29 in the sample score, Barrett comments:

Honestly I don't know what 'noisy constant' means, but it's sort of difficult because you're writing in real time and maybe another sound happened right after I started to write that, and I moved to the next one. So maybe it was supposed to be something that was more clear or made more sense or something. Or maybe it was 'noisy, constant' and I just forgot the comma.[10]

---

[6] *Ibid.*

[7] *Ibid.*

[8] G. Douglas Barrett, in correspondence with James Saunders, December 2009.

[9] Schaeffer, P., 'Acousmatics' in Cox and Warner, 2006, p. 77.

[10] G. Douglas Barrett, in correspondence with the author, December 2009.

The other sound common to all performances of *A Few Silence* is that of people writing. In quiet performance spaces in particular, it is likely that performers will notate the sound of notation in progress. Barrett is comfortable with this possibility if it surfaces, and points out that it often happens that the notation might contain a 'transcription of the piece's own performance. If it comes out, then it's fine. It often does happen that the next thing you notice is someone's pen on paper, a scratchy sound.'[11]

In the second phase of the piece, performers attempt to respond to their notation by making sounds that fit the notated descriptions, rather than as a response to the original sounds themselves. The piece is not primarily about recreating another environment, in contrast to Alvin Lucier's *(Hartford) Memory Space* (1970) which requires performers to 'record by any means (memory, written notations, tape recordings) the sound situations of [outside] environments' and then, using instruments or voices in the performance space, 'recreate [...] with the aid of your memory devices [...] those outside sound situations' (see Fig. 57).

Aside from the distance between the sampled environment and the performance environment, *(Hartford) Memory Space* differs from *A Few Silence* in that it defines recording as a memorising activity. The recording methods employed are to be used to recreate the original sound situations, acting as a trigger to memory. In *A Few Silence*, the original sounds are similarly captured by the notation, but performers attempt to read the resultant score autonomously and without reference to them. Barrett states:

> A question I often receive is 'am I supposed to recall the sound that this description refers to?' and I usually say no. I want it to be less about recording, recreating. So not thinking back 'that was a car driving by' so let me try to recreate a car driving by, but really to replay the mechanical written description. I've thought of it as an indexical use of language.[12]

Barrett acknowledges the importance of C. S. Peirce's writing on *indexicality*,[13] where a *sign* has a real link to the object it signifies.[14] Peirce's classic example is a weathervane,[15] whose orientation is indexically linked to wind direction, the thing it represents. Peirce states that indices 'represent their objects independently of any resemblance to them, only by virtue of real connections with them'.[16] So in *A Few Silence*, the link between the text written by

[11] *Ibid*.

[12] G. Douglas Barrett, in interview with the author, Huddersfield, 22 November 2009.

[13] In interview, Barrett made direct reference to Peirce as being influential on his work.

[14] Peirce contrasts this with two other categories of sign: *icon*, 'a sign which stands for something merely because it resembles it', and *symbol* (sometimes termed *token*), a sign which 'is related to its object only in consequence of a mental association, and depends upon a habit' (see Houser and Kloesel, 1992, pp. 225–6).

[15] Peirce Edition Project, 1998, p. 297.

[16] *Ibid.*, p. 461.

(Hartford) Memory Space

for any number of singers and players of acoustic instruments

Go to outside environments (urban, rural, hostile, benign) and record by any means (memory, written notations, tape recordings) the sound situations of those environments. Returning to an inside performance space at any later time, re-create, solely by means of your voices and instruments and with the aid of your memory devices (without additions, deletions, improvisation, interpretation) those outside sound situations.

When using tape recorders as memory devices, wear headphones to avoid an audible mix of the recorded sounds with the re-created ones.

For performances in places other than Hartford, use the name of the place of performance in parentheses at the beginning of the title.

Alvin Lucier, 1970

57 *Alvin Lucier,* (Hartford) Memory Space *(1970).*

the performers and the sounds that provoked them is indexical: the words are intended to describe the sounds.[17] Elsewhere Peirce also contends that:

> An index is a sign which would, at once, lose the character which makes it a sign if its object were removed, but would not lose that character if there were no interpretant. Such, for instance, is a piece of mould with a bullet-hole in it as sign of a shot; for without the shot there would have been no hole; but there is a hole there, whether anybody has the sense to attribute it to a shot or not.[18]

Likewise, in *A Few Silence*, the re-mapping of the notation onto a new set of sounds creates a fresh indexical relationship.

While in both Barrett's and Lucier's pieces there is a translation of one sound environment to another through the use of different sound-producing resources, the aim and result are different in each case. In *A Few Silence* there is a change of signification in the notated descriptions between the two phases of the piece. So consequently there is a difference between the change created by reading a notation which was suggested by a car driving by but which does not present the original context (Barrett) and the change when the aim is replication of the original sound (Lucier).

The score suggests a battery of instruments, and the categories listed present ideas which might be developed individually. Barrett sees this as 'a

---

[17] It is not an iconic link: the words do not resemble the sounds unless there is some sense of their being pictograms or onomatopoeic. It is also not generally symbolic: Barrett warns against referencing the source.

[18] Hartshorne and Weiss, 1931–58, para. 304.

question of exciting imagination, exciting possibilities',[19] encouraging the performers to adopt an investigative approach. The list at the beginning of the score implies the use of a (wide) range of instruments, rather than a single sound source used in a multiplicity of ways, although such a constraint is not explicitly excluded. In preparing a realisation, performers do have a choice over the instruments they might use in the piece, and it is likely that a smaller selection of these possibilities will be made during the performance, dependent on the events of the first five minutes.

As such, it could be useful to consider in advance what might happen in a particular environment, or to consider possible techniques of sound production if fewer resources are available. It may be practical to use instruments which are capable of producing a range of discrete or sustained sounds. The notational strategy of the first phase of the piece is also exemplified by the inclusion of a sample notation of sounds from the first performance as an appendix.[20] This provides a possible model for performers to follow, demonstrating the range of descriptive options available (including shape, contour, dynamic level, duration and the sound source), although it is potentially limiting in the way it might constrain realisations.

It is also worth noting that performances involving Barrett himself often have the performers sitting on the floor, and typically involve small groups of up to about eight performers,[21] although the score states that any number is possible. Performance locations have included conventional performance spaces (theatres, galleries), public spaces, and outside urban environments, presenting a wide range of possible soundscapes to sample in a realisation.

58 *G. Douglas Barrett,* A Few Silence (Berlin, 14 January 2009, 21:00), *realisation by (L–R) G. Douglas Barrett, Francesco Gagliardi and Kerstin Fuchs, at Miss Micks, Berlin.*

[19] G. Douglas Barrett, in interview with the author, Huddersfield, 22 November 2009.
[20] First performance: *A Few Silence (Big Orbit, 11 September 2007, 21:00)*, performed by Francesco Gagliardi, Lindsey L. Lodhie, G. Douglas Barrett as part of *Works in Translation* at Big Orbit Gallery, Buffalo, NY on 9 November 2007.
[21] Typically performances have involved three people, although the piece is often performed solo.

59 *G. Douglas Barrett*, A Few Silence (Belfast, 25 August 2008, 15:30), *realisation by (L–R) Richard Glover,*
G. Douglas Barrett and Scott Mc Laughlin, at Performing the City: An Urban Performance Workshop
co-presented with Francesco Gagliardi, ICMC 2008, Sonic Arts Research Centre, Queen's University.

60 *G. Douglas Barrett*, A Few Silence (Huddersfield, 23 November 2009, 14:20), *realisation by (L–R)*
James Saunders, Kate Ledger, Scott Mc Laughlin, Johnny Herbert, Joseph Kudirka, Richard Glover,
G. Douglas Barrett and Ray Evanof, at hcmf//2009.

Antoine Beuger

one tone. rather short. very quiet (1998)

Commentary: *one tone. rather short. very quiet*

one tone. rather short. very quiet
for two players

antoine beuger
1998

one tone.
rather short.
very quiet

once during the first half of each minute: one player plays the tone

once during the second half of each minute: the other player plays the tone

sometime one player ceases to play the tone and remains silent until the end of the piece

sometime the other player ceases to play the tone and remains silent until the end of the piece

duration of the piece: at least 30 minutes.

Commentary: *one tone. rather short. very quiet*

James Saunders

Antoine Beuger is one of the founders of the Wandelweiser group.[1] He describes composing as:

> not about creating or inventing differences or concatenations of differences. Each sound is going to be different anyway. I like the idea of a piece of music being just a few sounds, of performing music as just playing a few sounds. Composing seems to me to be about making a few basic decisions, that open up a specific, still infinite world of differences: just a few sounds.[2]

Beuger's works often appear in linked series, where a notational constraint or process is re-applied with small changes. Originally written in German,[3] *one tone. rather short. very quiet* (1998) for two performers is one of a group of pieces from 1997–9 which share similar sounds and temporal structures.[4] The piece uses different circumstantials of Location in time to express temporal relationships, specifying clock time measured in minutes, and relative time through the adjuncts 'sometime' and 'until'. Clock time is used to specify windows of activity for each performer to play the tone and an overall duration for the piece. Both 'sometime' and 'until' are used to suggest culmination of subjectively measured durations.

In *one tone. rather short. very quiet,* an instruction for sound production is found both in the title and the initial paragraph of the score. Players each make a sound which is rather short and very quiet. One player makes the sound in the first half of every minute, and the second player makes the sound in the second half of every minute. After some time, each performer then independently stops making the sound and remains silent until the end of the piece. Beuger comments:

> what is at stake here is the experience of separation: they can never come together, since they are separated in time. They can come very close, if one player plays near the end of his time and the other player plays at the beginning of his time. But this nearness has renewed distance as a prize: only after nearly [one minute] another situation of nearness may be established. So a very subtle 'communication' based on separation takes place. Or, in other words, being separated is established as the basis of a relationship, of 'two-ness'.[5]

---

[1] For an overview of their work, see Pisaro, 2009.
[2] Saunders, 2009, pp. 232–3.
[3] The original score in German has the title *ein ton. eher kurz. sehr leise*. Beuger prepared the English translation for this book.
[4] See also *ins ungebundene* (1997–9), *tout à fait solitaire* (1998), both for solo players, and another duo, *aus dem garten* (1998).
[5] Saunders, 2009, p. 233.

Beuger also emphasises the social relationship between the two players as being mediated by choices they make during a performance:

> the decision not to play the sound during a section implies not playing it anymore for the rest of the performance: it means leaving the other player alone. This very much reflects a love relationship: two people are together (which means: are in a situation of being separated) for a while (I am tempted to write: twogether). Ultimately they are separated forever, by parting or by death.[6]

The score specifies three distinct phases: both players making a sound; one player making a sound; neither player making a sound. There is no indication of the duration of these phases in relation to each other, with the score stating simply that the duration of the piece is 'at least 30 minutes'. The score takes two approaches to measuring time. The indication of when to play in each minute relies on clock time: the performers act in measured, 30-second windows. The duration of the first and second phases of activity in the piece are measured subjectively, contingent on the performers' interpretation of how long 'sometime' might be. This word suggests openness, but can be seen in relation to Beuger's practice, where extended performance durations containing few sounds are common. For example, his earlier series *calme étendue* (1996–7) alternates sounding and silent phases, with the sounding phases comprising a series of isolated sounds every eight seconds, set within a performance duration of between 45 minutes and nine hours. A complete performance of the related *calme étendue (spinoza)* lasts 180 hours. Beuger performed this in August 1997 at the Museum Schloss Morsbroich in Leverkusen for 26 consecutive days, playing for between six and ten hours per day (depending on the times at which the museum was open).[7]

Although the durations specified in *one tone. rather short. very quiet* give some flexibility over the placement of sounds within the sounding phases of the piece, Beuger is nonetheless keen for them to be observed accurately:

> I personally like to use a normal watch (analogue) when playing these pieces: it doesn't have this one-second pulse, instead I see the hand moving continually. But a watch or a clock is not always available, and some people like playing better with a stopwatch. For [*one tone. rather short. very quiet*] it is essential to have a timing device, since the time windows for the two players should remain separated from each other.[8]

---

[6] *Ibid.*
[7] For a recording of a 70-minute version of this piece, refer to Antoine Beuger, *calme étendue (spinoza)*, edition wandelweiser records EWR 0107, 1997.
[8] Antoine Beuger, in correspondence with the author, March 2010. Beuger goes on to comment on the use of timing devices in *calme étendue*, in which there is a clearer pulse, saying it 'should not be played with a timing device. The rhythmic irregularity which then happens is intended. For the timing of the silences in *calme étendue*, of course, a stopwatch should be used (the silences should not be counted: for the performer they wouldn't be silences anymore). So, in a performance of *calme étendue* I would have a stopwatch running, but when performing the sounds I don't look at it.'

In the third phase of the piece, both players are silent. The score does not state explicitly how to determine the end of the piece, but rather that after stopping making sounds, players remain 'silent until the end of the piece'. This implies that both players may understand when the end of the piece occurs, either mutually or through one player influencing the other during the performance, or by prior agreement. However Beuger comments that 'in this piece it is best to determine a duration beforehand', avoiding the possibility of ambiguity in performance.[9] He explains the context of the piece's composition and his reason for specifying duration:

> All performances until now have been 30 minutes. The piece was originally written for a project organized by Michael Pisaro at Northwestern University: he asked me to write a 30-minute piece (or a series of pieces), which would be played on 15 occasions in the course of three weeks. When I wrote the piece, I could imagine performances of longer durations. That's why I wrote: 'at least 30 minutes'.[10]

Variables are balanced very carefully in *one tone. rather short. very quiet.* Some aspects of the piece are dealt with precisely: 'one tone', 'once during the first half of each minute', 'one player plays the tone'. Others require interpretation by the performers: 'rather short', 'very quiet', 'sometime', 'at least'. By presenting both kinds of variable within a relatively short text, Beuger creates a directed indeterminacy in which the few decisions the performers must make have a large impact on the resultant realisation of the score.

[9] *Ibid.*
[10] *Ibid.*

George Brecht

***Time-Table Music* (1959) and *Time-Table Event* (1961)**

The Origin of 'Events'

Commentary: *Time-Table Music* and *Time-Table Event*

TIME-TABLE MUSIC

For performance in a railway station.

The performers enter a railway station and obtain time-tables.

They stand or seat themselves so as to be visible to each other, and, when ready, start their stopwatches simultaneously.

Each performer interprets the tabled time indications in terms of minutes and seconds (e.g. 7:16 = 7 minutes and 16 seconds). He selects one time by chance to determine the total duration of his performing. This done, he selects one row or column, and makes a sound at all points where tabled times within that row or column fall within the total duration of his performance.

George Brecht
Summer, 1959

TIME-TABLE EVENT

to occur in a railway station

A time-table is obtained.

A tabled time indication is interpreted
in minutes and seconds (7:16 equalling,
for example, 7 minutes and 16 seconds).
This determines the duration of the event.

Spring, 1961
G. Brecht

The Origin of 'Events'

George Brecht, August 1970

In 1958 and 1959 I was attending John Cage's classes in experimental music at the New School for Social Research in New York. My interests then were in such problems as making musical pieces with built-in chance durations rather than pre-determined ones (*Candle Piece for Radios*), or using game elements such as playing cards as musical scores (*Card Piece for Voice*). The pieces turned out quite theatrical when performed, as interesting visually, atmospherically, as aurally, though they were performed with as much economy, with as little fuss, as possible.

I was increasingly dissatisfied with an emphasis on the purely aural qualities of a situation, so that by the Fall of 1959 I had decided to call my first show (at the Reuben Gallery, of my more object-oriented work) *Towards Events*, my thought being that the word 'event' was closer to the multi-sensory (total) experience I was interested in than any other.

In the Spring of 1960, standing in the woods in East Brunswick, New Jersey, where I lived at the time, waiting for my wife to come from the house, standing behind my English Ford station wagon, the motor running and the left-turn signal blinking, it occurred to me that a truly 'event' piece could be drawn from the situation. Three months later the first piece explicitly titled as an 'event' was finished, the *Motor Vehicle Sundown (Event)*.

In 1960 the event-scores came copiously and arrived for several years after that (I still write one now and then). Curiously, the later ones became very private, like enlightenments I wanted to communicate to my friends who would know what to do with them, unlike the *Motor Vehicle Event* or a happening.

Later on, rather to my surprise, I learned that George Maciunas in Germany and France, Cornelius Cardew in England, Kosugi, Kubota, Shiomi in Japan, and others had made public realisations of the pieces I thought you had to wait for. (Pleasant surprise that the possibilities of realisation could not be foreseen.)

TO THE READER – A NOTE OF CAUTION

This is the first and probably the last time that I will write about 'events'. I have avoided it up to now out of a horror of being called an (or worse 'the') 'event-artist', as, for example, Allan Kaprow, who deserves more enlightened treatment than that, has been called a 'happener'. Events have always been a mode of experimenting, I only found a form (for myself) of putting them on paper (for others too).

Commentary: *Time-Table Music* and *Time-Table Event*

James Saunders

George Brecht was a Fluxus artist and research chemist whose work included making objects in various media and writing scores. He was one of the first people to make purely verbal scores, and these are collected principally in the Fluxus-produced *Water Yam*, a boxed edition of scorecards, with each card containing a single piece (see Fig. 63). *Time-Table Music* (1959) and *Time-Table Event* (1961) are early examples of these scores. Though the two scores bear a surface resemblance, they represent fundamentally different approaches, and represent Brecht's changing attitudes to the role of language in verbal notation.

63 *George Brecht*, Water Yam *(1972 edition).*

Brecht's work on scores can be traced back to his participation in John Cage's class at the New School for Social Research in New York, which he attended in 1958 and 1959. The class included a number of other emerging experimental artists, including Allan Kaprow, Dick Higgins and Al Hansen, for whom Cage's discussion of the role of chance in the creation of art was a catalyst to reconsidering the role of an artist in the production of their own work. Brecht had already been considering chance procedures, producing the essay 'Chance-Imagery' in 1957, which was drawn from his own experiments as a painter. It highlighted work by, among others, Duchamp, Pollock and, in a subsequent revision, Cage.

In the class, the practical nature of the work was important. Cage set exercises for participants to work on, and the results were often performed by members of the class, either as solos or ensemble pieces. The work was notionally musical, but often exemplified Higgins' idea of Intermedia Art as something which 'emphasized the dialectic between the media'.[1]

Time-Table Music is one of the first group of verbal scores that Brecht produced.[2] It provides instructions for using a train timetable to regulate the production of sounds by the performers. Like some of Brecht's other pieces composed at this time, including *Candle-Piece for Radios*, *Card Piece for Voice* (both 1959) and *Spanish Card Piece for Objects* (1960), *Time-Table Music* uses found material as a score. Here the use of timetables provides a chance-determined time structure, as their original purpose and function has been placed in a new context.

There is, though, still an implicit shape that might emerge based on typical journey schedules: there are likely to be fewer journeys in the very early morning for instance, with realisations of the piece tending more towards medium durations, and lasting no longer than 23'59". Brecht's choice of materials therefore shapes the realisation, something that he observes in 'Chance-Imagery':

> It is sometimes possible to specify only the universe of possible characteristics which a chance event may have. For example, a toss of a normal die will be expected to give a number from one to six. Any particular face will be expected to turn up in about one-sixth of a great many throws. But the outcome of any one toss remains unknown until the throw has been made. It is often useful to keep in mind this "universe of possible results," even when that universe is hypothetical, for this clarifies for us the nature of our chance event as a selection from a limited universe.[3]

Early drafts of *Time-Table Music* show how both the language and its implied performance practice developed during its composition, gradually becoming more precise. The first draft of the score, dated 13 July 1959, contains the main elements of the piece, that of obtaining timetables and using them to structure a period of time and control sound production by the performers (see Fig. 64). At this stage though, the location of the performance is open. Brecht suggests drawing on the immediate everyday environment:

> The piece may be performed in:
> a classroom, w/ pencils, pins, erasers, etc.
> a restaurant, w/ knives + forks, etc.[4]

---

[1] Higgins, D., 'Statement on Intermedia' in Stiles and Selz, 1996, p. 729.
[2] See Robinson and Fischer, 2005, pp. 300–2.
[3] Brecht, 1966, p. 5.
[4] Brecht, 1991c, p. 99. The note at the side of the page adds, 'Do at Sisti's!', a café in New York.

64 *George Brecht, sketch for* Time-Table Music *(Brecht, 1991c, p. 99).*

The possibility of using various performance locations was under consideration at this stage, with Brecht indicating in the revision the following day that it was 'To be performed in a railway station', and then in the following paragraph, 'The performers enter a (public place)' (see Fig. 65).[5] It is implied that the range of possibilities was discussed with other class members, as on both these drafts he indicates that, 'For a later generalization of this piece. (I am indebted to A. [lfred] Hansen for an element of this piece: the nature of the many places in which it may happen.)'[6]

The following two pages of the notebook seem to have resolved this question however. In a handwritten version of the score which appears later in the same notebook (see Fig. 66), dated 24 July 1959, Brecht now states that, 'The performers enter a railway station'[7] and this is confirmed by a typed copy of the score stuck to the facing page (see Fig. 67) with *Time-Table Music* being first performed by members of the class at Grand Central Station in New York.[8] This move from the general to the specific, thereby closing off potential realisations, is perhaps at odds with Brecht's later work in which the ambiguity of single words or groups of words opens up the realisation to more possibilities.

[5] *Ibid.*, p.105.
[6] *Ibid.*
[7] *Ibid.*, p.107.
[8] Robinson, 2009, p. 85.

For a later generalisation of this piece. →

Time-table Music

7.14

(Draft)

To be performed in a railway (tiled) station.

I am indebted to A.Hansen for one element of this piece: the nature of the many places in which it may happen.)

The performers enter a (public place) and, standing or seating themselves so as to be visible to each other, await a pre-arranged starting time, (origin") which might be a given clock-time (possibly chosen from the time-tables used below)

At the origin, each starts a stop-watch, and consults an ordinary time-table which determines the occurrence of programmed sound in the following way for each performer:

1. All times are interpreted in terms of minutes and seconds (7:16 = 7 minutes and 16 seconds). One time is taken from the page in a chance way to determine duration of the part.

2.

65 *George Brecht, second draft of* Time-Table Music *(Brecht, 1991c, p. 105).*

Elsewhere in the drafts of the score, ideas about the performance practice can be found. In an undated entry (see Fig. 67), Brecht suggests some 'Ideas arising in connection with TT Music', specifically questioning 'How "together" are the performers in space? (implies: who are the listeners?) (i.e. do the performers wander all over the station making sounds?' and then 'Comment: Ambiguities: 1. Are the performers free to move about the station once they have begun together?'[9] None of these thoughts find a place in the final score however. They are not central to the piece; in the published version, it remains possible for the performers to move, but they need not. The piece must however be performed by a group and the emphasis on ensemble performance is clear in the instruction: 'They stand or seat

[9] Brecht, 1991c, p. 106.

66 *George Brecht, another draft of* Time-Table Music *(Brecht, 1991c, p. 105).*

themselves so as to be visible to each other, and, when ready, start their stop-watches simultaneously.' This concerted action is a shared experience.

It should also be noted that even though Brecht refers to listeners in his notes, he leaves unspecified the extent to which the results of *Time-Table Music* are perceivable. Although performers are instructed to make sounds, there is no obligation for these sounds to be projected in such a way that the piece becomes noticeable to others. Performances may potentially be extrovert or private.

This range of possibilities is even more open in *Time-Table Event*,[10] the more generalised, separate piece Brecht developed from *Time-Table Music* in early 1961. The main differences with the later piece are the move from sound-based 'music' to a duration-determined 'event', and the use of the passive voice to obscure agency. Specifically, Brecht removes any reference to sound. By this time he was 'increasingly dissatisfied with the purely aural qualities of a situation... my thought being that the word "event" was closer to the multi-sensory (total) experience I was interested in than any other.'[11] As with his Fluxus colleagues, the consideration of performance as an inter-media experience was central:

[10] Both pieces are found in *Water Yam*, and as such have separate identities.
[11] Brecht, G., 'The Origin of "Events"', in Robinson and Fischer, 2005, p. 236. See also p. 111 of this book.

Ideas arising in connection w/ TT Music:
How "together" are the performers in space?
(implies: who are the listeners?) (ie. do the
performers wander all over the station making sounds?

Comment.
1. Are the performers free to move about the station
— once they have begun together?
2. Suggestion for performance:

Time-Table Music.

The performers enter a railway
station, and obtain time-tables.

They stand or seat themselves
so as to be visible to each
other, and, when ready, start
their stop-watches simultaneous
ly.

Each performer interprets the
tabled time indications in term
s of minutes and seconds (e.g.
7:16 = 7 minutes, 16 seconds).
He selects one time by chance
todetermine the total duration
of his performing. This done,
he selects one row or column,
and makes a sound at all points
where tabled times within that
row or columb fall within the
total duration of his
performance.

67 *George Brecht, page from notebook with first typed copy of score for* Time-Table Music *(Brecht,
1991c, p. 106).*

Composers, performers and auditors of music permit sound-experiences by arranging situations having sound as an aspect. But the theatre is well lit. I have to cough; the seat creaks, and I can feel the vibration. Since there is no distraction, why choose sound as the common agent?[12]

Time-Table Event simply uses a timetable obtained by the performer to determine the duration of an event in a railway station. In this later piece, Brecht removes the obligation for the performer to make sounds, or indeed to structure the performance based on the rows and columns of the timetable. The score states only that the timetable 'determines the duration of the event'. This is, as a result, a very different piece, but one which might be said to subsume the earlier one.

The performance situation is also reconsidered. *Time-Table Music* states that it is 'For performance in a railway station', while *Time-Table Event* is 'to occur in a railway station', although this change only occurred between the two drafts of the later piece (see Fig. 68).[13] This crucial difference is a result of Brecht's move towards the event as a structure, and away from the need to present work with any kind of overt theatricality.

In his short 1970 statement 'The Origin of "Events"', Brecht comments, 'In the Spring of 1960, standing in the woods in East Brunswick, New Jersey, where I lived at the time, waiting for my wife to come from the house, standing behind my English Ford station wagon, the motor running and the left-turn signal blinking, it occurred to me that a truly "event" piece could be drawn from the situation.'[14] Events can be observed, or thought about, as well as realised: a jotting on page 20 of his notebook in late March 1961 remarks 'perceiving is an act'.[15]

The sketches also make reference to the requirement that the tabulated times are 'chosen by chance',[16] an instruction which is also absent from the final score. Brecht's extensive research into chance as a formative process for making art is well documented, but the removal of this instruction from the score is partly as a result of its redundancy: timetables and their use in this piece, to an extent, promote chance inherently. *Time-Table Event* also removes references to the use of stopwatches and any sense of co-ordination between players. As a result it may be realised as a solo: there is no indication that it is for a group, as is the case with *Time-Table Music* ('the performers', 'they stand', 'each performer').

Brecht's move towards events can be seen within the context of his interest in creating multi-sensory situations. He states the case for event scores being equivalent to musical scores:

[12] Brecht, 2005b, p. 115.

[13] Brecht, 2005a, p. 21.

[14] Brecht, G., 'The Origin of "Events"', in Robinson and Fischer, 2005, p. 236. See also page 111 of this book. This situation can be linked to his *Motor Vehicle Sundown (Event)*.

[15] Brecht, 2005a, p. 20.

[16] *Ibid.*, p. 21

TIME-TABLE EVENT
(for performance in a railway station)

A time-table is obtained, ~~and A table entry~~ tabled time indication,
chosen by chance, is interpreted in minutes
and seconds (for example 7:16 equalling 7 minutes
and 16 seconds), to determine the ~~event~~ duration
of the event.

Spring, 1961
G. Brecht

Performance note:

A railway station is entered

TIME-TABLE EVENT   3/26

To occur in a
railway station.

A time-table is obtained.

A tabled time indication, chosen
by chance, is interpreted in minutes
and seconds (7:16 equalling, for
example, 7 minutes and 16 seconds).
This determines the duration of the
event.

spring, 1961
G. Brecht

68 *George Brecht, two drafts for* Time-Table Event *(Brecht, 2005a, p. 21).*

DRIP MUSIC (DRIP EVENT)

For single or multiple performance.

A source of dripping water and an empty vessel are arranged so that the water falls into the vessel.

Second version: Dripping.

G. Brecht
(1959-62)

69 *George Brecht,* Drip Music (Drip Event) *(1959–62).*

In composing music, the composer permits an experience by arranging a situation within which sound arises. If a musical score (sound-score) prepares a musical (sound) situation, the event-score prepares one for events in all dimensions (or outside of dimensions).[17]

The comparison of music and event can also be made in the composite score *Drip Music (Drip Event)* (1959–62) (see Fig. 69).[18] The instructions in the first part of the score imply that actions are intentionally carried out by the performer, even though the passive voice is used. But it need not be the case: there may be no intention, and an observed realisation might satisfy the score. This idea is formalised by the second version, which uses the present participle 'dripping'. Here the possibility of observing dripping, or it simply happening (somewhere), is now enough. The notion of a performer carrying out the activity is underplayed. Brecht confirms this in an interview with Michael Nyman, in which they discuss the duration of *Drip Music (Drip Event)*:

It depends whether you shut it off or whether you let the water run out. If you're using the piece I built with the glass vessel, you could just let it run

[17] Brecht, G., 'Events (assembled notes.)' in Robinson and Fischer, 2005, p. 226.
[18] See also *Comb Music (Comb Event)* (1959–62), where instructions for producing a sound by drawing a finger along the prongs of a comb are followed by four other versions of the piece: 'sounding comb-prong', 'comb-prong', 'comb' and 'prong'.

till it stops. But the *Drip Music* in the bathroom that we're hearing now, that will end when the reservoir fills. I can't hear it so well now because the refrigerator's running.[19]

Brecht also points out that he does not 'tell you what to try for'[20] and that 'the result of the score is beyond the score. It can't be deduced from what's on the card.'[21] Despite Brecht's openness to any realisation, he does at times express some preferences for found events, rather than staged ones. His comments, 'An event is a unit of experience'[22] and 'Events shrink experience to an immediate (as other than a past- present- and future) "now"',[23] emphasise this momentary observation of situations over the actual organisation of those situations. It is the recognition and consequent framing of the event which generates the experience, and this is focused and triggered by the score. As Brecht states, 'I would be more interested if the event just happened. If the telephone rings, then it's interesting if that becomes the piece. I'm not interested in arranging it first.'[24]

[19] Nyman, 1976, p. 262.
[20] *Ibid.*, p. 257. This is a response to Nyman's preceding comment 'Yours is an inner discipline, which the performer can…'
[21] *Ibid.*, p. 260.
[22] Brecht, 2005b, p. 112.
[23] Brecht, 2005a, p. 73.
[24] Nyman, 1976, p. 259.

Gavin Bryars

Far Away and Dimly Pealing (1970)

On Verbal Notation

Commentary: *Far Away and Dimly Pealing*

FAR AWAY AND DIMLY PEALING   Gavin Bryars

Cause sounds to occur at least one mile from the performer.

Do not use explosives and do not allow someone else to make the sound

for you.

The sound should be able to be heard by the performer

(the only attempt I ever made at this was thwarted by an express

train severing the means whereby the sound was to be made).

On Verbal Notation

Gavin Bryars, 2009

A lot of the people I worked with in the late 1960s were non-musicians or performers with limited technical ability. I was working in art colleges with students who simply didn't read conventional notation. So using text scores, or developing text scores, was a really useful way of making music together and of just finding out different ways of making pieces. Of course there were a lot of text pieces that existed before I started doing text pieces. I was aware of them – those in the La Monte Young *Anthology* and others – and there were some Cage pieces that involved text too. As a resource, I saw it as just another form of notation, but one that also helped free up performance. One of the common problems with conventional staff notation is that people are very tied to the notes. However much you encourage them to play freely, many performers will do exactly what is there and no more. Even in situations where people are being 'expressive' and making little gestures here and there, they won't radically reappraise the music. You can move away quite a long way from what is immediately apparent in a score, and graphical notation was one of the things that was used to encourage this, and this was a way to liberate the performers to some extent – and not just liberate, but enable them to engage more with the creative act of performance.

Text notation was a step further. Graphic notation was inevitably ambiguous, especially if you have the more extreme forms like, say, Cardew's *Treatise* where there's no explanation at all. When Peters Edition asked him to do a *Treatise Handbook* to explain it, he deliberately didn't do so. He gave lots of accounts about how the piece had been done in the past and so on. He didn't say things like 'this symbol equals that'. It was never a question of a one-to-one relationship between symbol and action. A lot of people like Stockhausen and the rest would use symbols to mean precise things. It was just a substitute notation, but it was not in itself anything conceptually different. It was just a way of doing things that could not comfortably be notated by stave notation. It was expedient rather than any significant advance, whereas the purer graphical notation became a form in itself.

There were people who were able to respond wonderfully to graphic notation but also many who had difficulties with it. In a way the extent to which you can be skilful or creative with graphic notation depends on your visual imagination, your ability to make the move from symbols to action. But with text notation one is using everyday language, it's a rudimentary thing that everybody has. And one of the things can be to keep the language as clear as possible. (I remember when I was studying philosophy it was stressed that one should not obfuscate through language, but keep it simple, as the ideas themselves were so complicated!) After that it's a question of how far you can go beyond what is literal to what is poetic, to what is metaphoric, and so on, and to what is instruction and what is suggestion. Text is another stage along that line of freeing up the notational concepts.

There seem to me to be two kinds of text notation. In the first place there are those text forms which are slightly mysterious, enigmatic and sometimes pithy. I'd put George Brecht's *Water Yam* into that category – and I think that it's a masterpiece – and it is probably the greatest collection of text pieces, and one that was a huge resource for English musicians in the '60s and immensely important for us. George lived in London at that time so he was accessible and was involved in performances. George was a visual artist, and so he came to this kind of work through Fluxus and the post-Happenings territory of art and performance. He was a major Fluxus artist and was very involved with it. So the Fluxus side of it, the art side of it, was very important for musicians working in text notation and George was probably the key figure in this area. With them there was this love of enigma and a lot of those people were very interested, probably via Cage, Alan Watts, Zen, in the idea of the koan, the inexplicable riddle for which you have to have this flash of sudden insight in order to come to some stage of enlightenment. There was that aspect to it, and so some of them were quite deliberately baffling – and those I always find incredibly rich and rewarding.

The second kind is closer to a form of instruction, which you get with a composer like Christian Wolff. Here a situation is set up where even with the most rudimentary ability you can start to do something, and then you move into a sort of improvisatory sphere. I'm thinking of pieces like *Stones* or *Sticks*, those pieces where you have the resources and how you shape the piece is then just down to what happens with the material. The text itself doesn't really do much about ordering the music, the shape of the performance. It sets up the situation and then relies on the kind of live interaction between the players (or the soloist if you were to do it alone).

So they are quite different and that's one of the nice things about text compositions: the range. There is this range not just of complexity but also the range of conceptual difference, and they fall into many different groups and sometimes overlap. Individual composers will move through several different areas of text composition. For instance Cardew's *Schooltime Special* is very different from his *Schooltime Compositions*. This is almost like a legal document in that you find your way through 'yesses', 'noes', 'tick the boxes', and so on. Whereas *Schooltime Compositions* involves a different process altogether, one much more in the spirit of George Brecht's *Water Yam*.

With my own text pieces, ironically, I think I was probably much more careful about writing them than I am with staff notation. I can write conventional notation quite quickly and have some things which are a bit loose, but with words, I was conscious that one redundant expression or an adjective too many would destroy the meaning. These pieces are probably harder to write in many ways. I suppose, that a *writer* who is a poet or a novelist would have no problem putting those together, but the intention is different if you're doing something for performance purposes, and at the same time you're trying to give an idea of the climate of the piece – the emotional colour, not just the technical things that need to be done, but the spirit of the piece. And then you have to be very, very careful, even as to what tense you use for a particular verb. I never used a thesaurus but it's the kind of situation where you might often need a substitute word, because you keep coming up with the same word. For example, the word 'reward' might come twice, but you wouldn't be able to use 'reward' the second time – you'd have to use 'gain' or 'trophy'. You'd have to find some other word and so the actual notation was quite hard. The concept of the piece would be reasonably clear, but it's always that notational thing.

Ultimately, whatever kind of composer you are, you have to have a clear concept of a piece and you make this concept as clear as you possibly can, and you do that through notation. In the case of text notation you've got to make it absolutely waterproof, almost like a kind of legal document. There should be *no loopholes*. Or if there are loopholes, they should be the kind of loopholes you can accept or even encourage. I have performed some kinds of process pieces where there are gaps in the logic and where, if you follow the loopholes to their logical end, you end up with something that the composer didn't necessarily want.

Commentary: *Far Away and Dimly Pealing*

James Saunders

Gavin Bryars' verbal scores first appeared in a series of multi-composer anthologies published by the Experimental Music Catalogue, which he co-edited with its founder Christopher Hobbs, and Michael Nyman. *Far Away and Dimly Pealing* (1970) is one of five Bryars scores in the *Verbal Anthology* (1972)[1] which are notable for his exploration of hidden or private music where, variously, the inner workings of the piece, or even its audible results, are concealed from the audience and potentially the performers. At the time of their composition, Bryars was in contact with George Brecht, who was living in London, and he cites the importance of Brecht's work to his own practice:

> I always liked that in George Brecht's work you may not even notice that a piece was happening. I remember in the Pop Art exhibition at the Hayward, in the '70s, there was one piece George Brecht presented which was *SILENCE*, and it's that. And it just looks like a fire notice. But eventually you realise that that is George's piece. But a lot of people would walk past that and think it was one of these public notices, signs, and it's printed in that way as well.[2]

By not drawing too much attention to an object or activity it might be stumbled upon accidentally, or go unnoticed, shifting responsibility to the observer or listener. In a conversation with Steve Reich, Bryars comments that 'by retaining a certain privacy within the piece, a certain kind of hidden area where everything isn't revealed... you're not laying all your cards on the table. If someone wants to find out what your cards are they've got to look very closely.'[3] In *Far Away and Dimly Pealing*, this privacy frames the score's personal challenge to the performer. It also physically distances the performer from the sounding object, in a similar way to the use of hidden sound sources in *Marvellous Aphorisms Are Scattered Richly Throughout These Pages* (1969), with its requirement that 'their activation and manipulation is outside public view' (see Fig. 71).

The directness of the first sentence of *Far Away and Dimly Pealing* is qualified by the rest of the text, which adds a series of constraints to the activity. These constraints do not make the activity impossible, but do require the performer to consider and plan how to realise the piece in some detail. The first sentence also suggests a number of further questions: 'cause' (how?); 'sounds' (what sounds? how many?); 'to occur' (when?); 'at least one

---

[1] The original publication was reissued by the Experimental Music Catalogue, now run by Christopher Hobbs and Virginia Anderson, in 2000. It is available from http://experimentalmusic.co.uk. Other verbal scores appear in the EMC's *Keyboard Anthology* (1972), *Visual Anthology* (1974), *Rhythmic Anthology* (1972).

[2] Gavin Bryars, in interview with John Lely and the author, Bath, 24 November 2008.

[3] Potter, 1981, p. 6.

MARVELLOUS APHORISMS ARE SCATTERED RICHLY THROUGHOUT THESE PAGES

Gavin Bryars

Any number and kinds of quiet sound sources

Concealed inside clothing in such a way that their activation and

manipulation is outside public view

Inside shoes, hats, coats, trousers

Bulky maybe, but quietly buzzing

A bottomless mine of useless information

First it was like Harpo Marx

John saw it like an old man on a park bench

I saw it like a prince among poets, constantly seeking out marvellous

aphorisms.

71 *Gavin Bryars,* Marvellous Aphorisms Are Scattered Richly Throughout These Pages *(1969).*

mile from' (how much more than one mile?); 'the performer' (who?). These are constrained further by the resources that the score specifies elsewhere: 'at least one mile'; 'the performer'; not explosives; not someone else; the sound.[4]

The other elements of the score – the title and the final anecdote – might also suggest ways that a performer might realise the piece, albeit by implying constraints rather than stating them explicitly. These additional elements provide more information about how the piece might be realised, and they may be read as documentation of Bryars' only attempt. They might also suggest the presence of a bell as the sound source (title), and a physical connection with the performer (anecdote). Bryars comments on his sole attempted realisation:

> Well it was in Goole, and where I was, I've forgotten why, but for some reason I had to go in a particular direction and it did cross the railway line, and I didn't have time, there wasn't a tunnel or anywhere nearby so I had to go across the railway line and I thought I had enough time but I'd mistimed the time that this express train was going to come and it just severed the rope, the string, before I had time to do it. And I thought, 'Oh sod it, that's it.'[5]

---

[4] It should be noted that initially Bryars refers to 'sounds', and later 'the sound'. This could be interpreted literally: sounds are to be made, but it is only necessary for one sound to be able to be heard. Or it could indicate that the initial sounds become the piece's singular sound event (perhaps the sound of bells ringing). Or it may be an error.

[5] Gavin Bryars, in interview with John Lely and the author, Bath, 24 November 2008.

Later in the same interview when asked about the sound source, he states simply that 'It was a bell'.[6] So although it is not explicitly defined in the score, using a bell is both poetic (the image of distant tolling) and practical (church bells are a common feature of the English landscape, and are designed to be audible from far away). According to the composer, central to the creation of the piece was the notion of a long-distance physical connection between performer and sound source:

> We had done this [Toshi] Ichiyanagi *Distance*, and that does involve producing sounds at a distance [...] it's nowhere near that [...] it's like three metres or so. I did that quite a lot at Portsmouth [College of Art], and there were some incredibly inventive solutions to that. I remember Jimmy Lampard, who was part of the [Portsmouth] Sinfonia. [...] He did this fantastic realisation of Ichiyanagi's *Distance* which involved a kind of length of chain and a box of matches and Andrews Liver Salts and all sorts of fizzing, it just went on and on, it was just sort of wonderful. So you've got that invention with the art students, and maybe that piece came out of that experience, but more extreme, a much more extreme version of it. You can see what you're doing. You've got to try and control it, but from a reasonable distance, the length of this room, but a mile is something else.[7]

However, the most explicit restrictions are imposed on the method by which sounds might be made to occur. The score states: 'Do not use explosives and do not allow someone else to make the sound for you.' While explosives are perhaps the most dramatic way to make audible sounds at a distance, they are not the most practicable: it is revealing that Bryars did not, for example, preclude using electricity as a triggering method.[8] This sentence also precludes other people from making the sound, but it does not prevent their involvement in the performance in other capacities, such as assisting in setting up the piece, or helping to solve problems.

However, the key phrase, the details of which may be easily overlooked, is the comment that 'the sound should be able to be heard by the performer'. This appears to mean not that the sound should be heard by the performer, but rather that it is *necessary* for there to be the *possibility* that the sound is heard by the performer. While one performer might decide that the composer's phrasing suggests that it is enough to make a sound and not to hear it (by triggering, say, something small and quiet), another performer may consider the possibility of hearing the sound to be an essential ingredient of the piece, and rise to the challenge.

---

[6] *Ibid.*

[7] *Ibid.*

[8] The question of an historically informed performance is relevant here, in respect to more recent technological developments. The issue is the same as with realising all music of a different period: should the initial conditions be preserved as far as is practicable in a contemporary performance?

Two Attempts

In November 2008, John Lely and I made a realisation of the piece as part of a series of performances of Gavin Bryars' music hosted by Bath Spa University. When preparing a realisation of *Far Away and Dimly Pealing*, we found that two principal, and interdependent, decisions needed to be made: how, and where. It seemed impossible to fix one without attending to the other as they enforce mutual constraints on the performance. Our starting point for the realisation was to begin discussing how we might make the piece. While it would have been straightforward enough to use recent technology, we felt that there needed to be something of the original context for the piece retained in our performance.

The account of the failed first attempt in the score also hints at a physical connection between the performer and the sound, so we began by exploring practical ways to achieve this. We settled almost immediately on the use of a suspended bell attached to a long piece of string. This was implied by the score, is a cost-effective way to make the piece, is easy to set up, and should be fairly robust given suitable materials.

After researching various types of string, we bought 3 km of three-ply sisal in four 750 m balls (which were about the size of footballs) to make sure we had enough. The string needed to be strong in order to prevent snapping when put under tension, but not so heavy that it would be impossible to pull. As it turned out, overbuying (a mile is c. 1660 m) was a good decision: during the first attempt I would run out of string after unfurling three balls – supposedly containing 2250 m of string – some 250 m short of the distance required. The string was to be attached to my father's old Great Eastern Railway station bell. In preparing the performance, we made numerous tests with short lengths of string tied to the clapper to determine the optimal means of producing the sound.

We were aware that the weight of the string might be such that once the clapper was pulled, the string could prevent it from returning to its original position, giving us only one chance to make the bell sound. By angling the bell with the handle pointing away from the direction of pulling, the weight of the clapper would provide it with the best chance of multiple strikes on release of the string. We mounted the bell on a wheeled tripod, placing it about a metre off the ground.

Once we had decided how to make the sound, our principal problem was to find a site where we could try a realisation. Bryars' parenthetical comment in the score served as a warning here: the likelihood of interference was high along what would most likely be an unguarded stretch of land. Sabotage could not be ruled out in a public space, so we looked at sites where either there was no public access, or the probability of being disturbed was low: it would most likely be a private performance. We considered beaches, remote parts of Norfolk, and open countryside before settling on an airfield as the most practical location. These are not generally accessible and have long straight tarmac runways.

Unfortunately many of them are less than a mile at their longest, which ruled out most of those within travelling distance. Other possible sites were in active, if only occasional, use and required a permit and sizeable fee to hire. After about a month of searching, we came across Upper Heyford near Oxford, a disused airfield now home to industrial units and small businesses. We were granted a day's use of the main taxiway,[9] which was more than a mile long and closed to the public.

On arrival at the airfield we measured out and marked the mile required using GPS and decided, taking into account wind direction, at which end to place the bell. The taxiway additionally had a line running down the centre, which served as a useful guide for walking. Next, we set up the bell, put the wheel-brakes on, and tied the string to the clapper. John then drove to the other end of the runway to await my arrival. Carrying the other balls of string in my rucksack, I walked the mile, gradually unfurling the string and tying additional lengths onto the previous one whenever a ball ran out. Arriving at the far end of the runway, and with the bell a tiny dot on the horizon, I attempted to cause sounds to occur a mile away.

Unfortunately, we were unable to ascertain whether the bell made a sound, since it was not audible at this distance; it was a blustery day and the wind direction may have changed. John drove to the instrument end of

72 *James Saunders preparing the bell.*

[9] We are grateful to Colin Theobald of Lambert Smith Hampton and the North Oxfordshire Consortium for providing access to the airfield free of charge for a full day.

73 *James Saunders walking the mile.*

the runway and tested it to make sure the bell was working. It was ringing, albeit fairly quietly, so he took the brakes off the stand, allowing the bell to be pulled more and gain a better release after each strike. This proved to make a much louder sound, but the bell was still inaudible from my end of the runway.

Fortunately we had brought along two backup solutions, a personal alarm and a pressurised air horn, and we tried both devices manually to hear whether or not they were audible from the other end of the runway. The personal alarm was inaudible, but the air horn could be heard quite clearly, if quietly. The air horn was placed facing the far end of the runway, on a metal platform. A large cardboard tube was lowered vertically over the horn, with a section of the tube removed at the front to allow the 'horn' part to poke through. The cardboard tube was fixed to the platform with tape. A piece of dowel was inserted horizontally through the tube from front to back, so that it was positioned just above the air-horn trigger. A plastic flowerpot was dropped down inside the tube, where the dowel supported it. The tube was then filled with large beach pebbles. We tied one end of our mile of string to a hook on the front end of the dowel, so that when pulled, the string would whip away the dowel, the weight of the stones would cause the flowerpot to push down on the trigger, and the air horn would sound.

While I stayed at the instrument end to monitor the new instrument, John drove back to the tugging end of the taxiway and pulled the string. The

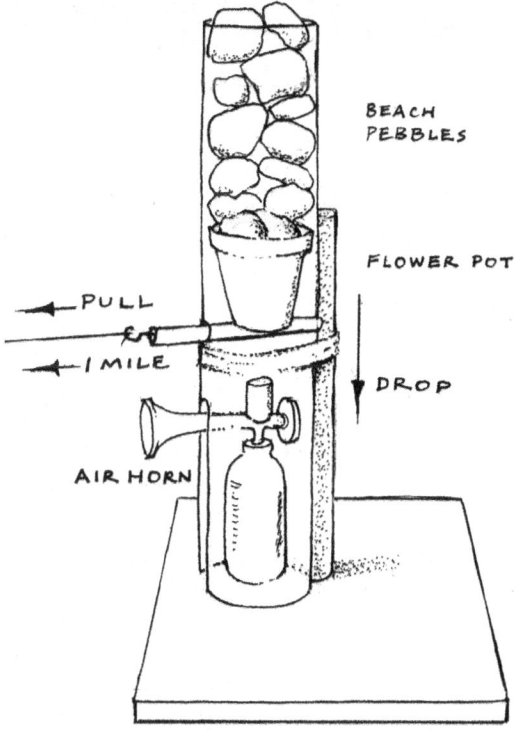

74 The air-horn instrument. *75 A diagram of the air-horn instrument.*

tension was taken up gradually, before a final tug released the pebbles. From a mile away, the air horn was just audible with its initial blast, which quickly subsided. I continued to watch the instrument from nearby and after a while the weight of the pebbles unexpectedly caused more of the compressed air to gradually seep out, and moments later the air horn regained enough pressure to make a second, sustained, dying and slowly falling sound, which again was audible a mile away.

76 *John Lely realises* Far Away and Dimly Pealing.

Arthur Bull

from *25 Scores* (1994)

Statement on Text Scores

In the evening, find a pond or bog
filled with singing frogs. Approach
the pond, noting how the peepers get
quieter as you get nearer, until there
are only trios, duets or solos. Then
walk away until the full chorus resumes.
Repeat several times, until you and they
have established a macro-rhythmic form
on their piece.

On a clear night, using rapid labial,
frontal and dental mouth sounds, take
a particular configuration of stars,
a constellation, say, as your score
following the shape until you have
returned to the first sound.

Statement on Text Scores

Arthur Bull, November 2010

I think what got me started was reading some text scores by the great impro-viser Hugh Davies in an American new music magazine. I was quite inspired by them and started thinking about writing something along those lines, especially the ones relating to natural sound, since I had recently moved to a remote region of Nova Scotia from Toronto. (I am also a musician and improviser, and was already familiar with Hugh Davies' work with New Music Company, etc.) I have since realized, with increasing humility, that this approach goes back to Fluxus and Yoko Ono and even before. Most recently I have been enjoying scores by Robert Filliou and George Brecht in the same vein. So I see myself as doing my own thing, such as it is, within a fairly well established genre.

The other impulse behind this writing had to do with my work as a poet. I was struggling with questions of voice at the time, that is, the rhetorical relation between writer and reader. This was giving me a lot of trouble, and, after chewing on it for some time, I started to think about the voice of cookbooks – such a simple and clear way of linking author to reader: do this, then do that, and you can try that, etc. It seemed a simple solution to an intractable problem. Soon I started reading all sorts of poems, including haiku and Chinese classical forms, as little scores, to be performed in the heart/mind of the listener.

Using the prose poem form shifts the medium from rhythmic line to syntactic and grammatical shape. This was also part of the attraction. Taking experiences like approaching the frog-orchestrated pond beside our house, or a long looking into the country night sky while singing, and putting them into complete, imperative sentences – that seemed interesting too.

John Cage

Solo for Voice 6 (1970)

Commentary: *Solo for Voice 6*

SOLO FOR VOICE 6

THEATRE

(IRRELEVANT)

DIRECTIONS

A series of numbers 1-64 each preceded by a plus or minus sign, one number sometimes written above another or others. The series may be performed completely or in part.

To prepare for a performance, the actor will make a numbered list of verbs (actions) and/or nouns (things) not to exceed 64 with which he or she is willing to be involved and which are theatrically feasible (these may include stage properties, clothes, etc.; actions may be 'real' or mimed, etc.). If these number 64, the tables given below (which relate numbers less than 64 to 64) are unnecessary. In any other case, the appropriate table below will enable the actor to identify which, for instance, of twenty-seven nouns and verbs the number 36 refers to. The minus and plus signs may be given any significance that the performer finds useful. For instance, a minus sign may mean "beginning with" or "taking off", etc.; a plus sign may mean "going to" or "putting on" etc. Or they may refer to the degree or emphasis with which something is done. Change of type-face may also be so interpreted. Where nouns or verbs indicating expressivity are included in the list, expressivity is obligatory. Otherwise perform impassively. Total time-length and duration of individual actions are free.

+ 40
+ 35   + 23

+ 28   − 55   + 54   + 58

+ 60   + 21   − 31   − 44   − 47

+ 46   + 61   + 4   − 63

− 12

− 38 − 38
+ 4

− 30

− 32
+ 61

Commentary: *Solo for Voice 6*

James Saunders

Solo for Voice 6 is one of the 92 solos that constitute John Cage's *Song Books* (1970), part of the series of indeterminate compositions that also includes *Concert for Piano and Orchestra* (1957–8) and *Rozart Mix* (1965) which Cage suggests might be performed simultaneously. It is an example of a score which requires the performers to use chance procedures to produce secondary notation for use when preparing a performance. Chance was central to Cage's compositional strategy by the 1970s, and *Solo for Voice 6* carries this approach through by instructing the performer how to prepare a new performance score by using chance-based procedures.

The solos in the *Song Books* can be realised in multiple ways, and in the general introduction to the score Cage states:

> The solos may be used by one or more singers. Any number of solos in any order and any superimposition may be used. Superimposition is sometimes possible, since some are not 'songs', but are directives for theatrical activity (which, on the other hand, may include voice production). A given solo may recur in a given performance.

This creates a large number of variables for a performer to consider when preparing a performance. It is necessary to determine how the material will be selected and realised by the performers, as well as the method for structuring the event. Experienced Cage performer William Brooks has directed many performances of *Song Books*, and explains his approach to preparing the piece:

> In a full performance of the *Song Books* given by a group of performers, there are some obvious questions: Which solos will be performed? By whom? Where? When? I usually begin by designating distinct performance spaces.[1] These may be dictated by circumstance (if, for instance, the performance is occupying many rooms, corridors, spaces); or they are artificially imposed (by dividing a proscenium stage into separate areas, often by means of a grid of some kind, as in *Europera*).[2] In each space only one solo will be performed at any one time.

---

[1] Brooks points out that this is his take on performing *Song Books*, adding, 'I can claim no special virtue in my performances, but I note that Cage congratulated me, beaming, after the Northwestern performance. But then, as we know, he had the (mis)fortune to be born an optimist.' For more information on other realisations, see Fetterman, 1996, pp. 149–66.

[2] Cage completed five *Europeras* from 1987 to 1991. They use superimposed fragments of operatic arias, instrumental parts, piano transcriptions, and recordings, with the chance-determined movement of performers, objects, and staging being related to a grid that is overlaid on the performing area.

Working individually and without consultation each performer then goes through the score, ruling out any solos deemed impractical. The remaining solos constitute (for that performer) the 'possible answers' to the question of what will be performed.

A matrix for the entire performance – time horizontally, locations vertically – is posted in a location accessible to all performers. Each performer then uses chance operations to fill in the matrix: choose a solo (by chance); choose a location (by chance); choose a start time (by chance); if the duration is unspecified, choose a duration (by chance). The performer's name and the name of the solo is written in the chosen location and a horizontal line is drawn blocking out that location for the duration of the solo. It's necessary that all the performers do this more or less concurrently, lest very few opportunities remain for a late entrant. [...]

In general Cage advocated multiplicity, and I've always instructed the performers to be quite active (without taking extraordinary measures).[3]

Solo for Voice 6 is a piece designated as 'theatre', and comprises a page of instructions and a page of numbers.[4] It is related to nine other pieces in the set through the use of similar notation. Solos *10, 19, 31, 76* and *77* use a near-identical method, each differing only in the set of numbers provided and the addition of a line which indicates the solo should 'overlap with preceding activity or song'. Solos *7, 9, 61* and *87* use predetermined words and phrases to suggest actions, rather than numbers that allow the performer to make selections from a personally prepared list.

While all of the solos include a verbal description of the means to realise the piece, many supplement this with stave or graphic notation. Of those that use solely text, some, such as *Solo for Voice 31*, have no further materials. Others, including *Solo for Voice 6,* have additional score pages containing words or numbers. Cage's score provides instructions for making a score for performers to follow in a performance that determines a series of actions, or objects with which the performer is 'willing to be involved and which are theatrically feasible'. The performer initially makes a list of up to 64 verbs and nouns, and assigns a number to each. The set of 23 numbers on the second page of Cage's score are then used to determine which of these words will be used in the performance. Where the performer has chosen fewer than 64 words for the list, numbers on the score page are assigned to the performer's words using one of 63 look-up tables that Cage provides elsewhere in the general instructions to the *Song Books*. In the example given

[3] William Brooks, in correspondence with the author, September 2010. The text by Brooks that is incorporated here is part of a commentary written following a request for information on how he has realised *Solo for Voice 6.*

[4] In the introduction, Cage explains that the solos belong to one of four categories: (i) song; (ii) song with electronics; (iii) theatre; (iv) theatre with electronics. He also states: 'Each is relevant or irrelevant to the subject: "We connect Satie with Thoreau."' Solo 6 is irrelevant.

in the score, where the number 36 on the score page must be matched to one of 27 chosen words,[5] the relevant table indicates that word 16 from the performer's list must be used in this case (see Fig. 79). In this instance, the process results in a set of 16 words to be used in the realisation, of which six appear twice. This happens for two reasons: either a number is used twice on the score page (e.g. 4, although the two instances use different typefaces), or the look-up table reduces two different numbers on the score to a single word on the performer's list (e.g. 30 and 31 both result in word 13 being selected, although again these numbers appear in different typefaces).

Cage does not specify the method for making the list. William Brooks observes:

> The question is: how will that list be made? What is *not* permissible, I think, is choosing particular items for aesthetic or theatrical reasons (i.e. because they will be funny, or beautiful, or unexpected). Either the list is defined by circumstances or a 'neutral' method is employed to construct it. I have advocated using a dictionary: creating a list of words by chance and setting about the task of realizing them. (Certain words, or overly literal realizations, will be rejected on moral or practical grounds: 'self-harm', for example. Cage offers the necessary escape clause: 'with which he or she is willing to be involved'.) I find the dictionary convenient, but there are many other, similar methods for assembling such a list. At Northwestern University in 1992 a student used the dictionary and wound up creating a very difficult and virtuosic performance.

27

1- 3 =	1	34-35 =	15
4- 6 =	2	36-37 =	16
7- 9 =	3	38-39 =	17
10-12 =	4	40-41 =	18
13-15 =	5	42-43 =	19
16-17 =	6	44-45 =	20
18-19 =	7	46-47 =	21
20-21 =	8	48-49 =	22
22-23 =	9	50-52 =	23
24-25 =	10	53-55 =	24
26-27 =	11	56-58 =	25
28-29 =	12	59-61 =	26
30-31 =	13	62-64 =	27
32-33 =	14		

79 *Table 27 from 'Tables Relating Numbers Less than 64 to 64', from John Cage's* Song Books *(1970).*

Another option is to choose a domain of actions, exercising taste in the choice, but then to choose the items themselves by chance. At the University of York in 2003 a performer with expertise in dance and martial arts used chance to select movements from a repertoire taken essentially from training manuals (or so I recall; it may have been somewhat different).

A third alternative (which in a sense is always present) is to allow circumstances to set the constraints. At the Orpheus Institute (2009) my own realization was largely determined by circumstance: at the start time for the solo I was already sitting on a chair; because of the nature of the space it was not possible to move widely or use extensive props; and when constructing the realization the only objects at hand were two

---

[5] Cage uses this as an example. The number 36 is not present on the score page of *Solo for Voice 6*, and 27 is one possibility for the number of words (which may amount to any number up to and including 64).

hats. The performance consisted of a series of poses, hat(s) in hand (or on the body).[6]

The score does not suggest the way to realise each word. However, relevant here are Cage's views on the performance practice of the related *Theatre Piece* (1960). He comments on a situation in this piece where two nouns and two verbs might be presented, stating:

> you're faced with the problem of a rose, a pencil and swimming, and sliding. How are you going to do that? And how are you going to do that in the right time relationship?[7] *What* are you going to do, in fact? If sliding comes after swim, comes after pencil, comes after rose, how are you going to work that out?[8]

Cage seems to be presenting a problem to the performer, one which should be resolved through a performance. Later in the same interview he underlines the experimental nature of these acts, criticising realisations where performers 'mostly do it in such a way that they don't have to confront new experience'.[9] His instructions later in the score of *Solo for Voice 6* indicate a preference for an impassive performance when realising the words. This recalls his requirement in *Solo for Voice 8,* a variant of the earlier *0'00''* (1962), that 'No attention to be given [*sic*] the situation', which is further exemplified by his comment that 'theatre is only another word for designating life'.[10] Cage makes a deliberate exception where selected words indicate expressivity. So if the word 'cry' were to be chosen as a verb, obvious expression would probably be inherent in the resultant action.

Cage allows for the interpretation of these words to be modified dependent on whether they are preceded by a plus or minus sign, and on the typeface used. According to the score the signs 'may be given any significance the performer finds useful'. Cage gives examples where the signs modify nouns, i.e. they indicate what can be done with the selected objects, for example 'putting on' in the example Cage gives. The score also states that they may 'refer to the degree or emphasis with which something is done', modifying the verbs in the list. These are only examples though: as the score states, usefulness to the performer is the primary criterion when determining their meaning.

The change of typeface 'may also be so interpreted'. On the score page, Cage uses ten different typefaces, with one appearing in two different sizes.[11] The typefaces are presented in contiguous blocks of between one and four

---

[6] William Brooks, in correspondence with the author, September 2010.

[7] In *Theatre Piece*, the numbers are placed on the page in time brackets that are measured using scalable rulers to determine precise start and end points.

[8] Fetterman, 1996, p. 236.

[9] *Ibid.*

[10] Cage, 1981, p. 165.

[11] The grouped +4 and two −38s use a smaller point size of the typeface used for the −30 at the bottom of the page.

numbers. A performer may decide to associate numbers in the same typeface with a single method of realising their corresponding actions. While the precise meanings of plus and minus symbols are contextually determined, they might broadly signify positive and negative change. The difference between typefaces may be more subjective, with contrasts in size, weight, and style being harder to map to parameters relevant to a realisation.

It is, however, ambiguous whether Cage's instruction that a change of typeface may be given significance also refers to a change of size and weight in addition to the change of style. Cage's use of different typefaces is a feature of much of his work with text, including the use of chance to determine aspects of the layout of *Notations* (1969), his anthology of experimental scores by other composers.[12] In *Solo for Voice* 6 though, it is used as a notational category to indicate differences in interpretation. In his 2009 realisation, William Brooks:

> sought to incorporate the differences in typefaces in *Solo* 6 (as well as the plus/minus signs that Cage explicitly discusses). I determined that each of the numbers in *Solo* 6 had several distinct properties: size; italic/ roman; serif/sans-serif; plus/minus; and the number itself. I then assigned different parameters to each of these. I made a list of body surfaces on which a hat could rest: head, face, back of head, shoulders (2), elbows (2), hands (2), back, knees (2), feet (2) – 14 places in all. Using an equal division of 64 (1–5, 6–10, and so forth) I determined the sequence of events (hat on elbow, on knees, and so forth). I used the size of the typeface to determine duration. Italic/roman determined which of two hats was used. Plus/minus determined whether the hat was right side up or upside down. Serif/sans-serif determined whether I was standing or sitting. (In truth, the mappings may have been somewhat different [...] But the principle is correct.) The result was a series of actions that were confined in scope and space because of constraints adopted at the outset, but which I had no way of predicting or influencing.[13]

In keeping with some earlier pieces by Cage, such as the *Concert for Piano and Orchestra*, the score does not give any clear indication of how the actions should relate to each other in time. Cage notes that durations of individual actions and the whole realisation are free, and that part or all of the series may be used. This is qualified by instructions in the preface to *Song Books* which states, 'Given a total performance time-length, each singer may make a program that will fill it', and that performers 'should make an independent program, not fitted or related in a predetermined way to anyone else's program. Any resultant silence in a program is not to be feared. Simply perform as you had decided to, before you knew what would happen.'

---

[12] In the Preface, Cage states: 'the typography too – letter size, intensity, and typeface – were all determined by chance operations' (Cage, 1969).

[13] William Brooks, in correspondence with the author, September 2010.

Actions may be selected from the 16 words produced by the notation of *Solo 6*. The ordering of these actions in lines on the page might suggest a sequence to be followed, and the three grouped arrangements of numbers might indicate a relationship between the actions they specify, but this is not an explicit indication. Given the openness of much of the score, when considering how to proceed when confronted by such a range of possibilities Brooks advises following Cage's views on realising his scores:

> In realizing the *Song Books* I have been guided by three precepts, all of which Cage made explicit in interviews and writings. (1) Observe the score; do nothing that is inconsistent with it, and seek to realize all nuances of notation. (2) Respect the circumstances; accept whatever constraints they impose. (3) For all interpretive decisions, and especially when the course of action is not clear, ask a question (or a series of questions), provide a list of possible answers, and use chance procedures to select from the list. It's important, I think, not to exercise imagination too early; let chance determine your 'instructions' as much as possible, and be creative only in resolving what seem at first to be impossibilities.[14]

[14] *Ibid.*

Cornelius Cardew

The Great Learning, Paragraph 6 (1968–71)

On the Role of the Instructions in the Interpretation of Indeterminate Music

Commentary: The Great Learning, Paragraph 6

The Great Learning, paragraph 6

FROM   Make or hear an isolated sound and hear out the following general pause. Then a set of four sounds, the first one synchronised.

THE EMPEROR   A pair of sounds, then a pair of optional sounds.

SON OF HEAVEN   Two sounds, the first synchronised. Between the two await the occurrence of a long pause.

DOWN TO   A synchronised sound followed by an isolated one. Then an optional sound followed by an isolated one.

DOWN TO   Five sounds; the second synchronised, the third isolated, the last preceded by a general pause.

DOWN TO   Two sounds, the first isolated. Then a set of four optional sounds, the second being loud or long. Finally an isolated pair of sounds (both made or both heard or one made one heard).

THE COMMON   Five sounds; the first isolated, the third optional, the fifth synchronised. Then wait for a general pause and at some point drop into it an isolated constellation of four sounds (made, heard, or part-made part-heard).

MAN   A pair of optional sounds.

SINGLY   Make a sound. Wait for a general pause and follow it with four sounds, the second isolated, the third loud or long. Wait for another general pause and follow it with three sounds, the first synchronised, the last two separated by an isolated pair of sounds.

AND   Wait for a general pause and follow it with four sounds, the first one synchronised. Then a pair of optional sounds and await another general pause. Finally one more sound.

ALL TOGETHER   Make four sounds, the first and third synchronised. Wait for a general pause and then make three more sounds, the first synchronised.

THIS   A synchronised sound, an isolated sound, an optional sound and an isolated sound in that order.

SELF—   After an optional sound await two general pauses. Then two optional sounds separated by a synchronised sound. Another general pause. Then a set of three sounds, the first one synchronised and loud or long.

DISCIPLINE   Make an isolated sound and hear out the following general pause. Then a set of five sounds; the first is synchronised and loud or long, and the last is optional.

IS   An isolated sound followed by an isolated set of three sounds. Then an optional sound followed by a set of three synchronised sounds (two or all may be simultaneous but in any case synchronised with another player). Then an isolated constellation of four sounds.

THE ROOT   Three sounds, the last two optional. Then wait for a general pause and end with a sound.

PERFORMANCE NOTES

Any number of performers move independently through the material in the written order. There is no obligation to reach the end. Performers dropping out or ending should signalise the fact in some way (e.g. if the performing space is well-defined, leave it).

Any materials may be used. Each sound from a different source or all sounds from the same source, or any gradation between. Stones, whistles, speech, song, gueros, etc. recommend themselves as occurring in other paragraphs of The Great Learning. In the case of speech or song, use the words written in capitals at the start of the sequence you are in. Anything from the whole word or group of words down to a single letter.

A "sound", with no qualifying adjective, means a rather definite type of sound with a certain amount of presence. Sounds are generally shortish and rather quiet.

"Optional sound" can mean a sound (as above), or an accidental or incidental (glancing) type of sound, or a quasi-accidental sound or no sound at all.

"Isolated" always implies the option of making the sound or hearing it, as in the first sentence.

"Synchronised sound" means make a sound simultaneously with another player.

In cases of failure to produce a properly "isolated" or "synchronised" sound, there is no limit to the number of attempts that may be made, but there is no obligation to make more than one.

"General pause" is when everyone is silent and still.

On the Role of the Instructions in the Interpretation of Indeterminate Music

Cornelius Cardew, 12 February 1965

The writing down of music is in process of disintegrating. In the past the notation of music was dependent on flexible conventions and a performer could use these to correct the tendencies of an aural tradition. In other words: by going back to study the notation of a piece a prospective interpreter could verify whether or not a certain popularisation by a famous virtuoso was justifiable. In the notation of music today two tendencies are apparent: 1) to so reduce the flexibility of the conventions that they become virtually inflexible (this means that and nothing else), and 2) to so increase the flexibility of the conventions that they in fact become non-conventional (this may mean this, that or the other, and not necessarily any of these). This is a simplification, and the examples I propose to discuss in this text are intended to show the complex situations that can arise with respect to pieces of music that are really delightfully simple and refreshingly primitive. (Everyone knows the anguish undergone by people who in the end come out with some gloriously simple remark like 'There is no other God but me' or '*Cogito ergo sum*'.)

I propose to use my own *Volo Solo* as an example to demonstrate the 'normal' situation encountered in indeterminate music, i.e. that there are certain notations, and then certain instructions about how these notations are to be read or understood. My other example will be La Monte Young's *X (any integer) for Henry Flynt*, a remarkable case of a piece that consists of no notations, and performing instructions that no one can agree on.

Many pieces (*Volo Solo* is one) contain internal implications some of which (not all) the composer is aware of. These he describes in his instructions. But there may be other implications which require that certain instructions should be waived and others observed. Performers have to be careful to realise the exact nature of the notation *apart* from the instructions before venturing to shift the piece's emphasis onto another aspect. The tones of *Volo Solo* are the nucleus of the piece. The notion of performing excessively fast is a relative one: an amateur's fast will be relatively slow, therefore slowness is not something alien to the piece, therefore some virtuoso (he would also have to be something of a mental virtuoso) might decide to play it at a leisurely speed. Even at that speed he might manage to make the instrument 'break apart', although that again, being a subjective experience, is not necessarily binding. So, in this case, the notes represent a sort of base camp, the instructions pointing out one route (or group of routes) to the summit which is a performance. The instructions are the imposition of a system on a mass of raw material, and no system, however closed, perfect and complete, can lay claim to being the only one, since what a system really represents is a human interpretation and ordering of given facts or material.

The case of La Monte Young's X *for Henry Flynt* is more difficult. What is the nucleus of that piece? What the instructions? We may deduce that La Monte's idea embraced the following categories and that he made decisions with regard to them (decisions are given in parentheses):

a) a sound (cluster, gong, bucket of bolts...)
b) repetition of a sound (uniform)
c) a time interval (1–2 seconds)
d) an articulation of the time interval (a relatively short silence between sounds)
e) a dynamic (as loud as possible)
f) (*not* total duration of the piece, but) Number of sounds
g) a number of performers (one).

These categories and their interrelationships constitute the matrix of the piece. The decisions relating to b, c, d are expressly given by La Monte. The decisions for a and f are definitely left open. e and g have been cursorily fixed, but without special mention. (g was altered by Rzewski, for example, in his performance in Rome with Hans Otte, and the piece was virtually destroyed). When we score the piece in this way it becomes apparent that everything may be altered (by altering the values in brackets) without altering the structure of the piece. Such alterations would produce a family of pieces, all 'topologically' identical. (Invent some.) But when La Monte insists on detail, he insists on his decisions for b, c, d. He *insists* on the variability of f, and *permits* the variability of a (this variability is from performance to performance, not within a single performance).

The foregoing analysis concerns itself with the *internal* structure of the piece. There are other angles. Let us for example take a frontal view: What is interesting about the piece in performance, from the audience's point of view?

1) Its duration, and proportional to that:
2) the variation within the uniform repetition.
3) the stress imposed on the single performer and through him on the audience.

(Note that none of these form part of the compositional structure of the piece. These elements occur rather *in spite of* the instructions, although naturally they are the *result* of them. What the listener can hear and appreciate are the *errors* in the interpretation. If the piece were performed by a machine this interest would disappear and with it the composition. Truly this piece is gladiatorial; what the audience comes to witness is a rosy crucifixion.)

Empirically then we can proscribe the 'area' of the piece (a subgroup of the family of topologically identical pieces): (Of course a different subgroup of that family might produce a different set of interesting and essential features in performance, e.g. with a large number of players the variation from uniformity is greater, but in the case of Rzewski's performance we have seen that this is just what diminished the interest of his performance. As in Homeopathy, perhaps the effect of the variation varies in inverse proportion to its magnitude.)

This 'area' then is:
a) one dense heavy decaying sound
b) repeated as uniformly and regularly as possible
c) at an interval of circa 1–2 seconds
d) with a short silence between each repetition
e) the sound is played as loud as possible
f) a relatively large number of times
g) by one performer.

Here we see that *a, c, d, f* are still free, but within fairly strict limits (and once the choices are made they must be adhered to uniformly), and *b* and *e* are relatively fixed (by 'as possible'), and g is fixed immutably (by the number 1).

Now we have to consider the internal implications in this piece of the words 'as possible', as they occur for instance in *e*: as loud as possible. Suppose the number of repetitions chosen is 3792, and the performer is in peak physical condition but has not played the piece before, and suppose also that he is playing it as a large cluster on the piano. The first cluster is very loud indeed, but after a certain number (say 600) he is physically exhausted and unable to control the movements of his arms beyond just letting them fall and then picking them up again with ever-increasing difficulty. He is still playing 'as loud as possible' but the variation in the sound has risen steeply; it is in fact no longer loud in the absolute sense, and it is unrecognizably deformed. So now suppose the performer has rehearsed the piece beforehand and realises the strain that he will suffer in the course of it. For the sake of maintaining uniformity he decided to play the cluster moderately loud and thus keep the variation within homeopathic limits. Some listeners might prefer this latter attitude, finding the spectacle of iron reserve and endurance an edifying one, whereas the spectacle of the physical destruction of a man is a degrading one (even though it be only temporary). Others may prefer the former attitude, on the grounds that 'there is more happening', or that the spectacle of destruction is necessary for the fortification – or understanding – of the constructive instinct, or purely for sadistic reasons.

So much for the words 'as possible' in connection with loud. Let us now look at their implications as applied to 'uniformity and regularity'. What is the model for this uniformity? The first sound? Or does each sound become the model for the one succeeding it? If the former, the first sound has to be fixed in the mind as a mental ideal which all the remaining sounds are to approach as closely as possible. (In practice the first sound too is an attempt to approach a mental image that exists already before the piece began.) If the latter method is chosen, constant care has to be taken to assimilate the various accidental variations as they occur. David Tudor has approached the piece in this way and tells how, on noticing that certain keys in the centre of the keyboard were not being depressed it became his task to make sure that these particular keys continued to be silent. This task of assimilating and maintaining accidental variations, if logically pursued, requires superhuman powers of concentration and technique. (It also presents the possibility that the piece might come to a 'natural end' before the decided number of repetitions has been accomplished.) It must be remembered that although uniformity is demanded ('as far as possible'), what is *desired* is variation. It is simply this: that the variation that is desired is that which results from the human (not the superhuman) attempt at uniformity.

These same remarks can be applied to the prescription 'as regularly as possible', with the added difficulty that there are two kinds of regularity: subjective regularity and mechanical regularity, besides various other regularities that may be created by dependence on characteristics of the sound. For instance, the sound might be cut off each time when it reaches a certain dynamic level, and thus the time-interval would vary in proportion to the variation in the loudness with which the cluster is played – which might be considerable, as we saw earlier.

What emerges from all this is that in the work of many composers (including Feldman, Wolff, Cage, myself, Rzewski, La Monte Young and even Stockhausen if he himself happens to be absent) the interpretation of the *instructions* for a piece has a decisive influence on the performance. We have seen that to say that the instructions govern the performers' interpretation of the notations does not cover the case. Very often a performer's intuitive response to the notation influences to a large extent his interpretation of the instructions. In a lot of indeterminate music the would-be performer, bringing with him all his prejudices and virtues, intervenes in the composition of the piece, influences its identity in fact, at the moment when he first glances at the notation and jumps to a conclusion about what the piece is, what is its nature. Then he turns to the instructions, which on occasion may explain that certain notations do not for instance mean what many people might at first blush expect, and these he proceeds to interpret in relation to his preconceptions deriving from the notations themselves. This is often a good thing. Since very often the notations themselves are the determining factor in the method of composition of a piece, and hence in the piece's identity and structure. And the composer often provides his instructions as an interpretation of the piece, and not a binding one (as is clear in many of Cage's scores). Often, then, these instructions are limiting (at best) and misleading (at worst) and their interpretation is a matter of great importance for would-be performers. And the most important matter for the performer to decide is: which instructions are interpretative (an interpretation provided gratuitously by the composer) and which ones are essential to the piece, i.e. are actually notations in their own right, in which case they must naturally be respected. Ideally then, we should while composing strive to eliminate all mere interpretation, and concentrate on the notation itself, which should be as new and as fresh as possible (hence less likely to arouse preconceptions in the interpreter – though if you have a good interpreter isn't it likely that his preconceptions will be good too?) and should contain implicit in its internal structure, without any need of any instruction, all the implications necessary for a live interpretation.

At the outset I said of my *Volo Solo* that the instruction, 'as fast as physically possible' was an interpretative instruction, and since an amateur's 'fast' is relatively slow, that 'speed' is not an essential of the work. But there is another instruction which says that the piece may be played by a 'virtuoso performer on any instrument', and if the piece is to be played only by virtuosi, i.e. people who are able to perform magic on their instrument, then it cannot be performed by an amateur, and this may lead us to conclude that speed is after all essential to the piece. But that is not the case – none of the instructions to the piece are essential, they are all interpretative, even the very title itself which might be taken to imply that it must be played by someone 'alone'. But no, I can very well imagine it being performed by several players. So none of the remarks that surround the piece are essential. In fact the most useful instructions are those which make it plain under what conditions the notation itself is not binding (i.e. when notes may be omitted, etc.).

At this point we may anticipate the probable end of the enquiry and assert – I repeat, this is only a probability – that what is implicit in the notation is this: that nothing whatever is binding, not even the well-tempered scale that I chose purely as a matter of convenience. I hope I have now made it clear that the writing down of music is in process of disintegrating. *Volo Solo* is evidence of the far advancement of this process at the present time, but I hope this will not prevent virtuosi and others all over the world from turning over its crumbling leaves during the short and precious duration of its half-life, on the off chance of deriving insight, edification or at least enjoyment from playing these notes that are not 'binding' (whatever that may mean), and perhaps even communicate something of this to a completely hypothetical and unlikely listener. It is a widely accepted doctrine – and I accept it myself with almost indecent alacrity since my survival depends on it – that even the meanest and most imperfect creature may be the unconscious bearer of a seed which, if by chance it fall on fertile ground, may take root and grow, and contribute, even if only infinitesimally, towards making Everything All Right.

Commentary: *The Great Learning*, Paragraph 6

John Lely

The Great Learning is a large-scale work by Cornelius Cardew, composed for the Scratch Orchestra between 1968 and 1971. Its seven Paragraphs employ a wide variety of instruments and notational strategies, and can be realised by what the score calls 'untrained musicians'. As with Cardew's other works from around this time, for example *Schooltime Compositions* and *Schooltime Special* (see Fig. 27, pages 39–41), in Paragraph 6 the notation appears to be treated as a mode of enquiry rather than the means to an end. The work is notable for the way in which it encourages each player's subjective perceptions of both the language of the score and the performance environment to influence the course of a performance. The score consists of two elements; the main section of text is the 'material' to be read through in performance, and the smaller text constitutes the 'performance notes'.

Performance Notes

The composer provides definitions for five types of event. The first definition is for a 'sound'. The indefinite article 'a' here counts as 'one' since, as will be seen, this type of event is intended to be discrete. Other composers have found the phrase 'a sound' convenient to use (see, for example, the English translation of Stockhausen's *RIGHT DURATIONS*, Fig. 138, page 361). Its convenience appears to lie in its impartiality and inclusiveness; 'a sound' admits any sound source, be it vocal (the score specifies that performers may use the Confucian text as a source), instrumental, environmental or found. The word 'sound' is qualified by the suggestion that it be 'a rather definite type of sound with a certain amount of presence [...] generally shortish and rather quiet'. Two other definitions of events provide qualifying adjectives for 'a sound'. An 'isolated' sound can be either made or heard, as in the first sentence of the material. 'Synchronised' sounds should occur in conjunction with other players. If players fail to produce properly 'isolated' or 'synchronised' sounds, they can keep trying until they succeed.

The inherent versatility of the phrase 'a sound' is supplemented by another type of event, an 'optional sound', which also promotes a broad range of possible interpretations. The performer has the option to make either 'a sound' or 'no sound at all'. Between these limits, the composer puts forward a range of other meanings. The definition of 'a sound' as 'rather definite' perhaps suggests a clear sense of intention on the part of the player. In contrast, the definitions provided for 'optional sound' emphasise a more ambiguous perspective on player intention. According to the score, an 'optional sound' may also mean 'an accidental or incidental (glancing) type of sound, or a quasi-accidental sound'. It is not specified whether 'optional sound' should be fixed to one single definition for a player, so its meaning can remain fluid during a performance. Interpretations of the terms 'accidental' and 'incidental' are likely to diverge. 'Accidental' could suggest a sound made unintentionally, the kind of sound that is traditionally considered extraneous, even objectionable in some musical performances: for instance a trombone slide tapping a music stand or a pen being dropped. It could also be interpreted as 'sounding accidental', perhaps like a recording of a bottle smashing.

Cardew's own view was that, 'a sound made intentionally has the characteristic of being intended; the same sound made accidentally has the different characteristics of accidentalness – regardless of whether you hear it as the same or different'.[1] If 'accidental' is interpreted as meaning something along the lines of 'unintentional', how can a player *intentionally* make an 'accidental' sound? As John Tilbury comments:

> Clearly, the precision demanded in the synchronisation of a sound with that of another performer involves a finer degree of intentionality than that demanded in the production of a 'glancing' sound – say if I casually knock a pen off the table with my elbow. But to what extent is the resulting sound of the pen falling on whatever surface *intentional* in the sense that the carefully intended synchronisation of two sounds is? In the former case the willed action produces an unwilled sound; in the latter the willed action produces a willed sound. Or was it in the former instance a case of producing an intentionally unwilled sound?[2]

The word 'incidental' suggests a slightly different meaning to 'accidental' – perhaps that of a sound that occurs as a by-product of an intentional action, like the sounds of a page being turned or an instrument being placed on a surface. Synonyms of 'incidental' include 'unimportant', 'peripheral' and 'resultant', and, perhaps more usefully, its antonyms include 'intentional', 'essential' and 'planned'. In parentheses is added the word 'glancing', which may suggest an intentional but fleeting contact between objects, or an unintentional, 'clipping' type of contact. It also perhaps recalls words like 'ricocheting' and 'rebounding', which are both suggestive of material processes beyond the immediate control of an agent.

Both 'accidental' and 'incidental' have as a root the Latin word *cadere*, meaning 'to fall', so this could be taken as a clue as to the physical manner in which the sounds might be made. The potentially unpredictable effects of gravity offer an immediately accessible way to explore non-intentionality. Cardew was familiar with George Brecht's *Incidental Music*, five pieces for pianist that feature several incidents of gravity-induced flux, including blocks falling into the piano and dried peas or beans being dropped on the piano keys (see Fig. 29, page 45). Brecht's interest was in what he called the 'incidentalness' of the resultant sounds.[3] The intended physical activity is prescribed in the score, but there is no mention of sounds – Brecht considered any resultant sounds incidental to a performance, a by-product

---

[1] Tilbury, 2008, p. 499.

[2] *Ibid.*, p. 500.

[3] Nyman, 1976, p. 257.

of the activity. According to John Tilbury, Cardew himself performed *Incidental Music* on more than one occasion:

> with a balletic grace and elegance, and in which his impeccable display of relaxed concentration, unflappability and sheer nerve would invariably serve to heighten the extreme tension built up during the performance.[4]

Prior to the composition of Paragraph 6, Cardew had been carrying out practical investigations into incidentalness and non-intention, particularly with his opera workbook *Schooltime Compositions*,[5] and with the improvising group AMM, which embraced incidental and environmental sounds as part of its practice.[6] Cardew's attitude to incidental sound offers insights into his general attitude to performance. He was, for example, critical of the traditional separation of the performer from the audience: in his short essay 'Sitting in the Dark', a text written to accompany *Schooltime Compositions*, he expresses his aversion to the 'pool of light' that is so common in opera, the 'thin veneer' that separates actor from audience.[7] On the other hand, he was also not completely opposed to framing a performance. John Tilbury relates an account of a solo performance that Cardew announced and gave at Morley College, which consisted of a sustained activity involving small objects (peas or dried beans) rolling down a slope onto an amplified metal surface. The stated formality of the occasion here sets up a tension, as Tilbury suggests, 'the indeterminacy and quiet anarchy of the beans offset by the palpable intentionality embodied in Cardew's simple act of provisioning'.[8]

Given Cardew's previous explorations of intentionality in performance, it is evident that the language of Paragraph 6 engages the players in a mode of activity that is calculated to occupy a similar realm. Cardew's precise, highly concentrated wording promotes divergence in such a way that a multiplicity of interpretations is bound to arise. The final definition of a 'general pause' occurs when 'everyone is silent and still'. Again, it is highly likely that players will have different interpretations of what actually qualifies as a 'general pause', and those different interpretations will in turn affect how each player progresses through the material.

Material

Cardew deploys these five types of event in the 16 short paragraphs that make up the performance material. The score states that performers move through the material independently, a process that Cardew had already encountered in the works of other composers. There are two pertinent examples of which

[4] Tilbury, 2008, p. 205.
[5] The first performance of which, incidentally, included George Brecht realising *Making A*.
[6] John Tilbury, in correspondence with the author, November 2009.
[7] Cardew, C., 'Sitting in the Dark', in Prévost, 2006, pp. 88–9.
[8] Tilbury, 2008, p. 356.

Cardew had direct performance experience prior to composing Paragraph 6. Both are relatively open in terms of duration. The first is Morton Feldman's *Two Pianos* (1957), which employs what Feldman called a 'race-course' notation, in which players begin together and gradually diverge at their own rates. The second is Terry Riley's *In C* (1964), a Scratch Orchestra favourite, in which, underpinned by a constant pulse, players independently progress through the same set of musical motifs, repeating each motif as many times as they want, thus creating multiple layerings of the same material.

These two examples demonstrate a gentle 'unsticking' of the vertical priority of traditional stave notation. In contrast, verbal notation can offer alternative ways to explore performer interaction and intentionality. In the case of Paragraph 6, when the score instructs performers to 'move independently through the material', this is not an arbitrary prescription. The nature of the material requires that every performer move through the material independently, though not wholly autonomously, since the notation compels performers to interact with one another in significant ways. Each performer's actions are influenced by the actions of other performers and the sounds of the environment. All performers are mutually reliant on each other for progress through the piece. As a result, there emerges an intricate, self-regulating network of social, acoustic and temporal correspondences.

The notation here creates a kind of resistance to each performer's individual progress, which is necessarily incremental, one sentence at a time. The notation demands an ongoing and disciplined negotiation of meaning, perception and intentionality. That sense of negotiation is perhaps reinforced by the way in which Cardew does not allow the language to slip into predictable patterns. Rather than simply listing the events, he articulates each in such a way that the player must remain alert. Some actions are very involved, yet the language remains precise. For instance: 'Wait for another general pause and follow it with three sounds, the first synchronised, the last two separated by an isolated pair of sounds.' There is also another surreptitious reference to gravity in the seventh paragraph: 'Then wait for a general pause and at some point drop into it an isolated constellation of four sounds (made, heard or part-made part-heard).'

In terms of the grammar of the score, one area for negotiation concerns ambiguities of connectivity in the language of the material. The score begins with an imperative clause, 'Make or hear an isolated sound', the outcome of which may be either a material process ('make') or a mental process ('hear'). The second clause, 'hear out the following general pause' is an imperative mental clause. There then follows the nominal group, 'Then a set of four sounds, the first one synchronised', which does not qualify as a clause because it does not centre around a verb. It cannot therefore take a mood, and so counts neither as an imperative nor a declaration of fact or existence. In the hope of turning this into a well-formed clause, one may decide to look backwards to the previous two clauses, and by carrying through the processes given in the first clause, one may infer that this is a short-hand version of the imperative, 'Then make or hear a set of four sounds, the first one synchronised.' However, if one instead decides to carry through the process given in the *second* clause, it may be inferred that this is a shorthand version of the imperative, 'Then hear out a set of four sounds, the first one synchronised.' Such grammatical ambiguities can be found throughout the score, but they may be resolved in the context of performance.

Although most qualifying adjectives are defined in the performance notes, others show up for the first time in the performance material. There is the option for some sounds to be 'loud' or 'long', and in the third paragraph there is also a 'long pause'. The discrete numbers, e.g. 'a pair of sounds', 'four sounds', emphasise the necessity for step-by-step progress, and reinforce the idea that 'a sound' should be 'one sound', a single discrete event. Note that there is never reference to 'some' sounds or 'a group' of sounds. All the sentences specify the number of sounds and even when sounds are 'optional' their number is still specified. Yet even with discrete variables there is room for interpretation. Is there, for instance, a difference between 'two sounds' and 'a pair of sounds'?

Whether one is waiting to hear a sound, or waiting out a general pause, or waiting for the opportunity for synchronisation, these moments of progress occur in incremental steps, in a suspended atmosphere of waiting. Each tangible moment provides a way forward, offering different solutions for different players. Given the sophistication of the notation and the personal responses that it can invoke, there is no substitute for performing this piece; experience will reveal unforeseen consequences. For example, the score suggests that there is no obligation for a player to reach the end of the instructions. In practice, though, a player may also discover that reaching the end is in fact an impossibility. A performance at the ICA in London in November 2009, by a group that included several Scratch Orchestra members, ended with a silence (or was it a 'general pause'?) of a little over two and a half minutes, during which one player waited patiently for an opportunity to synchronise his sound with someone (or something) else. That opportunity never arose.

Tony Conrad

Selected Pieces from 1961 Compositions

Word Scoring

PIECE

TO PERFORM THIS PIECE
DO NOT PERFORM THIS
PIECE

THIS PIECE IS ITS NAME.
THIS PIECE IS ITS NAME.

PIECE

TO PERFORM THIS PIECE,

COMPOSE IT,

AT LEAST.

PIECE

TO PERFORM THIS PIECE FOLLOW: THE INSTRUCTIONS FOR PERFORMING THIS PIECE

UNIVERSAL METACOMPOSITION.

To compose this { piece / art work }, form
the logical union of all possible
permutations of { words in your vocabulary / concepts of your acquaintance }

[N.B.: May also be appreciated as
concept art.]

— A. CONRAD   NOV. 6, '61

1.

This is the piece that is
any piece that is performed only
when it is written.

2.

This is another piece that is
performed only when it is written.

NOV 7 '61

a, This is the piece that is performed
whenever it is written.

b, This is the piece that is any piece.

c, This is the piece that is written.

d, This is the piece that is performed only
before it is written.

NOV 7 '61

Word Scoring

Tony Conrad, 13–14 October 2010

Today after a performance I'll get, 'That was really beautiful'. In the early 1960s 'beauty' was not the consensus criterion it's become today; fifty years have etched away at the critical issues that John Cage had set before serious music during the 1950s, and have left us with values that are registers of social consensus rather than problematic challenges addressed to a roiling arena of investigative artists. This move toward a larger social configuration has resulted from the terminal erosion of the old high-culture/low-culture boundary system – which was eaten away at both ends of the divide: the critical 'investigative artists' chewed up the 'high culture' aspects of music by *épat*-ing *la bourgeoisie,* while music *marketing* swallowed up the boundary with low-culture (mass culture).

But here, I'm asking a certain indulgence as I return/resort for a moment to that earlier position of privilege (in the early '60s) in which the fantasy of conceptual 'progress' was freely exercised as I and my fellow artists/composers looked for ways to move 'ahead' in our compositional practices, in our engagement with the Absolute where Muses still regulated the Mystery of Musical Beauty.

But we had already learned the lesson of taking 'beauty' in stride; we move ahead; we hope for high hurdles to leap. In the middle of the way ahead is the *score:* instructions to be obeyed by the necessary *performers.* The score is the instrument on which the composer performs, dancing across its staves and lines with increasingly careless preciosity. Then too, there ahead at the end of music is the *listener:* elevated by Cage to a post in this pantheon nearly as high as that of the composer or performer. And the *performer* could in significant respects be seen as controlling the whole operation. (This on the other hand was a gambit that 'mass media' played promiscuously – that what the music industry was producing was controlled, they said, by the 'choices' of listeners.)

The first model that impressed me for engaging with the problem of the score was a very early piece by David Behrman which was structured as a 'game'. If a composition is a game among the performers, the music produced is dependent on interactions among them, and far less upon the previous choices of the composer. The role of the composer is then shifted, radically; it becomes one of writing up the rules for the game that s/he invents for the performers to play. I liked this idea very much. Unlike the word pieces of George Brecht, that *commanded* the performer(s) with more or fewer instructions, or certain dada pieces of La Monte Young, that fundamentally problematized – and so trivialized – the listening activities of the audience, the game model generated a competitive (or cooperative) environment in which the listener's role was accurately represented as a spectator sport, and the composer became an arbitrator. If the players found themselves in a competitive relationship, this too provided a social reflection on the normative conditions of music performance – where arbitrary systems of competitive interaction are the norm.

During the first years of the 1960s word scores were accepted as a conceptual standard, largely without much careful analytical appraisal – this, in spite of the fact that both 'minimal' sculpture and Allan Kaprow's 'happenings' entailed subtle conceptual twists, and that Henry Flynt's 'concept art' and other innovations arose in a fundamentally analytical context. In any event, it appeared to me at the time that the dissociative tendencies word scores brought to the compositional process, and consequently to the social and cultural role of the composer as such, implied an opening for the score to *separate entirely* from the processes of music performance or listening. In my *This Piece Is Its Name*, for instance, there is no longer either any command structure nor any paradox for listeners.

The short word pieces that I wrote in 1961, by diverting the referential capabilities of the word score to point to the title or text of the piece itself, anticipate Acconci's early word poem, *here*, which referred to its own site on the page. Mine are however 'music', because they are to be understood as scores – they occupy the cultural site of prescriptive writing for action; Acconci's text on the other hand is 'poetry', as it occupies the cultural site of prescription for reading. In any case, my short pieces, which each displayed a kind of hermetic closure, fundamentally shut out their own possibilities for performance, and of course then for being heard. But this was not 'silence' in Cage's terms; it was conceptual silence, without place or time; in that respect, these pieces drew out a tautological presence that assumed form only in an abstract or imagined locus.

Properly speaking, then, these word scores were the antecedents of my 'minimal' music that followed: a continuous spatialized presence without compositional prescription, within which the performer(s) manipulated the acoustic environment directly, following a certain general 'game plan'. The game, in this instance, was a template or grid that derived from, and was intimately conjoined with, the timbral and harmonic infrastructure of a single tone.

Philip Corner

GAMELᴬOONY (2004)

----Music notation is about specifics*; Words are generalizations.**

Commentary: *GAMELᴬOONY*

GAMELOONY

structural essences from my "gamelan" series

Philip Corner

To be realized and improvised
on the basis of the principle of a strict correlation
between **pitch-heights**
and **time-lengths**

Usually this will be by arithmetic increments, as 1 2 3 4 5 6 7 . . . . .
correlated with the notes of a descending scale.   or (sometimes)
linked to an ascending line. Or even from the middle out.
The group texture may be formed by : systematic canonic pile-up
                                            simultaneous tutti
                                            unpredictable ins and outs
A longer tone could be counted against an imaginary fast beat; . . . .
or become in turn a new "one" at a slower tempo.
A very long duration (usually low) might initiate a progressive division by halves.
Or the principle of increments to be applied to irrational subdivisions.

Notes may doubled by neutral noise sounds — or that they at times fill in for
missing voices - - - - especially a "one", helping to keep the ensemble together.
An array of non-pitched percussion, in a clean pitch hierarchy, may play just
like other instruments. Also, the pitches, instead of single tones only,
might be made up of harmonic aggregates : like clusters, chords, intervals.

This strict linking of a scale-tone to a rhythmic duration
can also be realized melodically. Such a "tune" can be a line
supported by the above-described harmonic texture ; or appear without
any background, as a solo , or several encounterpoint.
In such a case all the elements would most obviously take part in the same
rational system . . . . . but also possible that each player has a unique
scale and/or tempo.

With the textures made up of repetitive pulsings, the players can exchange
pitches and rhythms.

formulated 2005

----Music notation is about specifics*; Words are generalizations.**

Philip Corner, 2009

* unless used as understood approximations, as in jazz, pop, folk, etc. (and Ives' 1st Sonata!). But then it needs a cultural agreement, which would be verbal if needed to be explicit.

** So if you want any kind of improvisation or indetermination beyond the usual range of expressive interpretation, some explanation is necessary. It has struck me that this requires some kind of intellectual understanding of the musical essentials---a kind of theory-in-practice, using a different part of the mind than that for note by note rote realization. I had found that desirable.

On one hand, i had it as an ideal to reduce the verbiage as much as possible.

A great model for that was George Brecht......one word!

But i finally "beat him": *OneNoteOnce* is only the title.

On the other, i always thought that Occidental writing was ugly and the trip to the Orient confirmed that. After a little study of calligraphy in Korea, i felt liberated to design my scores. Also to write free-hand when i wished to explain; so the two things come together. They, graphics and calligraphy may co-exist. or be separate.

Even with the designed scores i had usually a desire to exhaust the possibilities. This, for practical reasons, led to an accumulation of details which were always much more than any one playing could use. The sentences, on the other hand, subsume all the multitude---infinitude---of possibilities from which a single choice---the written-out composition----would be wholly arbitrary. An inherent contradiction. (Hidden, unremarked, in the delusive "best selection" of traditional fugues and sonatas.)

I want my musicians to understand what they are playing. There is always an Idea. (Actually, there always must be, even if, as in most cases, unconscious---i.e. "free".)

I might note that this affects the use of words, distilling grammar to present idea-essences with maximum directness to the unmediated eye. In this case the calligraphy can even serve beyond decorativeness to be expressively part of interpretive vision.

The recalcitrant nature of alphabetical writing, design to be cut in stone, resists imagery and so causes a tension between presentation and comprehension which i have long struggled to resolve. I must say that the solutions have been various. Favoring handwriting has also had a favorable effect on mechanical page presentation, layout and choice of fonts and such. Even traditional notes written by hand instead of music-program have been appreciated by some.

This approach makes one vulnerable......unscrupulous performers might (have) take a sloppy-minded approach to interpretation. But the reward is when they give you far more than you could have ever dreamed of. That, indeed----fortunate meetings with such musicians!---was one of the stimuli for my approach.

And it makes you yourself---obligation and opportunity----responsible for performances. Develop instrumental competence!

An additional professional "problem": author's rights; claims, credit, fame, ownership, jobs, money! A bit of generosity is required.

The performers must be considered co-creators.

What is wrong with having a useful job? What small-mindedness behind disdain for teaching. And i have never felt that working time interfering with creative production----the contrary----it stimulated it.

Ph.

Commentary: *GAMEL^AOONY*

John Lely

The score for *GAMEL^AOONY* (2004) exemplifies Philip Corner's broad and inclusive approach to how notation can function. His scores operate as open frameworks for performance, guided improvisation and new composition. The written language promotes multiplicities of interpretation and reference; there is a free flow to the movement of ideas, and always the possibility of connections back and forth between all scores, performances and improvisations. His works frequently quote or reference each other, with scores propagating new scores, improvisations suggesting scores, scores suggesting improvisations, scores being written years after an idea has been formulated, and so on.

Often presented on a single page, Corner's scores rarely take the form of straightforward instructions, but instead suggest generalised courses of action; the language remains provisional, speculative and reflective. This is in part due to Corner's generous use of modals such as 'could' and 'might' to ensure that each score remains flexible in its outcome. It is an approach reliant on co-operation: 'A bit of generosity is required. The performers must be considered co-creators.'[1] Performers are invited to take responsibility for aspects that may once have been solely within the remit of the composer, such as decisions relating to form, choice of notes and scales, choice of instruments, and tempo. The composer has faith in his performers; in the score of *C Major Chord* (1964), he writes:

> This music might be considered the most demanding piece in the literature. No demands at all are put on you, because there is no limit to what one can demand of himself.[2]

Corner's 'Gamelan Series', which began with *GAMELAN* (1975) (see Fig. 83), consists of approximately 500 works, of which most are published in three volumes by Frog Peak Music. These scores make use of a mixture of verbal instructions, graphic notations and regular staff notation. While the first gamelan works were created in collaboration with the experimental gamelan group Son of Lion, the pieces in this series are not limited to being performed using traditional Indonesian gamelan instruments. Rather, Corner uses the word 'gamelan' as a kind of homage, the series as a whole being very open:

> The 'Gamelan' series pieces are open structures, scored on graph paper, that require or permit either improvisation or realization, and are, within limits, indeterminate with respect to instrumentation and duration.[3]

---

[1] Corner, P., see p. 168 of this book.
[2] This work first appeared in *The Four Suits*, Something Else Press (1965).
[3] Corner, P., in Diamond, 1986, p. 32.

"GAMELAN"

Longest act to Lowest.

Be patient and progressively add in the parts.
Once in, they [stay] stay in.

A player on each

because waves of intensity flow control texture's clarity.

Best bells are 'untuned';
Begin with gongs,
A deal gamelan orchestra would be good,
Each plummeted note could be well
'thickened' by adjacent tuning.

At the ending, they drop out in reverse order — faster than before.
(But it could start up again.)

Kempul 6,6

Slentem (pelog) 1,2
Slentem (slendro) 2,3   1,2
Slentem (pelog) 5,6   3,5,6

Kenong 1   2
Demung 4,5...
Kenong (slendro) 5
(pelog) 4
Peking 5
Peking 7

64
32
16
8
4
2
1
0
½
¼
⅛

WESLEYAN   Feb 29, 1992
Gong

Evan
Rosalia
Rosalie

Larry
Barbara
(Mark)

◀ 83 *Philip
Corner,*
GAMELAN
(1975).

Gamelan means for me more than the name for Indonesian orchestras. I use the word the way, apart from Europe, someone might say 'Symphony': a basis of making music. So I have simply added a few wonderful ideas from the Orient, to what I am able to do.[4]

Corner's whole Gamelan Series represents a careful and sustained exploration of a very few compositional principles, or what the score of *GAMELᴬOONY* refers to as 'structural essences'. *GAMELᴬOONY* distils and describes these structural essences, and some of the ways in which they may vary from piece to piece. It is therefore a useful starting point for surveying correspondences and commonalities among some of the other gamelan works. The provisional characteristics of *GAMELᴬOONY* are not unique – all Corner's gamelan scores are inherently provisional, and remain open to different extents of variation. He explains:

I write generalized scores because I always glimpse many more valid possibilities than any written version could contain. Couperin said that he writes preludes for those who cannot improvise. I do not believe that Bach would ever have played a fugue exactly as he had written it.[5]

There follows a breakdown of each element of *GAMELᴬOONY*, with examples of how these principles are expressed in a cross-section of Corner's other gamelan scores, along with occasional statements from the composer about those principles. From the examples presented here, it is clear that the composer expresses these 'structural essences' in different ways from piece to piece, depending on context. Corner's scores are visually rich and, as can be seen from the three facsimiles, his use of language is occasionally quite fragmentary, with hand-written words scattered across the page, punctuation used very freely, and phrases hanging among other graphic elements. The layouts of the extracts below also give a flavour of this attitude.

'To be realized and improvised on the basis of the principle of a strict correlation between pitch-heights and time-lengths'

This is probably the most pervasive principle at work in the Gamelan Series, and it is also reminiscent of the colotomic principles of Indonesian gamelan music: broadly, the lower the sound, the longer its duration. In *GAMELᴬOONY* Corner does not specify what the correlation should be; for instance, it could also be 'the higher the sound the longer its duration'. But for many of the other scores there is a clear high–fast, low–slow hierarchy. This is a practical issue; generally speaking, low percussion sounds naturally resonate longer than high sounds. Corner explains the source of this principle:

---

[4] Corner, P., in Lukoszevieze, 2003, p. 70.
[5] Philip Corner, in correspondence with the author, July 2010.

It goes back to the premise on which I based the first piece. I had been doing metal meditations – strike one sound and then listen to it until it ends and then dance around – all irrational. But I didn't want to just transfer this to gamelan. Gamelan has something that is different from the richness of random sounds – it has uniformity and concentration, refinement, a tuning system, a homogeneity of color, a limitation of scale. The instruments invite you to play them together. So I began with the big gong. One stroke, and you listen as it fades away into silence, but I added a 64-second cycle, and the next instrument played at exactly halfway through the cycle. So what I added was a number, a rationality.[6]

According to the composer, after writing *GAMELAN* he noted that this principle is also used by Olivier Messiaen in his piano work, *Mode de Valeurs et d'Intensités* (1949–50). While this commentary was being prepared, Corner composed a number of new gamelan works, including *gamelan MESSIAEN* (2010) (see Fig. 84).

GAMELAN: 'Longest set to Lowest.'

GAMELAN II ("Number-Measure Increase Downward") (1975): 'start with highest pitch (this includes indeterminate percussion) at a rapid repeating of single strokes (play with one hand, not 2 alternating) … add successively lower pitches at increments of 1 added beat each'

gamelan ANTIPODES (1984): '2 notes are picked (one veryHigh . one veryLow) One of the extremes of INTENSITY is fixed to one, the other to the other. One of the extremes of DURATION is fixed to one, the other to the other. The playing and replaying will use only these two "sonic objects".'

gamelan ALMOST ANY (1985): 'No attempt is to be made to coordinate but, The Tempi (duration of each element) correlated with pitch levels – Highest = Fastest (but, by irrational gradients)'

gamelan AGAIN (1996): 'Divide the playing range onto pitch-areas approx 1/2 8ve in width [...] Each one represents a successive duration, of a progression which increases as it descends'

gamelan N(UMBER)S (1996): 'For each player: a central tone arranged in descending order in respect to the others, at intervals which will maximize the total range and preferably increasing in size towards the low end.'

gamelan SWELL (2002): 'Starts from the lowest note   Long and soft-ly   (may be repeated as-long-as – but eventually passes to) an added note, alternating   and the time is shorter. The 3rd note up makes the tempo even faster – and the 4th that-much more so.'

---

[6] Philip Corner, in Diamond, 1986, p. 28.

84 *Philip Corner,* gamelan MESSIAEN *(2010).* ▶

gamelan MESSIAEN

all the notes are in an area not larger than an 8ve.

(may be any number less than 12 .... consider'd ideal : 7)

There should be some <u>very</u> close intervals

These notes may be played in any order
either in regular rhythm
or with irregularity ("maximum freedom")

<u>drop out occasionally</u>

But there will be sections of formality .... principally

High — Low

the linking of notes to a
<u>scale of durations</u>

inversion

& scrambled

phasing of one parameter against another

Say : Durations against Pitches ...... by using a different number of each

<u>Dynamic levels</u>

PP — ff

can be treated in the same way
as an independent variable .

linked ;
freely contrasted

— Progressive order can occur

< >

in any & all
parameters

with more instruments

add levels

where lower levels proceed in
progressively slower tempi
(irrationally related)

Let there be no attempt to coördinate these strata.

Philip Corner
2010

gamelan TOM-TOM-TOM (2005): a number of adjacent ensembles, 'each with a different norm of register' play 'at a particular tempo, based on their position in pitch-space: High = Faster, Lower = Slower'.

gamelan PUNKTUS (2006): 'pitch = time-scale'

gamelan SITU (2008): 'let resonant durations increase towards basso [...] an intuitive hierarchy (rather than by strict counting)'

gamelan UNIMELOS (2010): 'The usual High–Low link to increasing time-values'

gamelan MESSIAEN: 'But these will be sections of formality.... principally the linking of notes to a scale of durations & scrambled phasing of parameter against another say: Durations against Pitches ...... by using a different number of each.'

'Usually this will be by arithmetic increments, as: 1 2 3 4 5 6 7... correlated to the notes of a descending scale or (sometimes) linked to an ascending line. Or even from the middle out.'

This sentence explains in more detail the relationships of note heights and durations. These relationships are often based on simple beat additions; for instance, in *Gamelan II* the highest note plays every beat, the second-highest note plays every second beat, the third-highest note plays every three beats, and so on. Other relationships based on slightly different systems also occur. Scales are very often left indeterminate in terms of tuning.

gamelan THE FLIGHT OF THE SYSTEM (1981): 'is based on the formal progression known as Cantor's series. Here the scale degrees involved increase arithmetically while the measure lengths increase geometrically – and each phrase is symmetrical.'

gamelan COLLABORATION II with Tom Johnson (1981): 'Arrange a series of pitches around a central tone (1). Set the other tones (2, 3, 4...), up & down. so that - there are left adjacent scale-steps, between them, corresponding to their position there: 1 space on either side of "1", 2 spaces [on either side of] "2", and so on.'

gamelan MOBILE (1981): 'Each note always sounds the same timing as its number'

gamelan ADAGIO (1981) (see Fig. 85): 'linear descent of pitches correspondence with expansion of durations'

gamelan DIV(is) (*"The choices of division"*) (1982): 'A number of predetermined pitch-class note-names is linked to a chosen exactly-measured duration so that Higher = Faster – Lower = Slower'

85 Philip Corner, gamelan ADAGIO (1981). ▶

ADAGIO   (from the "gamelan" series)

a slow version
of the structural idea   appearing for the first time
                            in "gamelan II" -- my second piece for
                            gamelan. (of course)
a simple arithmetic increment,
a "scale of durations", leads to complexity-------------more&more
                                    the more parts are added.
(Son-Of-Lion version :Folkways 31313: goes up to 9. A long desired
workshop this summer in Sumatra took gongs & drums to 33 parts, and
with counting voices in Java up to 48. But here the simpler beauty of
clarity is brought out---only 4 layers.)

quartet for anklungs

A simple calculation shows that, starting together,
1contra2contra3contra4   come together   after a measure of
12 beats.   This is where time stops.
And these bamboo rattles will fill in that space between ideas.
                                        (Shake that Thing.)

linear descent of pitches
correspondence with expansion of durations
at each repeat.............exchange.   Places; each takes an other timing
                                until all have had all.
No longer only a prepared piano solo for me.
Add now a procession of entering and exit.   In time always.
First performance last August. Special anklungs constructed by
Melati Abadi---the lowest one 12 feet big---possibly the largest
and the smallest anklungs in the world. at AMI/The Indonesian
Music Institute at Yogyakarta, Java.
We are now using more normal ones,
in a familiar tuning.

Philip Corner

gamelan MOUNT (1982): 'The lowest note The longest – equal to the same number of counts as there will be notes The sounded duration should always be natural .... let resonances die away; let held tones be just a single breath, or bowing.'

GAMELAN II – bonang version (1996): 'to be arranged in scalar order, so that the highest give the basic pulse of which each successive descending scale degree will be the equivalent beat multiple.'

gamelan LXXXXIX (2010): 'and of course will be linked to a descending scale of tones – : ideally – made of very small intervals and extending – through every instrument's range – from extremely high to the lowest.'

'The group texture may be formed by: systematic pile-up, simultaneous tutti, unpredictable ins and outs'

This sentence refers to the overall 'form' of the realisation. Players may enter one by one in a predictable way (systematic pile-up), all together (simultaneous tutti), or players may enter and exit at unpredictable times.

GAMELAN: 'Be patient and progressively add in the parts [...] At the ending, they drop out in reverse order – faster than before. (But it could start up again!)'

GAMELAN II ("*Number-Measure Increase Downward*"): 'never any backtracking, until the ending (where the beats are removed from high to low, systematically, and quickly.) But – at particular points, drop out all parts except 1 and one other'

gamelan GO! GOGO! GOGOGO! (1996): 'begin with an unbroken fast-pulsating .... on each single instrument – a single unmodulated sound. build-up – a progression of entrances: – from high to low'

gamelan N(UMBER)S: 'Not to keep a constant density: individuals should drop-out occasionally. And there may occur passages of limited density, even to prolonging a single line alone.'

gamelan SWELL: 'let this end by reversing the process – but much more quickly'

gamelan LXXXXIX: 'Note that the notes are added progressively from the top down.'

gamelan UNIMELOS: 'As this title implies the realization of the given structure is to be monophonic with the textural variety-possibilities ..... including their extension into heterophony [...] All together – starting on the first count.'

'A longer tone could be counted against an imaginary fast beat; or become in turn a new "one" at a slower tempo'

Many of the gamelan pieces, such as *GAMELAN*, begin with a long, low tone, with higher tones appearing with greater frequency as new parts are introduced. The 'imaginary fast beat' (echoes of the Javanese idea of the *balungan*) allows for the durations of very long tones to be accurate in relation to the other more frequent tones, so that when all parts are sounding simultaneously there will be a constant audible pulse. That a long tone can become a new 'one' at a slower tempo resembles Javanese changes in *irama*.

> gamelan *E-NUMERATE* (1996): 'There is a ubiquitous measure of one second, 1″ which is not to be heard, yet kept to.'

> gamelan *N(UMBER)S*: 'Note that pulse may be variable – by acceleration/ritards – or even suddenly provided that all can easily stay coordinated on it.'

> gamelan *UR-SCORE* (2008): 'The underlying count will be as fast as thinkable'

> gamelan *LXXXXIX*: 'Based on a basic beat. Must be fast, very fast, fast as possible, faster than possible.'

'A very long duration (usually low) might initiate a progressive division by halves.'

This is a very common principle in the Gamelan Series, but it is rarely expressed using words alone; Corner typically uses a mixture of traditional note-heads arranged in relation to one another, as can be seen in *GAMELAN*.

> gamelan *S–D* (1981): 'The whole-note, its progressive divisions: 1/2 1/4 1/8 1/16 1/32... arranged just as in this proliferation of exactly notated symmetries, makes the sound come out in syncopations'

> gamelan *KRYSTEL* (1989): 'The piece starts with the division by halves going to thirds and so on increasing by prime numbers – to any practicable limit.'

'Or the principle of increments to be applied to irrational subdivisions.'

That is, rather than using simple beat additions, the durations may be set through using 'irrational' subdivisions such as 4 in the time of 3, 5 in the time of 4, and so on. As a result, these subdivisions may create rhythmic patterns that are more complex than the standard 'grid' systems of works like *GAMELAN* and *GAMELAN II*.

gamelan P. .C (Prelude and Conclusion) (1979): 'The next tone enters ...... thirds. (add one note more) [...] This is the process, too, by which the next number will appear ... 4:3 5:4 and as far as the possibilities can take it. [...] There is hardly a need to hurry. Indeed – let the process enter a dialectic between the refinements of intellectual neatness (having degrees of vibrations nicely calculated around the struck precisions – yet never, even here, totally unsensual) and the growing energies of the physical (as the numbers become charged bodies).'

'Notes may [be] doubled by neutral noise sounds – or that they at times fill in for missing voices----especially a "one", helping to keep the ensemble together.'

Again, this is one way for the duration of longer tones to be counted accurately. It also means that the basic pulse can be heard by all the players, and that the pulse is not always marked solely by the highest instrument.

GAMELAN V ("ir-regularity") (1977): 'around a steady pulsing which is kept by a visual means only, is dancing! (drawn in air).'

gamelan N(UMBER)S: 'If an audible steady pulse be required, mark it, unpitched, softly ...... and dropping out when possible.'

gamelan IRIS (1997): 'The basic pulse "measured", by larger units – accented or in patterns; this could be elaborated as an ostinato. Pulses can be just tapped directly on the instrument's body.'

gamelan UNIMELOS: 'Also the 'one' counts could be marked by pulsing on a drum or idiophone.'

'An array of non-pitched percussion, in a clear pitch hierarchy, may play just like other instruments. Also the pitches, instead of single tones only, might be made up of harmonic aggregates: like clusters, chords, intervals.'

The gamelan pieces are scored for a wide range of instrumental resources, including traditional Indonesian instruments (bonang, anklung, etc.), voices, piano, dancers, string instruments, suspended metal objects, solo drummer and rock band. Often the resources are not specified in the score, but are decided on by the players. Corner explains:

When I started with gamelan, I felt I added something without taking anything away and so that some of the aspects of my previous music are still there and one of them is – I came up with a great phrase just now, 'non-compulsive indeterminacy'. I never thought of it exactly that way before. That is, there's always freedom, and the freedom sometimes re-manifests in terms of indeterminate performance which is, in a sense, improvisation. Or it can be a freedom to make a pre-thought realisation adapted to the performer and to the materials at hand. With the gamelan pieces I got more into a process of adding 'structure' in the narrow sense of small number patterns and recognisable forms and predictable things than I ever have. But no matter how rational those things are, how systematic, there's always some aspect in which the thing can be realised for different instruments.[7]

GAMELAN: 'A real gamelan orchestra would be good'

GAMELAN II ("Number-Measure Increase Downward"): 'With resonant instruments – mostly metal and some determinately pitched ones.'

gamelan SANTO (1980): 'Choose this and all subsequents by a sense of "harmony"* whatever that means; should mean whatever you know (you do) it to mean (rather than a "scale")'

even more for GAMELAN II "From The PulsePool": rondo (c. 1981) 'Whisper one's own number'

versions of GAMELAN II, using voices with objects (1982): 'Entrance of the parts by voices quasi-sung: pitch hierarchy according to the natural ranges of the performers' voices... '

gamelan TOM-TOM-TOM: 'When the instruments are very resonant, they could be played percussively, dry ..... let ring would be a special effect. [...] Assume timbre homogeneity for each ensemble [...] However favoring repeated articulated notes over melodic movement.'

gamelan SITU: 'for a multi-pitched percussion unit - clear Tone'd – and resonant... metalophones certainly but also idio-and membrano-phones, and (very good) struck-and-plucked chordophones plus another component: a wind -- or bowed string instrument (or a few of them) capable of gliss-andi'

gamelan ANGELSHEART I (1978): 'gongs and richly swelling resonances [...] The higher ones bright – – and bright enough to sound brilliant without overly hard onsets – – – and enough to resound to the end of their beats.'

---

[7] Corner, P., in Lukoszevieze, 1998, p. 16.

'This strict linking of a scale-tone to a rhythmic duration can also be realised melodically. Such a "tune" can be a line supported by the above-described harmonic texture; or appear without any background, as a solo, or several in counterpoint.'

Since each tone often has its own duration, as a result these 'melodies' are rhythmically quite ornate. Corner often puts constraints on how the melodies are constructed. Sometimes the 'tune' will be realised by several players in unison reading pre-composed material (prepared by the players), or be improvised independently by soloists playing at the same time.

> *gamelan*)) *A "austere with gorgeous tone"* (1978): 'There will be a numerical increment, from one endlessly out - - - Which means long sections of a strict application. [...] Numbers affect Melodic movement.'

> *gamelan AVE* (1980): 'Make melodies based on a scale in which the highest note is worth 1 beat and each successive, down adds a beat more. (rapid count)'

> *gamelan THE GOLD STONE* (1985): 'any number of independent, counterpointed or coordinated, parts.'

> *gamelan MONOPHO* (1989): 'From this [scale] a structure for performance is to be created, which is basically a unison-melody ..... colored by Klangfarbenmelody,harmonic resonances'

> *gamelan PUNKTUS*: 'melody rule: never an immediate note-repeat'

> *gamelan LXXXXIX*: 'a note can enter into free play – being returned to at pleasure (remembering to keep its correct rhythm number)'

> *gamelan UNIMELOS*: 'Once this Time/Space scale established, movement of the melody will be completely free (assuming of course the pitch-duration links always maintained.) No doubt a preliminary score will have to be composed.'

'In such a case all the elements would most obviously take part in the same notational system... but also possible that each player has a unique scale and/or tempo.'

This is also a very common principle, which allows for many different types of instruments to be played in the same performance; for instance, in several scores Corner suggests that Western instruments may be combined with traditional Indonesian instruments, their different scales played simultaneously, or sometimes intermeshed to create scales of more than 12 notes to the octave.

gamelan MOD (1992): 'a number (any number) of scales, gamuts, modes... [...] Each of the scales should have a distinctly unique pattern of intervals ; this may include various tuning systems. [...] a single player is free to move to another scale (They may occupy diverse places in the physical space) at any time. Two or more may join, playing together even in prepared forms of strict counterpoint or in an absolute unison.'

gamelan MESSIAEN: 'Let there be no attempt to coordinate these strata.'

'With the textures made up of repetitive pulsings, the players can exchange pitches and rhythms.'

In some pieces these changes occur using a strict method, whereby players exchange their pitches and/or rhythms (and potentially even their spatial location). These changes are sometimes prescribed in order to combine all possible permutations of instruments and rhythms, as in *gamelan ADAGIO*. In other works players are freer to make these exchanges in more fluid ways.

gamelan ADAGIO: 'at each repeat.............exchange.   Places; each takes an other timing   until all have had all.'

GAMELAN II (version for Medan, Sumatra) (1987): 'One or other of these components may at times predominate, or be alone (suggestion, FORM) start heterogeneous timbres, fade in & out others during the play, end "tutti".'

Gamelan II KHUSUS ("Special") (1991): 'sections of: steady pulsing, unaccented longer sections of: each in one's own rhythm = a duration which equates scale position with that same number of counted beats.' Players are arranged in a line according to their number, 'although persons, with their original instruments still, may exchange places. Then they must always take up the correct rhythm for that position; thus the pitch relations change.'

Bill Drummond

SHOW (2007)

MY SCORES & ME

SCORE

321. SHOW

VISIT A CITY.

ASK 100 RESIDENTS TO DESCRIBE
A SOUND IN THE CITY
THAT EVOKES EMOTION.
THE SOUND CAN BE
LOUD OR QUIET
BIG OR SMALL.

DOCUMENT THESE 100 DESCRIPTIONS.

SHOW THE DOCUMENT
TO THE RESIDENTS.

The17

100 people in Anchorage, Alaska
100 people in Milton Keynes, England
were asked to describe a sound in their city
A sound that evokes a personal emotion in them
A sound that could be loud or quiet
A sound that could be big or small

pb Beer Mat 101/A   the17.org/show

ANCHORAGE – ALASKA

**Two ravens fighting
over half eaten fries
in a McDonalds parking lot
on a mid-January afternoon.**

Kathleen Hesther

pb Beer Mat One   the17.org/show

The17

These 200 described sounds
have been printed on 100 different beer mats
A sound from Anchorage on one side
A sound from Milton Keynes on the other side
These beer mats have been distributed
in pubs and bars in both cities

pb Beer Mat 101/B   the17.org/show

MILTON KEYNES - ENGLAND

**The chippy van bell at 6pm
on Tuesday evenings.
The bell is hand rung
and the van has been coming
around our estate all my life.**

Megan who works in the flooring department
of John Lewis.

pb Beer Mat One   the17.org/show

MY SCORES & ME

Bill Drummond, 12 June 2009

The music of The17 existed inside my head for some years before it ever became an out there physical shared reality type of music.

When it only existed in my head I never considered scoring it. And even for the first two or three performances by The17 with real singers, I had nothing written down on paper. All I did was sit at the piano, explain and then play to the singers what I wanted them to sing. This worked. It wasn't as if there were long complicated passages they had to remember.

After that I started to write down, then edit, what I had been explaining to the singers while sitting at the piano. From these written down words I hoped anybody with a modicum of musical knowledge could lead 17 singers into being able to perform what I had been hearing in my head. It was only then that I started to think of what I had written as a score.

After this I had these 'scores' designed in the simple and bold way I had already been using in other areas of my practice. Then I had them printed as A0 size posters.

In main these compositions did not rely on time signatures or melody, this meant traditional notes on staves seemed irrelevant and would only make the reading of the scores vastly more complicated than need be. It would have been totally the wrong language to use. It was important to me that the music was about time, place, occasion, these conditions could be communicated far more readily in text.

Once I had written, designed and printed a few of these scores based on what I could hear in my head, they started to evolve. I could not stop some scores becoming more conceptual. These were not just about the making of choral music but about ways of thinking about music and the way we listen to it; our evolving relationship with it. The most important of these, I gave pole position and title Score One: *IMAGINE*, although it was not the first to be written. I always ask The17 to perform *IMAGINE* before any of the other scores are attempted.

It was after I had begun exhibiting these scores in the context of art galleries that people started to make comparisons with what Yoko Ono and Stockhausen had done decades earlier. I had never seen Yoko Ono's *Grapefruit* book or Stockhausen's *The Seven Days* scores before I had started on making scores for The17. But I am more than aware of how we are influenced by so many things without realising it.

This being influenced by osmosis via the ether is one of the many strands I explore in the book *17* that was published in 2008.

It is plain to me that the ways I use text to create scores for The17 have very real limitations, but for me they continue to work and evolve. And it is still the best way that I can communicate the music and thoughts in my head to the outside world.

Ken Friedman

Zen Vaudeville (1966)

Events, Scores, Notations

87 *Ken Friedman*, Zen Vaudeville *(1966)*. ▶

Zen Vaudeville

The sound of one shoe tapping.

1966

This piece was based on a graffito found
in New York in September of 1966.

Events, Scores, Notations

Ken Friedman, November 2010

My involvement with event scores began in August of 1966 when Dick Higgins and George Maciunas brought me into Fluxus. Dick introduced me to George Maciunas. George asked what I did. I described my ideas and projects and George invited me to participate in Fluxus. He planned a series of Fluxus editions based on my ideas. Jon Hendricks reproduces George's plan in *Fluxus Codex*, the comprehensive catalog of Fluxus editions.

When I met Dick and George, my projects and ideas had no name. They were a philosophical or spiritual practice that I enacted in a relatively systematic way in public spaces and parks, churches and conference centers, as well as broadcasting them on the radio or even on television.

These activities took place outside the art context. This made me different to the other Fluxus people. George Brecht, Nam June Paik, George Maciunas, Dick Higgins, Alison Knowles, Yoko Ono, Mieko Shiomi and others worked with event scores as artists and composers. My activities had no name. These artists and composers worked in such major art scenes as New York, Tokyo and London. I was a youngster in Connecticut and California. They took part in a global avant-garde network while I realized projects anywhere I could. But because I was not active in art or music, these artists did not influence me. My ideas were original.

George Maciunas suggested that I notate my repertoire of projects and activities as event scores, starting with the first piece I described to George, scrubbing a public monument in the spring of 1956. This became my first event score.

Notation in the form of scores is the key distinction that separates my activities before 1966 from those afterward. In 1956, I realized the first activity that I would later call an event. I developed a repertory practice of activities in the years between 1956 and 1966. These became scores at George Maciunas's suggestion, and I adopted the practice of designating and notating event scores when George brought me into Fluxus. Before then, I sometimes wrote instructions or descriptions of my activities in letters and bulletins, or private notes or diaries. I began to notate my ideas as formal scores for publication by Fluxus when George proposed that I do so.

Context determines the nature and status of social activity. I entered the art context in 1966. I performed the actions or realized the projects notated in my event scores from 1956 on, but these were not art works. Brecht, Knowles, Higgins, Ono, Watts and the others made art works and composed music. What I did had no name. The others worked in the context of art and music. I did not.

There remains an important distinction between my work and the work of later artists active in conceptual art and performance. While the older Fluxus people preceded me, this work was still uncommon in 1966. In 1966, only a dozen or so people did this kind of work. I was one of them.

Malcolm Goldstein

wood stone metal skin, with voice **(1983)**

Statement on Verbal Notation

6/4/83

wood

stone

sKin

metal

- for David Moss,
in friendship & music makin

wood stone metal skin, with voice

for David Moss, percussionist

~by Malcolm Goldstein

- a continous sequence (circle) of sounding materials, always in the order: wood, stone*, metal, skin, though with variety of articulation, quality, dynamics, etc. and with voice to be superimposed (as discussed below).

- a cycle of time/proportion durations for the sequence of sounding materials : 3·1·5·2 : that is a total/constant of 11 (seconds), though the proportion sequence/order can change, improvised as desired.

Details of performance:
   The four designated sound materials are generalized categories. there will be many different wood percussion objects, for example, to be sounded. The choice of which particular one is to be played is up to the percussionist at the moment/context of the sounding sequence. Seek variety of sound quality.

*(Note: the category "stone" might be too restricting. It is possible to seek out many kinds of stones, instruments made of stone, etc. — but it can also be expanded to allow for objects of clay/pottery, bone, etc.. So also "skin" could be animal, synthetic, etc..)

   Consider unique, "random" order of specific objects to be sounded, as well as incorporating repeated patterns (loops) of the same specific four instruments, now and then.

   Dynamics are free, to be shaped as desired, though

larger phrases can be created using dynamic shaping and/or with sections of contrasted interjections. Dynamics within each duration of sounding a specific object, can be constant or modified at will.

It would be good to have a variety of beaters available (or in hand) so as to create a variety of sound qualities; the hand itself can also be used when desired.

Pitch and non-pitch instruments are possible. It is possible to utilize unpatterned and patterned sequences of pitch within the shape of the music.

The time/proportion sequence can be altered every time the cycle is realized, i.e — 3.1.5.2 2.1.5.3, 1.2.3.5, 2.3.5.1, etc. — but it is possible, also, to maintain the same sequence of a cycle, like a loop, for a while as part of the overall changing structure. There should be no pauses between cycles, the music sounding continuously.

The manner of filling in the time of sounding can be:
       a) articulated by hitting, striking, beating, banging, etc., with patterned rhythmic articulations or un-patterned gestures;
       b) evoked by rubbing, scraping, caressing, etc..
There should never be any intentional silence.

The percussionist can also use their voice, superimposed upon this sound-object sequence/time duration cycle at any time — as an interjection, commentary or extension of the percussion music, or as a timbre/duration cycle on its own. All kinds of extended vocal techniques are possible.

The duration of each vocal timbre material is still to be within the framework of sound durations (1, 2, 3 or 5 seconds possible) ~ as a single vocal sound or in a cycle of vocal sounds or as part of a cycle of percussion sounds. The sounding of the voice can be as intermittent or as continuous as desired. The vocal material is free and varied, improvised as seems appropriate to the performer.

The overall structure of the music, as well as the details of sequence order and use of the voice, can be totally improvised and/or partially pre-set/organized as is the inclination of the musician.

Duration of the piece is a minimum of 5 minutes (about 28 time cycles), though longer performance time is preferable. The music stops abruptly at the end of a time cycle.

Brookline, Mass
6/4/83

Statement on Verbal Notation

Malcolm Goldstein, 2010

Notation as the practice/procedure of indicating what is to be done, to be enacted. All notations are possible, relevant to the needs of the work (music, etc.).

New music: new sounds and ways of making sound; an open and inclusive spectrum of possibilities of the physicality of sound qualities, textures, nuances and extremes all available; the fullness of sound activity necessitating a new notation.

The clarity of notation is essential; it can be a single word or pages of words, one image or a complex collage of images and words. Always the needs of the music determine the notation. Each work that I compose requires that I create a notation that is suitable for that piece of music; graphic, verbal, calligraphic, collage images, etc. all possible as is appropriate.

In verbal notation, as also in many new notation practices, the relation between the composer and performer is changed; it is no longer a through-composed musical structure in which the performer is relegated to being an interpreter of the will of the composer, but rather is a context in which the performer participates in the enactment of the creative process.

Improvisation becomes an integral ingredient in this new music. It is a collaboration; the composer offering the framework of the music with notation details as clarification of the spectrum of possibilities, which each performer realizes, each in their own way. Improvisation as the process of revealing the possibilities inherent in the notation, making it real in the presence of discovery; each time, moment to moment, a new music.

Daniel Goode

Relaxing at the Piano (1977)

Conceptual, Verbal, and Graphic Scores

Relaxing at the Piano

<u>Relaxing at the Piano</u> by Daniel Goode (from an idea of Elaine Summers)

Approach the keyboard of the piano as you would a bed, couch, a chair, or the floor: as a place to relax both mind and body: From a standing or sitting position, and exhaling naturally, let as much of your upper body as possible fall painlessly onto the keyboard —— stretching or curling up and gradually coming to rest ——— Let the sound die away.

To   extend   this   piece   from   one gesture   to   many:

From the position you have found yourself in:

(while you do this):

isolate one part of your body that is resting on the keyboard, stretch it by rolling or rotating it or sliding it gently to another position.

Bring your breathing into your consciousness

when a new position is reached, let the sound die away before moving again.

i s o l a t e   and   s t r e t c h   as many parts of your body lying on the keyboard, always letting the sound die away between movements

Finish anytime

Alternate titles:

"Relaxing at the Keyboard"

"Relaxing at the Harpsichord"

"Relaxing at the Organ"

"Relaxing at the Synthesizer"

© 1977 by Daniel Goode

Conceptual, Verbal, and Graphic Scores

Daniel Goode, 2010

A verbal score tells you how to make the music – in language, rather than in musical notation. There may be some musical symbols in a verbal score, may be a graphic, but you are being told how to make the music via language, not musical notes in musical staves to be played by specific musical instruments or voices (though the verbal score also can tell you what instruments should be played). The verbal score is the elephant-in-the-room of the Modernist and Experimental music traditions since it wipes clean the premises of musical notation. Moving from idea (expressed in words and maybe diagrams or sketches) to realization requires imaginative input from the performers on a level quite different from and more inclusive than what performers do with traditional musical notation. The verbal score can be difficult for a trained musician, and a godsend to a talented, but non-musically-literate performer. A verbal score may ask the performers to do anything, including making up their own sounds, or notes according to the instructions given. Call it the Platonic idea of musical composition because the idea precedes the actual notes, that is, the realization in sound.

Nothing more challenges music Conservatory training and tradition than the verbal score: that you can make music without that musical literacy which the Conservatory is in charge of instilling. The tool of the verbal score does an end-run around that pillar of cultural education, musical notation. It is radical, too, because it steals musical technique away from the medieval power-center of the Conservatory. Yoko Ono may have done the earliest ones in the mid-'50s. La Monte Young did a series in 1960 (sometimes these are called *conceptual scores,* or *conceptual music*. A full account would include the Fluxus artists such as George Brecht, Bob Watts, Dick Higgins, Philip Corner and others who developed 'Event Scores' influenced by John Cage's teaching).

The verbal score puts an intelligent agent in charge of finding the right performance for the composer's idea, but the performer is also the composer's partner, on the same level because s/he is in possession of the concept behind the music, expressed succinctly in words. Yet verbal scores can also be challenging because invariably there are questions about exactly what might be meant by the words, or sentences. And the musicians must be willing to give of themselves, to inhabit the ideas, to do, to compose what is needed to make the ideas into music. A spiritual commitment is required, and the building of a performance community, because there is no such thing as simply 'playing the score'.

Maybe just from this short discussion, the reader can sense what a powerful and flexible tool is the verbal score: first, because it addresses performers in their native language, their first language. And second, because it can say things that notes can't. In thinking about all this, it suddenly occurred to me to ask what if music notation from its beginnings had taken the form of human language, written and spoken, before it took its familiar form of notes and rests? Wouldn't the verbal score then be at the center of music culture and music teaching instead of at its periphery? Imagine writers and composers together, teaching the use of language to convey sound, idea, emotion, performance. This is a thought experiment we should all consider making.

Conceptual, graphic, and verbal scores challenge the immovable scholasticism of music theory as it has been taught since Medieval times in music theory courses world-wide, the kind of courses which discourage so many brilliant music students from studying music theoretically. Collections which bring this work to the fore start to redress the imbalance.

Note: This has been adapted from the liner notes to Philip Corner: Extreme Positions, *a 2CD set published by New World Records (2007).*

Lawrence Halprin

**'A Summary of the Characteristics of Scores', from
*The RSVP Cycles: Creative Processes in the Human
Environment***

'A Summary of the Characteristics of Scores', from *The RSVP Cycles: Creative Processes in the Human Environment*

Lawrence Halprin, 1969

There is no one method of scoring. Scores symbolize processes and cannot be separated from the process itself. As scoring processes vary, and involve different persons, the scoring techniques, methods, motivations and performance resulting from them will vary. Scores are at the heart of the process of creativity.

Since there is no one possible accepted method of scoring (only *scores*) I cannot give you a manual on how to score. However, I have found that scores exhibit some *fundamental characteristics* that seem to be universal. Here are some of these characteristics:

1. For a score to function the participants in a score must exhibit a commitment to the idea of scoring and be willing to 'go with' the specific score.

2. Scores themselves open up options rather than closing them down. As an example:
    a) scores say 'turn right', not 'do not turn left'.
    b) they say 'this area shall remain open' not 'do not build here'.
    c) they say 'I feel put down by that remark' not 'you should not have made that remark'.
    Wherever limitations exist they are under R or V in the cycle.

3. The way scores are presented has an enormous influence on the process itself and on the Performance (P). Nuances in scoring have great importance – often the scorer himself is not completely aware of how he is projecting himself and his own biases and preconceptions into the score. For example, here is a series of verbal scores which focus and define the quality and the nature of the experience:
    a) On trip from San Francisco to Sea Ranch stop after one hour and observe.
    b) On trip from San Francisco to Sea Ranch stop after one hour, interact with the environment.
    c) On trip from San Francisco to Sea Ranch stop after one hour, graphically represent what you see.
    d) On trip from San Francisco to Sea Ranch stop after one hour, wait until some event occurs in the environment which affects you.
    e) On trip from San Francisco to Sea Ranch stop after one hour,
       (i) record what you see.
       (ii) record how you feel.
    Each of these variations, though slight, would draw out marked differences in the Performance (P).

4. The element of *time* is always present in scores. Scores are not static; they extend over time.

5. Scores *themselves* are non-judgmental. That is, they do not moralize or preconceive what is to happen. (Selectivity when it occurs is determined under a different element of the RSVP cycles [V] not in scores.) Scores tell what and why, not how.

6. Scores are non-hierarchical, that is, they treat all persons, groups or elements involved in the activity as having the same importance in the score. As the process proceeds, that is, the score is played, the 'influence' of different inputs may be felt variously and weightings may change as activity continues, but the score itself does not preweight input. Scores are pluralistic.

7. Scores can be an end in themselves. They do not have to result in the process itself (which is another part of the RSVP cycles). Scores have a life of their own as distinguished from the Performance (P) of the score; for example, a plan for a building never built or a poem never read or a fantasy never lived out.

8. Scores relate very closely to natural processes since they are related to activity over time, are non-judgmental, equalize input, and are nonresult-oriented.

9. Though scores themselves have the non-judgmental qualities of natural systems they may be *used* for a variety of purposes and in many different contexts. To understand this configuration their relationship to the entire RSVP cycles must be understood clearly.

10. All parts of the score must be visible and clear at all times during the process. There cannot be secrets in scoring. This allows people to operate with a total view of the situation. Scores prevent 'hidden agendas'.

11. Scores can *energize* and *describe or control* processes. It is vital to determine *beforehand* which of these attitudes a score is going to express. Otherwise the participants will be confused about the expectation. In most scoring (as in most human relations) it is the confusion *between* these two attitudes that causes the focus of tensions and difficulty.

12. The question of whether scores energize or control depends on the relationship between scores and the other elements in the RSVP cycles. The elements of the cycle are as follows:

R   Resource: inventories resources, establishes motivations, enunciates purposes, determines requirements.

S   Score: describes processes leading to Performance.

V   Valuaction: incorporates change based on feedback and selectivity, including decisions.

P   Performance: establishes 'style' of the accomplishment of the process.

There are many interrelationships and weightings of the cycle but the major configurations are as follows: these describe the intent of the relationship *during performance* (P), not during the scoring itself or what has led up to the score.

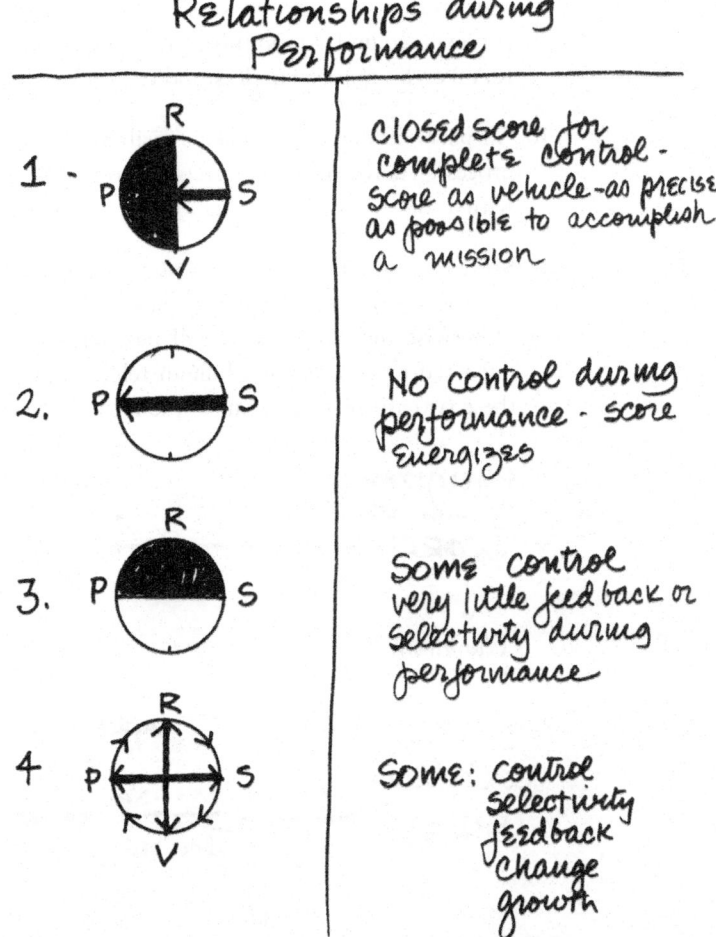

Relationships during Performance

1. Closed score for complete control - score as vehicle - as precise as possible to accomplish a mission

2. No control during performance - score energizes

3. Some control very little feedback or selectivity during performance

4. Some: control selectivity feedback change growth

Under I. in the preceding chart the score is simply a vehicle to carry out the program as part of Resource (R), that is, the score and the program are really identical. There is no feedback, no chance desired or allowed, and the score must be as precise as possible – there is therefore no irrational input and *no art process involved*. This category is similar to the systems-engineering approach to problem solving.

Examples: Moon shot[1]
                 Bank of America PERT chart[2]
                 Bach musical score (differentiate from Bach music)
                 Systems engineering

II. No programmatic (as part of Resource [R]) basis for scoring leaves a very close relationship between scoring and Performance (P). The Performance (P) evolves directly from the process which has been energized by the score. There is no selectivity except *during* Performance (P) by the persons involved and some selectivity established by the score itself. Such a relationship is exhibited by:

        Happenings
        New Music
        Driftwood Village event[3]
        Ecological scores

Note: Where only Performance (P) exists, without any score, what emerges is *improvisation*.

III. Where program as Resource (R) predates score and the two have sequential and equal weightings the Performance (P) reflects some selectivity and some control. The score has started from a basis established by the program and continues it in a creative way to energize processes. However, during Performance (P) very little or no Valuaction (V) occurs to influence the Performance (P) or the score as feedback. Such a score would be:

        Sports car rally
        Football score
        Architectural scores

IV. The ideal relationships in complex situations exists when Valuaction (V) becomes part of the entire procedural pattern and is used as a feedback mechanism to encourage growth and change during Performance (P). Valuaction (V) is here meant as an observation of process as well as

---

[1] See Halprin, 1969, pp. 44–5.
[2] *Ibid.*
[3] *Ibid.*

judgment and oriented selectivity. This relationship should ideally operate as the basis for:

> Community planning
> Theatre and other process-oriented arts
> Community interaction
> Personal interactions

This idealized relationship can be diagrammed this way:

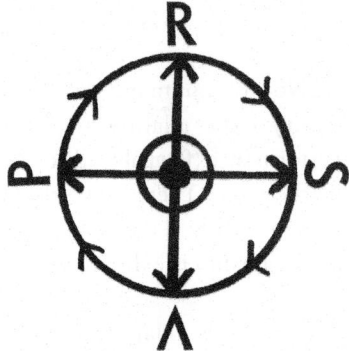

The ideal procedural relationships during performance in a multi-disciplinary environment.

It is, of course, possible to bypass the 'score' and proceed directly from Resource (R) to Performance (P) (with or without Valuaction [V]). Such a procedure leaves out the essential characteristics of the art process and *omits* creativity as a consciously organized process.

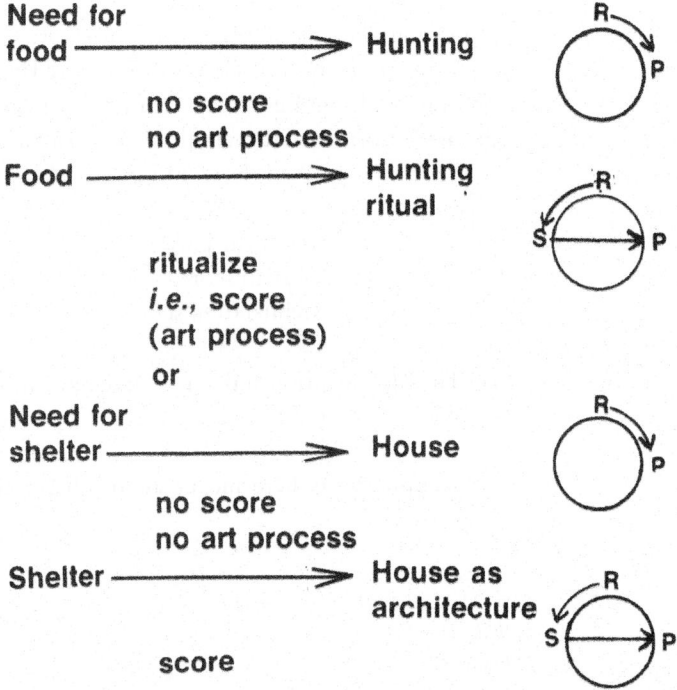

In some ways this is the obverse of the pure Performance (P) situation which leaves out RSV and is simply then a matter of improvisation. The first leaves out creativity as a consciously organized process while improvisation (though creative) also omits the consciously organized process aspect of the creative act.

13. Scores (particularly open scores) allow for great personal leeway. They call for and encourage the highest creativity from *all* participants, since performance as a creative act emerges as the result of scores. For that reason each person involved in scoring will have very high demands placed on him, involving self-imposed discipline, craftsmanship, and acknowledgment of his relationship to others in the scoring process – all as an extension of his own creativity.

14. Dreams are like scores for an existential life-script. They are the most important and revealing kind of score for the psychologist to understand. Life itself is the Performance (P) of this existential score (Fritz Peris).

15. In addition to the applications indicated in the book, the RSVP cycles have potential in the following situations:

> Interpersonal behaviour
> Group workshops
> Organizational charts for establishing new processes and
> methods of procedures

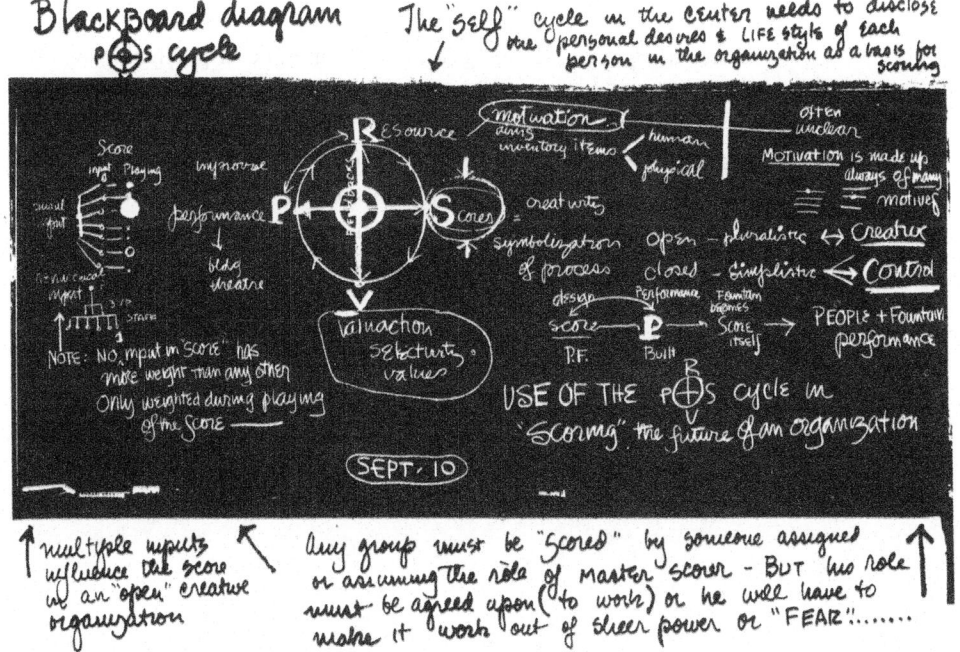

> Learning processes in all phases of education and all age levels
> Structuring any group or organization as well as artistic
> endeavors

For example, it is presently in use by the Dancers' Workshop Theatre as a guide in structuring a group that is living, working, organizing, teaching, and performing together.

The importance of pointing out the difference between 'scores' and a system is basic to the idea of this book [*The RSVP Cycles*]. A system is a closed and defined body with a beginning and an end. A system has a goal, and in order to achieve the goal establishes a specific way or technique of operation. A system is logical and sequential; it requires inputs but not feedback. A system implies order and regularity. A system relates things. A system starts with a preordained mission. There are systems to accomplish things; when things have gotten into good working order with everything functioning in a defined way they are called systems.

Scores have some characteristics of systems, but they differ profoundly. Scores are related to processes. Scores describe or initiate or energize processes. Scores include, in fact stimulate, elements of chance. Scores incorporate emotional states, include irrational elements. Scores require feedback as part of process. Scores are the essential ingredient of the creative process. Scores are not necessarily orderly, nor do they attempt to make things 'function well'. Scores are exploratory and not finite. Scores are open not closed. Scores help establish aims and motivation during scoring as part of process.

Systems, often, preamble scores. They can help factualize, inventory, give results of previous experience, store and evaluate knowledge. Scores, then, using the results of systems and including other inputs, guide the creative process.

Systems organize, scores guide. There may be 'a particular system' for accomplishing a specific end or product. But let us not view any particular score as the only and ultimate solution in the creative process. Scores are a means of revealing alternatives, of disclosing latent possibilities and the potential for releasing total human resources. They are a way of inviting the unexpected; of expanding consciousness, encouraging spontaneity and interaction; in short the score is a way of allowing the creative process to be 'natural'.

Tom Johnson

**The Big Rumble and the Tiny Blip, from *Private Pieces*
(1976)**

On *Private Pieces*: Piano Music for Self-Entertainment

The Big Rumble and the Tiny Blip

Once upon a time there was a tiny blip. (Play a very soft high note.) He was so small and so soft that you could not even hear him unless you listened very carefully. (Play the high note again, very softly.) He was always kind and friendly to everyone. But in the same neighborhood there lived a big rumble who was just the opposite. (Play a low loud rumble with your left hand and continue playing it as you read.) He was one of the meanest rumbles in town, so loud that you could hear him blocks away, and he had no respect for the tiny blip. Every time he saw the tiny blip, he laughed and scoffed, because he thought he was so tiny and ridiculous. (Try to make the rumble laugh and scoff a moment, and then stop playing.)

Now it so happened that the tiny blip was out playing one day (play a very soft high melody which sounds like the tiny blip out playing) when along came the big rumble. (Add the rumble music. Of course the tiny-blip music will not be heard against the loud rumbling, but play both parts anyway.) The big rumble, who was often rather awkward, was lumbering along in his usual loud way, when suddenly he tripped over a big log and fell flat on his face. (Stop the left-hand music in such a way that it seems to be tripping over a log and falling flat on its face. Continue the tiny blip music as you read.) Now the tiny blip was afraid to go too close to the big rumble, who had scoffed at him so many times, so he ignored him and continued playing as if nothing had happened. (Continue the tiny-blip music as if nothing has happened.) But after a time, he began to think about the big rumble, and started to worry that he might be seriously injured. (Try to reflect this worrying in your playing.)

The big rumble had not moved or made the slightest noise ever since his fall. The tiny blip stopped for a moment and wondered what he should do. (Stop the tiny-blip music.) He thought and thought and finally decided that he had to see if the big rumble was all right. He was still a little afraid, however, and approached the big fellow with some caution. (Resume the tiny-blip music, but slower. Perhaps you can make it tremble slightly to show fear. Follow the next episode as best you can.) When he examined the big rumble, he saw that he had cut his head, so he quickly bandaged it and tried to console him. Soon the rumble seemed to be better, and began to show signs of life. (Begin the rumble music again, but very softly.) When the big rumble saw who it was that had helped him, he was quite surprised and very grateful. (Play the rumble music as if it is very grateful.) The tiny blip said he was glad he could help him. (Play the tiny-blip music alone for a moment.) The rumble apologized for the way he used to scoff at the tiny blip. (Play the rumble music alone for a moment.) The tiny blip was pleased to hear this, naturally, and the two of them began to walk and talk together as if they had always been friends. (Now play the two kinds of music simultaneously, making them fit with each other as well as possible.) After that they became the best of friends. (Begin to build to a happy ending.) And to this very day, you are likely to see them together whenever you happen to walk down the block where they live. (Play a happy ending.)

Tom Johnson, 1976

On *Private Pieces: Piano Music for Self-Entertainment*

Tom Johnson

Preface (1976)

Most music is a social activity, designed for a group of musicians and listeners, but some is more intimate, and in extreme cases, such as these *Private Pieces*, it is doubtful whether the music could ever be presented effectively as a public performance. In any case, the pieces are intended to be read, played, and heard by individuals, in private.

It is of course tempting to try to deal with this volume from the comforts of an armchair, instead of from a piano stool. But those who do so will experience only the reading, will miss the other two thirds of the experience, and may completely misunderstand some of the pieces.

Some ability as a pianist is useful, but by no means necessary. The ability to read traditional music notation is obviously completely irrelevant here, and in general, *Private Pieces* can be approached on any level, from the beginner to the professional.

Remarks on *Private Pieces* (2010)

One of the main things on my mind when I wrote *Private Pieces* was that it would be nice to compose some music that could be played by amateurs who could not read written notation. Music for everybody. Music for anybody. Today though, I am not sure that this is really what the *Private Pieces* are about.

Indeed, sometimes I receive letters from piano teachers reporting how they use these scores to encourage beginners, and when I myself show one of these pieces to children, or to someone else who can't read music, they stumble through the instructions and have a bit of fun. But they rarely show any interest in playing the piece a second time. Musicians, on the other hand, sometimes play the pieces rather sensitively and want to do them again and again, gradually improving their interpretations, as with any other music. And often they are attracted by the idea that the music is only for their own pleasure, not to be played for an audience, because this is a new idea for them. So maybe it is music for musicians after all.

One example is the Italian composer/pianist Luca Miti, who became a fan of *Private Pieces* many years ago, was stimulated to make his own 'private' music, sometimes doing little performances of these pieces just for himself, or perhaps for one listener. He liked his private experiences so much that at one point he recorded one of them and included it on a CD. This was of course against the composer's wishes, as stated in the score, and he wrote me asking for permission, and knowing him, I decided to say OK. Now, when I listen to his recording, I sometimes feel that the music continues to be Luca's private experience, and will always be that, even if hundreds or thousands of people have heard the CD.

Composers can never be quite sure what they are doing, and sometimes the nature of the music turns out to be rather different from what they originally had in mind. But of course, all this is only my opinion. You have every right to your own private reactions.

Seth Kim-Cohen

Forever Got Shorter (from a t-shirt of the same name) (2010)

How To Write A Text About How To Write A Text Score (And Why)

Some Thoughts on *Forever Got Shorter*

Realising *Forever Got Shorter*

Forever Got Shorter (from a t-shirt of the same name)

Seth Kim-Cohen

For solo trap kit
Dedicated to Michael Lenzi

A drummer on a small platform plays a slow, heavy trap kit beat. Each time the drummer presses down on the kick drum pedal, he or she is also pressing down on a car jack. The jack gradually lifts the drummer's end of the platform until the drums and cymbals begin to tumble away. The drummer's seat is secured, ensuring that he or she will not similarly tumble. The piece is finished when the drummer can no longer reach any drums or cymbals.

Notes:
The specific arrangement of the car jack will depend on the model of jack employed. I consider solving this puzzle to be part of the performance of the piece. (Good luck.)

It goes without saying that the duration of Forever Got Shorter is a product of the frequency (or infrequency) of kick drum beats. (This parallels the correlation of heart rate to life expectancy in animals.) This equation should be considered in advance.

The choice of beat is left entirely to the performer.

How To Write A Text About How To Write A Text Score (And Why)

Seth Kim-Cohen, March 2009

Legato

1. Write the words, 'I don't speak "music"'. (In which the interior quotation marks cradle the delicate word 'music', so as to prevent it from breaking.)

2. Ask the question, 'Why can't I read or write musical notation?'

3. Answer (defensively, yet with a certain pride), 'I have been playing music for thirty years. At times, I have made a living solely writing, recording and playing music. I have written something like three hundred songs, a few dozen experimental musical compositions, and released eight albums. I have taken and taught classes about music, written books about music, hosted radio shows about music. But I can't read or write musical notation.'

4. Ask (hoping it will be taken rhetorically), 'What kind of ignoramus am I?'

   A brief interlude on cognitive style (to the tune of the ocarina part in the second movement of Ligeti's *Concerto for Violin and Orchestra*):

   > My mind doesn't function mathematically, hierarchically, systematically. I process information as magnetic particles, some attract, some repel. I process information as liquid, a little in this container, a little in that, a little spilled on the floor, a little evaporated. I process information as signs. It's not important to me that I'm hearing a 1–4–5 chord progression, it's important that what I'm hearing is relating itself to the blues: what, then, is the nature of that relation? Respectful? Antagonistic? Ironic? I group. I slurp. I engage. Derrida is never far from my thoughts: 'Il n'y a pas de hors-texte' ('There is no outside-the-text.') Conversely, and equally true: everything is (in the) text.

5. Justify this musico-logos-ical incompetence by arguing, 'Music isn't a set of numerical values, it's a set of ethical/ontological/epistemological values. That is to say, it's part of life and life's part of it. So, why should I feel compelled to adopt this invented, artificial, specialist language to produce, receive, and talk about music? The language I use every day, for everything else, ought to suffice. And, what do you know? For me, it does.'

6. Continue, beginning to feel like a dead horse is being beaten, yet wanting to persuade: 'I use text notation the same way I use everyday language:

descriptively, deceptively, instructively, ironically, generously, mischievously. The point is, we all relate to everyday language. We don't all relate to musical notation. If we're interested in the social aspects of art and music, then it seems wise to use the most inclusive language on offer.'

7. Being careful not to seem self-important, give an example from the work: 'I can whisper a text notation in the ear of an audience member and ask them to "pass it on" to another audience member, until it reaches the performer on the stage. This doesn't work as well with a little black dot on the end of a stick attached to the third of five horizontal lines, referring back to a cluster of little signs and some numbers.'

7a. Go on, another example couldn't hurt: 'I can describe sound as "stubborn" or "like a fruit bat", or designate its duration as equivalent to "completely opening and then closing a door". The subsequent sounds are now adorned with life-qualities that are unavailable to notation. As are the performer and the audience. Pretty neat, huh?'

8. Conclude by comparing attitudes toward life and music, implying that the former should guide the latter, 'I put no faith in higher powers, final answers, destiny. I do not obey a set of behavioural instructions determining my every movement, my tempo, my termination. Why then, would I ask music to submit to these unrealistic constraints? What right do I have to impose them on the listener? We're all in this together. Better yet if cake is served.'

9. Always say thank you, 'Thank you'.

Some Thoughts on *Forever Got Shorter*

Seth Kim-Cohen, September 2010

The date of composition is dependent on the date of realization. In keeping with post-structuralist theories of authorship, the piece wasn't written until Ross performed it and an audience heard/saw/interpreted it. That said, I first conceived of the piece in 2008.

Since I first read Mel Bochner's essay *The Serial Attitude* (1967), I've been haunted by this prescription: 'The completed work is fundamentally parsimonious and systematically self-exhausting.' I don't accept this as Talmudic law, but I do find it as valid a compositional aim as any other (harmony, symmetry, beauty). It is yet another mode of resolution. With *Forever Got Shorter*, the resolution is not proposed as failure, but as systematic self-exhaustion. The performance-as-organism fulfils its natural lifespan and dies. This is alluded to in step two of the score which equates the frequency of kick drum beats to the heart rate of animals. (Apparently, there is great consistency across species in terms of the number of times the heart beats in an average lifespan. Duration is determined by tempo. Hummingbirds exhaust their allotment of beats quickly, elephants more slowly.)

On the other hand, I chafe against passive radicalism: the safe, quiet, uneventful appropriation of revolutionary aesthetic modes. If one wishes to do violence to the prevailing order, then, please, do it violently. Whispering 'God is dead', under your breath, in the back of the temple, won't even make the rabbi blush. I spent a dozen years in a rock band. Towards the end, Michael Lenzi – to whom *Forever Got Shorter* is dedicated – and I adopted the practice of ending shows by wrecking the stage and destroying our instruments.

We smashed guitars, we dove into the drum kit, we kicked over amplifiers, etc. We did this because the 'fuck you' that rock and roll must be in order to validate its existence as a cultural form, had disappeared. All the gestures had been assimilated into a polite and tidy language, spoken by bands, fans and critics with equal ease. Now, I am fully aware that smashing instruments is a rock and roll trope like any other. And perhaps that's why I don't play rock and roll anymore. But in composition and in the gallery world, some rock-like gestures are still potent. You don't see the drum kit toppled at the Royal Festival Hall nearly as often as you did at CBGB. *Forever Got Shorter*, then, is an attempt to restore some violence to the radicalism of aleatory composition, conceptual practice, and avant-garde performance. Granted, it's not a steel bar to the teeth, but there nonetheless exists the possibility of harm to property, performer, and conventional practice, possibly even to the audience (like when a tire flies into the stands at a motor race).

The title of the piece comes indirectly from the title of a song by the '90s emocore band, Braid. Michael Lenzi created a handmade t-shirt bearing that inscription and wore it for the last few performances in the career of our band, The Fire Show. The title implies the disappearance of something that had been taken for granted as being permanent. It could reference a love affair, mortality, god, or values like truth and goodness. The drum beat employed in the piece, detached from other musical material, suggests eternal repetition, the beat returning to its origins at the start of each measure.

Yet, as pieces of the kit fall away, the beat must adapt to its newly-limited resources until, eventually, it has nothing to sustain it. Sound is always the product of the interaction of two (or more) things: stick and head, for instance. Even John Cage's realization that as long as we're alive there is sound, is a product of the interaction of plural biological factors, i.e. blood, veins and eardrums. When that plurality is reduced to singularity, sound stops, forever gets shorter. Ironically, gay-John Cage's sonic optimism finds its equally profound, pessimistic implications in the gay rights, AIDS-activist, slogan 'Silence = Death'. Mushrooms and Zen notwithstanding, we can't escape the real world of politics, power, and disease, *et al*.

As it happens, *Forever Got Shorter* has been followed by another drum violence piece. *Critique of Instrumental Reason (By The Use of Drums)* was performed in October 2010 at the exhibition *Non-Cochlear Sound* at Diapason Gallery in Brooklyn. This involves chucking a drum kit down a flight of stairs, collecting the drums in a wheelbarrow at the bottom, wheeling them through the gallery to the elevator, and back up to the top of the stairs – to be repeated for the duration of the exhibition.

Realising *Forever Got Shorter*

Ross Parfitt in conversation with John Lely, Summer 2010

John Lely: I know you've worked with Seth before, but how did you come across this piece?

Ross Parfitt: I overheard him talking about it sometime in 2008 and was immediately interested, chiefly, I think, because of the idea of this physical parallel of car jack and bass-drum pedal. The actions required to activate either of them are so closely related that the piece struck me as an interesting act of re-mapping, whereby a common action could have an uncommon outcome through a (conceptually) simple reconfiguring of physical materials. It reminded me of a section in Anne Michaels' book *Fugitive Pieces*, in which a typist shifts her fingers one key to the right but continues to type as if they were in the original position.

At the time that I eventually performed the piece, in a series of concerts in Sheffield with Steve Chase, it tied in with an idea of performing recursive pieces, in which the input to the piece depends upon its output. In *Forever Got Shorter*, the performer's ability to continue playing the piece is affected by the angle of tilt, the degree of collapse of parts of the kit, which is itself determined by what has already been played. This is fascinating – that the piece is essentially self-destructive.

John Lely: So when you finally saw the score, what was your approach to reading it?

92 Ross Parfitt performing Seth Kim-Cohen's Forever Got Shorter, *Bank St Arts, Sheffield, April 2010.*

Ross Parfitt: My initial approach is always to assume complete isolation of a score from all reference and influence, essentially to consider it as self-contained. From this position I look for clues within the score about what to do, starting with directly practical issues, such as resources required (space, equipment, people, etc.), obligations and logical infer-ences regarding obligations ('if I do *x* then what effect does that have on *y*?'), inconsistencies ('is it possible to do *y* if I do *x*?'), etc. Over many close readings of the score I want to increase the scope of examination to make sure I've understood it as fully as I can by, for example, considering more typical interactions with the given materials, unstated implications

regarding the manner of realisation, cultural references, my guess at intended meanings, metaphor, and so on.

As a principle, I feel it is initially crucial not to bring any musical or other assumptions to a score or to make any assumptions of the score. The reading of a score has to be detailed and focused, closely examining the meaning and connotations of the words, with the intention of gathering information from clues, and to ensure I'm taking it seriously and not doing it flippantly. For example, in the second section of James Tenney's *MAXIMUSIC* the performer is required to play until he or she is 'nearly exhausted' from the physical effort of playing loud and fast across a range of percussion instruments (see Fig. 46, page 63). As a performer you need to consider what is meant by 'nearly exhausted', and it could be tempting to aim for a lower threshold of exhaustion (it's pretty inconvenient and unpleasant to be exhausted), but reading the clues (the piece's title, 'sudden loud, fast', ending the section doing something 'as loud as possible', the contrast between the 'soft roll' which is later 'now inaudible', the precedent of Tenney's *Having Never Written a Note for Percussion* crescen-doing to *fff...*) it is clear that this is not about being a bit tired, or giving the impression to the audience (acting!) of being very tired, but it requires serious commitment to putting yourself into a state of near exhaustion.

A score which requires considerable physical activity is, to my mind, 'about' physical activity, and it is therefore against the spirit of the piece to scrimp on this, by being any less than fully committed to realising the physicality of it, whether that be exhausting, dangerous, embarrassing, etc. Lucier's *Music for Solo Performer* (see Fig. 10, page 19) is really important here because it cannot work unless you really are in this particular state – you cannot shortcut it or act as if you are in that state. If that means that there is no sonic output during a performance because the performer does not achieve that state then so be it. At least they really tried.

I also think it's important to consider omissions to be as important as inclusions and understand that they may be intended by the scorer. I always assume that the score is complete, that all aspects are as they should be and that no aspect could be better expressed in any other way – even logical inconsistencies may be intended. I don't like to assume that an omission is necessarily licence to do what is omitted.

Some of the clues I felt important in the score of *Forever Got Shorter* were:

- 'solo': one performer.
- 'trap kit': drum kit, but with what components?

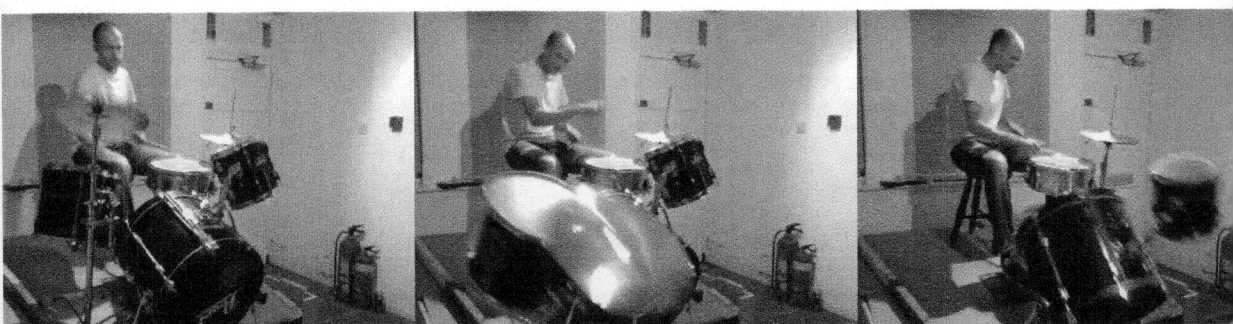

- 'small platform': what dictates its size?
- 'small heavy trap kit beat': non-specific, some fairly typical rock beat. No guidance on components of the drum kit, but surely it should look like a drum kit, so should include bass drum, snare and at least two tom-toms, hi-hat and at least one cymbal. Read the whole score for more info about musical content, then come back to this.
- Some details about the principles of operation of the tipping platform and connection between bass drum pedal and car jack are given. These details are crucial and need examining very closely for design requirements and flexibilities, plus further consideration of implications of any choices made here. Do they compromise any of the other requirements of the piece?
- 'The piece is finished when the drummer can no longer reach any drums or cymbals.' So the initial collapse of the kit might not be total, but has to be sufficient to put all elements out of the drummer's reach, which basically means being fully collapsed on the floor. More importantly this implies that the drummer continues with whatever parts of the kit are within his or her reach, and I take this to mean that the feeling of the music should be maintained as closely as possible, as if a rock drummer had dropped a stick or the guitarist had just kicked half of their drum kit over (they have to keep going). So the musical content must be flexible and responsive to the circumstances and there is a need for resolution to continue until total collapse.
- 'The specific arrangement of the car jack will depend on the model of jack employed.' So the platform and tipping mechanism need to be built by the performer to suit the model of jack they get. Crucially, though, Seth writes that this is 'part of the performance of the piece. (Good luck.)' So he obviously anticipates that it will be hard work and feels that the 'specific arrangement' (this is nicely understated; he really means designing and building) aspect is important enough to require additional emphasis in the score, rather than simply inclusion. Reading between the lines, I concluded that this is not just part of the piece but pretty much the most important aspect of it, apart from the collapse. It is a challenge to engage at a deep level with the process and practical details of construction and, again, short cuts are not appropriate.
- 'It goes without saying that the duration of *Forever Got Shorter* is a product of the frequency (or infrequency) of kick drumbeats. (This parallels the correlation of heart rate to life expectancy in animals.) This

equation should be considered in advance.' There is a spectacle involved in this piece and I feel it is important for it to occur gradually. Too short a duration and the drummer's position would go from normal to precipitous too quickly for the audience to really enjoy. There is an upper-limit of duration built in by relating each occurrence of the bass-drum in a drum-kit beat to a press of the pedal of a car jack. These things are built to lift a car relatively quickly so the issue of going on for too long isn't really present.

So imagine a typical rock-type beat – the bass drum occurs approximately two to four times per bar with a pulse c. 80–130 beats per minute. That gives a value of 40 bpm (i.e. 40 presses on the car jack per minute), if you take the slowest end of this rough rock-spectrum. Of course the relevance of this value differs according to the individual structure used, because the number of car-jack presses required to get the angle of the platform far enough to finish the piece will differ, possibly quite significantly.

But if we say, for the sake of the argument, that it might take around 100 presses to do this, then at 40 bpm the duration is 2½ minutes. Is that duration OK? My feeling was that this was too short and that something slower and sparser, in which the bass drum was a less-important musical element than in very typical rock, would enable this piece to unfold at an appropriate, gradual pace. Something between Led Zep's *Kashmir* and PiL's *Poptones* immediately came to mind, and I felt that a more thorough plan of the musical content just wasn't necessary. Rock drums are semi-improvised anyway but, more importantly, as you continue to read the score it becomes clear, because of the scant detail given to the exact nature of the musical content, that this is not what the piece is about.

John Lely: Seth says in the score that he considers solving the puzzle of how to build the device as part of the performance. Given the technical complexity, and the planning needed for the eventual presentation of the drumming element, do you think that your realisation perhaps began at the moment you heard about the piece from Seth?

Ross Parfitt: Well, my consideration of designing and building began at the point that I heard about it. The piece is so physical that at a very early stage it requires a mental image of possible structures and consideration of the complexities around this. So, yes, I think that the realisation started

in 2008 when I heard about it, though, of course, there were fluctuations in the amount of consideration I gave it – sometimes none, sometimes just pondering, sometimes drawing diagrams of possible constructions and wandering around DIY shops examining different car jacks. In 2010 I decided on a performance date, though I still didn't know how to do it.

John Lely: So how did you go about planning it?

Ross Parfitt: I know nothing about building/construction. I knew I needed strong materials and tools to work with them in order to build the structure. Basically I needed help from someone who knows what they're doing with these things and, as it happened, I knew a generous professional joiner and mechanic, Dave Cecil, and he was happy to collaborate. We drew up several different designs, trying to think as broadly as possible about problematic issues of each one, and of course they all had problems. The least problematic became the basis for the final structure.

As Seth suggests in the score, there were many issues to do with the dimensions of the jack itself that affected the design and build process – far more than I'd anticipated. A key consideration was my ability to activate the jack in a way that worked efficiently and did not require significant changes in the physical act of drumming. I felt that if such changes were required then I would be less able to concentrate on drumming and would be distracted by these unfamiliar playing requirements or by attending to the mechanism of the jack and platform. So the plans had to be very thorough and the structure had to be robust to enable this.

John Lely: And in the building stage – did the plans work?

Ross Parfitt: We managed to cover most of the key design issues before starting building, such as, crucially, measuring the angle at which the drum kit would tumble. But there were some other aspects that we had missed out, so the design had to change quite radically as we were building, when we realised how important these things were. I feel it's essential that performers of this piece should go through this process and consider these things for themselves, so I'm not going to go into real detail here, but there are a couple of very important things to think about. First, where is the pivot of the jack and how does that relate spatially to the platform and bass-drum pedal? Second, what surface does the jack rest on?

Through trial and error, and a fair amount of rebuilding, the structure that we ended up with was fantastic and it worked absolutely as well as I'd hoped it would when I first heard about the piece. I was so pleased. But I also took a planned risk by not fully testing it before the performance. We checked that the platform would tip sufficiently, that the drums could tumble (but not looking at how they would fall, or trying to plan for this – this is part of the beauty of the performance event), and also that I could drum easily and activate the jack efficiently. This was enough to reassure me that the mechanism would work and I really didn't want to know more than that, mainly so that I could enjoy the performance itself as naïvely as the audience, and as naïvely as I believe the piece requires.

John Lely: You've played other pieces by Seth, as well as various other experimental works for percussion. What was your approach to playing this one?

Ross Parfitt: It needed to be as similar as possible to playing a normal drum kit in a normal way; nothing extraordinary, so that the process of tipping would be as if incidental. I was concerned about the risk of the collapsing kit being a cartoonish or pantomime spectacle. Whilst there is certainly humour in what happens I did not want this to be overtly performative, and it took a while of thinking this through and discussing it with you and others to resolve this.

The eventual resolution was to do with Buster Keaton, who, you told me, is a hero of Seth's. Keaton became, for me, a fantastic model of performance attitude. He seemed to respond so directly to his circumstances, with minimal emotion or attempts to obtain sympathy. Run. Jump. Drive. That's what I wanted – simply focus on my task, responding as necessary to the changing circumstances as if they were mere interruption (don't be concerned about the tipping surface but about how to continue playing). Essentially my approach changed from performing a piece to doing a thing.

There appears, in this piece, something of a conflict between the attentive, detailed preparation and the naïve position required during performance. Again, this is the same as Keaton – he can only remain impassive to the wall of the house falling around him in *Steamboat Bill, Jr* because of the huge and careful effort that he put into preparing it. *Forever Got Shorter* does, therefore, require an amount of 'acting' during the performance (the performer has to pretend that he or she doesn't know that the platform will tip up), however this does not feel disingenuous because there is actually no engagement with the tipping (such as mock-surprise, panic or expressions of victimhood) other than to adjust my drumming as the drum kit collapses.

Most pieces of music can be realised more than once and this is usually a relatively simple act of repeated performance. A realisation of *Forever Got Shorter* is clearly not just a public performance, but has as a major concern the issue of solving the puzzle of the specific arrangement of the car jack. Using a pre-built structure or a design that has been standardised or previously realised is therefore a false solution, and so the structure I used has been taken apart and the wood reused (I think it's now part of a garage wall), because this process of considering, designing and building is so crucial to each realisation.

Bengt af Klintberg

from *Twenty Five Orange Events* (1963–6)

Peel an orange carefully...

from Twenty Five Orange Events

Bengt af Klintberg, 1963–1966

Number 1 (for Kerstin Aurell)
Try to find out which musical instrument you would first connect with an orange. Play it, as long as you like. Or pretend to play it for the corresponding time.

Number 3
Peel an orange carefully and arrange pieces in a row. Choose one of the pieces.

Number 4
Peel an orange carefully and place pieces here and there in the apartment. Eat them when you happen to pass.

Number 7
Eat an orange and, at the same time, listen attentively: to sounds of chewing, of sucking, of swallowing and external sounds that may occur.

Number 8 (for Pi Lind)
Eat an orange as if it were an apple. (Hold it, unpeeled, between forefinger, middle finger and thumb, bite big mouthfuls, etc.)

Number 10
Use at the same time an orange and a lemon, an orange and a die, an orange and a bucket, an orange and an apple, an orange and a phonograph, an orange and a shoe, an orange and a tangerine, an orange and an organ, an orange and a ski-track, or an apple and an umbrella.

Number 12 (for Staffan Olzon)
Fill all the drawers of a chest to the brim with oranges and depart for another part of the world.

Number 15
For umbrella, orange and sewing machine.

Number 16 (for Åke Hodell)
Regard two or three oranges for a long time.

Number 17 (for Folke Heybroek)
Leaning over a bridge parapet, look down into the water whirls of the Stockholm Stream. Between your two hands, roll an orange so that the peel becomes soft and will easily come loose from the orange. Quite often you will hear the rattle of trains, that are passing over the railway bridge in the neighborhood. At certain junctures you will also hear the bells of at least three churches ringing. When these two sounds reach you at the same time, start peeling the orange and let the peels fall down into the water.

Number 20
Paint an orange white and place it together with other oranges in a white bowl.

Number 21
Roll an orange over a floor, covered with hens' feathers.

Number 24
Stay for a long time in a room, in which there is silence. Breathe silently, move silently if you move. At a time that you choose yourself, crack a nut.

Number 25 ('Proposition')
Make a fruit salad of nuts and oranges and serve it.

Peel an orange carefully...

Bengt af Klintberg, September 2010

In the '60s I participated in avant-garde activities, some of which might be called music if you make a wide definition of music. But I am foremost a folklorist and poet, and I have expressed my thoughts about the similarity between Fluxus pieces and folklore in an article, 'Fluxus Games and Contemporary Folklore: On the Non-Individual Character of Fluxus Art'.[1]

My first encounter with verbal notation was when I read the instructions in George Brecht's *Water Yam*. Some of them were extremely brief and enigmatic. One example: *Saxophone Solo* – 'Trumpet.' Another example: *Two Elimination Events* – 'Empty vessel. Empty vessel.' A consequence of their brevity is that these scores may be performed very differently from time to time.

The event instructions of George Brecht and other Fluxus artists inspired me to explore this new genre (which might not be new at all). From a stylistic point of view most of my contributions consisted of sentences in imperative form. This has in all times been the favoured form for literature in which practical instructions are given, for example cookbooks. What characterizes these instructions is that their style is totally impersonal. You never hear an individual voice in them.

When you read a collection of verbal notations by Fluxus artists, such as Ken Friedman's *The Fluxus Performance Workbook*, you will find that the style is as impersonal as it is in the cookbook recipes. They consist of concise instructions in imperative form of how you can treat musical instruments, food etc.

George Maciunas' well-known definition of Fluxus is that it 'is the fusion of Spike Jones, vaudeville, gag, children's games and Marcel Duchamp'. Since I am a folklorist by profession, I have noticed that three of the characteristics mentioned are folklore genres: vaudeville, gags, children's games. I believe that this affinity between the Fluxus performance pieces and folklore explains why I became involved in Fluxus activities.

It was because Fluxus is at the same time avant-garde and anti-elitist, which might sound like a contradiction. The impersonal form and the social significance are what unite Fluxus performance pieces and folklore.

What I like about the verbal notations made by Fluxus artists is the lack of individuality. It would give me great satisfaction if, say, my *Orange Event Number 4* becomes transmitted orally and performed by people who have no idea from where it comes. In other words: that it becomes folklore.

---

[1] Klintberg, 1993, pp. 115–25.

Alison Knowles

Shoes of Your Choice (1963)

Commentary: _Shoes of Your Choice_

#6 —

Shoes of Your Choice (March, 1963)

A member of the audience is invited to come forward to a microphone if one is available and describe a pair of shoes, the ones he is wearing or another pair. He is encouraged to tell where he got them, the size, color, why he likes them, etc.

Premiered April 6th, 1963 at the Old Gymnasium of Douglass College, New Brunswick, New Jersey.

Commentary: *Shoes of Your Choice*

James Saunders

Shoes of Your Choice (1963) is one of a series of 23 pieces published by Something Else Press in a *Great Bear Pamphlet* entitled *by Alison Knowles*. Knowles made many of the pieces during the first Fluxus tours to Europe in 1962–3. As she explains:

> Most of those [scores] were written out of necessity because we were already performing in Germany and a lot of people followed us from city to city – we had to have fresh material, and we put the material together the night before so it had to be super simple, it had to have no theatre accoutrements, and it had to be for anybody in the group who was travelling with us [...] I composed them when we were touring and we did them the next day. It was very, very exciting.[1]

Shoes of Your Choice is such a piece, in that it requires minimal apparatus and the complexity emerges from a simple idea. It depends on the situation of performance and can be realised only in the presence of an audience. While the piece requires a member of the audience to become actively involved in the realisation, the instructions are expressed in the passive voice,[2] instead of the active voice (e.g. 'Invite a member of the audience to come forward...'). It is therefore not explicit who should invite the member of the audience and encourage them, or how this should be achieved. Knowles does this herself when performing the piece, as she explains:

> I read the piece [...] and then I'm used to waiting. People realise they're going to have to make it happen. [...] I can either [stand or] sit down, and if nothing happens after three or four minutes I'll start it off with my own shoes, but then I'll sit down again once they've gotten the idea, but then I always get a line of people. And once you get a couple of people, then you get egos stepping in. 'Well if Sam can do it, come on Steve, stand up there! Lucy, are you gonna let Steve... ' It builds on everyone wanting to do it suddenly.

> Mostly with *Shoes of Your Choice*, once they get started they don't want to go on forever.[3] They put their shoes [on] a music stand. The heels usually catch on the stand. And they'll say where they bought the shoes, why they like them. And then the person can step back and look at them along with the audience. I always use a music stand.[4]

---

[1] Alison Knowles, in interview with John Lely, Cambridge, MA, 27 September 2009.

[2] This is the only piece in *by Alison Knowles* that uses the passive voice.

[3] Knowles describes a performance at the ICA in London in 1963 which implies a more lengthy speech: 'Up stands Richard Hamilton, takes off his shoe and holds it for everyone to see, [in Dick Van Dyke cockney accent] "I bought these shoes, I did, when I was back in London, and they used to be brown and now they're getting a little beat up" and he goes on and on.' (Alison Knowles, in interview with John Lely, Cambridge, MA, 27 September 2009.)

[4] *Ibid.*

Knowles's preference for reading the score out during the performance perhaps gives the piece an objective quality. The reader communicates somebody else's requirements verbatim to the audience. It becomes a request from another party. Knowles feels that this can affect the way performers approach the task, commenting that:

> It gives it an authority I think, it's much better than, 'Could you please talk about your shoes?' The text is fixed, and people respond to the authority of the text, and they speak with more authority about their shoes.[5]

This is one possibility, and Knowles recognises that other presentations are possible, commenting: 'What you do with the score is just as correct as what I do with the score, as long as we follow it.'[6] The primacy of the text is therefore still the key to presenting the event and unlike George Brecht, who was open to all possible realisations of his event scores,[7] Knowles is uncomfortable with overly theatrical performances, or those where people want 'to load the score with other material'.[8] She explains the need to avoid a contrived presentation of the work:[9]

> I know that the people I tried to work with who were actually in theatre as actors or people who were in dance as dancers, are not attractive to me as performers. They don't step into the material for themselves, they think it's been put on like a musical score or like a dance performance, that there's something they're supposed to do. But these are just to be read, but they're to be read precisely, and if you get a theatre person, ah, I had this terrible experience, and I had no rehearsal: [in an overly dramatic manner] 'Please come up and speak about your shoes'. I couldn't get her off the stage.[10]

Knowles also feels that the presentation of the piece should be self-contained, and that it should avoid simultaneous performance with other pieces.[11] This is the practice adopted by many Fluxus artists, where pieces are presented as a sequence of separate events in a programme,[12] and contrasts with the intermedia presentations more common in happenings. Her pieces are focused events that require precision. Despite their apparent simplicity, 'they shouldn't be done sloppily, they shouldn't just be knocked off [...] I

---

[5] *Ibid.*

[6] Knowles, 2010.

[7] In an interview with Michael Nyman, when asked whether any realisation of his event scores is feasible, Brecht replies: 'Any and every. I wouldn't refuse any realisations.' Nyman, 1976, p. 259.

[8] Knowles, 2010.

[9] Knowles references a more natural approach to performance, suggesting, 'Whatever it is you have to touch and work with, you can make a kind of performance of it, but it has to be stripped of the hangings and accoutrements of theatre. What happens is that a kind of revelation, no an emptiness, opens up.' See Milman, E., (1992) 'Road Shows, Street Events, and Fluxus People: A Conversation with Alison Knowles', *Visible Language*, vol. 26, no. 9 in Friedman, 1998, p. 108.

[10] Alison Knowles, in interview with John Lely, Cambridge, MA, 27 September 2009.

[11] *Ibid.* When discussing simultaneous presentation of work, Knowles commented, 'I don't like this.'

[12] See Friedman 1998, p. 119.

think the vision of the composer is to actually pass it over to a performer. The precision of how it is done is usually for me a direct measure of the success of the piece.'[13]

This approach relates to one of the central concerns of the piece, that of creating a situation where the audience can observe other people who 'are not in a theatrical mode, they are not acting out a part.'[14] It is also apparent in other pieces from *by Alison Knowles*, such as *Proposition* (1962) (see Fig. 4, page 13) or *Child Art Piece* (1962), in which a two- or three-year-old child is the performer, and the piece is over when the child leaves the stage: no further activities are directly specified. Knowles sees it as a way to reveal characteristics of people involved in the performance, commenting, 'you get a wonderful reading of that person, the way they stand, the way that they pronounce the words, the way that they present them out to you, or don't'.[15]

This situation prioritises people and puts them at the centre of the activity, whether it be describing shoes or making a salad. While the activity gives a context, the core of the piece is the personality and choices made by the performers. Knowles is excited by the open nature of these situations. She sees the constraints the pieces place on their performers as a way to create a space which can satisfy the urge 'in human beings to step out into the unforeseen, for some people even if they don't know anything about art, they get driven to do something before people. To have them look at them, or to think what they say'.[16]

The results of these situations are unpredictable, and offer the opportunity for the unexpected to be acknowledged. Knowles is interested in people, and opening up 'a kind of spontaneous dialogue. So *Shoes of Your Choice* allows for that. You never know what's going to happen.'[17]

95 *Jackson Mac Low performing Alison Knowles,* Shoes of Your Choice *at The Viking Ship Hall, Roskilde, Denmark on 29 May 1985.*

96 *Ben Vautier performing Alison Knowles,* Shoes of Your Choice *at The Viking Ship Hall, Roskilde, Denmark on 29 May 1985.*

[13] Knowles, 2010.
[14] *Ibid.*
[15] *Ibid.*
[16] Alison Knowles, in interview with John Lely, Cambridge, MA, 27 September 2009.
[17] *Ibid.*

Takehisa Kosugi

South No. 3 (Malika) (1965)

Commentary: *South No. 3 (Malika)*

SOUTH NO.3 (MALIKA)

1. Performer considers S (O, U, T, H) as
sound and pronounces the letters as (s)
((a),(u),(θ),(θ)).
2. Performer considers S (O, U, T, H) as
forms for actions or actions to sound and
performs a movement to the shape of each
letter.

This piece may be performed as:
1) single performance of each letter either
   with sound or action.
2) multiple performance of each letter by
   single performer as sound or action.
3) simultaneous performance of S with H,
   O with S, U with O, T with U, H with T.
4) continuous performance with S following H immediatelly.
5) interrupted performance with a pause
   between each letter.

Any of these forms may be repeated any
number of times.

T. Kosugi, August 21,1965

Commentary: *South No. 3 (Malika)*

James Saunders

Takehisa Kosugi's event scores were first made in the early 1960s and appeared in Fluxus publications and performances. He was one of a number of Japanese artists who became associated with Fluxus, including his Group Ongaku co-founders Mieko Shiomi and Yasunao Tone, as well as Toshi Ichiyanagi and Yoko Ono. Kosugi's verbal scores explore the relationship between sound and action. He observes that:

> The sound object is not always music, but action, action. Sometimes no sound, just action. Opening a window is a beautiful action, even if there's no sound. It's part of the performance. For me that was very important, opening my eyes and ears to combining the non-musical part and the musical part of action. In my concerts, music became this totality, so even if there was no sound I said it was music. Confusing. This is how I opened my eyes to chaos.[1]

Kosugi made eight pieces bearing the title *South*, although only six remain in his list of works;[2] of these, only Nos. 1–3 are verbal scores. In *South No. 1 to Anthony Cox* (1962) the instruction is: 'Pronounce "SOUTH" during a predetermined or indetermined duration.' There is no indication of the length of this duration, simply that the performer must either know in advance how long it will be, or that it is not determined. *No. 2* is a variation of *No. 1*, with the instructions: 'Pronounce "SOUTH" during a duration of more than 15 minutes. Pause for breath is permitted but transition from pronounciation [*sic*] of one letter to another should be smooth and slow.' Although *No. 2* requires an extended duration, in *No. 1* this is not necessarily the case. A very short duration may result in a perfunctory delivery of the word. The meaning of 'during' is ambiguous however: the rest of the score does not define the pronunciation as a continuous activity or as a discrete point in the course of a longer duration. Kosugi comments that in *No. 1*, he 'didn't indicate to pronounce the word only one time, so that *South No. 1* and *No. 2* are totally different [to] each other'. This is clarified by his comment: 'No. 1 has been played [...] repeating the word many times.'[3] The use of the verb 'pronounce' suggests a correct or clear articulation of the word 'south'.

South No. 2 for Nam June Paik (1964) is similar to *No. 1* in its initial instructions, but with the addition of two constraints. It defines a duration of 'more than 15 minutes', and explicitly requires the performer to create

---

[1] Doris, D. T., 'Zen Vaudeville' in Friedman, 1998, p. 110.

[2] *South No. 1 to Anthony Cox* (1962), *South No. 2 to Nam June Paik* (1964), *South No. 3 (Malika)* (1965), *South No. 5* (1971), *South No. 6, Magnetism* (1973). Numbers 4 and 8 were abandoned, and there is no number 7. Kosugi also made *South, e.v.* in 1999 as an electronic version. There are therefore six extant pieces titled *South*.

[3] Takehisa Kosugi, in correspondence with the author, July 2010.

a smooth and slow transition from one letter to another. The combination of these two constraints results in an elongated pronunciation of the word 'south', accepting the ambiguity of 'during' once again.[4] This is in contrast to *No. 1*, where the word may be repeated. Writing about such slow-motion processes, Michael Nyman comments:

> when an everyday activity is subjected to slow-motion process all kinds of unforeseen, near-crippling problems are thrown up. This is also true of the transients of the word 'south'. Kosugi seems to have used the processes not as a means of taking the performer outside himself, but of making him more intensely aware of interior actions which he normally performs quite instinctively. As a result he is drawn outside the universe of his known physical functioning.[5]

It is worth comparing *South No. 1* and *No. 2* with Kosugi's *Anima 7* (1964), in which the score states:

> The performer chooses one action which would usually be completed in a short time and extends it to a time value of his choosing. For example, to take off a suit-jacket as one normally would in a few seconds, but extending it for a longer period – a half-hour, fifteen minutes, etc.

In a handwritten note on a plan for a concert programme featuring *Anima 7*, Kosugi further specifies:

> The following instruments will be used:
> String instrument, sound tape, film, light, large cloth bag with zippers, the word 'SOUTH', suit-jacket, etc...[6]

Although *Anima 7* is a separate piece, the extension of sounds and actions to longer than their normal duration may inform realisations of the *South* pieces, given the inclusion of the word 'south' in the list of instruments.

South No. 3 (Malika) (1965) differs from the first two scores in that it provides more information about how to perform the piece (see Fig. 97). It too begins with a description of how to pronounce the word 'south'. Here though the sonic quality is emphasised, asking the performer to consider the letters of 'south' as separate phonemes. In the printed score, the International Phonetic Association symbol θ is used twice, representing both the letters 't' and 'h' even though they form a digraph 'th'. Kosugi notes that this is a misprint in the Fluxus edition, and that 'one of them must be omitted'.[7] The score then gives an alternative way to realise the word as 'forms for actions

---

[4] *Ibid.* Kosugi explains that in *No. 2* the word 'south' is to be pronounced 'very slowly one time'.

[5] Nyman, 1999, p. 81.

[6] Reprinted in Hendricks *et al.*, 2008, p. 94.

[7] Takehisa Kosugi, in correspondence with the author, July 2010.

or actions to sound', with the description 'performs a movement to the shape of each letter', embodying Kosugi's view of music and action as a totality.

The score continues with five options for combining the indicated sounds and actions in a performance, suggesting how they could relate to each other. The first three options specify ways to realise each letter, as single, repeated, or simultaneous events. The first option is to give a 'single performance of each letter either with sound or action'. When compared with the second option, 'multiple performance of each letter by single performer as sound or action', the first option appears to imply that the performer should work through the letters in sequence before repeating any of them.

The second option suggests a letter could be repeated before moving to the next. It is the only place in the three versions of *South* that specifies the number of performers; it is possible that the multiple articulations of each letter could occur simultaneously by more than one performer if this was not stated. The third option complicates this however, by giving the possibility of a 'simultaneous performance of S with H, O with S, U with O, T with U, H with T'. The score does not prohibit a realisation by more than one performer for this option, which may result in a duo, or a single performer realising the piece through a combination of sounds and/or actions.

The final two options specify how each letter should be connected. Option four suggests a 'continuous performance with S following H [immediately]', such that the letters might be joined through a series of connected actions or sounds. Option five is for an 'interrupted performance with a pause between each letter', resulting in a series of discrete events.

There are three types of instruction for realising the sounds and actions which are specified at the beginning of the score. The numbered options one, two and three state the ordering and combination of events; options four and five state the way they are connected; and the final instruction in the score states that each option may be repeated. These three types of instruction combine to suggest a framework for a realisation. Kosugi is less prescriptive in his approach to realising the score however, stating: 'I think the text should be read in many ways. Each realization for performance must be different from each other. No standard for realization. No authorization, too.'[8]

---

[8] *Ibid.*

Joseph Kudirka

superstition's willing victim (2007)

Commentary: *superstition's willing victim*

superstition's willing victim

for three or more players

Each player chooses one sound capable of being sustained for at least a short period of time.

Each player chooses one other player, attempting to anticipate both when the other player will start their sound and end their sound, playing their own sound at the same time.

If your chosen player starts their sound before you, you may start your sound later and try to stop at the same time as them. If you start your sound first, you should continue sustaining it until your chosen player enters, trying to stop with them.

If the player you are trying to align with stops their sound first, you may keep sustaining your sound as long as you'd like.

All sounds should overlap at some point. So, if any player has stopped their sound before you've started yours, you should not play.

This process is carried out as many times as there are players, even though all players may not play each time. Your chosen player may be different each time. Naturally, someone must start each time.

Joseph Kudirka
2007

Commentary: *superstition's willing victim*

James Saunders

superstition's willing victim (2007)[1] is part of Joseph Kudirka's *Odd Objects* (2007),[2] a collection of nine solo and group activities. The performance instructions allow for a modular presentation of the constituent pieces, such that they may be presented alone, in sequence as movements, or simultaneously. Kudirka suggests ways in which simultaneity might be organised by presenting 'advice and rules' for doing so. Essentially pieces may be played any number of times, as long as each player only plays a given piece once; otherwise any overlapping is permissible, silence may occur, and any grouping of players may be made.

The aim in *superstition's willing victim* is for players to attempt to play their chosen sounds at the same time. They try to co-ordinate the beginning and end of their sounds with another player. Much of the score considers how to respond when failing to achieve this objective, highlighting its difficulty, the likelihood and acceptance of failure, and the use of a condition to generate resultant forms of activity.[3] Principally, Kudirka gives choices to performers if their sounds do not synchronise. He provides instructions for what to do if the chosen player starts before or after 'you' begin playing, and if the player finishes before 'you'.[4] These are the three situations where players make decisions about their actions.

It is worth highlighting the composer's use of the modals 'may' and 'should' in this respect. Compare the condition, 'If your chosen player starts their sound before you, you may start your sound later and try to stop at the same time as them' with 'If you start your sound first, you should continue sustaining it until your chosen player enters, trying to stop with them'. Here 'may' is used to give permission for or express the possibility of an action: you do not have to start your sound, but you could. Conversely, 'should' indicates an obligation or preference for sustaining the sound and stopping together, but it need not happen. Both sentences present options. Kudirka comments on the difficulties of opening up possibilities in this way, saying:

[1] The title is drawn from the 1935 publication *The Secret Museum of Mankind*, which comprises a series of photographs of people from around the world, described by unusual and often irrelevant or inappropriate captions. Kudirka has used these as a source for titles for a number of pieces. *superstition's willing victim* is drawn from vol. 3, 'The Secret Album of Asia', which can be found at http://ian.macky.net/secretmuseum/page_3.66.html#2 [accessed 1 September 2010].

[2] *Odd Objects* was published in the journal *Antennae*, no. 10, February 2009.

[3] Compare this with similar situations in Cornelius Cardew's *The Great Learning*, Paragraph 6 (1968–71) (see Fig. 80, p. 149), and Christian Wolff's *Burdocks (section IV)* (1970–1) which both rely on cueing networks. Cardew states, 'In cases of failure to produce a properly "isolated" or "synchronised" sound, there is no limit to the number of attempts that may be made, but there is no obligation to make more than one.' Wolff requires simply that players 'play as simultaneously as possible with the next sound of the player nearest you'.

[4] Kudirka uses the second person, 'you', to convey the instructions to individual performers in the section of the score that explains how to react to the other performers. Elsewhere he uses the third person plural, 'they'.

It requires a certain amount of precision, and it's a different kind of precision than describing a specific thing that you want to have happen. Whereas if it's one thing that the players need to make, described with text, actually I think you have more freedom in the language because they'll get it. You can use more adjectives. You can use more descriptive language. This language isn't descriptive. It's hard, because a lot of the words needed are generally not that precise. And I don't always know what people are going to think.[5]

As with much of Kudirka's work, there is openness in this piece with regard to some of the choices made by the performers. This openness is also apparent in Kudirka's use of adjuncts. For example, the phrase 'at least a short period of time' encourages the performers to consider what an appropriate duration might be, both for the chosen sounds and corresponding-ly for all aspects of the piece. The adjective 'short' does not have a fixed duration, and this indeterminacy is compounded by the adjunct 'at least'. Kudirka does not specify a measured duration: this would fix these relation-ships and reduce the subjectivity of a performer's response to the score. He explains this situation, saying:

I think I'm trying to get the precision to effectively carry out the piece through an interaction with the score. And sometimes to do that effec-tively, I think certain things have to become ambiguous within the score. So there are kind of crossing streams of precision and ambiguity. And sometimes things get added because I think, you know, I could go through this notation and I could do 'this thing'. And then I realise 'this thing' isn't the piece I want. What do I have to add to make it clear that it's 'this thing' and not 'that thing' you have to do? But generally it is about removal and subtraction from a definite way to make one version of the piece, in order to figure out what is essential to the piece and what opens up the most versions of the piece possible.[6]

The duration of the piece is also determined by the number of players in the ensemble. This too is a common feature in Kudirka's music. For example, in *Stuck 2004*, 'An action consists of each player sounding one note [...] at a time of their choosing, until all have played. This action is performed as many times as there are players', while in *Beauty and Industry* (2007), 'A performance of the piece is as many minutes long as there are players'. Kudirka explains the reason for this in relation to *Beauty and Industry*:

Listening might be a part of it, but I think what it really does is focus. There's something you have to think about every time you're rehearsing it. [...] If you have 10 players you're doing the 10-minute version that day,

5 Joseph Kudirka, in interview with the author, Huddersfield, 21 November 2009.
6 *Ibid.*

and then the 11 the next day. But it's also a kind of level of difficulty: you can't just miss a part out. If you miss a part, you're changing everything. So it changes the focus every time. [...] But it's also to do with the idea of 'portability'. You can think of it in terms of [...] picking it up and changing, but also this newer conception of digital portability. You can port this to other things.[7]

In *superstition's willing victim*, the choice of sound and manner of its production will determine much of the interaction between performers in the piece. If a clear action is required to start or end a sound (for example, striking and damping a bell, or bowing a cello), then it is relatively straight-forward to determine the point at which this might happen momentarily in advance. If however, the production of a sound involves a concealed action (for example, blowing through a low-pressure wind instrument such as a recorder, or where the action was not otherwise visible), then it is more of a challenge to synchronise the actions. So while any sound capable of being sustained for a short period of time is permissible, many possibilities create challenges when realising the piece. This is a central (and often unstated) concern in much music that contains elements of indeterminacy. Kudirka notes this, explaining that:

An important distinction which isn't spelled out often is that the 'x equals anything' which is often the case [...] isn't a case of 'x equals anything of everything which might be possible'. 'x equals anything, but not every-thing'. So when there's that openness there, and in my pieces, it's not that everything would work. It's not that every choice you could possibly make would work. Because there's this importance that it's taken into consid-eration and you find out what is going to work and there's maybe an infinite number of possibilities, but an infinite set can still exclude things from itself. [...] I think it's also an acknowledgement that I try to make that other people are really great at things that I'm not. People can do things, especially players, like really good instrumentalists, that not only I wouldn't think of, that other composers haven't thought of that these people come up with. And I think it's ridiculous to wait for a composer to talk to this one player and say, 'Oh, yeah, you've come up with that, and that's not in a piece anywhere – we'll have to make a piece out of that.' Why not give them a piece where if this thing that they do works, they can do it?[8]

This reliance on performer interpretation and contingency is central to the way the piece operates. After determining cueing players, it is likely that complex networks of players will result, although their constituency may be unknown to the group and subject to change between sequences. In larger

---

[7] *Ibid.*

[8] *Ibid.*

ensembles, the possibility of disconnected groups of mutually cueing players may emerge, although in many cases there will be at least one unilateral relationship which connects players to form a single group. Either way, the result of the rule system outlined in the score is a series of sounding and silent phases.

Sol LeWitt

Wall Drawing #960 (2001)

Wall Drawings

Doing Wall Drawings

CERTIFICATE

This is to certify that the Sol LeWitt wall drawing

number ___960___ evidenced by this certificate is authentic.

Wall Drawing #960
A straight line about 18"(45.7 cm) long is drawn; from
its midpoint, another line about 18"(45.7 cm) long;
from the midpoint of each subsequent line, another
line 18"(45.7 cm) long, uniformly dispersed covering
the entire surface of the wall.

Black marker
First Drawn By: William T. Clattenburg,
Justin Detwiler, Alexander K. Drinker, Kyle Ferguson,
Daniel C. Gargan, Daniel Kucer,
Jeffrey A. Larentowicz, Jeffrey S. Miller,
Michael C. Schantz
First Installation: Chestnut Hill Academy,
Philadelphia, PA
February, 2001

This certification is the signature for the wall drawing and must
accompany the wall drawing if it is sold or otherwise transferred.

Certified by _____
                              Sol LeWitt

100 *Bryan Eccleshall realising Sol LeWitt*, Wall Drawing #960 *at Site Gallery, Sheffield, May 2010.*

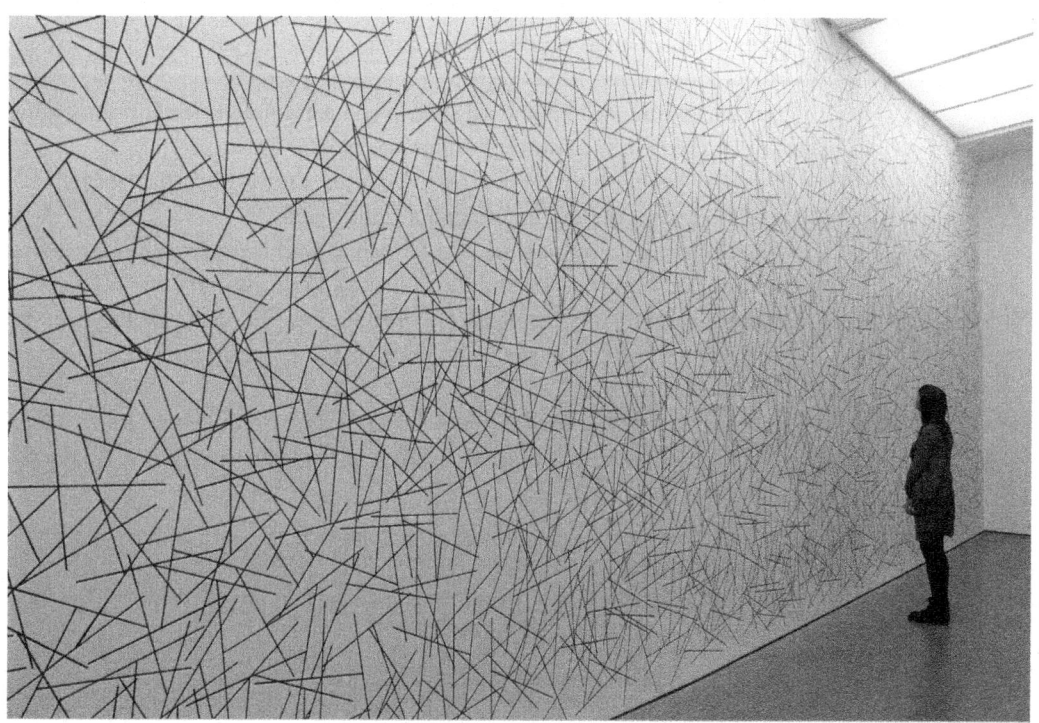

101 *Sol LeWitt*, Wall Drawing #960, *realised by Bryan Eccleshall and David McNab, Site Gallery, Sheffield, May 2010.*

Wall Drawings

Sol LeWitt, 1970

I wanted to do a work of art that was as two-dimensional as possible.

It seems more natural to work directly on walls than to make a construction, to work on that, and then put the construction on the wall.

The physical properties of the wall: height, length, color, material, and architectural conditions and intrusions, are a necessary part of the wall drawings.

Different kinds of walls make for different kinds of drawings.

Imperfections on the wall surface are occasionally apparent after the drawing is completed. These should be considered a part of the wall drawing.

The best surface to draw on is plaster, the worst is brick, but both have been used.

Most walls have holes, cracks, bumps, grease marks, are not level or square, and have various architectural eccentricities.

The handicap in using walls is that the artist is at the mercy of the architect.

The drawing is done rather lightly, using hard graphite so that the lines become, as much as possible, a part of the wall surface, visually.

Either the entire wall or a portion is used, but the dimensions of the wall and its surface have a considerable effect on the outcome.

When large walls are used the viewer would see the drawings in sections sequentially, and not the wall as a whole.

Different draftsmen produce lines darker or lighter and closer or farther apart. As long as they are consistent there is no preference.

Various combinations of black lines produce different tonalities; combinations of colored lines produce different colors.

The four basic kinds of straight lines used are vertical, horizontal, 45° diagonal left to right, and 45° diagonal right to left.

When color drawings are done, a flat white wall is preferable. The colors are yellow, red, blue, and black, the colors used in printing.

When a drawing is done using only black lines, the same tonality should be maintained throughout the plane in order to maintain the integrity of the wall surface.

An ink drawing is a plan for but not a reproduction of the wall drawing; the wall drawing is not a reproduction of the ink drawing. Each is equally important.

It is possible to think of the sides of simple three-dimensional objects as walls and draw on them.

The wall drawing is a permanent installation, until destroyed. Once something is done, it cannot be undone.

Doing Wall Drawings

Sol LeWitt, 1971

The artist conceives and plans the wall drawing. It is realized by draftsmen (the artist can act as his own draftsman); the plan (written, spoken or drawn) is interpreted by the draftsman.

There are decisions that the draftsman makes, within the plan, as part of the plan. Each individual, being unique, if given the same instructions would understand them differently and would carry them out differently.

The artist must allow various interpretations of his plan. The draftsman perceives the artist's plan, then reorders it to his experience and understanding.

The draftsman's contributions are unforeseen by the artist, even if he, the artist, is the draftsman. Even if the same draftsman followed the same plan twice, there would be two different works of art. No one can do the same thing twice.

The artist and the draftsman become collaborators in making the art.

Each person draws a line differently and each person understands words differently.

Neither lines nor words are ideas, they are the means by which ideas are conveyed.

The wall drawing is the artist's art, as long as the plan is not violated. If it is, then the draftsman becomes the artist and the drawing would be his work of art, but art that is a parody of the original concept.

The draftsman may make errors in following the plan. All wall drawings contain errors, they are part of the work.

The plan exists as an idea but needs to be put into its optimum form. Ideas of wall drawings alone are contradictions of the idea of wall drawings.

The explicit plan should accompany the finished wall drawing. They are of equal importance.

Annea Lockwood

From the River Archive (1973)

Statement

From the River Archive

Annea Lockwood

Find a brook or fast flowing river in as isolated a place as you can reach. Placing the microphone(s) near the surface at a spot where the water is creating a richly textured sound, make a tape recording at least a half-hour long. Note the name of the river, the place and date.

Play the tape back on a cassette recorder, in some public place, for one person at a time, (using headphones). Turn the listener's head very gently from side to side, tilted towards one shoulder, then towards the other as he or she is listening. Suggest that the listener closes his or her eyes to listen. Tell each other personal experiences with rivers/brooks/etc; dreams involving them; memories.

*   *   *   *

Find a place at which a river is passing through rocks or over logs, gently (i.e. not white water).

Search out every layer of the sounds the water is making until you can hear the whole intricate texture, until the river is flowing through your body.

Stay there from sunrise to night, or from sunset until dawn.

*   *   *   *

Choose a place where the river cascades through falls, over a weir, through a gorge or canyon, so that the sound approaches white noise.

Stay there all day, letting the sound change you and aware of those changes.

*   *   *   *

Statement

Annea Lockwood, 2010

Verbal notation has been a resource throughout my work. I use it to score pieces for which even graphic notation is too indirect: as in *Duende* (1998), a work for voice and pre-recorded sound composed with Thomas Buckner, in which the vocal part is formed from selected extended vocal techniques. The entire score is verbal and descriptive, for example:

> [At] 2:00   [shout] 'shaoh shayee' then in/out sighing leads to changing mouth shapes
> Goes to low tones w. lip buzzes and changing mouth shapes.
> Goes to brief yodelling w. tongue moving back and forth, voice placed front to back, changing formant from 'oo' to 'ee'
> 9:03   Tape gliss. Again

A common practice has been to devise symbols for such sounds, but an explanatory 'key' is always needed, adding another layer of information. Instead, Thomas Buckner underlines key words such as 'lip buzzes' but finds the complete text useful too. The emphasis is on clarity and concision.

I also use verbal notation to draw people into a listening activity, as with *From the River Archive*. Here, for me, the challenge lies in finding a balance between suggesting a focus and leaving the experience open, but possibly diffuse and generic. I think of it as 'enticing' rather than 'instructing' and have long admired the concision and openness of Yoko Ono's text pieces and of Pauline Oliveros' *Sonic Meditations*.

Alvin Lucier

Music on a Long Thin Wire (1977)

Notes on Verbal Notation

Realising Music on a Long Thin Wire

Music on a Long Thin Wire

for audio oscillator and electronic monochord

Extend a long metal wire (#1 music wire or equivalent) across or lengthwise down a performance space. Affix both ends to the far edges of the tops of tables or other similar platforms and tighten them with clamps, hanging weights over pulleys, or other tension-creating devices. Route the ends of the wire to the outputs of an amplifier, forming a current-carrying loop. Insert wood, metal, or other resonant bridges under the wire at both ends. Set a large magnet down on the table at one end of the wire; adjust the height of the wire so that it passes directly between the poles of the magnet. Attach microphones to the bridges and route them through amplifiers to loudspeakers.

Drive the wire with a sine wave oscillator, causing it to vibrate from the interaction between the current in the wire and the magnetic field across it, in ways determined by the frequencies and amplitudes of the driving signals and the length, size, weight, and tension of the wire. Design musical performances consisting of a series of any number of phrases which explore the acoustic properties of a single vibrating wire. Before each phrase, silently and freely choose a single oscillator frequency which will remain constant for the duration of that phrase. Within each phrase, however, raise and lower the volume controls of either the oscillator or the amplifier or a combination of both, in slow scanning patterns, causing the size of the excursions of the vibrating wire to vary, altering the tension of the wire accordingly, producing nodal shifts, echo trains, noisy overdrivings, rhythmic figures at low frequencies, phase-related time lags, simple and complex harmonic structures, larger self-generative cyclic patterns, stops and starts, and other audible and visible phenomena. At the end of each phrase, the length of which is determined by the nature of the sonic material in that phrase, reduce the volume to zero in order to silently retune the oscillator frequency for the next phrase.

Pick up the sounds of the vibrating wire with the microphones on the resonant bridges and amplify them for stereophonic listening through loudspeakers. Light the wire so that the modes of vibration are visible to viewers.

Commissioned by the Crane School of Music, State University College at Potsdam, New York, for the Live Electronic Music Ensemble, Donald Funes, Director.

Alvin Lucier, 1977

Notes on Verbal Notation

Alvin Lucier, 19 May 2010

4'33"

There are several kinds of verbal notation. There's the kind that gives more or less accurate instructions to the performers. Others are merely suggestive or poetic. They are often unperformable and merely present an idea to ponder.

Sometimes a prose score may begin as a set of specific instructions, then ramify to something more general. The score of John Cage's *4'33"* is first rather specific, furnishing the performer with exact timings. But then it becomes general with Cage's statement: 'The work may be performed by (any) instrumentalist or combination of instrumentalists and last any length of time.' The specific version, particularly as played by David Tudor, is a sure-fire concert work; the more general version is less focused and may be in danger of boredom, particularly if it has no time limitation. Both versions are meant to focus the listener to the surrounding sounds of the environment. The specific version helps the listener; the general leaves him or her up to his or her self.

Stones

Most verbal scores are by their very nature indeterminate. They often come into existence because the music or action cannot be notated graphically or by conventional notation. Performers have to be careful not to impose ideas about structure on a work that does not suggest one. In Christian Wolff's prose score *Stones*, for example, the players are simply asked to make sounds with stones. There is no mention of timing, structure or interrelatedness among the players. Every once in a while a performer will suggest moving the sounds across the room in the shape of a mandala or other such formal arrangement. The openness of the score lures players to be overly creative, to bring in their own ideas. Christian simply wants the sounds to be scattered, each player playing separately, not reacting consciously to another player, no eye contact, and no visual or sonic cueing. There is nothing in the score that asks players to superimpose their own ideas on the performance. Performance of *Stones* reminds me of the complex sound situations of localized bio-systems.

Vespers

The reason I wrote a prose score for *Vespers* (1970) was because basically the work is about the articulation of a given space. And since I never know much about a space before I get into it I have no way of choreographing the players' movements to certain points in space or indicate speeding up and slowing down the pulses emitted by their handheld pulse wave oscillators.

Nor would I wish to impose a grid of any kind upon a real-time exploration of an acoustic space. The score specifies a task to be accomplished, not a composer's idea of a fixed object. One would miss so much of the room's sound by the presence of specific instructions. There would be no way to pin down the variables. Nor would I want to pin them down. They change themselves as the performance progresses. The work is not site-specific. It's meant to be an exploration of any room.

Realising *Music on a Long Thin Wire*

Hauke Harder in correspondence with John Lely, Summer 2010

John Lely: How did you first become involved with Music on a Long Thin Wire?

Hauke Harder: In 1989, together with the visual artist Rainer Grodnick, I founded an organisation called Gesellschaft für akustische Lebenshilfe in Kiel, northern Germany. During the 1990s we organised several activities in contemporary arts, with a strong focus on contemporary music. From time to time we collaborated with Knut Nievers from the local gallery, who in turn invited us to curate a show in his house. *Music on a Long Thin Wire* was considered for that show from the beginning, since the building had a gallery formed as a 50 m quarter circle and the wire seemed to fit there very well. The exhibition changed its concept and finally turned into a Lucier show. *Music on a Long Thin Wire* was presented, as well as other sound installations, concerts and talks.

John Lely: How much of your experience comes from working with the score, and how much comes from working with Alvin Lucier himself?

Hauke Harder: When I invited Alvin, I knew the score, the CD and probably a photo, so I knew that it should work well in the space. I hadn't seen the installation live. Since Alvin was coming himself, I just followed his instructions. He brought most of the necessary material, while I organised tables, mixers, amplifiers and speakers. He showed me how to set it up. We installed it like this: two tables were placed in the gallery facing each other. The position allowed a long version of 35 m, but left enough space for people to walk around the installation. The wire was fixed with clamps to the outer edges of the tables; bridges with contact microphones were inserted under the wire on both tables. On one table a magnet was placed with the wire positioned between the two poles. The two ends of the wire were routed to a power amplifier, which amplified the signal of a sine wave generator. The interaction of magnetic field and electric current made the wire vibrate. The resulting sound of the wire was picked up on each side with the microphones attached to the bridges and was amplified using mixers and conventional amplifiers and two speakers on each side.

Since the show was running for six weeks, I went there several times to tune the wire and so I learned quite a lot about the work. Before Alvin returned to the US, he asked me if I would like to keep his magnet, so that I could set up the work for him in Europe. From that time on I just went on installing it in the way I had learned from Alvin, adjusting to the characteristics of the space.

104 *Alvin Lucier's* Music on a Long Thin Wire (1977), *at Stadtgalerie Kiel, 1995.*

John Lely: What are the physical principles at work in Music on a Long Thin Wire?

Hauke Harder: The basic principle to make the wire vibrate is that an electric charge moving in a magnetic field undergoes a force changing the direction of the movement, the so called 'Lorentz force', something people have probably learned in school in connection with the 'right-hand rule' mnemonic, which relates to the working principle behind most loudspeakers, cathode ray tubes, and so on. In *Music on a Long Thin Wire* an electric sine wave signal is fed into the wire, which is placed between the two poles of a magnet. Due to the change of the direction of the electric current, the resulting force on the wire changes direction and makes it vibrate. The force is perpendicular to the plane formed by the direction of the magnetic field and the movement of the current. Because with the magnets we use the magnetic field is parallel to the floor, the wire in this case tends to vibrate up and down.

John Lely: From a technical perspective, there are a number of elements that Alvin deliberately keeps very general in the score: the type and length of wire, what sort of magnet to use, and so on. Why do you think this is?

Hauke Harder: In my experience Alvin keeps his scores quite open since he is interested in the exploration of a special acoustical phenomenon and he accepts different approaches to arrive at an interesting result. He once said: 'I have to decide whether to write them [scores] in a practical way, making them easier to distribute and perform, or in a more general or visionary way, emphasizing the ideas behind the pieces.'[1] The score of *Music on a Long Thin Wire* refers to that generality, to that concept, and allows for ongoing research. The pieces take shape with the experience of various realisations, and Alvin often omits several possibilities that the score suggests when he performs or installs a work by himself. I believe it is important to take into account his experience rather than following the score, at least for some pieces. Only then do you get close to what the piece

105 Music on a Long Thin Wire *at Stadtgalerie Kiel, 1995.*

[1] Lucier, 1995, p. 192.

is really about. I would always suggest this as the starting point. When he started to work on the piece, the wire was rather short and he was performing the piece by lowering and raising the volume of the oscillator, driven at a fixed frequency for a single phrase. But after a few attempts he omitted this possibility, since he found out that the wire, if carefully tuned, undergoes marvellous changes by itself or by minimal changes in the surroundings. He found this 'doing by itself' much more interesting than any performance would allow. So he abandoned the possibility of performances, even though it is mentioned in the score, and now presents the work exclusively as an installation.

If Alvin had written a practical score with all details, we would be stuck with one type of realisation that he himself didn't find completely satisfying in the end. In this ongoing research, the wire is nowadays stretched to lengths that seemed to be completely impossible at the beginning, and this allows the use of new technologies as they are achieved, for example in the material sciences.

John Lely: What do you think are the characteristics of a successful realisation?

Hauke Harder: A successful realisation is one where the wire undergoes significant changes by itself, resulting in various acoustical phenomena, like beating patterns, the sudden occurrence of complex harmonies, and so on. I believe Daniel Wolf has correctly described that the step from a short wire to a long wire goes hand-in-hand with the move from linear to non-linear physics or deterministic chaos[2] which can also be found in other works by Lucier. I would consider this as the main principle behind the piece, besides that mentioned before.

The set-up is obviously an example of non-linear physics with two vibrating systems. The interaction of the electric current and magnetic field makes the wire vibrate, but the frequency of the driving force (the frequency of the sine wave) and the frequencies of natural harmonics of the wire might differ. Depending on the set-up, the wire might vibrate either quite regularly or chaotically. If the wire is short, it behaves quite regularly. Thus the possible complexity is achieved by more than the combination of two vibrating systems. It seems that only Alvin's choice of a long wire leads to this behaviour. When I was visiting a workshop on Zither manufacturing, someone explained the properties of a thin string. An instrument is built with rather thin strings or with low tension in the strings in order to obtain a rich sound with lots of harmonics. This is exactly what is needed for *Music on a Long Thin Wire*.

Thus, with a long, thin wire, one is able to find a tuning of the wire such that the vibration develops and alters over time, sometimes with sudden changes, and several acoustical phenomena are audible. Let us call this for simplicity 'chaotic behaviour'. This chaotic behaviour might

---

[2] Wolf, D., 'A Composer in the Gallery' in Harder and Nievers, 1995, p. 17.

be quite different for each installation, but there are similarities often overlooked.

For this purpose, I would like to characterise some set-ups. There is the set-up where you haven't reached the chaotic behaviour. In such installations, one basically hears a sound similar to a sine wave or drone, with just a few harmonics changing from time to time. This is musically not very interesting and in my opinion in this case the crucial aim of *Music on a Long Thin Wire* has not been achieved.

Then there are set-ups which show chaotic behaviour. Some of them may produce a very rich sound. However, probably because of the richness of the sound, the listener may not experience or focus on changes in the system and may not stay attentive for a long period. The most interesting set-ups are those where the wire undergoes significant changes and this often happens in a regular way. This is quite typical for non-linear physics.

In my experience of *Music on a Long Thin Wire*, the wire, let's say, is at first quite silent, one or more harmonics become more and more vivid and suddenly the wire breaks into complex harmonies, then returns to near silence, starting another cycle. Other acoustical phenomena may happen within these cycles. Thus the wire might undergo cycles, but they may change more or less with each cycle and after a long time the wire may tend to find an equilibrium, where it is rather silent (probably after some hours).

This behaviour is what I am aiming at when I install the work and I have experienced it with most of the (successful) set-ups. As an example we can take track three on the CD released by Lovely Music.[3] In the beginning the cycles are very short. A short sound like a drone or sine wave (only a few seconds) is immediately followed by a very vivid sound with complex harmonies for about one minute. But towards the end of the track the cycles get significantly longer (a few minutes) and less vivid. If we consider track one, the cycles are not (so) obvious, and it seems the wire changes all the time without going through these cycles. I believe this is probably the most interesting result but also the most difficult to achieve.

Only set-ups with these changes, more or less dramatic, are musically interesting. But they are not easily achieved even with the right equipment since tension, tuning and the strength of the interacting force must all fit together and sometimes it just takes time and patience to get to this point.

An increase in tension would cause a normal string to sound a bit higher, but for these long wires a small change might lead to a totally different characteristic. Once when I installed the wire in Hamburg, the tables were placed on a wooden floor and below one of them was the sinewave oscillator. Thus to change the frequency I had to step close to the table. This movement on the wooden floor changed the tension of the wire in such a way that it simply stopped sounding. When I stepped back it sounded again. Alvin has described an installation in Kyoto where the wire was installed in a dance studio with a wooden floor and where the movements of the visitors lead to

---

[3] Lucier, A., *Music on a Long Thin Wire*, Lovely Music CD 1011, 1980/92.

wonderful changes in sound. This sensitivity to a change in tension is surely the main reason that the system responds to the surroundings.

John Lely: Have you found what you would consider an optimal set-up? For instance, is there an optimal length? What kind of mistakes might someone make in setting it up?

Hauke Harder: My experience might be different from other people who set up or have set up *Music on a Long Thin Wire*. Thus, opinions about an optimal set-up might differ. Two things seem to be relevant to producing an optimal set-up: the dimensions and tension of the wire and the strength of the interacting (Lorentz) force. My experiences are based on (steel) music wire with a diameter of 0.25–0.3 mm. Typically I use a 200 W mono signal (referring to an impedance of 8 Ohms, the power when the wire is driven is significantly lower) and a magnetic field around 200 mT from a horse-shoe magnet (alternatively I use rare earth magnets which are slightly stronger). The amplifier has to be driven near maximum power, the one I use is clipping or close to clipping.

With this kind of set-up I have been able to get the chaotic behaviour and thus interesting musical results in a range of around 20 to 40 m, though in fact for some versions I don't know how much power the amplifiers actually had. Significantly below 20 m most of the versions didn't work perfectly for me. It seemed more difficult to tune the wire to obtain the ongoing but regular changes in the movement of the wire and to get the sudden complex harmonies. From this, my guess was that the diameter at these lengths should be smaller, around 0.2 mm, but first attempts at around 11 m length have not yet proved promising. I have only set up a significantly longer version once, the longest so far, with 65 m. In this case I faced a completely different problem. Due to the length of the wire, the resistance was so high that an enormously strong amplifier was needed. So I ordered one, but the protection system didn't allow the amplifier to reach the requested power level and we had to test a different one, which finally worked. To avoid problems at very high powers, I would tend to work with thicker wires above 40 m, probably with a diameter of 0.35 or 0.4 mm or with material other than steel.

Something I haven't mentioned yet, which is also important, is that these results are based on a tension of the wire that can easily achieved by hand, thus not being very high, but also not too low (when the wire would probably also stick to the magnet).

Based on these experiences I consider a range of 15–50 m as a good length of wire to work with, completely contradicting the statement in Alvin's book *Chambers* from 1980, where a possible maximum length of 11 m (36 feet) is mentioned.[4] Things and opinions have changed a lot! Nevertheless I believe it might just be a matter of what equipment is used, and I am sure an optimal set-up depends on the length chosen. Difficulties are different for shorter and longer versions, thus mistakes might be of a quite different nature. I believe

---

[4] Lucier and Simon, 1980, p. 164.

a thorough investigation of set-ups using different material at various lengths might be very helpful to clarify some of these aspects and I am planning this for the future. In any case, for visual reasons I prefer lengths of more than 15 m.

It might be useful to discuss the interaction which makes the wire vibrate. The Lorentz force is proportional to the magnetic field and the square root of the electric power. As previously mentioned, I am typically using a 200 W (8 Ohms) mono signal and a magnetic field of around 200 mT. Only very strong magnets reach this value and it is difficult to get this strength without using magnets made of rare earth elements. It is necessary to compensate for a significantly weaker magnetic field with higher electric power, which needs to increase by a power of two, and you could easily end up with 1000 W amplifiers. This can be dangerous and the use of such high power levels and voltages is not to be recommended without a strong technical background. Thus a strong magnet is important.

So, the mistakes that could be made are manifold and I hope this discussion may help in the avoidance of some of them. However, even with the right equipment it takes time to tune the wire and experience is very helpful. When I say 'to tune', this incorporates more aspects than just changing the frequency (which is typically between 50 and 150 Hz), though that might be the most important part. It includes also varying the amplitude of the sine wave and, if necessary, changing the tension of the wire and the positions of the magnet and the bridges.

As mentioned before, the wire tends to reach a musically less interesting state of equilibrium. Since the system responds strongly to any minor change there will probably be an interesting sound after a new adjustment, but the question is how fast will it reach the equilibrium, i.e. how long will it stay interesting? One has to listen carefully to its development for an extended period. Once you have found a good tuning for which the wire has been quite vivid, even if the wire reached a state of equilibrium at a certain point, it might return to its vivid state by small changes in its surroundings. These are mysterious moments.

When I install the work, I generally schedule two days. The first day is basically for the setting up of the technical equipment and the second for the tuning. It could be done within one day, but one never knows how the wire will respond or what problems will occur.

John Lely: The work is nowadays presented as a long-term installation. Can you describe how installations have differed?

Hauke Harder: As I mentioned before, the musical result depends on many factors, so it's difficult to say, for example, a short version will sound like this and a longer version like that. If you compare the tracks on the CD, though they are from the same set-up, they sound quite different, due to the chosen tuning. I would like to give two examples in order to emphasise one important aspect. After years of setting up the wire, it became more and more clear to me that there was a regularity in the changes of the wire and that this regularity – the cycles were quite stable – meant the changes in sound were found mainly within the system, rather than being due to sensitivity to the surroundings. This seems counter-intuitive, and you often see people blowing at the wire and then wondering why it doesn't change sound.

For me, the ultimate test was an installation I realised with Winfried Ritsch at Schloss Kalsdorf, Austria, where the wire was stretched across the inner courtyard of the castle. At a certain point it started raining and raindrops were falling on the wire. However, the changes in the general sound of the wire, its development, seemed to be unaltered. It remained similar to during the period before it started raining, except for the extra pizzicato-like sounds from the raindrops. Thus, so long as the main features, such as tension and amplitude and frequency of the sine wave, are unchanged the system can remain quite stable.

However, the surroundings can easily change the tension of the wire (temperature, steps on the floor...) and sometimes this leads to a sublime change in sound, as happened with the longest version so far, in Milwaukee. Alvin was invited by Joe Ketner to present the wire at Milwaukee Arts Museum, where it could be stretched to a length of 65 m. Once the known technical problems were solved, it sounded wonderful and was at its most beautiful in the late afternoon. The wire was stretched along one of the corridors of the museum's Santiago Calatrava wing with a continuous glass wall running the length of the corridor. In the afternoon the sun shone on the wire and it is probable that the sunshine brought a slight change to the system, resulting in a marvellous, rich sound.

John Lely: In the score Alvin writes, 'light the wire so that the modes of vibration are visible to viewers', and elsewhere he mentions placing coloured beads on the wire to reveal the nodal patterns. What has been your approach to the visual presentation of Music on a Long Thin Wire? *Do you regard it as an important aspect of the work?*

106 Music on a Long Thin Wire *at Milwaukee Arts Museum, 2006.*

Hauke Harder: I regard the visual as an important, if not very important aspect of the work. However, things have changed in this regard. Nowadays Alvin is less interested in special lighting and I believe this is because the piece is now presented as an installation, where you can more easily watch the wire vibrating than in a performance situation. Furthermore, the set-up itself – stripped down to its simplest form – already has strong visual qualities. There is the wire, as Alvin once mentioned, making

107 Music on a Long Thin Wire *at Schloss Kalsdorf, 2008*.

one line in space, like a drawing, and the set-up has sculptural qualities, once you pay attention to the equipment used and the setting. Alvin brought perfectly made bridges and special excentre clamps for fixing the wire. I prefer hi-fi equipment to PA equipment since it often looks better and is mostly in better condition.

The normal set-up uses two tables of the same type and Alvin once said: 'I would clamp the ends of the wire to tables that I found in whatever place I was setting up. I didn't want to make tables or bring them along with me. I wanted to find them.'[5] By this 'finding' you can adapt visually to the space. When I installed the wire in Kiel, I found the most appropriate tables in the laboratories of my physical chemistry department. They were workshop tables and the department kindly offered to refurbish them. In Milwaukee I was asked to buy tables, so we drove to many stores but I couldn't find anything reasonable. Then I walked through the workshop and offices of the museum and found a type that really worked well.

For me, the tables, together with the wire stretched from one side to the other, make you aware of the architecture, define the space, and so I prefer this set-up. I believe it is for this reason that we avoid diagonal versions, even though they might be a little longer.

However, other interesting versions have also been realised. In Ghent, Belgium, the wire was placed in the restaurant of the Handelsbeurs, which was also used as a concert hall. Due to this double function, the wire had to be at a height above the visitors. The space had a window front with a view of a canal. In front of this was a steel pillar to which one of the platforms, the one with the magnet, could be fixed. It was a wonderful combination: the window front with the canal, and the wire and magnet at around 3 m height.

John Lely: *In what ways has your experience of Alvin's work informed your own practice?*

Hauke Harder: My decision to start composing was strongly motivated by my knowledge of American experimental music. In the beginning I was influenced by the work of John Cage and Morton Feldman and I didn't pay so much attention to the subsequent generations. But this changed over the years. Especially due to my friendship with Daniel Wolf, a former student of Alvin, I became more and more attracted by Alvin's work and this of course grew stronger when I started working for him. I admire his way of clarifying things, the way he is practical in realising things, his honesty and modesty and I love his humour, to mention just a few things. He and his work are an orientation and encouragement 'to stay the course' – as he would say – and I still regard it as a wonderful gift that he asked me to work for him.

[5] Lucier, 1995, p. 526.

George Maciunas

In Memoriam to Adriano Olivetti (1962)

Commentary: *In Memoriam to Adriano Olivetti*

108 *George Maciunas*, In Memoriam to Adriano Olivetti *(1962), original version, 20 March 1962. Overleaf*

IN MEMORIAM to ADRIANO
OLIVETTI

by George Maciunas
                    March 20, 1962

Any used tape from an
Olivetti adding machine
may be used as a score
for this piece.

Tempo
Preferably fast (1 to 3
beats per second) and
regular. A conductor may
direct the group if
necessary.

Zero
Stands for silence or
lack of action of one
beat.

Blank Space
Instead of row stands for
silence of one beat.

Each horizontal row must
be performed simultane-
ously.

Performance Variations
Variation no. 1:
Each performer pronounces
one vertical row of num-
bers in any language he
wishes. All pronounce
horizontal rows simulta-
neously in even tempo and
voice.
Variation no. 2:
Each number represents a
pitch sounded on chordo-
phones, aerophones,
membranophones or voices.
Variation no. 3:
Each number represents a
sound or soundless action
as for example:
No. 1 scratching any
       material
    2 sniffing wet nose

3 smacking lips
4 clearing throat or
   lungering
5 creaking chair,
   door etc.
6 ripping (fast or
   slow) paper
7 drop of water into
   pail
8 shake foot
9 shake coins in
   pocket
Other sounds or actions
may be substituted to
obtain louder, softer
more or less dense sounds

```
              .00 T
X            8.74
X             .02
X             .00
X         17 48 T

             8.74
            17.48
            26 22 T
              .00 T

             8.74
             8.74 T

           874.00
            17.48
           891.48 T
X            8.74
X            1.02
X             .00
X          891.48 T

X             .00 T

X          556.60
X            2.52 -
X             .00
X      140,263.20 TC

            .00 TC

           556.60
             2.50 -
              .02 -
```

```
            47.23 -
           109.41
           616.26 T

           431.06
           616.26 -
           185.20 TC

              .43
              .43 T

           185.20
           118.05 -
            67.15 T

            43.10
            43.10 T

           185.20
           118.05 -
            67.15 -
              .00 T

           431.06
           118.05
            67.05
              .10
           616.26 T

           146.00
            67.15 -
            78.85 T

           280.00
           118.05 -
           161.95 T

            41.41
             3.75 -
            37.66 T

              .06
              .06 T

           266.58
             3.75
            44.57
           314.90 T

           314.90
           266.58 -
            48.32 T
```

Commentary: *In Memoriam to Adriano Olivetti*

James Saunders

In Memoriam to Adriano Olivetti (1962) is a set of instructions for making use of found tape from Olivetti adding machines as performance scores. The digits[1] on the tape are used to represent predetermined sounds or actions. The order of performance events will depend on the specific ordering of numbers on the tapes, so is a simple way of creating a complex and unpredictable set of actions which will be different with every realisation. This is one of George Maciunas' scores from the inaugural period of Fluxus, with the first version dated 20 March 1962. It underwent many subsequent revisions, with each new version containing slightly different instructions and performance information. While the differences have the potential to produce significantly varying results, Philip Corner's observation that, 'I would not give much credence to score instructions – George didn't',[2] implies that, in Corner's view, it is the general conditions of the piece that are of primary importance.

109 *George Maciunas,* In Memoriam to Adriano Olivetti, *performance at Fluxus Festival, Hypockriterion Theater, Amsterdam, 23 June 1963.*

[1] Maciunas refers to 'numbers' in the scores. The current text makes the distinction between a 'digit', which may occur on the printed tape as part of a larger number (e.g. the number 1,465 contains four digits), and 'number' as a reference for the action to be undertaken by the performer.

[2] Philip Corner, in correspondence with the author, July 2010.

110 *George Maciunas,* In Memoriam to Adriano Olivetti *(1962),* ▶
revised version 8 November 1962.

It is, however, worth examining the changes of meaning that result when the instructions are altered.

The original 1962 version outlines the general concept for the piece, that of using adding machine tape as a score (see Fig. 108). It specifies that a zero or blank row represents silence or lack of action, that there is a fast tempo (at 60–180 beats per minute),[3] and that each horizontal row must be performed simultaneously. Each row on the tape represents one beat in performance, with performers reading the tape line by line in time with a conductor.[4] The Performance Variations that follow indicate how performers should articulate the digits found on the tape.

Variation No. 1 assigns a vertical row of digits to each performer, and each digit is pronounced in any language. So using the example tape included with Maciunas' score, the performer reading the right hand column would pronounce the digits in the sequence xx42x8x482 (where 'x' is a rest) on successive beats, and the performer reading the third column would pronounce the digits in the sequence xx8xx7x876. In this version, performers reading left-most columns would pronounce the fewest digits.

Variation No. 2 substitutes pitches, sounded on instruments or sung, for the spoken digits. It maintains the assigning of columns to performers. This also happens in Variation No. 3, where each digit indicates a different action. Maciunas also notes that, 'other sounds or actions may be substituted to obtain louder, softer more or less dense sounds', emphasising the provisional nature of the suggestions included in the score and the latitude to create alternative versions.

The original version of the score differs significantly from the later revisions, as it requires performers to read a particular column and realise each digit in that column. It results in performers needing to realise up to nine digits each as sounds or actions. In comparison, the first revised version from 8 November 1962 states that, 'Numbers (including zero) represent specific sounds or actions, each of which is assigned to separate performer', and again that, 'Each horizontal row is performed simultaneously' (see Fig. 110). Assigning digits rather than columns to performers reduces the complexity of the piece, as each performer only needs to perform a single sound or action. It also reduces the variety found in the original version where, for example, different people performing even a single action, such as 'smacking lips', might produce a range of results. This revision of the score also assigns an action to zero, while maintaining the blank row as a rest for all performers.

---

[3] This tempo is specified differently in other versions, with the November 1962 revision suggesting a 'fast tempo such as 2 regular beats per second', and the 1966 Fluxfest version 'about 100 beats per sec'. (Presumably this is an error!)

[4] Later versions also suggest the use of a metronome.

ny used tape from an Olivetti adding machine may be used as a score for this piece.

PERFORMANCE INSTRUCTIONS

Numbers (including zero) represent specific sounds or actions, each of which is
assigned to separate performer. When performed by fewer than 10 performers, the
unassigned excessive numbers represent silences. Same number can also be assigned
to more than one performer if the tape contains more than one of same number per row.
In such cases the second or third performer performs only when 2nd. or 3rd. of same
number appear on the row.
Each horizontal row is performed simultaneously at preferably fast tempo such as
2 regular beats per second. A conductor or metronome may direct the group if necessary
Blank row represents silence of one beat.

VERSION 1. (poem)
Each performer pronounces his assigned number in any language.

VERSION 2. (ballet) performers to be formally dressed (except no.9,in military uniform
Performers perform the following actions assigned to indicated numbers:
0 - lift bowler hat from head when first 0 is indicated,place on head when next 0 is
    indicated, repeat action for succeeding indications of 0's.
1 - point with finger at someone in the audience (arm outstreched) whenever 1 is
    indicated. Point at different member of audience for each separate indication of 1.
2 - point with finger at ceiling or floor
3 - sit down on a chair when first 3 is indicated, stand up on next indication, etc.
4 - squat down when first 4 is indicated, stand up when next is indicated, etc.
5 - strike floor with cane or umbrella on each indication of 5
6 - open umbrella over head on first indication of 6, close on next, etc.
7 - bow down (towards or away from audience) on first indication of of 7, raise on next
8 - stamp floor with foot on each indication of 8
9 - give military salute with hand on first indication of 9, lower hand on next, etc

VERSION 3. (ballet)
Each performer to use different kind of hat. Perform as in Version 2 (zero)

VERSION 4. (chorale)
0 - smack with lips smartly (sound like drop falling into water) on each indication of 0
1 - smack with tongue (click like opening corcked bottle)
2 - lip-fart (through tight lips)
3 - lip-fart (with tongue between lips)
4 - draw air (upper teeth over lower lips)
5 - draw air, open mouth, vibrate deep throat (pig like sound)
6 - blow air between lips vibrating them
7 - dry spitting
8 - lunger
9 - sniff wet nose (wet nose with water if necessary)

VERSION 5 (string quartet or ensemble)
0 - strike body with mallet or stick
1 - knock against floor (cello) or table (violin)
2 - shake body (have pellet or pellets placed inside beforehand)
3 - with stick scrape edge of sound hole (obtain squeek or screech)
4 - place instrument in playing position and in non-playing position on next called beat
5 - place bow over strings in playing position   ,,   ,,   ,,
6 - (replace beforehand a string with electric heating coil) scrape coil
7 - pluck heating coil
8 - (replace beforehand a string with rubber band)- pluck rubber band smartly
9 - open etuis, close it on next called beat.

VERSION 6 (for string quartet only)
1 - pizzicato C
2 -   ,,   C+$\frac{1}{2}$ (tone)
3 -   ,,   C-$\frac{1}{2}$
4 -   ,,   C $\sharp$

Any sounds or actions of any versions may be combined in any way to form new
versions or new sounds and actions substituted.

EXAMPLE (combined version 2 and 4)   8 performers (1,3,5,6,7,8,9,0)

16387 - point finger,open umbrella,sit on chair,lip-fart(8),bow down
0086 - lift bowler hat,list boater-hat,lip-fart,close umbrella
1057 - point finger elsewhere,place bowler hat on head,draw air(pig-like),raise-up
608   - open umbrella,lift bowler hat,lip-fart
300   - get up from chair,place bowler hat on head,place boater-hat on head.
3798 - sit down on chair,bow down, give military salute,lip fart

etc.

The November 1962 revision also suggests that where a digit appears more than once in a row, other performers may realise the extra occurrences. So if '2' appears three times on a row, such as line 10 of the example which contains 26.22, then two other performers may also realise action/sound '2' alongside the first performer. This implies that all performers read from the same score, because it is only possible to know if the additional articulations are required if the information is common to the whole group. This seems at odds with the evidence presented elsewhere in the score, and in photographic documentation of performances.[5]

Alison Knowles confirms the use of unique tapes by each performer in early performances, and suggests an alternative way to realise repeated numbers. She comments that: 'The scrolls were run off from adding machine rolls. Each was different. The umbrella holder also had her own roll in order to perform the piece, albeit with difficulty [...] Each performer selects a different number and raises his/her hat when that number appears in each line. If the number appears more than once the hat may be raised multiple times.'[6] It is worth noting however that none of the versions explicitly state whether all performers may use the same tape, or whether they each have a different tape. This is partly confused by the use of the words 'tape' and 'ribbon' to indicate a quantity of these materials that does not distinguish plurality.[7]

The revised version of the score also clarifies and expands the variations of the original, renaming them 'versions' and giving them descriptive classifications such as 'poem', 'ballet' or 'chorale'. Version 1 is the same as Variation No.1 in the original, but the others are all different. Each specifies a related range of actions or sounds to be made. Version 2 was frequently performed,[8] and features controlled theatrical actions. Here the digits are assigned to individual performers, associating them with specific, repeated actions, in contrast to the original version, where each performs a variety of actions. Versions 5 and 6 specify an instrumental ensemble and demonstrate the change in density when fewer than ten actions are specified. Both may be performed by a string quartet, which would result in only four sounds per

---

[5] The only exception seems to be where a performer cannot use both hands to hold a roll, such as when operating an umbrella. In a photo of the performance on 23 June 1963 at the Hypokriterion Theatre in Amsterdam, the umbrella performer is reading the tape of the neighbouring performer (see Fig. 109). This is also the case in the Düsseldorf performance on 2 February 1963.

[6] Alison Knowles, in correspondence with the author, July 2010. Knowles refers to Version 3 (ballet), where each performer should 'use a different kind of hat', which is either raised or lowered when performing an action. This is also confirmed by Philip Corner, who states: 'One could not have reproduced a same roll for everyone so they must have been different.' Philip Corner, in correspondence with the author, July 2010.

[7] 'I have a lot of ribbon' and 'I have lots of ribbons' might both indicate the ownership of many individual pieces of ribbon. Only the first sentence allows for a single, very long piece of ribbon however.

[8] Most of the photographs of early performances are seemingly of this version, given the presence of a bowler hat, umbrella, military hat, bowing, etc.

George Maciunas: In memoriam to Adriano Olivetti   Performers follow used adding machine
paper ribbon as a score. Each horizontal line on this
ribbon represents a metronome beat. Each performer
is assigned a number. When his number appears in the
line he performs upon that beat, precisely and sharply.
This version will consist of sharp, short and percussive
lip and tongue sounds only such as clicks, pops,
smacks etc. pronounced into microphones. If microphones
are not available, hunting whistles can be substituted.
Microphones are not necessary if performers are very
proficient in producing loud lip sounds or room is small.
Metronome time about 100 beats per sec.

111 *George Maciunas,* In Memoriam to Adriano Olivetti *(1962), version from Proposed Program for a Fluxfest in Prague (1966).*

version. As the performance instructions indicate, 'the unassigned excessive numbers represent silences', so it is likely that fewer actions or sounds will be made. Maciunas concludes the score by giving an example of how the first six beats of a performance combining Versions 2 and 4 might occur, demonstrating how to apply the final instruction, 'Any sounds or actions of any versions may be combined in any way to form new versions or new sounds and actions substituted.'

One further version of the score has a different status to the previous versions. It is included as part of a *Proposed Program for a Fluxfest in Prague, 1966*[9] (see Fig. 111), and is presented alongside a list of pieces by other Fluxus artists, each of which is accompanied by Maciunas's description of how it is to be performed in the festival. This document does not generally include the original instructions for each piece. The descriptions are not the pieces themselves, but secondary texts that give an insight into the contemporary performance practice of such works. They mostly extend the text of the original score, adding interpretative ideas and focusing on particular aspects of their potential content. A comparison of George Brecht's *Symphony No. 2* (1962) with Maciunas' directions for its performance reveals this change:

Symphony No. 2
(turning)

FLUXVERSION 1
Thick score books are positioned on music stands in front of orchestra members. As soon as conductor begins to turn the pages of his book, orchestra members start turning theirs. The books are leafed either at a different rate or same rate of speed, but always to the last page. (contact microphones on scores?)

[9] Reprinted in Hendricks, 1983, p. 165.

In Memoriam to Adriano Olivetti is included in 'Concert No. 2 – Piano and Chamber Group'. Here the text concisely summarises the instructions presented in the revised version, and fixes the sounds to be used as 'sharp, short and percussive lip and tongue sounds only such as clicks, pops, smacks, etc. pronounced into microphones'. It also notes that the sounds should be articulated 'precisely and sharply'. The description does not alter the original score as much as happens with work by other composers in the programme, but Maciunas nonetheless includes a detailed description of the performance practice, making reference to the practicalities of performing the piece in a particular space.

While the changes made between the different versions of the score do not in general alter its basic premise,[10] they do raise questions about how a performance could be realised. At its heart, *In Memoriam to Adriano Olivetti* provides a method for converting a found sequence of digits into a series of actions or sounds. In the different versions, Maciunas presents a variety of ways to achieve this. Other approaches might also be considered within the framework he proposes however.

[10] A number of other variants appear elsewhere, often scaled to fit the available space on the page or the context of their publication. Another 1966 version appeared in *Film Culture No. 43* (Winter 1966), again as part of anthologised collections of scores by a range of Fluxus artists. Here the text reads: 'Each performer chooses any number from a used adding machine paper roll. Performer performs whenever his number appears in a row. Each row indicates beat of metronome. Possible actions to perform on each appearance of the number: 1. Bowler hats, lifted or lowered. 2. Mouth, lip, tongue sounds. 3. Opening, closing umbrella, etc.' In *Tulane Drama Review*, vol. 10, no. 2 (Winter 1965), a foldout page featuring a photograph of the named performance is captioned with a further variation, principally adding an instruction for the conductor: 'A used Olivetti adding machine paper roll is used as a score. Each performer chooses a number. Metronome beat indicates time of each horizontal row of numbers. Performer performs sharply and exactly on beat whenever his number appears in a row. Version 2: Performed by Fluxorchestra at Carnegie Recital Hall, 1964. Performer raises bowler hat on first appearance of his number and lowers Hat over head on next appearance of his number, raises on 3rd, lowers on 4th, etc. Conductor uses a top hat.'

Benedict Mason

telling, from *outside sight unseen and opened* (1999)

outside sight unseen and opened

find a simple abstract music
that is still telling through
the real illusory or imaginary use of sound

eschewing context consequence
development and artiface
or musicality as we have come to know the term

find things at the extreme edge
or balanced skilfully between
showing another kind of virtuosity and control

be free to develop a personal potential
and expression with the instrument

not 'musicky' music with all its
idiosyncratic parameters
but the sound the instrument makes
and what happens when it
activates and energises the acoustical space

not exercise or study nor 'avant-garde' art piece
but steering a subtle course in between
testing and using what is seen and heard to work

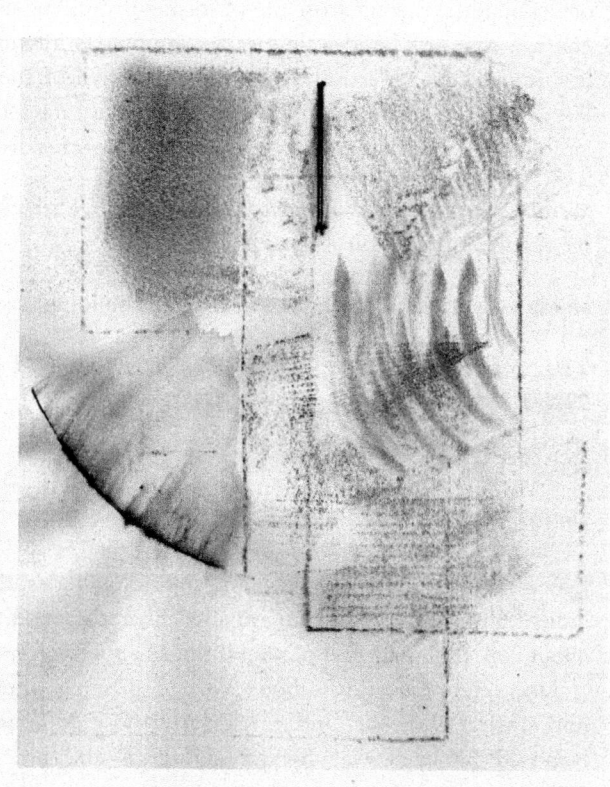

outside sight unseen and opened

Benedict Mason, October 2010

Texts, images, to read, perform and imagine.
Drawings, photographs: Benedict Mason
pencil, wax, charcoal, graphite, coffee, wine on paper.
© 1999 www.benedictmason.com

This is a hand-made, hand-printed book of 130 texts and drawings. Much of the material therein arose out of ideas surrounding my *Music for Concert Halls*, a series of large-scale pieces composed in the mid-'90s to be played in any hall, but objectively germane to the hall of the given performance. Pieces composed for among others, Ensemble Intercontemporain, London Sinfonietta, ASKO ensemble, and various orchestras, for example:

Second Music for a European Concert Hall: Ensemble Modern/Freiburg Barockorchester/Benoît Régent/Mozartsaal

and later works, (including the instrument-building involved in):

THE NEURONS, THE TONGUE, THE COCHLEA....THE BREATH, THE RESONANCE

and

felt | ebb | thus | brink | here | array | telling

Doing these pieces in *concert halls* (and not galleries, theatres or redundant industrial spaces and so on) was a deliberate decision: they are as much about concert-giving and presentation, as about perception.

One intention of this book was to promote these ideas to a wider non-musical audience, and particularly those administrators who seemed bemused by what was for me a logical and necessary compositional endeavour.

So the pieces in this book can be read and enjoyed by non-musicians as well as musicians, acousticians and artists.

Most simply, they can exist in the mind of the reader, whose imagination may well devise private virtual spaces and scenarios which cannot ever be practically realised.

The musicologist, Richard Toop put it very well, the way the whole book is to be made use of. The following is from his foreword to the book:

There is a short story by Borges that describes a unique book – *The Book of Sand* – whose randomly numbered pages are infinite, impossible to find a second time, and so slender that one could never locate either the first or the last of them. Ideally, this [Mason's book] would be just such a work. Alas, since – unlike Borges' mythical tome – it actually exists, its dimensions have to be finite. Yet by nature, it aspires to the same utopian condition: it too wants to offer glimpses of the infinities of thought, which, even in a seemingly limited area, always go far beyond what we could ever dream of writing down.

The sympathetic reader will want to respect these aspirations. While nothing can prevent prosaic left-to-right reading, from first page to last, to do so seems quite contrary to this (unpaginated) book's intentions. It is a kind of book of hushed revelations, to be dipped into, and privately pondered.

The ideal reader will also be a listener: more precisely, an inner listener. These many fragmentary texts are, above all, about listening and imagining. But they are also about the fluid intersections and interdependencies of hearing and seeing, especially at the margins of perception, [...] and about the paradoxes of near and far [...] sometimes almost reluctantly [about music], in the sense that hearing 'music' (as composition, as structure) is viewed as a potential obstruction to perceptions of sound and space.

By the same token none of these pieces need necessarily be only subjective and conceptual: they are also designed to be produced by performers in front of an audience (inside or outside the tradition of the text piece and graphic score), played separately, or in combination, and with the only proviso that they are produced as imaginatively as possible.

All the works in the *Music for Concert Halls* series functioned in terms of highly detailed and exacting notation, not only conventional musical notation, but also one defining a variety of non-musical and visual requirements, like movement.

In my book, text itself becomes a surprisingly precise type of notation. Layout becomes crucial, while punctuation is renounced, seeming almost a hindrance. Clarity should balance freedom: the necessary essentials of the idea are described, while its realization freely invites the reader and performers to use the resources available, and in language available to everyone, however much the instructions might vary between a direct imperative and a more descriptive third person.

Furthermore the pieces don't preclude being transcribed into a more formal detailed notation. They can also serve as the basis for precisely and fully notated pieces in all requisite parameters: musical, spatial, acoustical, performance... and so on. Everything connects, but similar departures tend to arrive at different concerns.

The images are more ambiguous. Richard Toop again:

And for each brief text, there is a complementarily fragile image. The relationship between the two is not banally illustrative, but softly discursive: it is as if the two facing pages – one verbal, one more overtly visual – were whispering to one another, inviting the reader to overhear.

However, this is not just a compendium of dreams about what *could* happen, and maybe will do so. Let's wake up: within Benedict Mason's own works, much of this already *has* happened.

Kenneth Maue

from 'Ideas Around the Experiences', in *Water in the Lake: Real Events for the Imagination*

from 'Ideas Around the Experiences', in *Water in the Lake: Real Events for the Imagination*

Kenneth Maue, 1979

It is the *notation* of a piece – its instructions – that gives it form. The skill in creating notations is one of the most valuable skills that I, or that anyone, can have. In notation lies the creation of process. What a successful notation requires is lucid ambiguity. That means it must be very clear, and at the same time leave open spaces for multiple interpretations.

A notation must reflect a consideration of beginning, middle, ending, parts, and transitions – the chronological unfolding of a piece – even if much of that consideration is communicated implicitly. [...] A piece is a coherent unit of experience, and it needs its own internal, organic connections.

I do not build meanings into the pieces. This is so that part of doing a piece is the discovery of your own meanings. I am certainly not interested in meaningless activity. And although I don't build purpose into the pieces, I do require of a notation that it specify an activity that suggests some basic human worth. When I write a notation, I ask myself: Do I want to do this myself? Is asking other people to do the piece an expression of my respect for them? I cannot imagine asking other people to do a piece that I wouldn't want to do. What I am pointing to here is intrinsic value, prior to any meanings. Value is deeper than any meanings we create; it allows for multiple meanings; it is a quality akin to spirit itself. I want the pieces to allow the breath of spirit to pass through what we do.

The second dynamic of process learning is *ensemble* – the quality of the relationships of the parts within the whole. Musicians use the term ensemble (which means 'together') to speak of the group of people who are playing together, and more importantly, to refer to the sensitivity of their interaction. Thus we speak of 'good ensemble' and 'poor ensemble' when the musicians are and are not sounding together. Well-developed ensemble means that the players are interacting with sensitive and supportive teamwork. It means a balancing of the intentions of all the individual players with each other, and with the needs of the group as a whole. In learning ensemble, we meet the universal question of the balances between individual freedom and social imperatives.

Ensemble is a sensibility that we practice and gradually master. There are many different kinds of ensemble, which are set up by the given notation. Ensemble can be more and less interactive, demanding more and less inter-nalized skill of the players. We can also notice what kinds of roles are being set up. Does everyone have the same role, or are there differentiated roles? Do different roles fall into a hierarchy? Are people equally involved, or are some more central while others are more peripheral? Are there provisions for players entering or leaving the piece?

I extend the sense of ensemble to mean the interrelationships of all the parts within the whole. That means everything: the time and the place, the circumstances and surroundings. If a piece happens outdoors, it means the land we're standing on, the sky and the air we're breathing, the sounds we can hear, the quality of the light. In learning ensemble, we can attune ourselves to a single unified field of sensitive awareness, and experience that field as a single organism. Within this field, we make our human interactions. The ensemble we learn in the pieces is a model for what we do together in life.

Improvisation is the third dynamic of process learning. By improvisation I mean simply the act of making the most of a given situation. It is the freedom, large or small, constructive or destructive, that we choose to exercise within fixed limitations. In terms of the pieces, improvisation means the actual use we make of the notations. Improvisation thrives best in a climate of good ensemble among the players, that is, where there is trust and mutual understanding. [...]

People ask, 'What are the pieces all about?' Different people give very different answers. My own answers change from day to day, from year to year, even with pieces I repeat. The pieces seem to me like houses – I may be interested in the architecture or the decor, but what really matters is the life that goes on inside them...

Book of Lives

Get a blank bound book, and over a week or two, collect sixteen one-sentence autobiographies in the book. Approach people, tell them what you're doing, and ask them to contribute their life stories. Each autobiography must be stated as a single sentence. Add your own autobiography as the sixteenth contribution.

... I want to contact people in ways that set aside our familiar patterns, that open us to unexpected experiences. I surprise you with my request. How to encapsulate an entire life in a single sentence? It is an invitation to accidental poetry, to fresh insight, to the courage of self-revelation. My gift to you is to ask you who you are...

Eureka Space

A group of players sit together in darkness. Each pursues an inner path of thought, feeling, reflection, meditation – whatever fits the circumstances. If and when you make a discovery, some moment of 'Aha!', light a match, and let it burn for an amount of time proportional to what you feel is the magnitude of your discovery – briefly for a minor insight, longer for a more significant awakening. Continue until there have been no match lightings for a long time, and it seems that there won't be any more.

... Doing the events is, for me, a risky activity. My mind wants to tell me, Oh, I get the idea just by thinking about doing it, or, there's no point to that, it's not important. My mind tells me a lot of things, to keep me from plunging into an activity that I can't fully grasp with my reason. What's the risk? That

I will have wasted my time, that I will be doing something of no clear value, that I will make a fool of myself...

Moving Things

Take a long walk, perhaps through a wooded area. Find things that appeal to you. From time to time, pick something up and carry it for a while. Then put it down somewhere, perhaps in a place carefully chosen, perhaps just anywhere. Sometimes carry more than one thing at once. Do this as if you were a natural part of the surroundings, carrying out some function that fits with the space. Continue until you decide that you have moved enough things. Be careful about how you make that decision.

... What I look for is a sense of 'fit'. Fitting the walk into my day, fitting the event into my walk, fitting the individual items into the landscape. I want to be casual enough, and also decisive enough. I want my placings to blend with the environment, and also to bear some trace of distinctive quality. I want to do just enough, for just long enough. I want to connect intimately with the surroundings, without becoming heavy. Questions of balance. And I want to achieve all of this without a thought, or calculation, or effort, at conscious aesthetics. Just something simple – the fresh spontaneity of real 'fit'...

Points of Reference

Choose five places in your area. Go to each one. In each place, make a distinctive marking in that location. Perhaps spread this activity over several weeks, and possibly over a very large land area. In later times, when you want to know where you are in relation to other things, take your bearings from these five points of reference.

... Where am I, anyway? What's fixed? Value-systems change; belief-systems change. I may be locating myself in relation to my memory of the home I grew up in. What if it's been paved over? What if my memory has altered it through time? I may recall that I have academic degrees, but what if these mean nothing to people I'm with? Everything keeps changing, and I keep looking for something that is dependably fixed. When I am lost, I refer to my markings. They tell me nothing; yet they help me to remember something. I feel a physical connection to these marked places. Being lost is not the same as not knowing where I am...

String Give-Away

Give away 30 pieces of string to people you walk up to in public places, and keep a record of your give-aways. Use two balls of string, with different colors. Give people their choice of color and length.

With each person, keep notes of color chosen, length cut, and information about the person (age, sex, height, clothing, regional speech accent, other). When you finish, organize all this information into a report, perhaps add your own conclusions, and mail a copy of the report to a relevant institution, asking if they wish to contract you for further research studies.

… A parody? Of what? Advertising and promotions? Poll-taking? A practical joke? A stunt? A novel way to meet people? A political statement? Street theater? Or perhaps just itself, no double meaning, no implications, just what it is – a string give-away. Purpose can accumulate around life experiences to the point of obscuring the experiences. The way to reconnect with our purpose is to do things that seem, at first appearance, to lack purpose…

2^n Durations Music

Mark a series of durations, beginning with one second, then continuously doubling (2 sec, 4 sec, 8 sec, 16 sec, 32 sec, and so on) until a maximum duration is reached, then continuing with an immediate repetition of that longest duration and proceeding with successively halving durations, down to an ending that is a mirrored repeat of the beginning (… 8 sec, 4 sec, 2 sec, 1 sec). Do this as a continuous series, marked by strikings of a gong or other ceremonial observations, and precisely timed. Perhaps add a celebration to start and another to end the whole series.

… I have done this twice. The second time, we did a seven-month version, the longest durations in the middle being about 24 days each. These occurrences have left me with lasting impressions, as if those two series of durations consisted of time somehow different from other time in my life. I recall getting together with the other people, in the room where we kept the gong and official clock, often at odd times of day and night. And I remember how the expanding first sections of the event gave me a deep sense of the whole world expanding, and how the contracting sections gave me a sense of moving inward to a center point. I recall the impression of being inside something like a cathedral of time.

Book in the Freezer

Put a book in your freezer and leave it there.

… I am doing this now for a second time. I've had a book on California earthquakes in my freezer for a year and a half now. People seeing the book there invariably ask me why it's there. There are many answers, and no answer at all. During this time I have moved twice. Each time I wrapped the book in thick layers of newspaper and transferred it from one freezer to the next as quickly as possible, to keep it from thawing out […]

When you move from reading the pieces to doing them, be careful about your expectations. I find that expectations about doing a piece are usually quite different from the experience itself. (There's an expectation right there!) It would be foolish of me to say, 'Don't have expectations', but I do suggest some awareness here. Stay conscious of what you may be expecting, and don't let your expectations cut you off from direct experience.

When you do a piece, take your time; don't rush. Sometimes people want to do pieces quickly, as though getting through the instructions efficiently were all there were to the experience. Each piece requires its own beginning, its own unfolding in cycles and transitions, and its own ending. I avoid specifying amounts of clock-time in the notations, because part of doing a piece is to find its natural shape and size in time. Take the time to let a piece fill itself in its own proper way. [...]

In using the notations, I urge you to play close attention to the wordings. The difference between a piece that works and one that doesn't often lies in the clarity with which the instructions are stated, and the attentiveness with which the players absorb them. The exact phrases in the notations, and the little details of structure, are invitations to lucid awareness of what we're doing. None of the specifications is arbitrary or capricious; that kind of activity does not interest me. All the instructions come out of a sense, which experience has taught me, of how organic balances are created, and how diverse possibilities are opened up and brought together in natural conclusions [...]

The endings of pieces are challenging enough to merit special attention. It takes time to learn how to end a piece, when to end a piece. An extra sensitivity is required when different people want to end at different times. Since talking about a piece is almost never allowed while a piece is in progress, these questions require awareness and intuition. In all cases it's important to end pieces while there is still energy happening in them, and not to wait until everyone has run out of ideas. In that way the ending itself is a conscious, dynamic act.

Max Neuhaus

LISTEN (1966)

LISTEN

BROOKLYN BRIDGE-SOUTH STREET for Joe Jones   Max Neuhaus 1976

LISTEN

Max Neuhaus, 1988, 1990, 2004

The impetus for the title was twofold. The simple clear meaning of the word, to pay attention aurally, and its clean visual shape – LISTEN – when capitalized. It was also its imperative meaning – partly I must admit, as a private joke between myself and my then current lover, a French-Bulgarian girl, who used to shout it before she began to throw things at me when she was angry. It was my first independent work as an artist in 1966. As a percussionist I had been directly involved in the gradual insertion of everyday sound into the concert hall, from Russolo through Varèse and finally to Cage who brought live street sounds directly into the hall.

I saw these activities as a way of giving aesthetic credence to these sounds – something I was all for – but I began to question the effectiveness of the method. Most members of the audience seemed more impressed with the scandal than the sounds, and few were able to carry the experience over to a new perspective on the sounds of their daily lives.

I became interested in going a step further. Why limit listening to the concert hall? Instead of bringing these sounds into the hall, why not simply take the audience outside – a demonstration in situ?

The first performance was for a small group of invited friends. I asked them to meet me on the corner of Avenue D and West 14th Street in Manhattan. I rubber-stamped LISTEN on each person's hand and began walking with them down 14th Street towards the East River. At that point the street bisects a power plant and, as I had noticed previously, one hears some spectacularly massive rumbling. We continued, crossing the highway and walking along the sound of its tire wash, down river for a few blocks, re-crossing over a pedestrian bridge, passing through the Puerto Rican street life of the lower east side to my studio, where I performed some percussion pieces for them. After a while I began to do these works as 'Lecture Demonstrations'; the rubber stamp was the lecture and the walk the demonstration. I would ask the audience at a concert or lecture to collect outside the hall, stamp their hands and lead them through their everyday environment. Saying nothing, I would simply concentrate on listening, and start walking. At first, they would be a little embarrassed, of course, but the focus was generally conta-gious. The group would proceed silently, and by the time we returned to the hall many had found a new way to listen for themselves.

Of course, there were a few 'mishaps'. I remember one in particular at a university somewhere in Iowa. The faculty must have thought I was actually going to give a talk. They were nonplussed when I told the students to leave the hall, but fortunately not quick-witted enough to figure out a way of contradicting the day's 'guest lecturer'. The students were more than happy to escape and take a walk. Several hundred of us formed a silent parade through the streets of this small town – it must have been Ames. The faculty was so enraged that, to a man, they boycotted the elaborate lunch they had prepared for me after the lecture.

A number of years later, when Murray Schafer's soundscape project became known, I am sure these academics didn't have any problem accepting similar ideas. But the reality – not being safely contained between the covers of a book – was quite another matter. I suppose the real definition of this series of works is the use of the word LISTEN to refocus people's aural perspective. I began to think of other ways of using it. (The Iowa experience had blacklisted me as a university lecturer.)

The largest version of the work (1 million people) was certainly an opinion editorial, which I wrote for the *New York Times* in 1974, condemning the silly bureaucrats of the Department of Air Resources for making too much noise. Unable to do their real job of cleaning up the air that New Yorkers breathed, they naïvely applied their energies to 'cleaning up' the sound of the city. To keep their pot boiling, they published a pamphlet entitled 'Noise Pollution Makes You Sick'. I countered with 'Noise Propaganda Makes Noise', the basic point being that by arbitrarily condemning most man-made sounds as noise they were making noise where it never existed before. The worst result of their meddling is the people one has seen blasting their ears out (quite literally) with walkmen while riding the subway, convinced that they are protecting their ears from the subway sounds which are, in fact, not nearly as loud as the ones inside their ears from their walkmen.

There were other manifestations of the idea. I organized 'field-trips' to places which were generally inaccessible and had sounds which could never be captured on a recording. I also did some versions as publications. One of these was a poster with a view looking up from under the Brooklyn Bridge, with the word LISTEN stamped in large letters on the underside of the bridge. It came from a long fascination of mine with sounds of traffic moving across that bridge – the rich sound texture formed from hundreds of tires rolling over the open grating of the roadbed, each with a different speed and tread.

The developers of the South Street seaport project, which is near the bridge, always felt that its sound would limit real estate values in the area. In the late '80s they succeeded in convincing the city to pave over the open grating with asphalt. Afterwards, they discovered that this tremendous added weight caused serious structural problems in the bridge. There is still a sound, but it is not as interesting as it was before the repaving.

In 1978 I published a do-it-yourself version – a postcard in the form of a decal with the word outlined in open letters, to be placed in locations selected by its recipients.

Pauline Oliveros

Ear Piece (1998)

Commentary: *Ear Piece*

Ear Piece

by Pauline Oliveros (1998)

1) Are you listening now?

2) Are you listening to what you are now hearing?

3) Are you hearing while you listen?

4) Are you listening while you are hearing?

5) Do you remember the last sound you heard before this question?

6) What will you hear in the near future?

7) Can you hear now and also listen to your memory of an old sound?

8) What causes you to listen?

9) Do you hear yourself in your daily life?

10) Do you have healthy ears?

11) If you could hear any sound you want, what would it be?

12) Are you listening to sounds now or just hearing them?

13) What sound is most meaningful to you?

Commentary: *Ear Piece*

James Saunders

Since 1957, Pauline Oliveros has been involved in the practice of Deep Listening, an activity which she describes as coming 'from noticing my listening or listening to my listening and discerning the effects on my body–mind continuum, from listening to others, to art and to life', and which 'is intended to heighten and expand consciousness of sound in as many dimensions of awareness and attentional dynamics as humanly possible'.[1] Oliveros defines it as:

> a philosophy and practice [...] that explores the difference between the involuntary nature of hearing and the voluntary selective nature of listening. The result of the practice cultivates appreciation of sounds on a heightened level, expanding the potential for connection and interaction with one's environment, technology and performance with others in music and related arts.[2]

The practice is taught through workshops, which include a series of exercises that focus on the sound environment and our perception of it. Such exercises include Oliveros's *Sonic Meditations* (1971–89), a set of 25 verbal scores that suggest approaches to individual and communal listening. Her more recent *Deep Listening Pieces* are an on-going series of occasional activities composed in part as responses to situations and places. These include *Ear Piece* (1998), commissioned by the WDR Studio Akustische Kunst as part of her project *Deep Listening Through the Millennium* with the aim of promoting and encouraging listening internationally from 1999–2001 in order 'to listen to change – listen in order to change – listen for change'.[3] This was first realised as a *Hörspiel*,[4] with the 13 questions that comprise the score being answered by Cologne residents in their native languages in a variety of locations. These were then mixed alongside an environmental recording to produce the final piece, with the verbal score being published separately.

Ear Piece is an example of a score which uses questions. These can take the form of *WH*-interrogatives which request missing information (open), those that offer a choice from a set of alternatives (options), and yes/no clauses which request a binary response (closed). Question types therefore affect certain freedoms afforded to the addressee, which is a central concern for much verbal notation.

Questions appear in a relatively large number of Oliveros' scores, with the context varying considerably. In *Any Piece of Music* (1980), an imperative instruction directs participants to answer the questions 'in as many ways

---

[1] Oliveros, 2005, xxiii–xxiv.
[2] Oliveros, 2010.
[3] Oliveros, 2005, p. 33.
[4] *Hörspiel* is a German term for a radio play.

as possible'. *Earth: Sensing/Listening/Sounding* (1992) is given an explicit performance context, specifying that participants 'Make a circle with a group. Lie on the ground or floor on your back with your head towards the centre of the room', before asking a series of questions that explore the relationship with the listening environment. The 22 texts that form the *Deep Listening Meditations – Egypt* (1999) were intended to be performed singularly, one per day. The focus of these meditations is intensified by their separation and realisation over time, so that the activity suggested by the question 'In a group or crowd can you hear with their ears?' might develop in parallel with the establishment of the group as a social environment. *Sonic Images* (1972) comprises 17 multi-part questions, mixing closed and open forms (for example, '6. Have you heard a sound lately which you could not identify? What were the circumstances? How did you feel?').[5] It was presented at a conference for architects and designers. The most extensive set is Oliveros' *Listening Questions*, published as a separate text in *Deep Listening*. Its 40 questions summarise her approach to investigating individual responses to listening, and a consideration of its role in our lives. They encompass ideas taken from other scores, and present them as an exercise in developing aural awareness.

Of the 13 questions found in *Ear Piece*, eight of them are closed, four are open, and one question presents options. While it might be expected that there would be more open questions, given their implicit requirement to present a choice from a wider range of possibilities and encourage deeper interaction, the activities which are linked to the closed questions are not straightforward. For example, although the first question, 'Are you listening now?' may be considered closed with a yes/no answer, it could also elicit an open response, as an explanation of the degree of listening may form part of the response to, or reflective consideration of, the question. In addition to assessing whether listening is taking place, the question also fixes the activity in time, specifying it as happening in the present. Attempting to consider the question distracts from the activity.[6] The question therefore requires continual monitoring and is not fixed to a single point in time (although this is implied to an extent by presenting the questions as a numbered list). There is also no object specified: to what are you listening? While closed questions offer the opportunity to answer simply 'yes' or 'no', they often also allow for a fuller answer, as in this case.

The next three questions engage the addressee with a further consideration of their current listening: 'Are you listening to what you are now hearing?', 'Are you hearing while you listen?', and 'Are you listening while you are hearing?' These questions consider the relationship between hearing

---

[5] Oliveros, 1984, p. 53.

[6] This is explained by Oliveros' distinction between attention and awareness. She comments: 'Attention is narrow, pointed and selective. Awareness is broad, diffuse and inclusive [...] Attention seems to equate with mental activity and to be aroused by interest or desire. Awareness seems to equate with the body's sensory receptivity. It is activated, or present, during pleasure and pain [...] When either attention or awareness predominates or becomes out of balance, the other tends to drift or become unconscious.' *Ibid.*, p. 139.

and listening,[7] asking how attention is managed over time. The first four questions are closely related, serving as a starting point for the piece's exploration of personal listening.

The next two questions consider the role of memory and time in the listening process: 'Do you remember the last sound you heard before this question?' and 'What will you hear in the near future?' While they are phrased as closed and open questions respectively, both point towards a descriptive response. They are qualitatively different to the first block, which questions the mode of activity being undertaken; these questions discuss the context and outcomes of those activities, as well as their temporal relationship. They are also connected to question 7, which asks, 'Can you hear now and also listen to your memory of an old sound?' This too is speculative, inviting the addressee to think about the distinctions made between the information-gathering mode of hearing and the deeper processing of listening.

Questions 8–11 are of a different type again. While the first seven refer to the immediate listening environment, this third block opens up the activity to a reflection on the addressee's general approach to listening. To this point, the addressee might be involved in a realisation of the score in the form of a private or imaginary performance, where interaction between the score, reader and environment creates an event in the mind of the reader (there are no instructions for deliberately making sounds). These next questions weaken that position, as attention is taken away from listening in favour of thinking about listening. They are qualitatively different, operating outside of the temporal domain established by the opening part of the score and examining the importance and motivation for listening in a more abstract way, separated from the immediate environmental context. They deal with stimulus ('What causes you to listen?'), the addressee's role in the soundscape and their response to it ('Do you hear yourself in your daily life?'), (meta)physical well-being ('Do you have healthy ears?'), and personal preference and aspiration ('If you could hear any sound you want, what would it be?').[8]

The final two questions follow the forms already established. Question 12 returns to a consideration of the immediate environment, asking, 'Are you listening to sounds now or just hearing them?' This could be read as an attempt to check whether engaging with the preceding questions has engendered change in the reader. It is the only optional question in the piece, and once more examines the difference between hearing and listening. Question 13, 'What sound is most meaningful to you?' is similar to question

---

[7] The *Oxford English Dictionary* defines 'hear' as to 'perceive sounds with the ear' and 'listen' as to '1. make an effort to hear something; 2. attentively hear a person speaking; 3. give attention with the ear'.

[8] It is worth noting the use of 'hear' in questions 9 and 11. Oliveros comments earlier in *Deep Listening*, 'I differentiate between "to hear" and "to listen". To hear is the physical means that enables perception. To listen is to give attention to what is perceived both acoustically and psychologically.' (Oliveros, 2005, p. xxii)

11, although there is some ambiguity in that it could also be applied to the current context and/or general listening.

Ear Piece originally served as a way to generate source material in the original *Hörspiel*, where respondents literally answered the questions. Oliveros thinks of it 'as a score that generates a radio piece'[9] and explains the process of making the realisation:

> There were people who went out and did interviews. At the WDR I was struck by all the sounds going on in the building, for example doors opening and closing and reverberating as well as a lot of other sounds that were below consciousness. I asked the recording engineers to record the building with all of the ongoing sounds. This, along with the interview material, became part of the mix for the *Hörspiel* called *Ear Piece*.[10]

The nature of the activities suggested by the score might vary considerably however. Oliveros recognises this possibility, while emphasising her preference for a recorded compilation of responses:

> *Ear Piece* can be done just as a series of questions to a group of people for their mental contemplation or writing with a person asking the questions or the questions delivered by projected media or a recording. Best though is the act of interviewing and recording on location then returning the material for editing and mixing.[11]

In the context of her own practice, the reflective aspect of the piece is emphasised by its potential inclusion in Oliveros' Deep Listening Class. Here performances of sound pieces contribute to the participants' training,[12] alongside breathing and listening exercises, journal writing and improvisation. In her short text 'Notational Range', reprinted as a preface to the collection from which *Ear Piece* is taken, Oliveros explains: 'The notations for sonic meditations [*sic*] were presented in written form only after many trials with oral instructions given to many different people. Even though sonic meditations are in print, I often vary or revise the wording I use to transmit the instructions in new situations.'[13] So Oliveros takes a provisional attitude, and is open to re-wording the questions in response to local conditions.

According to the composer the aim of the questions, though, is 'to set an attention process in motion within a participant and among the group that can deepen gradually with repeated experience. A definitive performance can vary considerably even though the integrity of the guidelines will not be

---

[9] Pauline Oliveros, in correspondence with the author, August 2010.
[10] *Ibid.*
[11] *Ibid.*
[12] See Oliveros, 2005, pp. 1–4.
[13] Oliveros, 1998, p. 22.

disturbed and the piece will be recognizable each time.'[14] Whether *Ear Piece* is performed through a mental realisation, or as a written or spoken exercise, this aim is still embedded in the activity. It would be '"sonic" in the sense that sound and hearing, both active and receptive, are the foci of attention and stimuli of awareness.'[15]

[14] Oliveros, 2005, p. 29.
[15] Oliveros, 1984, p. 141.

Yoko Ono

RECORD OF 13 CONCERT PIECE PERFORMANCES

Instructions for Bath Spa University (2010)

Statement

RECORD OF 13 CONCERT PIECE PERFORMANCES
... since most pieces consist of
just titles or very short instructions,
passing words as to how they were
performed previously has become a habit...

HIDE PIECE

Hide.

This piece was first performed in New York, Carnegie
Recital Hall, 1961, by completely turning off the light in
the concert hall including the stage and a girl hiding in a
large canvas sheet on the stage while two men made soft
voice accompaniment. In 1962, Tokyo, also in total
darkness, performers hid behind various things on the stage,
while a male solo performer struggled to get out of a bag
on the stage he was put in. In New York, 1965, performers
and audience, using Canal Street subway station as a place
of performance, hid from each other by using their own
methods. In London, 1966, Jeanette Cochrane Theatre,
Yoko Ono brought out a 3 foot pole on the center of the
stage and hid behind it ½ hr.

SWEEP PIECE

Sweep.

This was first performed 1962 in Tokyo, Sogetsu Art Center
by a solo male performer during 4 hour concert of works by
Yoko Ono. The performer covered the areas all around and
in the concert hall. It was performed again 1966 London,
Jeanette Cochrane Theatre, as a solo piece by Yoko Ono,
sweeping from one end of the stage to another.

CUT PIECE

Cut.

This piece was performed in Kyoto, Tokyo, New York and London. It is usually performed by Yoko Ono coming on the stage and in a sitting position, placing a pair of scissors in front of her and asking the audience to come up on the stage, one by one, and cut a portion of her clothing (anywhere they like) and take it. The performer, however, does not have to be a woman.

BEAT PIECE

Listen to a heartbeat.

This was first performed in 1965 at the East End Theatre, New York, by people coming on stage and lying on each other's body to listen.

WIND PIECE

Make a way for the wind.

This was first performed in 1962 Sogetsu Art Center, Tokyo, with a huge electric fan on the stage. In 1966 Wesleyan University, Conn., audience was asked to move their chairs a little and make a narrow aisle for the wind to pass through. No wind was created with special means.

PROMISE PIECE

Promise.

This was first performed in Jeanette Cochrane Theatre in London, 1966. Yoko Ono, as the last piece of the night, broke a vase on the stage and asked people to pick up the pieces and take them home, promising that they would all meet again in 10 years time with the pieces and put the vase together again. Second performance was by a male performer in Tokyo calling a female performer in New York, 1964, at the Plaza Hotel; third performance by a solo performer calling a person in Kitazawa flat, 1962; fourth performance by a man in Chinatown phone booth, New York, calling a person at Chambers Street loft, New York, 1961; fifth performance, an elephant in Paris calling a parrot in New Guinea, 1959 – all calls being about future meetings. Call or write about future meetings or any other plans.

WHISPER PIECE

Whisper.

This piece was originally called a telephone piece, and was the starting of the word-of-mouth pieces. It is usually performed by the performer whispering a word or a note into an audience's ear and asking to have it passed on until it reaches the last person in the audience.

BREATH PIECE

Breathe.

First performed at Wesleyan University, Conn., U.S.A., in 1966. A large card with small lettering saying "breathe" was passed three times among the audience.

FLY PIECE

Fly.

This piece was first performed in Tokyo, Naiqua Gallery, 1964. Each person who attended the night flew in his/her own way. It was performed again in London at Jeanette Cochrane Theatre, by the audience who came up on the stage and jumped off the different leveled ladders prepared for them.

QUESTION PIECE

Question.

This piece, was first performed in Tokyo, 1962, Sogetsu Art Center, by two people on stage asking questions to each other and not answering. At the time it was done in French, but it can be done in any language or in many different languages at one time. The piece is meant for a dialogue or a monologue of continuous questions, answered only by questions. It was also performed in English on Voice of America Radio Program, Tokyo, 1964, and in Japanese on NTV (Japanese Television) by six children from the audience, 1964.

DISAPPEARING PIECE

Boil water.

This piece was first performed in New York, 1966, by only five people. This was not deliberate, but probably due to the subway strike in New York at the time. The water was boiled in a still, until it came out of the other side of the still, which took two hours. In London 1966, Mercury Theatre, the boiling of the water, the size of the pot in which the water was boiled, etc., was announced on the stage. The actual boiling of the water was performed at a Notting Hill Gate flat. The complete evaporation of the water was announced from the stage as the ending of the piece.

CLOCK PIECE

Usually a clock is placed on the center of the stage and audience is asked to wait until the alarm goes off.

TOUCH PIECE

Touch.

This piece was performed many times in different places in Europe, United States and Japan. Usually, the lights are put off and the audience touches each other for ten minutes to sometimes over two hours. In Nanzenji Temple in Kyoto, 1964, it lasted from evening till dawn. In London, people started to whistle the theme song of "Bridge of River Kwai" during the performance which became a chorus.

Instructions for Bath Spa University (2010)

1. Perform one of the following pieces in the way you have decided to perform.
2. Report to someone how the performance went and share your experience in that manner.
3. Bury a set of records of your performance in a place only you will remember.

yoko ono June 2010

Tape Piece I

Collecting Piece

Earth Piece

Snow Piece

Map Piece

Mirror Piece

Pieces for Orchestra

Statement

Yoko Ono, 22 October 2009

Initially, I was a haiku poet. Those poems could have easily become instructions. That is the form side of things – where it came from for me. But my instructions are quite often less minimal than a haiku poem, though the spirit of it is still very much connected with haiku.

Grapefruit was a book of instructions for others.

Those pieces which are apparently impossible to perform are very much related to Gyo in Zen Buddhism.

They come very quickly. It only takes the time to write it out.

I like the idea that Art work can become scores, just like music, so it can be 'played/performed' by others.

I put ideas on paper which were not possible for me to realize – either because I did not have the means to, or it was something that only belonged to the conceptual world – like science-fiction.

The word scores may be notated, but it gives you a space to use your creativity. Just like in music scores, if the notation says play pianissimo, you have to find the degree of pianissimo you feel comfortable in.

In *Water Piece*, I will perform in the way what water means to me at the time. I might go to the bathroom and pee. I might use water to clean rice before boiling. I might invite friends and watch the water evaporate – as I did as a performance in N.Y., 1966. Right now, I think I will just get a glass of clear water and drink it thinking at the same time, to heal me, and therefore, my son, my daughter, and the world. I believe in simultaneous healing. And the world urgently needs healing.

I will be very pleased if my work will inspire others to make their own.

Michael Parsons

Walk (1969)

Commentary: Walk

WALK   Michael Parsons

for any number of people walking in a large open space.

Each person chooses 3, 4 or 5 points, of roughly equal distance from
each other, and walks from one to another of these points, using pairs of
randomly chosen numbers to determine:

i)   speed of walking from one point to the next
ii)   length of time spent standing still at the point reached.

All begin together. Standing at one of your chosen points, read your
first pair of figures. The first figure tells you how fast to move to
get to the next point (0= very fast, 9= very slowly): the second
figure tells you how long to stay at the point reached (0= no time
at all, 9= a very long time). Then set off, at the determined speed,
for another of your chosen points; having arrived and waited there for
the indicated length of time, read your second pair of figures, and
set off accordingly for another point (or back to the first point:
choice of which of the 3,4 or 5 points to move to for each journey is free).
Always go from one point to the next by the most direct route.
Continue until all have completed an agreed number of journeys.

Commentary: *Walk*

John Lely

In Michael Parsons' *Walk* (1969), performers independently make their way across a large open space, using sets of randomly chosen numbers to determine their rates of walking and the times spent at a number of different spatial locations. The score consists of instructions explaining the performance procedure in detail. Within the constraints imposed by the score, the performers are given specific choices: they can choose, for instance, where to walk, and how to interpret fairly broad descriptions of walking speed and duration.

As with much of the composer's work, *Walk* mixes strict compositional constraints with performer intuition. Any performance of *Walk* will produce a range of unpredictable spatial and temporal arrangements, which arise out of a combination of the constraints of the score, the performers' own input, and the space of performance.

As well as *Walk*, Parsons has composed other pieces that involve movement through space, including *Walking and Measuring Piece* (1973), *Slow Motion Walking Piece* (1973) and *Echo Piece at Muddusjarvi* (1976) (see Fig. 32, pages 50–1), and has for many years been attempting to walk the entire coast of the British mainland, joining up sections of coastline on different stages. This walking project exemplifies his compositional approach: first a constraint is quite strictly formalised; it is then approached with a high degree of openness to contingency and to where the boundaries of that constraint might lie. The constraint may then be revised in the light of experience. For instance, in practice walking around the intricate coast of Scotland has been found to be too time-consuming, and remains under review. So constraints are always present, but the composer is open to reassessing their conditions. Parsons regards his whole output as work in progress, and is always prepared to re-evaluate and recompose pieces for new contexts.

Walk was originally composed in the summer of 1969 after the first practical meeting of the Scratch Orchestra, held at St Katharine Docks in London. The piece was first publicly performed on 8 November 1969 at Islington Town Hall, and the score was later published in 1974 in Michael Nyman's *Experimental Music: Cage and Beyond* and the Experimental Music Catalogue's *Visual Anthology*. The piece was actually conceived while walking in London:

> I can remember exactly where I was – the idea for *Walk* came in a flash. I had the idea as I was crossing a road, and by the time I'd got to the other side of the road the idea essentially was complete. I just had to work out the details. I had this picture of people walking in straight lines and intersecting each other. And when I think of *Walk* I still think of that particular crossing.[1]

---

[1] Michael Parsons, in interview with the author, London, 2 August 2009.

The composer recognises the influence of La Monte Young's *Composition 1960 #10 to Bob Morris* (1960) (see Fig. 153, page 425), 'Draw a straight line and follow it', which Parsons describes as 'the ultimate single-minded directed activity, where you make a decision and just keep going whatever happens'.[2] Another influence was Samuel Beckett's *Watt* (1953), a novel saturated in the exhaustive permutations of words and objects. For example, for three pages the character of Mr Knott moves first himself and then various items of furniture around his room in a meticulous sequence of combinations:

> Here he stood. Here he sat. Here he knelt. Here he lay. Here he moved, to and fro, from the door to the window, from the window to the door; from the window to the door, from the door to the window; from the fire to the bed, from the bed to the fire; from the bed to the fire, from the fire to the bed; from the door to the fire... [3]

Parsons is interested in using systems to generate unforeseen results. From 1970 until 1990 he was a visiting lecturer in the Department of Fine Art at Portsmouth Polytechnic, where he made links with the Systems Group of visual artists, who explored ways in which strict formal systems could be employed to create visual work. As Parsons explains, their work is:

> based on the choice of a limited set of elements and the use of consistent principles to determine how those elements are combined. Single straight lines, for example, may follow numerical rules which determine their length, position and direction; the rules are not hidden from view but are made clearly evident in the work itself. There is an interest in working in series, in which a network of relationships is perceptibly transformed from one work to another. Rational procedures are seen not as a means of complete control, but as a method of inquiry: within a defined field, further relationships can be discovered.[4]

Parsons recalls a particular teaching exercise instigated by Michael Kidner: A chair is placed on a table at eye-level, and its four legs are labelled from left to right in the order they appear in the visual field, e.g. A, B, C and D. Students slowly move around the chair, taking note whenever there is a change in the order that the legs appear in their own visual field. This practical method creates its own unique set of orderings, wholly reliant for its generation on the viewer's own observations of physical space. Parsons comments:

> This always intrigues me about any kind of movement. But you become very aware of it when you walk. You only have to walk a very short

---

[2] *Ibid.*

[3] Beckett, 1953, p. 176.

[4] Parsons, M., 1976, pp. 815–18.

distance for this lamppost to be in a completely different position in relation to this building. If you take any given points of reference and walk in relation to them they change positions in the visual field in a way that is like a change-ringing permutation.[5]

In the case of *Walk*, it is clear that the walking constraints can create a wealth of opportunities for temporal and spatial arrangements and coincidences. The composer expresses an interest in the unexpected ways in which the space of performance is articulated by the movement of people walking:

> I think of each walk as drawing a line in a space. As you walk it's a sort of dynamic re-articulation of the space. [...] The piece is concerned with redefining awareness and perception, of space and of the passage of time, through the activity of walking. The perception of space is continually reconfigured by changes in the position and visual field of each performer and by the changing relationships between the positions, movements and directions of all the performers. So there is this idea of the space being explored and reconfigured, really recreated. What you're actually doing is recreating the space as you move.[6]

That observational ethos is reflected in the composer's concern with which elements of a score create indeterminacy. For Parsons the language of a score must function to create a specific class of movements and interactions in performance. The score of *Walk* makes clear which elements are indeterminate: for instance, the pairs of random numbers for walking and waiting, the subjective scaling of walking speeds and waiting times, and the choice of points for arrival and departure. He explains:

> In writing verbal scores, I take into account the inherent unpredictability of the performance situation, but I am not concerned with the ambiguity of language as such. I try to specify as clearly as possible what is to be done. Indeterminacy arises not so much from the individual performer's interpretation of the instructions, but as a result of interaction between performers, with each other and with aspects of the situation beyond their control.[7]

So it appears to be important that a performer has a specific constraint in mind. The speed and duration scales act as guides, which may be interpreted with differing degrees of exactitude. Parsons considered this type of notation to be an effective way of engaging the different temperaments of the Scratch Orchestra members, who came from a wide variety of disciplines and vocations. *Walk* is an example of what Michael Nyman has called a 'people process', as Parsons describes:

[5] Michael Parsons, in interview with the author, London, 2 August 2009.
[6] Michael Parsons, in interview with the author, London, 6 March 2008.
[7] Michael Parsons, in correspondence with the author, February 2010.

The idea of one and the same activity being done simultaneously by a number of people, so that everyone does it slightly differently, 'unity' becoming 'multiplicity', gives one a very economical form of notation – it is only necessary to specify one procedure and the variety comes from the way everyone does it differently. This is an example of making use of 'hidden resources' in the sense of natural individual differences (rather than talents or abilities) which is completely neglected in classical concert music, though not in folk music.[8]

The grammar of the score reinforces this attitude of independent activity. While the sections that describe the general conditions of the piece are marked for the declarative mood, i.e. 'Each person chooses...', those that describe each performer's individual actions are marked for the imperative, and address the performer directly, i.e. 'read your first pair of figures'. The composer suggests that an objective, clear approach to the activity of walking will promote a climate of reflection and observation among participants:

They should be trying to keep to the differentiations of the speeds and the lengths of time as closely as they can, estimating them subjectively or measuring, whichever way they choose to do it. So there is a discipline involved, they shouldn't just be wandering around aimlessly or just waiting for as long as they feel like, or responding to something in a subjective way. There should be that structure in the back of people's minds while they're performing.[9]

Since its original conception, Parsons has performed *Walk* on various occasions, and has produced a set of variations on the 1969 score. Each new version is made for a specific circumstance, with variables being given different emphasis and weighting, in turn altering the equilibrium of each performance. These new versions are informed by the composer's own experience of exploring the world on foot. In preparation for a performance he will make expeditions in search of effective spaces and routes, taking into account topography, acoustics and other practical matters, and the structure of the activity will change in light of these things.

For the first performance of the 2008 version, *Walking Piece (Intersections)*, the venue was Finsbury Avenue Square, London EC2.[10] Prior to the event the score was distributed to potential performers in the form of a postcard, complete with a hand-drawn diagram of what to do when you meet a boundary (see Fig. 117).

Comparing the 2008 version with the 1969 version, there are several notable differences. First, there is no longer the requirement to use a random

[8] Parsons, M., in Nyman, 1999, p. 6.
[9] Michael Parsons, in interview with the author, London, 2 August 2009.
[10] The other piece on the programme was John White performing Philip Corner's *OneNoteOnce* (1975) on a helicon, inside the 55-foot Richard Serra sculpture *Fulcrum* (1987), near Liverpool Street Station.

WALKING PIECE (Intersections)

Walking (x, y): Standing still (z)

x (number of paces): 4, 8, 12, 16, 20
y (walking speed): slow, medium, fast
z (duration of standstill): 20", 40", 60"

Alternate walking and standing still (repeat ad.lib.)

Each time, choose different values for x, y, z.
For each movement, choose a new direction (NE, E, SW etc.)

All movements in a straight line, except when reaching a wall, obstacle
or spatial boundary: then, either (a) direction is reflected at angle of
incidence, or (b) make a right-angle turn.

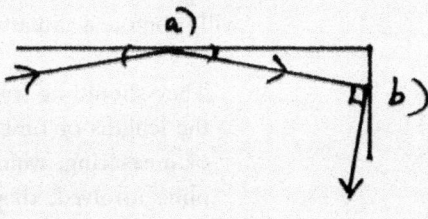

117 *Michael Parsons,* Walking Piece (Intersections) *(2008).*

number table for speeds and durations. In the 1969 version performers need to refer to pairs of randomly selected numbers throughout a performance. In the 2008 version, the numbers, like the directions for walking, may be chosen moments before setting off. The list of numbers for pacing (all multiples of four) is now easily remembered and, when appropriate, each performer mentally selects a number from this list.

Second, there are no longer any points to be determined prior to performance. In the 1969 score each performer chooses 3, 4 or 5 points in space. Since these points are to be determined beforehand, a performer must stick with this initial decision for the whole of the performance. Each discrete walk is therefore focused on specified points of arrival and departure. Combined with a constant speed of walking, there emerges a particular type of predictability to this whole movement. However, in the 2008 version, rather than subjectively choosing points for arrival and departure prior to performance, each performer chooses the direction[11] and number of paces for each discrete walk. The points of standing still, originally predetermined, now emerge as a by-product of the activity of choosing a direction, walking and counting. The performer is also no longer required to remember fixed points.

Third, in the 1969 version, performers take 'the most direct route' between points, so a performer may need to negotiate around, over, under or through

[11] In the score, compass directions refer to relative direction, with 'North' being taken as the direction of the previous walk.

any obstacles; paths of walking therefore may not be in straight lines. In the 2008 version a walker's path is reflected by a wall, obstacle or spatial boundary, thus ensuring that performers can always move in straight lines. According to the composer, the specific environment of Finsbury Avenue Square, which features raised flowerbeds, benches, architectural elements and a grid pattern on the ground, suggested this rule.[12]

Again, the performer is given a clear choice of two possibilities for the angle of reflection, either the angle of incidence or a right angle. The notion of reflection also features in another event that Parsons was preparing at this time, *Echo Piece at Canary Wharf* (2009), in which musicians with brass instruments slowly make their way through the Canary Wharf business district in London's Docklands, exploring the resonant and reflective sonic potential of the office-block facades and open stretches of water.[13]

The 1969 and 2008 versions of *Walk* may bear a surface resemblance, but the moods of performance are strikingly different. In the case of the 1969 version, the points are known. There is a fixed overall state, as it were, which is gradually articulated through performance. However, in the 2008 version, performers stop and wait in many different locations. The dynamic is different, less a sense of arrival and departure, more provisional and indefinite. A common characteristic of many performances of *Walk*, particularly in urban spaces, is that this disciplined activity of walking merges with the environment, and other passers-by may, while going about their business, intersect the performance space and unwittingly make a contribution.

The duration of the 2008 Finsbury Avenue Square version was determined (11 a.m. to 12 noon). Within this duration, individual performers could join in and drop out as they pleased, and towards the end of the hour the participants gradually dispersed.

---

[12] See the front cover of this book.
[13] *Echo Piece at Canary Wharf* was first realised on 20 July 2009.

Ben Patterson

Solo for Dancer (1962)

On Solo for Dancer

SOLO FOR DANCER

benjamin patterson

a pulley is hung from ceiling. a rope, both ends reaching floor,
is hung through pulley. dancer ties loop in one end of rope,
lays self on floor face down, up, left, or right (or all four
possibilities), places feet (or foot) through loop and hoist
self using free end of rope. dance may end upon achieving
ceiling, failure of a pre- or indetermined number of attempts,
or exhaustion.

wiesbaden, june 1962

119 *Alison Knowles performing Ben Patterson,* Solo for Dancer, *Old Gym, Douglass College, New Brunswick, New Jersey, 6 April 1963. (Photo by Peter Moore © Estate of Peter Moore/VAGA, NYC.)*

On *Solo for Dancer*

Ben Patterson, October 2010

I 'composed' this dance in 1961 solely in my head... meaning that I did not try to perform it before Alison Knowles gave the first performance in the Nickolai Kirche in Copenhagen during the Fluxus Festival in 1962. I and everyone watching gasped in awe, to see that the piece actually worked and Alison did 'achieve ceiling'... about 10 meters above the floor. 20 years later, during the 20th anniversary Fluxus Festival at the same site, Alison attempted the piece again... but only ended hanging up-side-down about 2.5 centimeters above the floor. Why didn't it work? ... wrong technique, weak muscles, or something else? In theory it should work. I would be interested to learn what experiences anyone else has had with the piece.

Michael Pisaro

Only (2005–6)

Ten Encounters (A Personal Text Score History)

Commentary: *Only*

Only [harmony series no. 17]
      for one musician

            to Manfred

Void Only

Time like glass
Space like glass
I sit quiet
Anywhere Anything
Happens
Quiet loud still turbulent
The serpent coils
On itself
All things are translucent
Then transparent
Then gone
Only emptiness
No limits
Only the infinitely faint
Song
Of the coiling mind
Only.

                    —Kenneth Rexroth

In a large, open space (possibly outdoors).
For a long time.
Sitting quietly.
Listening.
A few times, playing an extremely long, very quiet tone.

                                    June, 2005/May, 2006

Ten Encounters (A Personal Text Score History)

Michael Pisaro, February 2009

I would like to narrate the chain of experiences that led to my present understanding of the usefulness, richness and elegance of the text score. This method of writing music remains an ongoing stream, in which, as is often the case in experimental music, the potentials are linked up work by work, amongst different composers, rather than in the development of a personal prose-score style. Our orientation in the field comes as often as not from the points in this landscape that have moved us rather than from any particular desire to write text. This list is organized by the approximate order in which these encounters occurred in my musical life.

1. *Stones* and *The Prose Collection* of Christian Wolff

It is immediately clear that anyone can perform these works and that they are engaging and enjoyable in many circumstances. They are, for the most part, portable. What becomes clear over time is that they can also be distinctly challenging (*For Jill*, for example, or *Pit Music*) – and that with some hard work in rehearsal, beautiful and unexpected. Prose likes collections (poems and stories too).

2. The score to *4'33"* by John Cage

When I finally saw it, I realized that this revolution was accomplished in two pages, one of which is nearly blank. The description of an event is entirely disproportionate to its impact.

3. *The Great Learning* by Cornelius Cardew

It is hard to think of a text score that surpasses the physical beauty of this one. Reading the score is a complex pleasure: it is an elaborate instruction manual, a philosophical poem, a calligraphic drawing and music all at once. Lest one think its impact is purely visual, let's all sing Paragraph 7 once again.

4. *Water Yam* by George Brecht

A silent explosion in a box. Take the pieces out, if you can, one at a time, and let them fall quietly on the table, reading them as they fall.

Satisfying just to think about, occasionally necessary to perform. Indeed with these works Brecht underlines the undecidability between reading as a complete experience of a piece, and the conceptual and physical requirements of performance required to turn word into event – an event that somehow translates the brevity and lightness of the description into a temporal frame. A very difficult task.

5. *0'00"* (John Cage)

Deciphering the (one assumes, intentional) contradictions of this work is a science. The score might be the musical equivalent of the Russell Paradox. Also, years later, reading in the work of Alain Badiou about the untraceable origin of an event, I recognized that Cage had discovered this in his own way: the duration of the title is significant – it is *real*.

6. *A certain species of eternity* (1996) (author)

This work led me to widen my understanding of what a score means and what a score can do. The conceptual foundation for the piece was a brief comment by Benedict Spinoza in *The Ethics* that seemed to propose a kind of time we might be able to experience in music. The score is a challenge, open to any musician, to create this time (a sense of infinite duration) as something real (thus, local). Text scores can be like Wallace Stevens' *Jar in Tennessee* – easy to carry and to place just about anywhere, but with the power to transform the landscape by a minimal intrusion and, especially, the engaged participation of readers, players and listeners. The form is that of a disturbance rather than of a package. In the terms of artist/film critic Manny Farber, they are Termite rather than White Elephant art.

7. Antoine Beuger's *l'horizon unanime* (and other works of the period – 1997/98 – *ein ton, eher kurz, sehr leise; tout à fait solitaire*, and *ins ungebundene*)

The explicit influence of Friedrich Hölderlin and Stéphane Mallarmé on these scores leads to pure poetry (but with a mechanical function). The scores can be read in five seconds, but the experience of them may take years to unpack and to understand: their brief resonance, their long duration, their uncanny quality of disappearing before your eyes. Unlike the similarly compact scores of George Brecht, these *must* be performed to be understood. The unmeasurable relation between description and experience, between score and sound (and silence) reaches, for the moment at least, a limit in these works. The beauty of the concept, of the text and of the sound is equivalent but not identical.

8. Manfred Werder's date pieces and Yoko Ono's *Grapefruit*

The work of Werder (and, as I only later discovered, through Manfred's suggestion, Yoko Ono) is life work. Art can impose on life in ways that improve life and that help the people living it become more sensitive to each other and to their environment. It can challenge them to discover the extraordinary event buried under piles of everyday detritus. But it can only do this if it is a vector or a detour. It must be small. It should be transparent and open to anyone. It is also usually quite odd. In fact the work doesn't know how to do this for you, but it tells you that *you already know how to begin*. The work by encouraging you, gives you courage: to try, to fail, to try again.

9. *The Postal Pieces*, James Tenney

Sound capsules in which an entire musical aesthetic is made to fit onto a postcard. As time went on, Tenney expanded individual cards into whole repertoires: *Having Never Written A Note For Percussion* for John Bergamo for example. It is indeed one note (and thus perhaps not a text score?) – but its 'oneness', its shape and its length are really everything necessary to fully realize the piece. Furthermore, this *gestalt* (as Jim would have called it) is transportable and repeatable in various formats and under different conditions.

The collections of features are distinct from one card to another (no doubt because of the variety of musics represented by the people to whom the pieces are dedicated). It is a constellation of forms and thus totally distinct from the formulaic repetition in the wonderful postal work of On Kawara. Hearing them, no one would confuse *For Percussion Perhaps, or....* for Harold Budd with *MAXIMUSIC* for Max Neuhaus.

What better demonstration could one have of the experimental music conspiracy network than the addressing of these works to their dedicatees?

10. *Harmony Series* (author)

My work on this collection of thirty-four pieces began as a response to Tenney's *Swell Piece for Alison Knowles* (another one of the *Postal Pieces*). The experience of beautiful, imaginative and unheard or newly heard harmony that is created under the conditions of the piece's independent 'swells', *without* specifying which pitches would be played, had for me the force of revelation. Maybe, despite my years spent with just tunings, harmony was something more, or even something *other* than the relationship between frequencies. This I know contradicts the conclusion of Tenney's wonderful essay, 'John Cage and the Theory of Harmony': that harmony must be defined as harmonic relations between *pitches*.

What the work in the *Harmony Series* says is that these pitch relations are always there, they are a given – and that their rational *and* irrational relations are ultimately beyond summary. It says that what we understand, as listeners, to be harmony, is, or at least can be, the entirely local and specific set of relationships between a whole set of variables: some known and some unknown; some created, others simply heard. The shape of the sound, the timbre, the exact moment of onset or release – those things in fact which traditional scores struggle (and usually fail) to indicate, may, in the end be a stronger net of relation, of musical knitting than the ratio of their frequencies or the sense of interval. Harmony here is the spontaneous set of responses to a specific situation, carried out by human beings under the auspices of a minimal set of rules. In this situation the score functions, to refer to Wallace Stevens again, as a 'Description without Place'. That place, the one where the imaginary comes into contact with the local and the real, is what we strive to create.

Commentary: *Only*

James Saunders

Only (2005–6) is one of 34 pieces in Michael Pisaro's *Harmony Series* (2004–6), each of which has the same format, comprising an existing text (a poem, or short quotation) followed by the instructions for performing the piece. The title of each piece is drawn from the quoted text, which in many cases has a structural relationship with events in the piece.[1] Pisaro comments on the way in which poems are 'in their own way completely wrapped up in sound', and that the aim in these pieces was:

> to see if embedding that kind of language in a score would affect, and how it would affect, a performer. [...] Obviously [it is] something that was never meant to instruct musicians, and doesn't in these cases. In no case here can you read a poem and know how to do the piece: you still need to be told what the piece is. But I wanted it to be more than a quotation at the top of a piece that may in some way suggest something. I wanted it to really be right there in the midst of it so that at some level you're encountering it again and again. And in some cases, as in the case of *Only*, it's much more of what's written there than what I write. But I never wanted to define what that was [...] For me that would be pretty uninteresting, to try to instruct somebody how to read Rexroth and have it affect what they do in that piece. For me it's enough that it's just there as a central feature of the score itself and truly see what happens as a result of that.[2]

In *Only*, lines from Kenneth Rexroth's *Void Only* (1974) have a literal relationship with the instructions, which is not characteristic of many other pieces in the series. The section, 'I sit quiet/Anywhere Anything/Happens/Quiet loud still turbulent', describes the principal activity of Pisaro's piece, that of 'Sitting quietly. Listening.' This information is presented in two formats: one poetic, one instructional. Pisaro points to the use of a poem to slow the reader down, preparing the presentation of the instructions. He suggests that:

> by the time you get done thinking about what Rexroth was trying to describe, and then you read a set of instructions that say 'well, you might do something like this', you're involved at a level that's a little different than a postal score piece,[3] something that's a few lines on a score that you can grasp instantaneously. [...] I think the process of reading something that you know is a real text, it's not instructions, is a little bit more intense at first than reading instructions. You're already kind of thinking along

---

[1] For example, the 13 lines of William Carlos Williams' poem *The Locust Tree in Flower* quoted at the top of *In flower* (2005) define all 13 of the 30-second sections of Pisaro's piece. The line breaks between the poem's stanzas are translated as additional 30-second silences.

[2] Michael Pisaro, in interview with John Lely, Los Angeles, 14 October 2009.

[3] See James Tenney's *Postal Pieces*, a collection of single-card scores which includes *MAXIMUSIC* (See Fig. 46, p. 63).

the lines of the piece hopefully by the time you've gotten done with the poem, before you even know what the piece is.[4]

Pisaro's other work often explores extended timescales and minimal sonic activity, offering a space for reflection during a realisation, an approach encouraged by the gentle direction found in *Only*. He makes the following comment:

> You could think of a thousand ways of saying or doing something in which you're going to add a tone to the environment, and everybody has a different judgement about what might be 'just enough', but if you have a little familiarity with this other kind of music that I've been involved in then the notion of 'just enough' is a kind of specific one.[5]

Pisaro also emphasises the importance of preparation. Although the text describing the sound is relatively brief, he explains how he settled on the indefinite article to describe the sound:

> When you're in a sense using language to specify that exact thing, that one thing, you're saying this piece will consist of one thing. And under those conditions to say 'a sound' is a much more interesting way of approaching it, or was for me at least, than to write a whole-note B flat, which I could easily have done of course. But when you say 'a sound' you might be saying 'any sound', but because it's singular there's also this pressure on the performer to think of what this 'a' might be. 'Any' kind of implies I'm going to find something and we'll do it. 'A' seems to say there's nothing here and I have to put one sound in that place, and my experience with that so many times was I better feel good about that sound because I'm going to be doing that for the next five hours, you know in some of those early pieces. That's all I have, that one thing.[6]

In August 2009, at composer Jason Brogan's invitation, 21 people made realisations of *Only*, and the documentation was posted on the *compost and height* website.[7] According to the performers, the choice of sound to be made was mostly pre-planned, although in some cases this choice ended up being contingent on the circumstances of the situation. For Joseph Clayton Mills (see Fig. 121):

> it seemed appropriate [...] on several levels, to perform this piece using one of my late grandmother's hearing aids. When clasped in my palm, the hearing aid produced quiet, gently modulated feedback; on opening my hand, the feedback ceased. I spent approximately one hour sitting, listening, and occasionally responding to the surrounding space or the course of my own thoughts by closing and opening my hand.[8]

---

[4] Michael Pisaro, in interview with John Lely, Los Angeles, 14 October 2009.
[5] *Ibid.*
[6] *Ibid.*
[7] http://harmonyseries.blogspot.com/ [accessed 2 February 2010].
[8] http://harmonyseries.blogspot.com/2009/09/joseph-clayton-mills.html [accessed 2 February 2010].

121 *from Joseph Clayton Mills' realisation of Michael Pisaro's* Only.

The careful preselection of a sound was common to many of the realisations, including Jason Kahn's large steel bowl, bought at a flea market in Zurich and played with one hand using a soft vibraphone mallet (see Fig. 122), Adam Sonderberg's oscillator playing a 82 Hz sine tone (see Fig. 123), and Sarah Hughes' chorded zither activated with an e-bow. For Julia Eckhardt however, the decision was limited by what was to hand at the point she decided to make the realisation. She comments: 'I had no regular instrument with me (no space to carry the viola, no time to decide on something else), so possibilities were singing or whistling, of which I very much preferred the second option because of its more objective or straight quality.'[9]

Sam Sfirri decided to play sine tones on his computer 'out of practicality and a lack of inspiration to find a better "extremely long, very quiet tone", while still able to sit quietly and listen'.[10] Richard Kamerman, despite spending a long time considering which sounds to use, also found himself with a limited selection of equipment such that he 'had to perform in a manner that did not require plugging into an electrical outlet. [...] However, most of my battery-powered equipment is not capable of maintaining continuous, non-changing sounds, so there were only a few options left for me in my kit. I turned to a pair of piezo buzzers.'[11]

Performers also determined the location and time of performance in a variety of ways. Knowledge of the immediate environment informed Jason Kahn's decision to realise the piece:

[9] Julia Eckhardt, in correspondence with the author, November 2009.
[10] Sam Sfirri, in correspondence with the author, October 2009.
[11] Richard Kamerman, in correspondence with the author, October 2009.

122 *Jason Kahn realising Pisaro's* Only.

in the Swiss Alps, about an hour's hike from the village of Brüsti in the state of Uri. [...] I'd been to Brüsti several times with my family for holidays, so I knew the area relatively well and was confident I could find a good spot. [...] After arriving in Brüsti I walked further up in the mountains, trying to find a place away from the hiking trails. I settled on a small ridge rising between two valleys, with a view of the Vierwaldstättersee (Lake Lucerne) in front of me. The elevation was around 2000 meters (6000 feet). I spent a good deal of time finding the right position. [...] It became immediately apparent how far removed this site was from the cliché of the alpine idyll, as a steady background of cowbells, rushing water, wind and the occasional airplane made for a very dense and sometimes loud environment.[12]

Sam Sfirri used increasing familiarity with a location to frame his realisation (see Fig. 124), commenting:

I had decided to spend some time in Prague for a few days following the [Ostrava] festival, and found living quarters in a quiet hostel in Prague 7. Every day I would walk by a small porch (maybe 4' x 10' with a bench for

[12] http://harmonyseries.blogspot.com/2009/08/jason-kahn.html [accessed 2 February 2010].

123 *The oscillator used in Adam Sonderberg's realisation of Pisaro's* Only.

124 *Sam Sfirri realising Pisaro's* Only.

two) as I climbed the stairs to my room. It was somewhat hidden around a corner, yet not completely out of view from the stairs. This seemed to be the most practical place to perform, as I shared my bedroom with a rotating cast of six to eight young, college-age people at a time. On August 31st, I found myself at the hostel on a quiet afternoon and decided to perform the piece.[13]

Although Richard Kamerman initially selected a site through personal preference, this was later changed. He comments that:

I immediately knew where I wanted to record the piece: the little park at the cul-de-sac on East 58th Street in Manhattan, overlooking the FDR drive and the East River, early in the morning. The combination of sounds there is great. The highway and the Queensboro Bridge and various electrical and ventilation noises off of the neighboring buildings and a surprising number of birds and it was summer so the odds of some cool boat noises were in my favor too. But mostly, it is a calming place for me. One of those particular locations I go to be quietly alone and clear my head.

However, circumstances prevented this realisation, 'and then all of a sudden, we were in Redding, CA. And I took a walk for dinner and realized it was a pretty nice spot to record a performance of *Only*',[14] with the realisation taking place in the parking lot of the Deluxe Inn (see Fig. 125).

---

[13] Sam Sfirri, in correspondence with the author, October 2009.
[14] Richard Kamerman, in correspondence with the author, October 2009.

125 *from Richard Kamerman's realisation of Pisaro's* Only.

126 *from Michael Pisaro's realisation of* Only.

Michael Pisaro explains simply that he was staying in the Austrian town of Neufelden, and 'walked along a path following the Grosse Mühl until I came to a nice peaceful spot to spend a long period of time' (see Fig. 126).[15]

For others, practical realisations also had a bearing on the choice of location. For Julia Eckhardt (see Fig. 127), decisions were:

> taken for practical reasons: the hour (8 a.m.) because I wanted to play the piece for at least an hour (it was in the end one hour and 20 minutes), and since I was on family vacation, that was the only possible hour: the children were still asleep. It was also a beautiful hour air- and light-wise, and relatively still [...] I had been wondering about the place: should I do the performance at the most obvious place at the seaside, which is the beach? After some consideration I realised it would have been an artificial choice to not use this *grand décor* for such a minimal performance.[16]

---

[15] http://harmonyseries.blogspot.com/2009/08/michael-pisaro.html [accessed 2 February 2010].

[16] Julia Eckhardt, in correspondence with the author, November 2009.

127 *from Julia Eckhardt's*   128 *from Julia Holter's realisation of Pisaro's* Only.
realisation of Pisaro's Only.

For Julia Holter, the choice of Union Station in Los Angeles (see Fig. 128) shaped the performance as it 'only closed for one minute everyday. The hour before this minute must be really different than all of the other hours. The performance took place during the first half of that hour. I wasn't there for the minute.'[17] Conversely, external reference initiated Sarah Hughes's decision to perform in a field, a result of 'reading John Berger's essay "Field", which questions whether one views the field as an environment awaiting an event or event in itself. *Only* presents the same questions and to perform one must first consider their relation with the situation with which they have chosen to play.'[18]

The balance between personal preference and decision-making processes determines the form of these realisations. Pisaro sees this engagement as a central aspect of the piece:

There is something so special about it. This is somebody really performing. This is not casual any longer, at this moment the person is embedded in some process. They haven't just gone into a field and played a sound. They've been looking for a specific way to do that, and I think this surfaces in most of those realisations, the sense that even though just about anything could pass [...] There's no way to be even slightly critical because in a sense it's truly open, but then the sense that each musician takes the responsibility of that tiny little bit of instruction that they're given so seriously, I found that really impressive.[19]

This search for a specific way to realise the piece is also apparent in the methods the performers used to determine the duration of their realisations.

[17] http://harmonyseries.blogspot.com/2009/09/julia-holter.html [accessed 2 February 2010].
[18] Sarah Hughes, in correspondence with the author, December 2009.
[19] Michael Pisaro, in interview with John Lely, Los Angeles, 14 October 2009.

For Sam Sfirri, the objective use of chance to determine parameters removed the possibility of an intuitive response to the situation. This secondary composition process used chance to fix:

> the duration of the piece, the frequency of the tone, the amount of times I would play the tone, the moments in time that I would begin the tone and the duration of the tone. [...] Because of the use of fairly open text (how long is 'extremely long?'), I decided on coming up with an equally open range of durations, frequencies, etc. that could suit the situation and still remain loyal to the piece (and also remain loyal to the sounding range and battery life of my laptop). I don't remember any of the ranges, except for the total duration, which was thirty minutes to three hours, and anywhere in between. I was hoping for a longer duration, but drew 40'11".[20]

For Sarah Hughes, a response to the environment mediated the length of her performance, with the duration being 'dictated by the chorus of sheep in an adjacent field'.[21]

Some performers sought to find an interdependent relationship with the 'large, open space'. Jason Kahn's aim when playing:

> was to somehow find a way of co-existing with the sonic environment up there on the ridge. In a way, I didn't want to concentrate as much on my playing as on all the sound events occurring around me. I'd have to say that the first time I played the bowl [...] after sitting still and listening for around ten minutes, I experienced the strange sensation that I was somehow encroaching on the natural sound environment, so alien did the steel bowl sound in relation to everything else. After several minutes of playing I started to feel more comfortable with my role and found a way into the sounds around me.[22]

Julia Eckhardt also comments on the importance of a personal experience of place when performing *Only*, saying: 'What counts is that it is done, not what is sounding. Then also I performed for the birds, the joggers, the people with their dog who didn't look at me, and what they also didn't know: they performed with me. I was performing the beach, the light and the early morning hour, whoever was aware of these things at any place in the world at that moment, performed with me. It's a matter of performing with instead of performing for.'[23]

This connection with an environment, where a sound and a place briefly co-exist witnessed by the performer and any passing observers, is at the heart of the piece and reflects the harmony of the series title. It is a piece which specifies action and an environment, an event.

---

[20] Sam Sfirri, in correspondence with the author, October 2009.

[21] Sarah Hughes, in correspondence with the author, December 2009.

[22] http://harmonyseries.blogspot.com/2009/08/jason-kahn.html [accessed 2 February 2010].

[23] Julia Eckhardt, in correspondence with the author, November 2009.

Erik Satie

Performance Indications

To Whom It May Concern[1]

I forbid reading the text aloud in the course of musical performance. Any failure to observe this requirement will incur my righteous indignation against the presuming party.

No special cases will be allowed.

Erik Satie

[1] Note in the margin of the original edition of *Heures séculaires & instantanées*, for piano, E. Demets, Paris, 1917. [...] Contamine de Latour relates (in *Erik Satie intime, Souvenirs de jeunesse, Comœdia 3/5/6 Aug 1925;* see *Satie Remembered*, p. 270), how Satie decided one day, with great jubilation, to replace the standard tempo marks (*'lent'*, *'grave'* etc.) with his own made-up expressions ('Without pride', 'With amazement', 'Even whiter if possible', etc.) which addressed the pianist's feelings rather than his or her technique.

After meeting the great pianist Ricardo Viñes, late in 1912, and making him a privileged accomplice for a number of years, Satie – now in the middle of this 'fantasist' period – started to enjoy thinking up performance indications and tempo marks which mixed poetic humour with a taste for the absurd ('On yellowing velvet', 'On the tips of your back teeth', 'Light as an egg'), and which seem to be driven by a desire to disrupt the player's presumably rational approach, in order to make him more easily receptive. These performance indications ended up developing to the point where they began to look like little stories, and charmed a number of pianists and concert organisers to the extent that they started reading them out in the course of musical performance. This provoked the wrath of Satie who could not tolerate these voices over the delivery of his music, whether or not the words were his own work. He declared once and for all that 'these indications are a secret between the performer and myself' (footnote by Ornella Volta, in Satie, 1997).

Performance Indications
(translated by Antony Melville)

A bit hot

A bit rococo but slow

Advise yourself most carefully

A little cooked

A little warm

Alone, for a moment

Alone, opposite

A lot of expression and slower

Almost invisible

Apply within yourself

Apply yourself to renunciation

Arching your back

As if you were congested

As quiet as Baptiste

Assertively

Attaching too much importance

Attentively

At the top of your voice, don't you think?

Avoid any sacrilegious excitement

Be an hour late

Be-dig yourself

Be fixed

Behave yourself, please: a monkey is watching you

Behind

Be invited

Be unaware of your own presence

Be visible for a moment

Blackish

Both hands together

Bounce back scantily

Breathe

Broad as possible

Broadening your head

Broaden your impression

Brutal

Bury the sound

Caeremoniosus

Calm and profoundly gentle

Calm without slowness

Carefully

Caressing

Carried away

Carry that further

Casually

Cautiously and slowly

Cloisterly

Coldly

Continue without losing consciousness

Convince

Corpulentus

Courageously easy and obligingly alone

Cultivate renunciation

Cumulatively

Curtain

Dance inwardly

Dancing

Deferentially

Detached but not dry

Determined

Do as I do

Do not change your physiognomy

Do not come out of your shadow

Do not cough

Do not eat too much

Do not go out

Do not inflate

Do not look disagreeable

Do not lose your bearings

Do not speak

Do not swallow

Do not sweat

Do not torment yourself

Dry as a cuckoo

End for yourself

Energetic

Energetically

Enigmatic

Enthusiastically

Epotus

Even duller if you can

Even whiter if possible

Fairly alert
Fall till you are weak
Fascinatedly
Fast
Fatten
Fidgety
Fierce and forbidding
Flat on the floor
Floating
Fold carefully
Fold gently
From a distance, bored
From afar
From the top of yourself
Full of subtlety, if you believe me

Gaily
Gawp
Gently
Genuinely
Get late bit by bit without
    equivocation
Get soaked
Gird yourself with perceptiveness
Give orders quietly
Go away!
Go down
Go on
Good-naturedly
Graciously
Grandiose
Grandly forgetting the present
Grow bigger
Grow pale
Gummy

Haggard in your body
Half way
Hard as the devil?
Have a drink
Heavy
High
Hold back
Hypocritically

Illusorius
Imbibe
Imitativus

Impassive
Important
In a very peculiar manner
Indubitable
Inevitably
Inflexible
In force
In one breath
In the back of your throat
In the best
In the deepest silence
In the pit of your belly
In the ribs
Into the slow
In your head
Ironically
Is your feeling mellow?

Lacquered like a chinaman
Lastly
Laugh without anyone knowing
Learnedly
Light as an egg
Light, but decent
Light, but loud
Lightly animated
Lights out
Like a beast
Like a gentle request
Like a nightingale with
    toothache
Look closely, that is all
Looking at yourself from afar
Looking at it twice
Look like a fraud

Meanly
Melancholy
Moderate and very bored
Moderate joy
Modestly
More intimately
More relaxedly
Mysterious and tender

Naturally
Neapolitan
Necessarily

Nice
Nobly
Nocturnally
Nocturnus
Noiselessly, believe me again.
Not too rare

Obey
Obligingly
One step at a time
On fire
On the tip of your mind
On the tips of your back teeth
On yellowing velvet
On your tongue
Opacus
Open your head
Out of the corner of your hand
Outward, painfully

Paedagogus
Pale and priest-like
Paululum
Peacefully
Perfect
Physiognomical
Play out, don't you think?
Play right out
Pleasurably, without shyness
Plenty of action
Positively
Preciously
Push apart
Put yourself in the shade

Questioning
Quite blue
Quite slow
Quite well done
Quiver like a leaf

Rather cold
Rather slow, if you would
Riddled
Rise on your fingers
Rising
Rocking
Run

Sad
Sad and more and more calm
Same assertiveness but more inward
Scratch
Second helping
Seriously but without tears
Shake yourself
Silently, please
Sing
Sing seriously
Skilfully
Slow and grave
Slow and painful
Slow down good-naturedly
Slow down kindly
Slow down mentally
Slow down politely
Smile
So as to make a hollow
Sombre
Sound surprised
Stay (half a second) right in front
   of you
Steady as she goes
Sticky
Stir it up inside
Straight in front of you
Subitus
Substantialis
Superstitiously
Supple

Take your hand off and put it in
   your pocket
Tell yourself about it
Tender
Tough as the devil
Try some more
Turbulent
Turn pale

Under the pomegranates
Up on your fingers

Very affectionate
Very boring
Very carefully

Very Christian
Very down to earth
Very far away
Very lost
Very much
Very nice
Very sheepish
Very shining
Very sincerely silent
Very sticky
Very suitable
Very Turkish
Very white
Virtuous
Visible for a moment

Weep like a willow
Weighty
White
White and immobile
Whiter
Wholly and completely
Winking
With a broad view
With a full chest
With a healthy superiority
With amazement
With both hands
With camaraderie
With ceremony
With conviction and stern sadness
With delicate intimacy

With great goodness
With great seriousness and
    courteous gravity
With inane but appropriate naivety
Without batting an eyelid too much
Without getting annoyed
Without grandeur
Without hurrying
Without ostentation
Without pride
Without trembling too much
Without wickedness
Without your fingers blushing
With righteous anger
With sadness
With sadness and inevitability
With shy piety
With slowness
With tears in your fingers
With tenderness
With the flow
With the tips of your eyes and
    holding back in advance
With timid piety
With your body
With your bones dry and distant
With your hand above
With your hand on your conscience
With your head between your hands
With no shine

You see

Craig Shepard

***Lines (1)* and *Lines (2)* (1999)**

Use of Text Notation

Lines (1)

one performer

for Carlo Inderhees and the *3 Years* project

The performer will need a pencil, and a standard letter size piece of paper.

Holding the paper in one hand, and the pencil in the other, the performer draws five lines across the paper.
Each line runs the length of the long end of the paper, roughly parallel to the edges. (in the case of 8.5x 11 inch paper, each line would be close to 11 inches long.)

Between the drawing of lines, there is silence.

Each line is drawn as slowly as possible, maintaining a steady, present and clear sound.

Craig Shepard
December, 1998—April, 1999
South Windsor, Connecticut
USA

Lines (2)

for choir

The choir as a group chooses one pitch in the low range, just high enough to be comfortable for all singers in one of two octaves (baritone and tenor in the low octave, alto and soprano in the high octave).   All singers use only this one pitch for the entire performance.

Singers sing as softly as possible while maintaining a clear and steady tone.

Each singer, independently of the rest of the choir, chooses only one vowel (no consonants) on which to sing, using that vowel for the entire performance.

Each singer takes his or her individual beat from his or her heartbeat, following it as closely as possible.

Each singer rests for a number of his or her beats equal to the number of singers in the choir, and then sings, holding his or her sound for 7 beats.
Each singer continues to rest and then sing, rest and then sing, and so on, until 15 minutes have passed. After 15 minutes, singers finish their individual cycle and remain silent. When all singers have finished, the piece ends.

Craig Shepard
January 1999
South Windsor, Connecticut
USA

Use of Text Notation

Craig Shepard, 2009

Text notation is one way to clearly and directly communicate musical ideas and concepts to the performer. I use text to, 1) give directions on how to perform a piece, like a recipe, 2) to describe mood, feelings, and concepts behind pieces, and 3) as a supplement to describe symbolic notation. The central question concerning notation is communication: how can I communicate musical ideas most effectively to someone who is performing my work? The answer to this question depends on the needs of the piece, the capabilities of the performer, and the situation of the performance.

In *Lines (1)*, it was important to communicate very fine variations and fluctuations. At the same time, it was not necessary to control them. So the score needed to set up the system within which these fluctuations could take place, and to communicate that to a performer who may not be able to read music. Text was a practical means to achieve these ends.

In *Lines (2)* the ideas of perfection and deviation are central to the piece. It is written for a choir making tiny deviations from a perfect unison/octave, which results in changes in the harmonic structure of the overtones. While choirs can generally read music, I wanted the score to be something that could be memorized and performed without sheet music. So I described the system within which these fluctuations could take place using a short text. I also wanted the piece to be able to be performed by those who may not be trained to read music.

Kunsu Shim

PLACES with Airhorn (1999)

Statement: Verbal Notation

PLACES *with Airhorn*

the performance takes place over several consecutive days, each day at the same time. it requires two performers: one to play, and one to listen.

the performers sit opposite each other at an appropriate distance. for each day of performance, decide on new positions within the performance space, taking into account the properties and characteristics of the location.

for each performance, the player performs one action:
the action consists of the sustained pressing of the control button of an air horn, ship horn or melodic car horn, in a way that produces a very soft, continuous sound. instead of an air horn, a different sound source may be used, e.g. a sine wave generator.

duration of the action: in any length, with subsequent silence.
the listener is sitting still for the full duration.
the entire performance is to be carried out in a calm and serene manner.
one is a part of the place.

-----

versions for an indoor space.
version 1.   through the deployment of microphones, relay the environmental sound to the performance space. then play a very quiet sustained sound, using an instrument, object or other sound source, for example a sine wave generator, a piano string with e-bow, a microphone with feedback etc.
version 2.   play the environmental sound as recorded onto tape or cd. within the space, play a very quiet sustained sound, using an instrument, object or other sound source.
the environmental sound or its recording should be transmitted or played back at a low volume. the sound being played live should be somewhat quieter still.

1999
kunsu shim

Statement: Verbal Notation

Kunsu Shim, October 2010

We have come to accept as a matter of course that music can be notated in different ways. I employ text scores mainly for musical performance art. To convey music in words, i.e. through verbal notation, is not suitable if its parameters are complex, dependent on simultaneity or result-oriented, i.e. fixed. However, it is certainly helpful for performance-based sound art, which builds on creative and open situations. To me, verbal notation is not an instruction but a proposal. It is free from coded systems – unlike staff or graphic notation, which are both more or less representative of time and space and require an explanation. This is why I regard verbal notation as an elemental way of transmitting and realising a musical idea. Oral transmission may be more authentic still yet it is dependent on the actual presence of the author.

Mieko (Chieko) Shiomi

Event Scores (1963–4)

Text Notation

Mieko (Chieko) Shiomi, event scores (1963–4). Overleaf

MIRROR

Stand on the sandy beach with your back to the sea.
Hold a mirror in front of your face and look into it.
Step back to the sea and enter into the water.

Chieko Shiomi, 1963

EVENT FOR THE TWILIGHT

Steep a piano in the water of a pool
Play some piece of F.Liszt on the piano

Chieko Shiomi, 1963

BOUNDARY MUSIC

Make the faintest possible sound to a boundary condition
whether the sound is given birth to as a sound or not.
At the performance, instruments, human bodies, electronic
apparatus or anything else may be used.

Chieko Shiomi, 1963

PIECE FOR A SMALL PUDDLE

This piece is performed by several performers.
Each performer takes position around the puddle.
Each stands or squats according to ones own
chosen rhythm looking at the surface of the puddle.

C. Shiomi   June 1964

EVENT FOR THE LATE AFTERNOON

Suspend a violin with a long rope
from the roof of a building
till it nearly reaches the ground

Chieko Shiomi, 1963

Text Notation

Mieko Shiomi, 2010

- Text notation can be used for works in various genres such as music, performance, installation, dance, film, etc.
- Sometimes it needs to be assisted by musical notes or graphic illustrations.
- A text score must convey a clear concept.
- It must be suggestive.
- It should make its possibilities and limitations clear.

- Text notation must be stylistic.
- Descriptions are better kept short.
- It is located somewhere between poem and instruction.

- A text score has its own destiny.
- It always risks being misunderstood.
- In some cases it can inspire even more imaginative performances than the composer expected.
- A person who writes text scores must endure any undesirable performances which were realized from his/her scores.
- However text scores themselves are not damaged by any poor or messy performances.
- This is because text scores always maintain their original concepts.

Hugh Shrapnel

Houdini Rite **(1970)**

Verbal Music

Hugh Shrapnel

Houdini Rite

All performers securely bound (feet together, hands behind back).

They play only when so bound.

If they work themselves partially free they play only with the limb(s) still bound.

The performance can be said to have ended when all performers have worked themselves free or are untied by someone else.

Solo Version:

One performer only (maybe a virtuoso) is subjected to the above treatment; the rest play 'normally'.

August 1970

Houdini Rite

(who thereafter assumes a passive role)

One person, finds the hands
the (behind ~~each other~~ the back) and feet of ~~all~~
each ~~performer~~ rest who may play only
when so bound; performers should not
try to escape, but if they ~~become~~ free use
in a work themselves free, they may ~~play~~ use
only ~~with~~ the limbs ~~it~~ still bound. The rite
ends ~~when~~ for each person when he ~~too~~ x
works himself completely free or is untied
by someone else.

The hands (behind the back) + feet of each
performer are securely bound by one person

Verbal Music

Hugh Shrapnel, July 2010

Why verbal pieces? At the time (from c. 1968 onwards) it just seemed the thing to do – they were in the air (as it were). During the time Chris Hobbs and I and others were studying with Cornelius Cardew at the Royal Academy in the late '60s. Cardew was writing *Sextet: The Tiger's Mind* and *Schooltime Compositions* as well as working out ideas, including improvisation rites that came to fruition in the Scratch Orchestra. Also there were Christian Wolff's *Prose Collection* for the Scratch and, in the recent background, La Monte Young's 1960 pieces and his *Poem*. During that time we all wanted to escape from the museum of the mainstream music world and the hermetically sealed 'guaranteed germ free' Darmstadt stuff that in the '50s and '60s had constituted 'new music'. Cornelius Cardew was the great liberator here and encouraged us all to believe that anything was possible.

One of the most interesting things about experimental music is the exploration of what music is, should or could be (the term 'experimental music' incidentally is one I have always disliked as it suggests experiments hatched up in a laboratory). Verbal scores were the ideal medium for this and could be a poem, a piece of theatre, a concept or anything else. Perhaps the difficulty in writing a good verbal piece is no different to writing a fully notated 'musical' one, the trick being for the end product to have an identity and life of its own.

In his foreword to his book *A Year from Monday*, Cage criticises the role of the composer as: 'simply someone who tells other people what to do. I find this an unattractive way of getting things done.' Given that one of the aims of experimental music was to liberate the performer, it is ironic that the composer of a verbal score is literally telling people 'what to do'. In a verbal piece the performer has no shield from the direct commands of the composer, which the musical notes of a traditionally notated score can be said to provide by allowing the performer a certain degree of 'expressive' freedom. However there are compensations; verbal scores undoubtedly give the performer other 'freedoms' and are an ideal form of notation for non-music readers, thus enabling amateurs and non musicians to take part in new music, as in the Scratch Orchestra.

My verbal scores were mainly written during the Scratch Orchestra period from 1969–72. In some of them I was inspired by Nam June Paik's *Danger Music*, Psi Ellison's wild performances in the Scratch and also perhaps by Michael Chant's stated desire at the time to write 'dangerous' music.

My attempted forays into the outrageous (perhaps done with a typically English reserve) include tying up performers (*Houdini Rite* – I really wanted someone like Sir Malcolm Sargent or Yehudi Menuhin to be the star soloist, not poor John Tilbury!); throwing things at a grand piano, but having a care not to actually damage the Steinway (*Projectiles*); lacerating long stretches of silence with very short, very loud sounds (*Silence*, my 'answer' to *4'33"*); lampooning that most elevated classical instrumental combination, the string quartet (*Accompaniment*); filling out the markings on a wooden floor with chalk (the result looking a bit like a poor man's Jackson Pollock) and amplifying the process with contact mikes (*Floorboard Music*); attempting to wipe out hallowed masterpieces (*Erasure*) – this, incidentally, inspired by Rauschenberg's act of rubbing out a de Kooning drawing.

Other verbal pieces of mine are comparatively old-fashioned in that they have purely musical aims, e.g. *Tripos* and the two *Waves* pieces, the first of which is a chip off Karlheinz's workbench. Others, including *Space-time Music*, *Shadows* and *Sing* belong to the long-lost escapist '60s 'beautiful sounds' aesthetic. Still others, including *Tone Poem* and *flit*, are really poems which can however be interpreted into sound.

After a very long gap I have returned to writing verbal scores in the last few years. Why? Maybe it represents a bit of a relief from writing chamber music and songs, which I have been doing during the last 20 years or so. My recent verbal pieces include a series of Landscapes for various instruments, some using pre-recordings. The first is for musical saw, bottles & swanee whistle, and written for Simon Allen, Bob Coleridge and myself to perform; the third was written in support of the Lebanese people against Israeli aggression and uses a traditional Lebanese tune; the fifth is a 'send up' of grand opera (I had in mind the Marx Brothers' *Night at the Opera*).

More recently I have written *Crosspatch*, a kind of satire on Stockhausen's *Kreuzspiel*; composed for the same instruments it lampoons various aspects of contemporary music (from Stockhausen to Michael Nyman). *After 40 Years* was written for and first performed at the Scratch Orchestra's 40th anniversary celebrations put on by Resonance FM in May 2009. It, rather appropriately, incorporates tunes from the 1940s.

What is the future for verbal scores? Bright, as long as they continue to be written and I, for one, have a mind to do more.

Howard Skempton

for Strings (1969)

On for Strings

for Strings

Waves

Shingle

Seagulls

On *for Strings*

Howard Skempton, 17 October 2010

for Strings was written in 1969 for Cornelius Cardew's Experimental Music class at Morley College. The class met for four hours every Friday evening. Members would arrive around six and the first part would be devoted to discussion, instruction and rehearsal. After a break in the canteen, the remaining time would be given over to performance or free improvisation.

The major project for the Morley College class in its first year – it started in 1968 – was the second paragraph of Cardew's *The Great Learning*, and we were all encouraged to bring drums. I was prompted to write a short text piece called *Drum No. 1*.

The first performance of *Drum No. 1* proved a great success and impressed Cardew who observed that it was a piece which was also not a piece. Indeed, it became the first of the *Improvisation Rites* in *Nature Study Notes*.

Some weeks after the call for drums came a call for stringed instruments. These were not exploited in any disciplined way, but my response again was to write a short text, *for Strings*.

Photocopying was available in 1969 but in its infancy. A copy made at the library would have been a negative: white writing on a black ground. For this reason, I made half a dozen original copies of *for Strings*, two of which I still have.

The five words of the text were written carefully in black ink, using a drawing pen, on white cartridge paper. A sheet was taken from a sketch pad, folded in half and cut with a penknife. Three sheets therefore made six copies (or maybe four were used to make eight). Each sheet was quarto, so each copy was 5 x 8 inches (127 x 203 mm). A pencil line was ruled vertically a little over an inch from the left-hand side to form a margin, and lines were ruled horizontally for the four lines of text. I imagine that the horizontal lines were ruled first, and though it seems unlikely that precise measurements were made in this operation, the two copies in my possession are almost identical: uniformity, albeit casual, would have been the aim. Each copy is in portrait format, the text occupying the upper half of the page. There is no other information: no name, no date, no copyright advice. Once the text had been written and the ink had dried, the pencil lines were carefully rubbed out.

DRUM No. 1.   HOWARD SKEMPTON

Any number of drums
Introduction of pulse
Continuation of pulse
Deviation through emphasis, decoration,
contradiction

135 *Howard Skempton*, Drum No. 1 *(1968)*.

Mark So

Some forgotten day (sparse winter) (2009)

text | composition – scores and structure after 4'33"

Some forgotten day (sparse winter)

    mark so

[1 person, using ordinary means

[an ordinary open place, indoors

The poem of these things takes them apart
    – John Ashbery, "Five Pedantic Pieces"

very simple and soft

realize 1 word at a time from the following page
any sequence, each once for some duration
spaced freely in time

22 april 2009
park city

cloud

snow

horizon

fir

hare

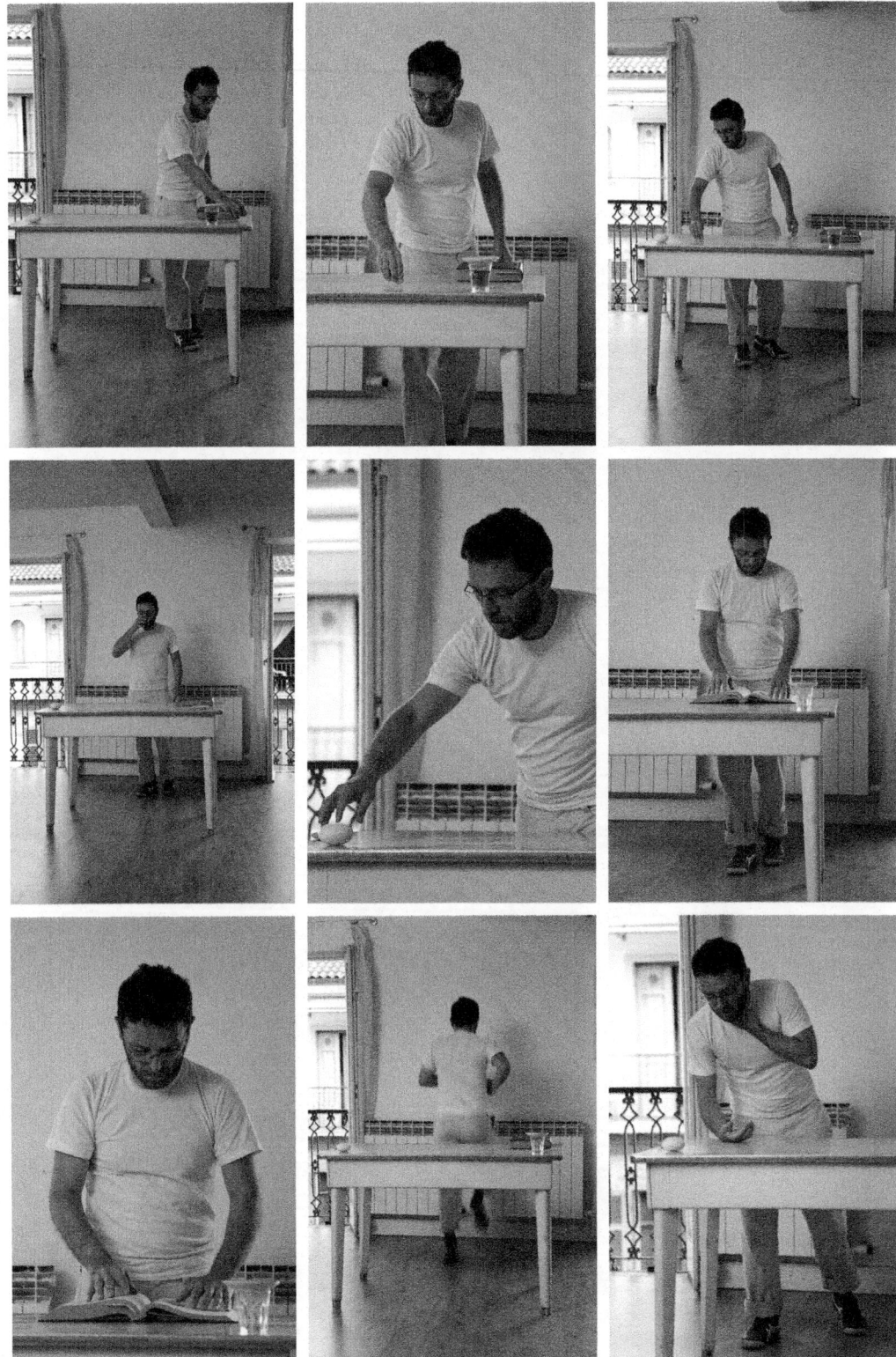

137 *Francesco Gagliardi realising Mark So's* Some forgotten day (sparse winter), *28 June 2009, Associazione 15 febbraio, Torino, Italy.*

text | composition – scores and structure after 4'33"

Mark So, 2010

As I consider my own scores, it's impossible not to be general about how text serves. Often, it defines activity to be undertaken; number and arrangement of participants/materials involved; lengths of time; degrees of intensity; formal proportions; spacing; conditions of harmony, continuity, and setting; etc. Typically, I use an imprecise language of designation – a few sounds, a long time, quite soft, unhurried, somehow overlapping, independent or somehow together, in an ordinary room open to the outdoors, etc., these dicta being vague and purposely diffident as to specifics, generally indifferent to material contingencies and open to, quite radically speaking, *whatever* realization. In other words, I tend to make a deliberately 'boring' foray into ordinary experience, to cast my score in a soft, yielding form, nonchalant in regard to what it will encounter in life; to set water upon sand, so to speak.

The 'common' language I use stands in keen relation to the under-stated, subtle responsiveness of idle chatter, and to the ebb and flow of normal perception. It seems to formulate a poetics suitably receptive to real complexity in simple circumstances, a kind hand greeting life in the embrace of conversation. Against the umbrella-jab of formal imposition, intended to suss out its shape amid the noise, a language rather of the caress, engrossed in the edge between the provisionality of setting out and the community of involvement, within the fluid margins of the encounter; the grammar of this formulation perhaps emerging and disappearing along the subtle arc of its utterance, at once unremarkable and baffling as a desert spring. Instead of calibrating the form of a hard solid, which, when hurled at the wall, stops dead, I want my score to somehow foster communication, to find an angle of permeability, and to slip and weave through the interaction, even/ever potentially to be lost in it.

Perhaps somewhat paradoxically, in coming to grips with the score as a basically formulaic text, comprised of generic textual matter while precisely aimed at the possibility of a singular encounter, I've found that the role of score-writing does not retreat into the circumspect flavor of its (somewhat arbitrary) materials, a purely detached, internally consistent conceptual artifact – that what the score becomes and how it functions is far from arbitrary. If no longer the painting, then surely the score is *drawing*: genre of immediate, just perception; harbor of discoveries as yet unrealized; sharp and incisive, yet necessarily provisional. A language to draw near and touch what can only be discovered in life: a touching question. And it must touch, for its aim is to move duration to song. Anything less garners only the sound of death in the arbitrariness of textual regression, 'about such and such...'. The quality and precision of the question, in other words, show not in the cleverness of what is said to be known by it, but in whether it *works*. There are shapes the pencil makes which the brush knows nothing of, shapes of communication, of trying-out and getting to know, of making and holding contact; the fragile line turning along the path of seduction that draws mind and world into mutual subjection, the track of impressionable insightfulness only after and upon (over) which painting may deduce. What good is a 'comprehensive' question if it fails to instigate the musicality of the subject it addresses – if it fails to touch? A good question yields not answers, but a community of the question (not necessarily a group of people, no society, but all that comes together in perception), gathered along the spreading seam of contact, formulating a discourse through which, in the deepening bond of embrace, the sensation of reality doesn't narrow but explodes.

I know nothing of comprehensive approaches, only small things: what strikes me in the course of a day, reading a poem or some experience of life, etc. For me, this is the only way to set out, an encounter which simply moves me to some sense of its life, and I hold language like a drafting pencil; I want the prick of perception to register in the score, to locate a point and gain access to some avenues onward from it. Like any sequence of drawings, this process doesn't hold still; the very nature of it is restless and experimental, perpetually refreshing, moving on, getting closer, getting involved again and again, and in so doing, learning and getting better at it, making each approach less beholden to its legs and more immediate, more faithful within the nature of the situation. Any system has a baseline of criteria and limits that in a sense lies settled beneath/before even the first mark. This baselining of formal terms is antithetical to the musical situation. It comes to the crossroads only to mark its end, its dire inadequacy to continue, and then forever point back ignorantly to the consistency of its rhetoric, the soundness of its rules, and so on. But language has no such baseline, at least not necessarily so. Language is not an imaging system, but a drafting procedure. Its functions are inherently musical, the development of which require musicianly practices (skills and instincts), perpetually inventing and discovering ways to continue the discipline of an exploratory drawing that moves from text into life. (This, after all, is all that reading is.)

In summary, I would venture that scoring with text involves the combination of these four basic, musical functions of language:

enumerative   instructional
propositional   poetic

Certainly not unique to text scores and arguably prevalent throughout all the history of writing, these functions power the versatile practicality of writing across all its conceivable applications, from banal commerce to poetry. And now, for the first time, the score has come fully into the field of *writing in general*. As the score has passed from its old role as a special kind of representation – somewhere between painting and writing; repository of the proper image of the musical work; surrogate for the mastery of the composer's hand – and into the field of writing (pure supplementarity), compositional structure has become solely the province of realization.

It is hard to imagine a clearer gage of the score's new role than its coming into a condition of ordinary language: manifestly fragmentary, vital supplement to something yet to come, the shape of our setting out... What the score loses in giving up representation, it gains in the elemental utility of language as a vehicle of perception – how the world can arrive in a word, naming our affectionate point of contact with it; how writing makes object of our attentive affection just like drawing does, exquisite marking of our involvement that entrances and incites us to further affection. Not to say that there can no longer be other styles of score besides the strictly text-based (I frequently use them myself): standard notation, graphic diagrams, other schematics both written and otherwise, etc.; nor that the principle of generic formulation necessitates formal imprecision (but this categorical 'paper precision', within the terms of a given formula, will differ fundamentally with the singular precision of what happens, and the composer must accept this as a given). But such considerations are all bracketed by the functional capacities of language, understood entirely within the preliminary role of score-as-text in the wake of *4'33"*, having now become a form of writing in general: like the page beneath this print, definite in shape yet open and speechless, waiting for *whatever* to take place. In this light, the text score reads not as an image of the musical work that preserves its compositional structure, but a text which may initiate it.

All was silent except the pedals
of the loom, from which a tapestry streams
in bits and pieces. "I don't care how you do it."

John Ashbery, *Lost Footage*
(http://docsouth.unc.edu/support/citing/detail/mla_poem.html)

Karlheinz Stockhausen

RIGHT DURATIONS (1968)

Commentary: _RIGHT DURATIONS_

may 7, 1968

for circa 4 players

RIGHT DURATIONS

play a sound
play it for so long
until you feel
that you should stop

again play a sound
play it for so long
until you feel
that you should stop

and so on

stop
when you feel
that you should stop

but whether you play or stop
keep listening to the others

At best play
when people are listening

do not rehearse

Commentary: *RIGHT DURATIONS*

James Saunders

Karlheinz Stockhausen completed 32 verbal scores in two sets, which were published under the titles *AUS DEN SIEBEN TAGEN* (1968) and *FÜR KOMMENDE ZEITEN* (1968–70).[1] In both sets, the constituent pieces are presented in German and English,[2] as well as French in the case of *FÜR KOMMENDE ZEITEN*. They each contain texts that are examples of Stockhausen's concept of 'Intuitive Music', which he defines as music that:

> results from the musicians' spiritual attunement through short texts. To me, the term "improvisation" no longer seems appropriate to describe what we are playing, since improvisation is always associated with the idea of underlying schemata, formulas, stylistic elements. It thus somehow moves within a musical language, even though one temporarily – during so-called "free improvisation" – goes beyond the limits of such a language.[3]

Stockhausen emphasises what he sees as the distinction between improvisation (whether free or stylistically located) and Intuitive Music, focusing on the need to avoid clichés. He comments that: 'playing purely intuitively is an innovation in *all* traditions. Intuitive music is no longer improvisation either. It goes beyond improvisation...'[4]

In *RIGHT DURATIONS*, one of the pieces from *AUS DEN SIEBEN TAGEN*, the instructions specify that long sounds should be played. This immediately limits the types of actions that can be made. Although elsewhere in the intuitive pieces there is more scope for personal imagination, here responses are made within a relatively narrow set of parameters. There is, however, still space for players to respond to the text. As Hugh Davies notes, these pieces:

> place the musician in a very different framework of thinking and reacting from that of the improviser. Given such basic definitions to characterize a particular composition, the performers are then required to be as imaginative as possible in their interpretation, to produce music that they did not know they were capable of producing – the very opposite of drawing on clichés. [...] Stockhausen himself is happiest when he is surprised by the imaginative qualities in the music that results, and – provided that his score has clearly been followed (which hasn't always been the case)

---

[1] Although there are 32 scores in the two collections, the final two pieces in *FÜR KOMMENDE ZEITEN, JAPAN* and *CEYLON,* both rely on a significant fragment of stave notation.

[2] The titles of the two sets translate as *FROM THE SEVEN DAYS* and *FOR TIMES TO COME.*

[3] Stockhausen, 1969/1993, p. 12.

[4] Stockhausen, K., 'Intuitive Music' in Stockhausen, 1989, p. 36.

– welcomes interpretations that are very different from those of his own performing group.[5]

Many of the scores in the two collections rely on decisions from the performer to determine duration and structure. In *RIGHT DURATIONS*, the instruction is to 'play a sound/play it for so long/until you feel/that you should stop'. Here the decision to stop the sound is based on a performer's unspecified feeling that it is necessary to do so. Stockhausen focuses on the intuitive response in his short commentary on *RIGHT DURATIONS*, stating:

> Thus the duration of a note is *not* – as in all earlier music – to be determined by movements of the body or counting, by the clock or by optical signs, by prescribed or agreed-upon timings given by the sounds themselves, by group reactions or rhythmic patterns, but rather by each individual player, always purely *intuitively*, purely *musically*: "until you feel that you should stop". Only this kind of heard out duration is adjudged right in this context. But the duration of each sound depends on the previous, simultaneous and even subsequent sounds: "but whether you play or stop: keep listening to the others."[6]

This final qualification of the earlier instructions also promotes listening as a criterion for the performers to judge when to stop playing. Stockhausen references this further with the clause, 'At best play/when people are listening', stating that when considering the duration of sounds, 'each player is influenced by the listeners'.[7]

The reliance on listening is also a factor when determining the number of players in a realisation. *RIGHT DURATIONS* is 'for circa 4 players' and is one of the few pieces in *AUS DEN SIEBEN TAGEN* to specify ensemble size.[8] According to the composer, this is partly to regulate texture, in particular promoting lower densities of sound, as he explains:

> That is why I always say that the mass begins with 7; with more than 7 all becomes too dense. Exceptional personalities are needed when the group is larger than 7 – say 8 or 9 – players. The best number is 4 or 5. Even with 6, in my opinion, one needs a lot of self-discipline to stop playing for relatively long periods of time during the performance, and to know exactly when the right moment has come, so that also solos and duos and trios occur – not just sextets all the time.[9]

---

[5] Davies, 2002, p. 28.

[6] Stockhausen, 1973, pp. 32–3.

[7] *Ibid.*

[8] The majority are for 'ensemble', with only *GOLD DUST* (small ensemble), *ARRIVAL* (any number of musicians), *COMMUNION* (ensemble at first for 3 then for 4, 5, 6, 7 players, singers) and the theatre piece *HIGH AND LOW* having other requirements.

[9] Stockhausen, 1971, pp. 80–1.

Stockhausen also notes that the nature of the chosen sounds is a factor when determining their duration, adding: 'One automatically *takes into account all the properties* of a sound (its pitch, timbre, volume, its place in a sequence or group or mass) in seeking to *sense* its *right* duration.'[10] So decisions made by the musicians as to the nature of the sounds might also affect the duration of the sounds.

Despite the transcendent aim of his Intuitive Music, Stockhausen is quite clear about what constitutes a successful realisation of pieces from *AUS DEN SIEBEN TAGEN*. He focuses principally on the need to avoid repeating or emulating known music, and for players to listen to each other. He explains this at length in an interview about Intuitive Music in 1971:

> The first sign of rubbish is the emergence of clichés: when pre-formed material comes out; when it sounds like something which we already know. Then we feel that it is going wrong. There is a sort of automatic recording within us, which also automatically spits out all the recorded stuff – also the garbage – and then one stops. [...] While playing Intuitive Music it becomes extremely obvious which musician has the most self-control; the musicians soon reveal whether they are critical, whether the physical and spiritual sides are in a certain balance, etc. Some musicians are very easily confused, because they do not listen. That is the usual reason for rubbish – rubbish in the sense that they produce dynamic levels which erode the rest for quite some time, without realising it themselves. In certain situations some become very totalitarian, for example, and that leads to really awful situations of ensemble playing. The sounds then become extremely aggressive and destructive; they operate on a very low level of communication, and destructive elements prevail (I hope we understand one another: I do not only mean simply 'ugly' or 'beautiful' when I say 'low' level; I mean bodily, physically destroying each other). Then they all play at once. This is one of the most important criteria, that one must constantly remind oneself: 'Do not play all the time', and 'Do not get carried away to act all the time.[11]

The final instruction in the score – 'do not rehearse' – serves to create the optimal conditions for producing such critical playing. By rehearsing, it becomes more likely that a contrived realisation will result. As John McGuire notes, 'all is lost if we attempt to prescribe a specific realization. The text must help to free, not enchain, the performer's intuition.'[12] It is however revealing that, in Stockhausen's view, different performances of the same text from *AUS DEN SIEBEN TAGEN* generate particular shared characteristics. So despite the wish to create something new each time, he sees it as an aim of this work to reveal the essence of the situation that is specified in the score:

---

[10] Stockhausen, 1973, pp. 32–3.

[11] Stockhausen, 1971, pp. 78–9.

[12] Ritzel, 1970, p. 87. McGuire took part in Stockhausen's intuitive music project *Musik für ein Haus* in Darmstadt in September 1968.

Even though each realisation of a text is substantially different in many respects from another realisation of the same text, it has nevertheless become apparent that several realisations of the same text have certain features – music-genetic characteristics – in common. Thus the point is, to discover – by way of the different texts – different archetypal musical processes, each of which leads to very characteristic musical events.[13]

[13] Stockhausen, 1969/1993, p. 13.

Jennifer Walshe

dirty white fields (2002)

Commentary: *dirty white fields*

dirty white fields

This piece is intended to be played by one performer, who both sings and plays violin. Though this is the preferred mode of performance, the piece can be performed by two different performers. The violin part does not require very much violin training beyond bowing. The most important thing is the ability of the performer to be sensitive to how the sounds are made.

The piece consists of four short movements. The notation for each movement consists of three elements:

1. a textual description of the idiom for that movement

2. notated descriptions of the sounds used in that movement

3. audio-visual clips of the sounds used in that movement

This notation constitutes a controlled framework for improvisation. The performer should internalise the idiom for each movement and memorise the sounds. How these elements function locally is up to the individual performer.

Each of the movements should last for ca. 3-4 minutes, and the performer should pause for 20-30 seconds between movements.

one: fizzing bruised white

idiom

Very cold day, biting wind. Sitting by the sea, on rocks. Everything is white and grey, occasional splotches of green, but always mottled with grey and white and dirty white. Listening to the waves coming in and going out, the white noise sound in different parts of the space. There is a wave that is starting next to me and then receding at an angle to the rear left distance. There are bunches of fizzy white noise in the rear-right corner and to my left. Now and then a plane or a train in the far-distance. Perhaps not even this.

The sound abruptly diminuendos when I jump off the rocks and turn my back. You can hear my foot-steps fade up as I walk away. Then cut.

violin sounds

Strings usually muted using the fingers of the left hand (place gently on strings). These are "white-noise" sounds.

1. Bow on shoulder of instrument, hard and soft pressure.

2. Bow in dip of instrument.

3. Bow on shoulder, left-hand side, hitting IV from time to time.

4. Bow on bridge, keeping pressure light.

5. Bow on I, both straight and elliptically.

voice sounds

Air sounds, coloured and dirty. All long, drawn-out sounds. Intakes and expellations on all sounds.

1. [s] s as in sue. Bring tongue back a little – high-pitched whistling sound.

2. [ss] ss as in mission. Low in mouth. Can push to whistling noise.

3. [ci] c as in cat, i as in slid. Slightly low in throat.

4. [co] [po] o as in hot, p as in push. Low in throat.

5. [poo] [coo] [foo] f as in fat. Bring lips into pout, amplify air sound against them.

6. [f] Low in throat. Bring bottom lip up to meet front teeth – spitty, fizzy sound.

7. [di] [du] d as in door, u as in thud. Tiny tips of tongue, as if bursting spit bubbles.

two: filmy smoke white

idiom

Up at Sauce's Creek, or maybe on top of a mountain elsewhere. The West of Ireland. Kerry. There's mist in the air, mist everywhere, there is grey everywhere. It is impossible to tell where the sun is in all this. There's rain beating gently, sprinkling and spackling down on the hood of your rain-coat. You know that every hair on your head is in a curly frizz from the moisture in the air. In the distance, you can maybe see gentle smoke from the chimney of a cottage. The cottage was white, but is dirty white from the sea and the water. You know the smoke is turf smoke, it's just gently soaking into the air above the cottage. The occasional sheep runs by. He's drenched and dirty and the red and blue colours on his coat are running and vivid locally. The sea is far off – you can see it, but hear it less.

violin sounds

Hold violin flat on lap for this movement.

1. Long sounds, melting in and out of nothing. Run the flat of the left hand (palm or fingers) up and down the strings, from the nut to the bridge.

2. Gentle pattering. Use the fleshy pads of the fingers of the right hand to gently tap the strings around the bridge.

3. Soft touch: sweep and patter on the body of the instrument, using fleshy pads of fingers and fingertips of right hand.

4. Circling: swipe the strings around the bridge in a circular motion, using fleshy pads of fingers of right hand.

5. Caressing the scroll and tuning pegs with left hand.

6. Moving the violin around on lap (noise of wood sliding on cloth).

voice sounds

Make very few vocal sounds.

1. Mouth very slightly open, humming far away in the back of the mouth. Two notes, a major second apart, isolated in time. No vibrato. Hum on "m."

2. Mouth closed. Bleating sound – push with belly.

three: silver-spit white

idiom

The Ice Queen. You're on a vast plain. It's covered in snow, very delicate powdery snow. It's also snowing this delicate powdery snow, but it's so fine in the air it's hard to tell if it's mist or just the fading light or snow. It's late afternoon, looks later than it is because of the clouds in the sky, because of the grey and white-ness. What little light there is seems to come from everywhere at the same time. The Ice Queen (and with her the thought that Aslan might die and the fear and sadness and enormity of this) swishes away in her sled, which is pulled by silent creatures just as the field begins. She's gone, and you're left alone. You still know that she's there, somewhere, even though the space is huge and empty and very, very cold.

violin sounds

Prepare the violin by clamping a clothes peg on II, so that it leans over on I and under III. Place the mute on IV. Hand in muting position

1. Ragged uneven tremolando on II, behind and on bridge.

2. Bowing gently on IV and III, far side of left hand.

3. Ricochet bowing on IV and III, molto flautando.

4. Light scrubbing on IV and III.

5. Right hand banging on I, as if aggressively fingering a fast, complex melody (no bow).

6. Silence.

voice sounds

1. Sniffs and short intakes/expellations of breath. Very very cold/scared.
[ha] ha as in had. Warm, at back of throat [ts] ts as in shorts. On intake of breath.

2. Little hoops of sound, at back of throat, like fragment of scared noise.

3. Longer breath sounds.

4. Silence.

four: dark splotchy white

idiom

It's night and dark. Out in the middle of bloody nowhere, the cold is becoming very biting and the wind is whipping up. Everything is dirty dark-white and black with blotches of jet green in it. It's becoming difficult to see anything, just different-size snow-flakes blowing in all directions at the same time. Occasionally there's a lull, but not so often. Sometimes you think you can hear a voice in the storm, in the wind, like perhaps the car turning the corner is the one you're waiting for, but it always recedes, always drives past you in the wet sound.

violin sounds

Prepare violin by inserting a business card between the strings. The card should be threaded over III and II and under IV and I. The card should be positioned so it is half over the fingerboard, half off.

1. Long bows on the strings, both the outer and card-covered inner, bow positioned in the centre of the card. Different levels of pressure.

voice sounds

All sounds with pitch. Pick up on the pitches contained in the violin sounds. Use following phonemes/modes:

1. Inhale, catching a weak pitch.

2. [ng] [n] ng as in spring. Very nasal.

3. [s] s as in vision – dirty sound with interference

4. [wa] wa as in wall. Try to get a hollow harmonic (lips form a small "o")

5. [m] [n] Clench nostrils, amplify the air coming through them.

Commentary: *dirty white fields*

James Saunders

Jennifer Walshe uses a range of notation types in her pieces, in order to create context and convey information to performers. In addition to standard stave notation, many pieces use text and graphic notation, or objects, sometimes explained further by the use of audio-visual documentation. As well as being a practical strategy for conveying the techniques used in the piece, the choice of notation type also says something about the nature of the music.

Walshe explains that she strongly believes, 'the method of notation should reflect the overall philosophy of the piece – you should learn something about the piece just by looking at the way the information is organised notationally'.[1] For example, in the case of *THIS IS WHY PEOPLE O.D. ON PILLS/AND JUMP FROM THE GOLDEN GATE BRIDGE* (2004) (see Fig. 6, page 15), a piece which involves the performer learning to skateboard in preparation for a performance, the score is printed on a T-shirt. In her food-preparation meal plan pieces, such as *MMP #112: 'dear hero imprison'd'* (2004), the scores are printed on small recipe cards presented in vellum envelopes (see Fig. 140).

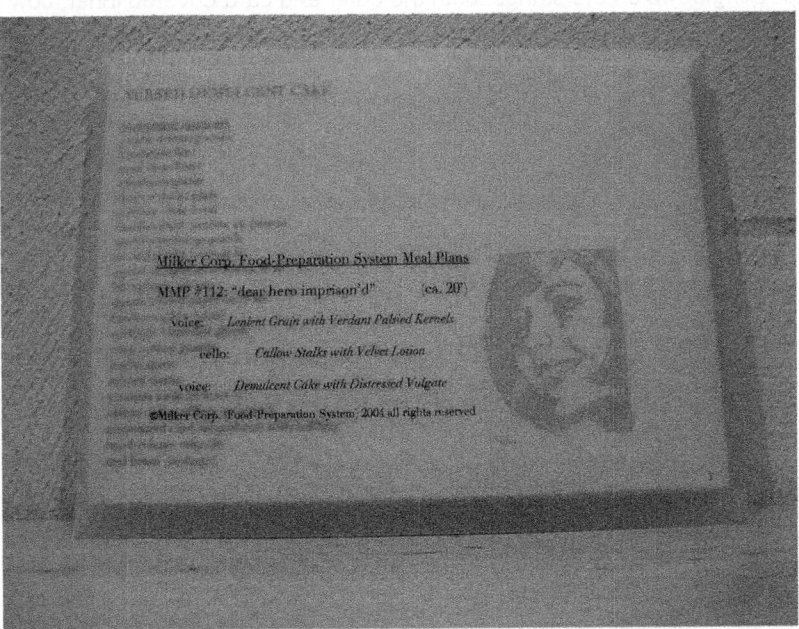

140 Jennifer Walshe, *MMP #112: 'dear hero imprison'd'* (2004).

In *dirty white fields* (2002), a piece in four movements for a solo violinist–vocalist, Walshe presents three different types of notation for each movement, stating that the 'notation constitutes a controlled framework for improvisation':

---

[1] Saunders, 2009, p. 349. Walshe also recognises the influence of Edward Tufte in her consideration of how to present information. See Tufte, 1990, 2001 and 2006.

1. Textual description of the idiom.
2. Notated descriptions of the sounds.
3. Audio-visual clips of the sounds.

These notation types present complementary information. The descriptions of sounds give a technical explanation of their production, supported by the examples given in the audio-visual documentation. The description of idiom provides a context for their production, placing the sounds in a loose semi-narrative structure that shapes their deployment in a performance. Each notation type helps to clarify ambiguities raised by limitations in the others: while a demonstration of a technique (3) suggests the sound to be produced, it does not explain how it is made, especially where it relates to an internal vocal articulation, whereas the description of technique (2) explains how to produce a sound, but says nothing of its character and context (1).

In each of the four movements, the textual description of idiom provides a way of explaining what to do with the sounds, imbuing them with a range of possible meanings and interpretations. The idiom descriptions present an environment. Mostly, these are relatively static, such that any changes caused by events are paced very slowly. Examples include: 'Now and then a plane or a train in the far-distance', 'There's rain beating gently, sprinkling and spackling down on the hood of your rain-coat', and 'Sometimes you think you can hear a voice in the storm'. Each of these creates a context, either through the evocation of physical (sonic) distance, or through continuity.

In contrast, in 'fizzing bruised white', the final separate line does specify distinct, and discrete, events: 'The sound abruptly diminuendos when I jump off the rocks and turn my back. You can hear my foot-steps fade up as I walk away. Then cut.' Here the shape of the event is specified, and an implied structure for the movement as a whole emerges. This is the only movement treated in this way, and the only one to present the idiom predominantly in the first person, although the implied reader is also present in the environment: 'You can hear my foot-steps'. All the other movements place the reader in the environment alone, or with other tangentially involved participants (the Ice Queen and her silent creatures, sheep, the cottage owner, and the plane or train). In the final line, the focus is transferred from the implied author describing her experience, to the point where she leaves and the narrative is directed at the reader, a situation which then remains for the rest of the piece.

The idiom in the first movement also gives the most explicit description of sound, but this is not typical of the piece as a whole. In general, the other movements describe the environment in visual terms, with only very few references to its sound. This is in keeping with Walshe's synaesthetic approach to sound:

My connection with the types of sounds I use is quite visceral. When I write a new piece often I draw up a sort of a mood-board, the way a lot of fashion designers would, beforehand, where I think about colours, textures, smells, anything. And the sounds will often grow out of this – so choosing beige, off-white, dirty cream and pastel milky blue colours, with felt, greasy metal and shaved suede textures, chalk stinging your nostrils and dust mites blinking in dry light, thinking about crackling and spitting and sounds which create tiny clouds of dust, sounds like a lighter bristling into flame or spray cans of water articulating irritated text or vitamins fizzing in water with radio static beside them.[2]

In *dirty white fields* this is the foundation of much of the notation of idiom. The main categories of description are the physical environment, weather and light, colour, time, proper nouns, and the emotion, perception, or physical situation of the reader. This variety highlights the strategies Walshe uses to elicit a response from the performer: environment, emotional state, and cultural knowledge are all used to suggest a point of departure.

This is clearest in 'silver-spit white', where references to C. S. Lewis[3] and winter serve to colour both the physical environment and the reader's psychological state. A protagonist, 'The Ice Queen', is suggested, evoking the threat of this specific character in Lewis's work, as well as the term's more general meaning as a cold-blooded or ruthless woman. Towards the end of the paragraph, though, it is found that she has recently left the immediate environment, such that her absence and possible proximity might inflect the emotional state suggested at the opening. The fact that 'you're left alone' while '[you] still know that she's there, somewhere' creates an element of suspense. This is coloured by the more specific prompt that her appearance gives rise to 'the thought that Aslan might die and the fear and sadness and enormity of this', a culturally specific description which requires passing familiarity with Lewis's work.

The rest of the text of this movement describes the landscape. It focuses on the size of the space, 'a vast plain [...] huge and empty', and the way the light, weather and time of day suggest a specific atmosphere. A particular kind of snow is projected into this environment, creating the potential for gradual change in an otherwise static landscape.

By presenting the reader with this information first, Walshe ensures that the approach to making sounds will be conditioned by the response to the idiom. So when in 'silver-spit white' the voice part specifies the production of 'Sniffs and short intakes/expellations of breath. Very very cold/scared', there is already a context present. Walshe explains this approach in relation to her work in general, saying:

---

[2] *Ibid.*, p. 344.

[3] This movement makes reference to C. S. Lewis' series of children's books *The Chronicles of Narnia* (1950–6), especially *The Lion, The Witch and the Wardrobe* (1950). In contrast, in 'filmy smoke white' the specific location of Sauce's Creek in County Kerry, Ireland is suggested together with the optional 'or maybe on top of a mountain elsewhere'. It is less likely that a performer will know this precise location from personal experience, in contrast to the more readily available Lewis novels. This separates potential realisations more than elsewhere in the score, where the imagery is more generic.

In the past I've also worked with sounds which are imaginary, sounds which function as conceptual descriptions. A lot of the time this involves textual notation, just pure text with no standard musical notation involved. I did a series of 'cooking' pieces which described sounds in highly-detailed imaginative terms. The performer for example might be required to imagine the inside of their body as the interior of a mountain full of mines, feel the blood moving through their veins as tiny carts carrying diamonds to and fro through a tunnel system, and then tip these tiny imaginary diamonds into their lungs to prepare for creating a sound. The audience of course can't *see* the performer creating blasts of white light in their lungs to pulverise the diamonds they just tipped into them. But my intention is that all this preparation and delicate attention means that when the performer emits a vocal sound which atomises the diamond dust, creating a crystalline mist through the air, there's a quality to the sound which comes from these imaginings.[4]

While the descriptions of the idioms are predominantly atmospheric, the explanations of how to make the sounds are more concrete, referring to physical actions that limit the range of possible results. There is however a noticeable difference between Walshe's approach to describing the violin and vocal sounds. The violin sounds are described in relation to the action to be completed: they are a kind of tablature. The vocal sounds, however, in most cases also include a reference to the quality of the sound that is to be produced. So, for example, in 'filmy smoke white', the direction is to place the violin flat on the lap and then perform actions which include: 'Soft touch: sweep and patter on the body of the instrument, using fleshy pads of fingers and fingertips of right hand.' There is no precise indication of the sounds which will result from these actions. In contrast, the vocal sounds in 'fizzing bruised white' are contextualised by the general instruction that they should be: 'Air sounds, coloured and dirty. All long, drawn-out sounds. Intakes and expellations on all sounds.'

The detailed descriptions that follow all include an indication of the phonetic component of the sound, linked to a vocal technique, and in most cases a description of the result of the action. So, for example, this movement specifies '[s̱] s̱ as in s̱ue. Bring tongue back a little – high-pitched whistling sound.' or '[f̱] Low in throat. Bring bottom lip up to meet front teeth – spitty, fizzy sound.' This gives the performer something to aim for. The action is made, and assessed in relation to the description of the sound. Both of these approaches are supported further by the audio-visual documentation of the sounds. These comprise recordings of each of the stated sounds, and documentary evidence where this is possible. So in 'dark splotchy white' the violin set-up is explained further through providing a photograph to accompany the text (see Fig. 141):

---

4   Saunders, 2009, p. 344.

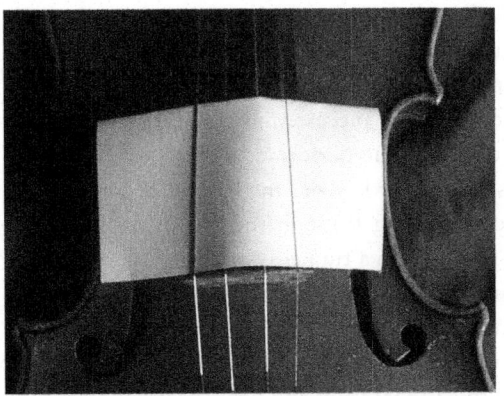

141 *Card preparation of violin in Jennifer Walshe's* dirty white fields.

Prepare violin by inserting a business card between the strings. The card should be threaded over III and II and under IV and I. The card should be positioned so it is half over the fingerboard, half off.

1. Long bows on the strings, both the outer and card-covered inner, bow positioned in the centre of the card. Different levels of pressure.

Walshe's palette of sounds is drawn from her own experimentation, focusing on extended techniques and instrumentalising objects. She comments on being 'particularly taken with "dirty" sounds – sounds we might commonly regard as flawed, or as by-products of normal techniques of playing an instrument, or even as by-products of life, rather than objects worthy of attention.'[5] This juxtaposition of seemingly unconnected sounds in her work is mediated through Walshe's concern with their provenance, and the way in which their associations change when placed in a different context. There is also an element of transcription in her approach:

> I'll have an idea for a sound, and then try and re-create that sound with instruments or find it. Like the sound of a brush scrubbing wet tiles. A lot of the times the sounds might be described as the Foley sounds in a film – when I watch films I am always very interested in the sound design, in how light-bulbs sound as they flicker on, a dog's nails clipping on lino. It's especially interesting knowing that what you are hearing from a Foley track probably wasn't made with the implements you see. If you watch a Foley track being made the disconnect between the objects they use to make the sounds and what you see on the screen is quite wonderful. This appeals to me hugely because the way I think about sound can be very visual, and it's nice to twist that a bit. Often I find myself writing a piece which is basically the Foley track of a film I can see very clearly in my head.[6]

Given the importance of both description and narrative as ways of colouring the physical production of sound in Walshe's music, her use of text either as the sole notation medium or as a significant component in a mixed approach, as in *dirty white fields*, is clearly pragmatic.

[5] *Ibid.*, p. 343.
[6] *Ibid.*, pp. 343–4.

Manfred Werder

2005[1]

Text Scores – Statement (1)

Statement on Indeterminacy

Commentary: 2005[1]

ort
zeit

(klänge)

place
time

(sounds)

2005[1]
manfred werder

Text Scores – Statement (1)

Manfred Werder, March 2009

A beginning of music as beginning which is not yet Music.

This beginning happens in an indetermined field where pure *incidence* may turn into *coincidence* – (something) *occurs*.

Much later Music and Discourse would follow.

Communication systems – language, notation – endure an intrinsic tension between the institutionally established system and their nature: no second use of a sign or a word has remained the same – words and language have already changed, permanently they *differ* (their inherent quality of iteration allows language to become what it is).

So, the precision of a kind of notation becomes a lack of precision because, notation is permanently differing, and emerging through a contextual proliferation.

When I'm hearing the sounding of the world, I sense a beginning of music touching me, transparently, without imposition on but immersion in the world.

Inclusion. Cheerfulness. By sensing and experiencing the vertiginous infinity of mere *occurrence*, something like dignity in relation to the world would appear.

The Score – a sheet of paper.

The plane of the score, be a field of *incidence* – unassignable unpredictability.

Not unlike the performance moment: its inherently environmental drift merely *incides* – and then, performance moment and environmental drift *coincide*.

Insects, plants, geographies have begun to populate my scores – a whole flora and fauna is emerging through the plane of the score.

The *degré zéro* of both a score and a performance is not an accurately prepared blank situation, but in fact *is* the world.

The moment of a score.

Onto that plane of the score, the world is reflecting its abundance, and the lighter the sheet of paper has been inflected by our wish, the more lucidly the reflection of the world on this sheet of paper is manifested. Each letter marks our wish, and therefore inflects the world's reflection onto the score. Wishes incline to the production of monuments. The letters in the score tend to both represent our wishes and produce monuments.

So, there is a precise though chaotically indeterminable economy both of letters and their impact in the world.

Words, a score, a performer, a place, a listener, they all are permanently drifting – drifting along, they meet contingently as part of the world's abundance. Meeting contingently they actualize their potentiality and, permanently become what their drift implies.

Language seems to happen as uninterrupted speech without corresponding reply. Not unlike birds we hear and sing – though we intend to talk to each other. Not unlike birds we adjust ourselves every day to what we come across. There is in a beautiful moment that which has been called the *event* – not only that of a single work but – *of the Écriture.*

Statement on Indeterminacy

Manfred Werder, February 2010

> *Une « époque » ne préexiste pas aux énoncés qui l'expriment, ni aux visibilités qui la remplissent.*
> (Gilles Deleuze: *Foucault*, 1986)

Indeterminacy happens as intrinsic unavailability (*Unverfügbarkeit*) of world, and the occurrence of scores such as Cage's *4′33″* or Brecht's *Water Yam* is beautiful evidence of the efforts to be made in order to trace this unavailability.

These efforts remain, residing somewhere in the scores as evidence (*énoncé*) of the epoch.

But Indeterminacy has become an artistic strategy, and the resultant practice of producing musical situations (encounters referring rather to sound) reflects these efforts of the potentiality of the score, though in a rather chaotic and unpredictable way.

Language oscillates between power and unavailability. A score reflects this structure.

An encounter referring rather to sound and occurring as intrinsically unavailable, could it have emerged through a notation where the quality of iteration of language and notation has been locked and where letters and signs have become mere representatives?

Scores as such occurring as *incident*.
Unavailability.
Regarding their possible realisations, perplexity.
Trace elements of a world.

Commentary: 2005[1]

John Lely

Manfred Werder's practice may be illustrated by a phrase appearing in several of his scores: 'to itself, clear and objective. simple'. Since the mid-1990s his work has moved from finely constructed quarter-tone music for mixed ensemble, for instance *vierteltonklavier und weitere instrumente* (1995), through 4000-page scores to be actualised only once (*stück 1998*), to short texts made up solely of, for instance, lists of geographical terms or philosophical quotations (2008[3], 2008[1]).

Werder has relinquished what he has called the 'differential thinking'[1] of his previous compositional attitude by no longer focusing on materials such as pitch-structure and instrumentation within a score, but rather on the potentiality of the sounding world. He now recognises as 'material' the general conditions of any given situation. He explains, 'I'm not interested in differences as differences, but in nature/life/world, where pure difference exists. So it is the fact *that* (this) exists, rather than *what* differences'.[2] His scores are notable for their refined attention to the details of language, and the experiential opportunities they offer for those involved. 'Each new score is a fine alteration of a situation already existing: the presence of a person actualising the score and the occurrence of sound. Each new score makes me think this situation in a slightly different way.'[3]

Werder's 2005[1] exemplifies this practice. The score comprises three words in German and three words in English, in two spatially distinct groupings. According to the composer,[4] he wrote the whole score by considering how the words would look in both languages, rather than writing the score in one language and then translating it. Given the economy of the score, the use of the two languages provides a degree of context.

In isolation, the English words have several potential meanings; they could be regarded as nouns, or as verbs. However, if one assumes that the two groups of text have congruent meanings, the German words act to qualify the meaning of the English words: in German the words 'ort', 'zeit', and 'klänge' can only be interpreted as nouns. According to the composer, it was his original intended meaning that all the words be nouns.[5]

In the English section, the lack of a definite article, i.e. 'a' or 'the', as in 'a place', 'a time', etc. may suggest broader philosophical meanings, as in the general concepts of 'place', 'time' and 'sounds'. Werder explains the absence of the definite article in German:

> The article 'Die/Der/Das' is called *bestimmter Artikel*, definite article in English, and its use or not substantially changes the meaning or atmosphere in German.

---

[1] Manfred Werder, in correspondence with the author, August 2008.
[2] *Ibid.*
[3] *Ibid.*
[4] *Ibid.*
[5] Manfred Werder, in correspondence with the author, September 2010.

If you say: 'Die Zeit', you imply a shared understanding of what you're talking about in terms either of a possible content or the term itself.

If you say: 'Zeit', the word refers much more to an abstract (indefinite) materiality, and its signification and style is much more floating.[6]

According to Werder, in *2005¹* the words 'ort/place' and 'zeit/time' refer to the 'where' and 'when' of an actualisation. These are the things that are determined by someone actualising the score.[7] The brackets around the words 'klänge/sounds', along with the slight spatial separation from the other words in each group, are intended to signify that while time and place are determined, any sounds that occur might or might not be intentional; intended sounds are optional and there will certainly be sounds occurring in the environment anyway.

The slow, thoughtful designating of a place and time for each actualisation is characteristic of Werder's practice.

I carefully determine both the place and the time, usually this is a quite long process of revisiting a place, and in order to propose a specific form of encounter for guests I'd like to invite (audience). With 'specific form of encounter' I mean the ways in which people and a place come together and form a kind of extension.

Often I realise projects outdoors in the intersection of urban environments and parks, gardens. The selected parks and gardens are usually rather small and insignificant: at most, neighbours and casual passers-by notice and value them for rather simple things like having a rest and eating. There are often home to a beautiful and rich flora and fauna.

No world on stage but just life, and where I love to be.[8]

In order to give a more detailed sense of what informs his decisions of 'where' and 'when', in October 2010 Werder provided descriptions of two events in Zurich. The first description is of a set of actualisations of *2005¹* that had already occurred; the second is of an actualisation of his work *2010²* (see Fig. 143), which was, at the time Werder wrote the description, still to take place:[9]

September 1–30, 2009, each day at 9 p.m. for about 25 minutes, on the shores of the River Limmat in the industrial part of town, it's dark,

---

[6] *Ibid.*

[7] In comparison, Werder's *2006²* suggests simultaneous realisations at different locations: 'orte/ places, eine zeit/a time, (klänge/sounds)'.

[8] Manfred Werder, in correspondence with the author, September 2010.

[9] This took place on Wednesday 13 October 2010, from 6 a.m. to 9 p.m. at Leuengasse, 8001 Zurich.

le mot VERRE D'EAU serait en quelque façon adéquat à l'objet qu'il désigne ...
commençant par un V, finissant par un U, les deux seules lettres en forme de vase ou de verre

(Francis Ponge, Le verre d'eau (25 mars [1948] (matin)), 1961)

manfred werder, 2010^2

143 *Manfred Werder*, 2010².

an open but highly diverse space, very active fauna, lots of traffic of all kinds at a distance, all is in movement: different national train lines, trams, buses, all on various viaducts, the river runs fast, also the clouds moving and reflecting the city lights, planes, all kind of insects near water, passers-by. The short actualisations allow immediate contact with guests: Many evenings the events were followed by beautiful conversations, sitting on the shore with a few guests, some of whom have come several times, pondering what's happening in such a place at such an hour, or in ourselves, and exchanging about many other things.

Or the 15 hours of next Wednesday: it's a rather static and calm place, inhabited by neighbours and passers-by, only few tourists (Lenin's flat is in view, but not adjacent to the square). One extended atmosphere without the possibility of any immediate response through language: some people will come and stay rather for a longer time, maybe several hours, maybe coming back later in the day once more, but the guests and the person actualising the score keep their experience mainly for themselves. A very different extension of experience here, less abundant but more extensive, possibly more introvert, reflective.

There's nothing significant about all these contexts, but it's a way of sensing the world, of being part of the world. In this sense, I really think, it's essential to consider where to locate our work.[10]

144 *Manfred Werder, actualisation of 2010², Leuengasse, Zurich, 13 October 2010.*

[10] Manfred Werder, in correspondence with the author, October 2010.

As the second description makes clear, Werder sometimes presents single events of extended duration. For example, in 2008 he hosted a 24-hour concert at his Zurich home. Such events have tended towards sustained periods of inactivity, with performers only very rarely making sounds intentionally. Werder suggests that this sparseness of performance material, taking place within an extended duration, can produce a profound effect on the listener's perception: 'lack of information magnifies the parameters of experience'.[11] Over the course of an unusually long period of listening, a listener may become hypersensitive to the sonic environment; performance sounds co-exist with sounds of the world. Everyday objects, the acoustic qualities of the space, local atmospheric conditions – all may be magnified and become aspects of the experience. As in John Cage's *4'33"* (1952) (see Fig. 14, page 23), Werder's *2005¹* brings environmental sounds to the listener's attention. However, whereas in *4'33"* the performer remains silent, in *2005¹* the person actualising the score can make sounds. Werder distinguishes his general approach from Cage's: '[My work is] not about exploring new sounds, but exploring a new relation to what the world sounds – as we are actually as much a part of the world as the very phenomenon of sound itself.'[12]

The sparseness of the score for *2005¹* is reminiscent of some of the event scores in George Brecht's *Water Yam*, an influence that Werder acknowledges. In scores such as Brecht's *Word Event* (1961) (see Fig. 31, page 47), the meaning of the single, isolated word 'EXIT' is indeterminate; is it a verb? is it a noun? By privileging one meaning over others, the reader has already begun to realise the score. When asked whether any realisation of his event scores was possible, Brecht's response was, 'Any and every. I wouldn't refuse any realisations.'[13] Werder himself has publicly realised events from *Water Yam*, usually choosing just one score to interpret, and he offers an insight into his own attitude to how to interpret these scores:

> Reading through *Water Yam*, my experience is that music has never been more poetically condensed than in the finest of [Brecht's] work. It's so beautiful that my experience of performing out of it has often been irritating, somewhat disappointing because, I have felt it so difficult to transpose the glimpse of intensity or beauty into the temporal plane of the performed situation. My strategy in Brecht realisations has been to look for, or maybe 'celebrate', a purely condensed occurrence where time and place would hopefully coincide.[14]

Many of Brecht's scores do not necessarily engage directly with sound. In works like *Incidental Music*, the sounds made by the performer are not the main focus of the activity, but an 'incidental' result of those actions (see

[11] Manfred Werder, in correspondence with the author, August 2008.
[12] *Ibid.*
[13] Nyman, 1976, p. 259.
[14] Manfred Werder, in correspondence with the author, August 2008.

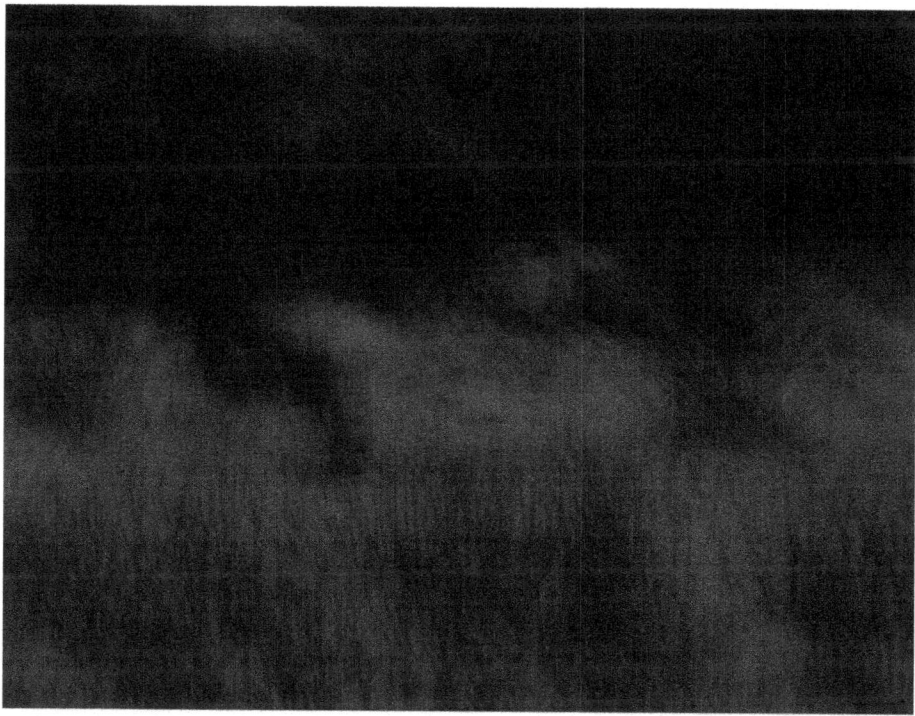

145 *Christoph Nicolaus and Manfred Werder, actualisation of 2006¹, Rosengarten, München-Giesing, Munich, 14 January 2010.*

Fig. 29, page 45). Other event scores may be found to be occurring, or might be realised in a physical form. However, in Werder's own work the concern is with a situation relating primarily to sound. He explains:

> Brecht created the musical genre of the 'event', opening the 'traditional' delimitations of the separated media (music, theatre, dance, literature, etc.). I'm more interested in 'opening' the 'phenomenon of sound' to its place/time specific potentiality/context/dimension. In this sense, I feel like somewhere in between *4'33"* and *Water Yam*.[15]

According to Werder, any person actualising the score should prepare *2005¹* in the knowledge that 'it doesn't have to be "performed", but it can simply be experienced'.[16] He speaks of a person finding a way of making an actualisation 'fit' with its place and time. 'What does not appear in the score should not appear in an actualisation except as its contextual "material", (celebrating the world).'[17] If a person does decide to make sounds, the choice of sound-source remains open. Werder has spoken of making use of objects found at the site of the event, 'non-musical' objects, or possibly regular musical instruments, 'perhaps for reasons of sentimentality'.[18]

[15] *Ibid.*
[16] *Ibid.*
[17] *Ibid.*
[18] Manfred Werder, in interview with the author, Zurich, 23 August 2008.

John White

Newspaper-Reading Machine (c. 1971)

Statement on Verbal Notation

Commentary: *Newspaper-Reading Machine*

NEWSPAPER-READING MACHINE

John White c. 1971

Material: (photo-) copies of a column about a
page long from a newspaper article.

Performers: more than 5.

Procedure: after an agreed signal to start, read
through the material 8 times
continuously, following the stated
instructions (at own speed, no
co-ordination with other players).

1st x: silently.

2nd x: mumbled "sotto voce".

3rd x: silently except for the word "the", sung staccato,
high in the voice.

4th x: text mumbled "sotto voce", the word "and" spoken
sostenuto, low in the voice.

5th x: silently, except interpreting [commas] with the
quiet, firmly spoken sound "tic".

6th x: text mumbled "sotto voce", except interpreting
[full stops] with the quiet, firmly spoken sound "toc"

7th x: silently.

8th x: silently, except interpreting [commas] "tic",
[full stops] "toc", the word "the" sung high and
staccato, the word "and" spoken low and
sostenuto.

At the end of the reading remain silent and
immobile until all the performers have completed
the material before breaking "performer silence".

Statement on Verbal Notation

John White, July 2010

In 1969 I stopped improvising, because most of the improvising situations in which I found myself consisted of a lot of people playing very loudly for a long time to the edification of no-one in particular. I didn't want to return to tonality-orientated narrative composition at the time, but was interested in a kind of lightly controlled randomness in the way that sounds happened in time. 'Lightly controlled randomness' became, in those days, a desirable condition of music in which the sounds were given a chance to 'speak for themselves' in a relaxed way, rather than in over-tightly bundled compositional packages or uncontrolled improvisational eruptions.

Procedures like traditional church-bell ringing, rows of prime numbers, the musical encoding of winning lottery numbers, numerical anagrams of various sorts, in short: systemic procedures seemed a reasonable escape from what had become the very predictable outcome of 'free' music. Hence 'Machines', in which the performers followed clearly defined rules of behavior but didn't lead to a fixed end-result, became for me the genre of the moment.

Newspaper-Reading Machine was the result of a conversation with Michael Parsons during a train journey in which we discussed the ease with which a 'Machine' could be created: in this case a few easy-to-follow instructions regarding the reading and re-readings of an article from a newspaper. 'Easy-to-follow' instructions were a direct statement of opposition to the exaggerated complexities of the 1960s 'inner-circle-Darmstadt' school of musical thought.

Verbal scores are still economic ways of creating desired effects in certain compositional situations. In my own music, simple traditional notation is usually OK for what I need these days.

Commentary: *Newspaper-Reading Machine*

John Lely

Newspaper-Reading Machine (c. 1971) is an example of a score that instructs performers to make use of a found text, in this case a newspaper article, as a secondary score for performance. There are two types of notation at work here: first, a verbal score in the form of instructions describing a general procedure; second, a symbolic form of notation reminiscent of traditional stave notation, in which symbols are associated with particular actions. The composer uses the first type of notation (verbal) to describe the second (symbolic). The found newspaper article is divorced from its original meaning, and instead used like an analogue sequencer. White associates commonly occurring textual elements – the words 'the' and 'and', as well as punctuation marks – with particular vocal sounds. The performers must independently work through the found newspaper article making the appropriate sounds whenever they see the corresponding element in the text. As with some of White's other 'machines'[1] from this time, in *Newspaper-Reading Machine* there is an interest in a spacious, relaxed yet controlled sound world, and its compositional ethos can perhaps be best appreciated through consideration of the context in which the work was originally composed and performed.

In 1969 John White was named 'musical adviser' to the New Arts Lab, Robert Street in London. His brief was to organise a musical performance every Sunday afternoon for a year. White invited fellow composers and musicians to collaborate on various performances of extended duration. Usually any available rehearsal time was greatly out-weighed by the projected duration of the performance. This format was therefore conducive to the very compact 'machine' scores that White composed around this time, which could be explained to performers relatively quickly, and unpacked in full during a performance. In a 1971 interview with Michael Nyman, White explained:

> The sound and activities of the performer are fed like raw materials into a machine or process and emerge as a pattern unique to the occasion on which the particular machine is being performed. The sounds tend towards a rugged consonance, the procedures usually involve much repetition, with changes happening almost imperceptibly over large spans of time, and the atmosphere is usually pretty calm and unruffled however fast the pace of the music.[2]

As well as providing economical ways to generate performances of extended duration, the compositional procedures of works such as

---

[1] Other machines that White composed around this time include *Drinking and Hooting Machine* (1970), *C-Major Machine* (1970), *Gothic Chord Machine* (1970), and *Jew's Harp Machine* (c. 1970).

[2] White, J., in Nyman, 1971, p. 27.

Newspaper-Reading Machine appear to have been designed to encourage, in light of the composer's previous experiences with free improvisation, a relatively formal and disciplined approach to performance. As White comments:

> By 1970 I felt impatient with the complacent attitude of the purveyors of 'free music' with their implied attitudes of indiscipline and lack of regard to the effect on its audience, and felt that there had to be a new approach to the kind of statement that composer/performers needed to make.
>
> To be kept: a certain element of randomness, 'letting the sounds speak for themselves', a relaxing of the strictures of the (by then) traditional 'Darmstadt/New Music' ethos, and a general feeling of sonorous and procedural inclusiveness.
>
> To be discarded: careless and selfish behaviour towards other performers and the audience, a wastage of sounding resources through unintentional cluttering and self-indulgent excess in performing attitude, and obfuscation of all kinds.[3]

This period saw the formation of the Promenade Theatre Orchestra (PTO), a group consisting of White, Alec Hill, Christopher Hobbs and Hugh Shrapnel, all composers, all active members of the Scratch Orchestra (SO). Despite the individual members' associations with improvisation, the group's approach was rooted in composition; an advertisement for a PTO concert in 1971 proclaimed, 'All musical material guaranteed thru-composed. NO hit or miss improvisation!'[4] According to White:

> The PTO was born out of the need to address musical matters at a time when the Scratch Orchestra had become increasingly focused on political issues. There was also an increasingly evident division among the SO between those who had not studied music (notation, etc.) and those including myself, Hobbs, [Michael] Parsons, Shrapnel and Hill, who had been, and continue to be, interested in situations involving precise notation as well as the aspects of what was later to be known as 'performance art'. What started as a splinter group (who met up and rehearsed each others' pieces separately from SO meetings) became an actual alternative to the SO, as we felt that our work was becoming of no interest to the SO and was regarded as elitist.[5]

Performing mostly in art galleries and educational institutions, PTO performances were often presented as part of the environment, a 'sound-orientated performance art', and works composed for the group commonly took this

---

[3] John White, in correspondence with the author, July 2010.
[4] The advertisement appeared in *Contact* no. 3, Autumn 1971, p. 37.
[5] John White, in correspondence with the author, July 2010.

attitude into account. The PTO were regular contributors to the New Arts Lab events. The group met on Sundays in White's front room to play through music composed by members in the previous week and select material suitable for performance. According to Adrian Jack, as performers the PTO were 'hermetically sealed'.[6] This attitude appears to have been in direct response to performance tendencies within the Scratch Orchestra. White recalls being frustrated by the manner in which pieces were presented to the public during Scratch Orchestra events:

> The frustrations came from the mix of performers from different backgrounds. Us 'musos' tended to regard performances, even of non-musical material, as periods of isolation from normal life, and total concentration on the conditions of the piece, whereas the 'non-musos' took a far more casual attitude, and felt free to wander off, chat and continue to lead their lives.[7]

This attitude of 'total concentration on the conditions of the piece' is exemplified in White's score for *Newspaper-Reading Machine*, with its description of 'performer silence' at the end of the score, and the manner in which sounds should be made: 'quiet, firm'. White's use of Italian terms, '*sotto voce*', '*sostenuto*', 'staccato', perhaps also reflects his compositional roots, and while much verbal notation is accessible to those who are not conversant with musical terminology, this piece does require some specialist knowledge.

According to the composer, a performance of *Newspaper-Reading Machine* should be 'somewhat stylised', the sounds made boldly and deliberately rather than as 'the accidental results of people going about their business'.[8] For Christopher Hobbs, the main performance requirement is 'seriousness of intent!'[9] A performer may be tempted to read through the silent sections quickly. However, Dave Smith, who has long been associated with White's music, recommends that 'participants read silently at the same speed as they read aloud'.[10]

> Before attempting a run-through, I always ensure that performers will be mumbling loud enough and are able to interpret the other instructions properly (usually not everybody can): in other words – each performer's approach should be as identical as possible and a bit of rehearsal (it doesn't need much at all) should make this possible. Also, it's important to stamp on the chuckleheads and the grinners, self-congratulatory, self-conscious or otherwise – a pre-requisite for any work of this sort, of course, but something more than likely to arise with anybody participating in this

[6] Jack, 1972, p. 24.
[7] John White, in correspondence with the author, July 2010.
[8] John White, in interview with the author, 10 July 2010.
[9] Christopher Hobbs, in correspondence with the author, July 2010.
[10] Dave Smith, in correspondence with the author, July 2010.

for the first time. I wouldn't say that a 'good' performance is necessarily guaranteed by sorting those matters, but you'd certainly be well on the way.[11]

There are ambiguities surrounding White's machines. Some of them were never written out in score form, and accurate dates of composition are hard to ascertain from the composer. The only previously available published score of *Newspaper-Reading Machine* was a shortened version to be found in Brian Dennis' *Projects in Sound*, a book designed for use in classrooms.[12] The *Projects in Sound* version of the score was, according to White, probably written out by Dennis through his own recollections of previous performances.

Importantly, the Dennis version does not specify that players should read through the same material, but that 'each player selects a newspaper article containing eight fairly substantial paragraphs (all the material should be as different as possible)', thus altering the process considerably. The Dennis version also ends with performers reading the whole text silently and then repeating the last five words 'starting low and quiet and then getting louder and more frenzied until out of breath'. According to White, these last instructions were 'pretty subjective, OK by me, but not an integral part of the original concept'.[13]

The score for *Newspaper-Reading Machine* that is printed here is a new version made by John White in 2010, the instructions having in the past been explained to performers orally or with reference to the Dennis version. As is common with some of his other machines, the composer recognises that over the years there have probably been various versions 'doing the rounds', each being adapted slightly to fit with circumstances – a flexibility that seems quite in keeping with the way the work was originally conceived.

---

[11] *Ibid.*
[12] Dennis, 1975.
[13] John White, in correspondence with the author, July 2010.

Michael Winter

for Sol LeWitt **(2009)**

Relativity and Scalability with Respect to Sound and Silence

for Sol LeWitt

1 glissando; 4 sustained tones

a glissando:

- that has a minimal, almost imperceptible slope.

- that starts and ends at the midpoints in time of two sustained tones with the same duration (at most half the duration of the glissando); the first of which ends and the second of which begins in unison with the glissando.

- with a midpoint in pitch that is equidistant to two (other) sustained tones with the same duration (at least three times the duration of the glissando); the first of which ends and the second of which starts at the midpoint in time of the glissando.

the entrances of the sustained tones are preferably accented with percussive attacks that decay slowly and the exits are preferably accented with percussive attacks that are punctuated.

long; clear; not loud.

–michael winter
(february, march, april 2009;
new york city, san francisco, los angeles)

Relativity and Scalability with Respect to Sound and Silence

Michael Winter, 2009

The (dis)organization of musical elements and parameters typically consists of a set of definitions (automatically complemented by what is left undefined). Most often, the definitions apply to each element independently. For a simple example: a certain instrument is scheduled to sound a tone with a certain pitch at a certain time.

Alternatively, definitions can be relative. That is, elements are not defined independently, but by how they relate to other elements and/or the whole. For a simple example of this: an instrument is defined by its similarity (or conversely; dissimilarity) to another instrument and sounds a tone with a pitch that is defined in relation to another pitch and at a time relative to another sound.

In visual art, this type of organization is exemplified by Sol LeWitt's work. Many of his scores define how elements are related to each other. For example, LeWitt will indicate a location for each element relative to the locations of other elements.

This trend also has precedence in music. James Tenney's seminal text, *Meta∤Hodos*, proposes analyzing sound and silence partially by factors of similarity and dissimilarity. Also, many of his works are largely defined by similarities and dissimilarities (or more general relativities). For example, in the score of *Critical Band,* Tenney calls for 16 or more sustaining instruments; a definition exclusively by commonalities. Many of Christian Wolff's works are also defined relatively. The score of his work *For One, Two or Three People* indicates the possible beginning and/or end of each sound in relation to ('before', 'after' or 'with') the beginning and ends of other sounds. Such examples are actually ubiquitous in music.

Relativity can result in scalability if relativities are proportional as opposed to absolute. For example, telling a person to move three feet from their current location is not scalable; however, telling them to move a distance half the height of the closest person is. Time dilation is a common example of scalability in music. Composers can prescribe scalable temporal relations between elements instead of assigning each element an absolute time.

The concept of scaling a piece without disturbing its structure can be expressed in terms of computability. Let us assume that a given piece can be generated by a computer program. The program takes as input a set of variables that, when changed, alter (or scale) the piece without compromising its structure. In the LeWitt case, for example, the input would be the size of the wall. In concrete terms, modifying a variable that hardly affects the size (in bits) of the program and greatly affects the amount of information the program outputs may imply a scaling with negligible change to the piece's structure. We can illustrate this idea through a piece of music that is scalable in length such as Tenney's *Having Never Written a Note for Percussion* (1971). Changing the length of the piece (so long as it satisfies the instruction 'very long') does not change the structure of the piece at all. If one considers a computer program that generates the piece, changing the length variable of the piece hardly changes the size of the computer program as compared to what could be a radical change in the length of the piece.

In music, total scalable relativity (or at least to the extent possible) is less common. By total scalable relativity, I mean that a variable structure remains consistently and completely isomorphic from realization to realization because scalable relations apply to every aspect/dimension/parameter of the piece. I deeply considered total scalable relativity after experiencing Sol LeWitt's *Wall Drawing #248: The location of a straight, not straight and a broken line, a square, a triangle and a circle.* In this piece, structural isomorphism can never be broken. The piece retains its structure independent of the size of the wall because it is relative to the size of the wall, making the piece completely scalable.

After such considerations, I decided to write what would become *for Sol LeWitt*, which is essentially an attempt at defining a work of music primarily by relativities such that the piece is scalable to the extent possible (as in the LeWitt work mentioned above – hence, the namesake/dedication).

Whether or not I fully achieved my intentions is certainly an uncertainty. Hopefully, the piece is beautiful nonetheless. The score – despite its brevity – took a long time to solidify itself. The final version was preceded by several sketches in which the text was supplemented by graphics and more traditional notations. But the algebra and geometry of the piece are perhaps best communicated by text alone and imagined in mind. It became clear that anything but text alone actually reduced the variability and scalability of the possible realizations.

Daniel James Wolf

The Long March (2009)

Notes with or without Notes

D.J. WOLF

THE LONG MARCH

for four off-the-shelf melodicas

for *Taylan Susam*

Preparation: Compare all unison pairs among the quartet, determining the beat rates, due to mistuning, in beats per second. Make a numbered list of these pairs in terms of beat rates, from fastest to slowest. Only one pair with a perfect (beat-free) unison should be included on the list, any other such pairs omitted. Using chance operations, a selection of these pairs, the number of which shall vary with the available program time, shall be listed, in the form of a score with four staves, one for each player. In the score, the numerical order of the list shall be maintained although not all items have been selected, so that the tone pairs played in score order will have a gradual decrease in beat rates, until a beat-free final unison.

Performance: The four melodica players should be positioned in four equidistant positions around the audience. The space should be darkened except for small individual music lamps for each player. Each unison pair should be played with the duration of a single long breath, beginning as closely together as possible without an audible or physical signal but expiring individually. Tone attacks should avoid dynamic changes but releases should have a light fade without relaxing the pitch. If a pair of players did not play the previous tone, their new pair of tones should begin as immediately as possible with the expiration of the previous tone pair. If a player plays in two tone pairs (or more) in succession, enough time for a breath should be allotted between tones.

Morro Bay, California
1 February 2009

Notes with or without Notes

Daniel James Wolf, October 2010

What advantages and disadvantages does a score in the form of a prose text offer a composer as an alternative to the conventional use of graphic music notation? Under which musical and practical conditions might a prose score be an optimal form for a composition's notation?

Along the Notational Continuum

As distinctly exceptional as a prose-only score may seem to the tradition of notated music, it is useful to remember that the received conventional notation is not exclusively graphical in nature and typically includes several components which are essentially in verbal form, dynamic levels,[1] tempi, technical instructions, and expressive markings among them. Moreover, the graphic display of the Western staff is more a historical and regional exception to the wide variety of alternative notation based instead upon some combination of symbols borrowed from writing or number systems.

One caveat: many of these verbal forms are internalized by practising musicians as if they were graphic symbols; in part this is due to the fact that although the words have been extracted from real spoken languages, by their placement in the context of written music, they have been removed from that linguistic context, which may well become obscure, foreign, and/or archaic to musicians. There is, naturally, some loss of subtlety in this process: non-Italian-speaking musicians readily interpret a bold-faced italic 'p' as 'quiet' and a bold-faced italic 'f' as 'loud', without giving a second thought to more accurately translated terms like 'soft' or 'strong', let alone *piano* or *forte*.

While it would certainly be possible – and several attempts along these lines have been made – to replace these verbal or ex-verbal markings with graphic symbols entirely, and perhaps even to achieve graphic systems for these musical attributes which offer greater precision and less ambiguity, it is probably correct to conclude that within these parameters, the received verbal or abbreviated verbal notations are generally considered to be adequate and to have been successfully interpreted by working musicians. Moreover, it may be assumed that the lack of precision and possibly the presence of ambiguity in these parameters has conventionally been considered, and positively so, to belong to the individual musician's range of interpretative license.

---

[1] Loudness levels are conventionally verbal, albeit often in abbreviated form (*p* for piano etc.) while dynamics proper, i.e. changes in loudness executed over some length of time have come to use both verbal and graphic elements and frequently a combination of the two, for example a 'hairpin' connecting piano to forte, *p < f*, with the length of the hairpin, in its physical length on the page and placement relative to individual notes in the score co-determining the development of the dynamic in time. The interpreter's convention of describing such a dynamic as a shape further illustrates the interplay here between graphic and verbal representations and the acoustical experience of music.

Notes

Neither a word, phrase, sentence nor paragraph in a prose score is necessarily identical to or coterminous with the event construed in conventional notation or what ordinary musicians talk of as a 'note'. There are examples, however, where this may be the case, among them one form of Japanese *shakuhachi* notation, *kinko ryu*, in which a single character is simultaneously a recognizable *katakana* character and a musical pitch with duration indicated by an added mark.

However, the individual, aurally-transmitted performance practice traditions may read particular combinations of these 'notes' as dense, multi-parametric events, thus indicating something more than a Western note.[2] The oldest form of Chinese *qin* notation is a verbal tablature, describing the physical production of sounds, yet as many of the events described involve transient tones or groups of tones, the correspondence to a 'note' is approximate at best.

A contemporary notation practice based on linguistic glyphs can be found in the typographic notation of Danyel Franque. In the first example below (see Fig. 149), letters from the *Kufic* (the ur-Arabic script composed of straight lines and verticals) alphabet are used to indicate pitches (which have not been precisely defined), and Arabic numerals, replicating thirteenth-century Arabic notational practice, are used to define duration. In the second example (see Fig. 150), a Roman alphabet set with diacritical marks is used to notate individual tones as consonant–vowel–consonant syllables, with each letter corresponding to an aspect of the tone, respectively, the attack; the timbre, pitch, and pitch-accent (the diacriticals corresponding to those used in ancient Greek); and the release. Again, Arabic numerals are used to indicate durations.

Although some verbal notations may correspond one-to-one to conventional musical notes, in many prose scores, composers have taken advantage of the fact that this correspondence is not necessary. A prose score may then – and efficiently so – indicate everything from single events to large complexes of events, from single tones to groups, simultaneities, tunes or even successions of chords or entire melodies with minimal but suggestive language. An instruction to an orchestra to play descending scales, without defining the scales any further as to content or as to their coordination, for example, as Christian Wolff does in *Burdocks*, is an efficient means of reaching a complex stochastic texture.

[2] This echoes an older tradition in the West, in which a 'mode' is not just an abstract, scalar list of pitches, but a way or style of singing or playing within a specific collection of pitches, often involving a hierarchy among the tones, transient events, ornaments, accents and other ways of uniquely articulating the connections of pitches to one another.

149 *Danyel Franque,* Abstract Composition IV *(1997).* ▶

ABSTRACT COMPOSITION IV

Für 4-6 archaïsche Instrumente

rab 🐦

Jedes Zeichen bedeute einen Ton (ein leeres Feld eine Pause); Alle Spieler lesen aus derselben Stimme, jeder für sich; Man beginne in einem beliebigen Feld & bewege sich zu einem angrenzenden Feld weiter. 4 kufische Buchstaben entsprechen 4 Tonhöhen, je klarer die Tonhöhe des Instruments, desto enger die Intervalle; überschreitet man eine Doppellinie, so ändere man jeweils einen der 4 Töne. Die Zahlen in der rechten Marge bezeichnen Dauern für alle Felder der entsprechenden Zeile. 🐦 19/8/97 o.z.

P'IRI

FÜR 1 BLASINSTRUMENT

JEDE Sylbe entspreche einem Ton; der 1. Consonant bedeute den Ansatz desselben, der Vocal sein Timbre, der 2. Consonant sein Verklingen. Die Akzente auf den Vokalen bedeuten: í - subtile Aufwärtsbewegung, ì - ebensolche Abwärtsbewegung, î - ein besonderes Vibrato. Es gebe (abgesehen von Inflexionen) nur 3 Tonhöhen, ° bedeute die höhere Octave derselben. Die Ziffern in der rechten Marge bezeichnen die Dauer aller Sylben auf dieser Höhe.

28/08/96 05:40:01

sehr ruhig

b	S	T	h	*m*	D	'	p	k	p	b	l	p	R	d	D	p	b	
â°	ô	à	ó	ý	a	ê°	I	û	y	ì	ó°	a	a	o°	ú	ê	i	**3**
P	w	'	b	S	w	b	h	t	T	r	h	s	L	r	'	b	s	
...	...	:	-	.	-	:	...	...	,	.	.	,	.	:	:	-		
s	W	t	b	r	m	k	m	l	s	t	H	D	H	d	Q	m	d	
y°	e	i°	ù	I°	ý	ú°	a	Ì	y	à°	à°	ì	a°	e	ý°	ó°	ô	**2**
P	w	t	b	p	d	r	s	r	d	h	p	W	'	h	S	h	b	
:	.	-		-	:	:	-	...	,	,	-	.	;	,	-	,	-	
d	p	'	B	d	D	b	m	t	l	q	T	p	r	m	h	d	'	
ì	u	é°	a	y°	y°	ý°	i	ù	u	y	á°	ò	ò°	u	é°	ê	ú	**5**
w	t	p	H	t	*m*	p	p	h	r	d	q	m	l	w	t	d		
,	.	,	:	,	.	:	:	,	...	:	.	:	...	.	;	,	;	
s	B	t	h	m	T	t	k	s	T	p	l	'	w	h	h	s	w	
o	U°	u	u°	e	é	í	a°	ê°	o	ô	ó°	á°	Y	ú°	a°	ê°	Ú°	**1**
'	d	w	r	d	d	'	P	'	p	l	m	r	q	'	l	b	l	
-	,	,	.	.	,	;		-	...	,	:	:	-	,	:	,		
p	W	k	'	s	p	'	w	q	m	B	r	p	p	h	k	w	d	
u°	é°	e	E	y	e	E	i	u°	Í°	À°	à	à°	i	a°	a	u°	u°	**2**
t	T	m	S	d	*m*	w	'	m	r	r	r	w	r	p	r	H		
...	-	:	'	.	...	;	:	;	:	...	...	.	...	-				
t	M	t	'	k	p	'	s	B	l	'	w	h	t	s	w	t		
o°	y	ê	ò	e	o°	Ó	i°	Û	i	e	o	à°	Y	i°	e°			**4**
b	*m*	l	q	h	r	D	'	w	w	b	S	t	L	'	B	k	'	

fin

◀ 150 *Danyel Franque,* P'iri *(1996).*

Recipes

A prose score may represent one stage in an extended development of a musical work. In some cases, it may be considered to be pre-compositional. It may even be thought of as a score whose performance results in the production of a conventional graphic musical score.

Henry Brant made a practice of writing 'prose reports' prior to composing his works, identifying the resources required for the work and then describing, in a mixture of specific and general terms, the succession and character of larger sections or events in a work. Brant described this tactic to me as one which 'removed anxiety' from the composition of the final conventional score, but he also used similar prose reports as functional scores, describing in general terms the materials, character, style and succession of events for performances which he identified as 'instant composing'. I believe that Brant intended to distinguish and distance his own pieces which were so realized both from improvisation and from scores with aspects which were indeterminate with regard to performance, which he viewed as representing rival aesthetic traditions to his own.

Ben Johnston's *Four Do-It-Yourself Pieces* includes one piece specifically described as a *Recipe for a **, but each of the four can be understood as recipes, structured with a list of ingredients and a procedure for their application and combination in the work within a specified time frame. The individual performer realizes the piece very much in the same spirit that one follows a recipe or the instructions for the DIY assembly of Ikea furniture or model airplanes.[3]

The vast majority of these recipe-like prose scores are likely, however, to have been written after considerable experiment and/or a – for the composer – successful performance or series of performances, indicating a final form of the work. There may have been any number of provisional notations used in the process, but this final form is usually the acknowledged public notational form of the work, the score from which additional performances may be derived without further input from the composer. This post-compositional form of the score resembles even more closely the performance practice used in cooking according to received recipes. The published notated prose form of many of Alvin Lucier's musical works and installations is usually the result of such a process, with many of the early performances conducted by means of verbal instructions and only limited written materials or diagrams, if not without a written score altogether. Some of the published scores to works by John Cage, including items in the *Variations* series, were similarly put together after first performances.

---

[3] The research project, as practised, for example, by the Scratch Orchestra (see, for example, their realization of George Brecht's *Land Mass Translocations* in the form of a *Realization of the Journey of the Isle of Wight Westwards by Iceberg to Tokyo Bay*), may be understood as an extension of this recipe concept.

Generic and Specific

It may appear trivial to note that a conventional graphic musical score is more specific than a prose score, except when a prose score is more specific than a conventionally notated musical graphic score. However, each alternative form of notation is likely to be a more efficient notation for specificity within particular parameters.

Generalists and Specialists

Conventional graphic music notation requires (or assumes) a certain amount of familiarity and fluency in interpretation and realization of the notation, attained via a non-trivial amount of training and experience with the conventions and possibilities of the notational system. A prose notation may but does not necessarily advantage a musician with conventional training. Indeed, a prose notation may advantage a conventionally untrained or even non-musician.

When a prose scores has a specific detail, there is a strong tendency towards an arcane, arbitrary, whimsical or witty quality to the specificity (i.e. the numbers in a Christian Wolff prose score), while highly specified details in a conventionally notated score can be read/heard as exquisite, picayune, or precious.

Literacy

A prose notation requires (or assumes) an ability to read a text and to interpret the text so as to realize a musical work. Accurate reading and faithful interpretation are non-trivial skills. The design of prose scores for use by young people or larger groups of players may usefully consider clarity of language to be more important than the inclusion of linguistically ambiguous or obscure elements.

Particular and Universal

As a prose notation is usually made within a single, particular language, it is generally assumed that interpreters will have fluency in that particular language. A text score may well need to be translated in order to be useful to musicians not fluent in the particular language.[4] Conventional Western musical notation has come to have a user base that extends well beyond linguistic boundaries.

Identity

A work may be identified, and defined by its extents and limitations, as much

---

[4] Creative misinterpretations of prose scores by musicians not fluent or even the least familiar with the actual language used in the score may be an interesting source of new performance styles or even new repertoire. There is, of course, a long tradition of similar practices with conventional notation.

by the characteristics of its successful realization as by unsuccessful realizations. Imaginative and enlightened misreadings and inspired but unfaithful interpretations are non-trivial skills.

Idea and Instance

A prose score may be understood as the generalization of the terms and concepts of work realized in one or more conventionally-notated scores. My own *The Long March* for four off-the-shelf melodicas is an example of a recipe for the realization of an indefinite number of more-or-less conventional scores, each depending upon the specific instrumental resources of the realizing ensemble. However variable in detail particular realizations may be, I believe that the instructions in the score will reliably produce performances which are similar enough in character to be recognizable as the same piece.

A prose score may include sufficient variable or indeterminate elements, and/or exist at such an abstract or conceptual level relative to individual realizations in performance or as derived scores such that the relationship between the individual realizations is obscured, or not immediately – or even ever – audible. As a composer, I sometimes find the production of such a prose score to be a useful 'clearing house' for the ideas shared in whole or part by a series of more conventionally-notated works.

Function

A prose musical score may function in domains parallel to, indeed even independent of, musical performance proper. Often, this is a direct result of the suitability of the score to realization by non-trained players, lending itself to pedagogical use. The 'piece' may occupy territory that is not unambiguously musical – theatre pieces for example, but also dance, visual arts, and audio-visual media. La Monte Young's or Karlheinz Stockhausen's collections of text scores, for example, included work which might more readily be described as theatre than music. The entire Fluxus prose piece repertoire cheerfully straddled the borders between music, theatre, dance and the visual arts well before the term 'performance art' had any currency. (George Brecht's preferred term for his performances, 'event', was perhaps the more accurate contemporary term of art.)

The prose-scored 'piece', no longer restricted to musical performance, soon became useful in domains beyond the arts in general, from private – meditation, values clarification, physical or psychological therapy – to social (or even political) settings, including educational, motivational or organizational exercises. Examples: Tom Johnson, *Private Pieces*, Pauline Oliveros, *Sonic Meditations*, Kenneth Maue, *Water in the Lake*, Robert Ashley, *Public Opinion Descends Upon the Demonstrators*.

The work of Kenneth Maue deserves particular attention. Originating as academic work, within the World Music Program of the Wesleyan University Music Department, the scope of Maue's pieces quickly went well outside of any conventional boundaries associated with the discipline of music. Indeed, his doctoral dissertation, bearing the title *Encyclopedia* and consisting of some 50 pieces notated in a shared five-line format, was defended more as a work of philosophy, albeit a form of philosophical performance and demonstration rather than conventional discourse, argument, or proof.[5]

Maue's anthology of pieces, *Water in the Lake,* ranged from the specifically musical to the social and even sacred, and was, for a time, widely used by educators and therapists. One piece of Maue's, for example, instructs the performer to write a list of the names of every person he or she can remember meeting; another instructs the performer to put a book in a freezer and leave it there. These pieces clearly move out of the conventional domain of music as, at a minimum, an acoustic event, but just as clearly, they each require the performance of a disciplined action in time, for which musical performance practice is definitely the model and point of departure.

Prose and Poetry

I have used the word 'prose' here in preference to 'verbal' or 'text' scores, given my own focus, as a musician, on scores containing concrete instructions for the realization of a piece. There are, however, important works in this broad tradition which cannot be easily described as works of prose, but are better described as concepts, images or even poetry. La Monte Young's *Composition 1960 #15 to Richard Huelsenbeck,* which consists only of the text: 'This piece is little whirlpools out in the middle of the ocean' is a strong example of the kind (see Fig. 153, page 425).

It clearly describes an event with sonic and temporal dimensions, i.e. essentially musical dimensions, but the terms of its realization, as a piece to be performed and heard, are far from clear. Is it just concept or image, is it a poetic description of natural phenomena, or is it an invitation to bring – by means undetermined – such an experience into a formal performer/audience environment? The answer is, usefully, open.

Advantage Prose

As a student and journeyman composer through the 1980s, I composed many prose scores. Prose scores appeared to be an efficient and appropriate way of making interesting music with the resources, musicians – many amateur – and rehearsal time – never enough – with which I then primarily worked. Later, around 1990, making scores in conventional notation then appeared to be a more urgent concern, for both my own musical uses and for the players interested in my work.

Thus, it was after a significant break that I returned to writing prose scores in 2008, with the composition of a set of three études for the pianist Hildegard Kleeb. I chose the prose form for a number of reasons, the first

---

[5] There is a decided irony in Maue's prose scores in that they are never verbose, favoring compact instructions over any explication.

of which is that she is a highly imaginative musician, also active in improvisation, and the prose form was ideal for setting her a series of musical tasks designed to take full advantage of those qualities.

Further, in these pieces, I was interested more in an exploration of natural phenomena (i.e. resonances of speech sounds, or the inertial movement of a player's hands) than in a particular arrangement of the sonic results of these phenomena. Moreover, as Hildegard is also active as a teacher, I wanted to write études that might be useful to her in that setting, which could be shared with her students and not only performed as a professional concert work. The études, *Dr Wolf's Complete & Correct School of Piano Levitation* have since had a lively and diverse performance history, by professional and amateur musicians and in a wide variety of settings. This liveliness and diversity was due not least to the advantages of the prose format.

Christian Wolff

Stones (1968)

On Verbal Notations

Commentary: Stones

Stones

Make sounds with stones, draw sounds out of stones, using a number of sizes and kinds (and colors); for the most part discretely; sometimes in rapid sequences. For the most part striking stones with stones, but also stones on other surfaces (inside the open head of a drum, for instance) or other than struck (bowed, for instance, or amplified). Do not break anything.

On Verbal Notations

Christian Wolff, February 2009

I've called them prose compositions. First did them in 1968 when travelling around Britain doing talks about my music, mostly at art schools, wanting as much to do that by having students (audience) trying to play the music as just myself talking about it and playing it alone. At the art schools, though there was usually a handful of guitarists, almost no one could read music, so verbal description of what to do was the way to make the pieces performable, and accessible to 'non-musicians' (really a non-category: anyone could be a musician of some kind, and may have some desire to make music).

That's why first I used verbal 'notations'. Actually all notations, verbal or (standard) visual-symbolic, are simply instructions for what and how to play. The latter, when using grids (staves, measures or recurring metric spaces), allow a certain kind of specificity. Words are different, in some sense less exact in specifying. Words of course frequently accompany standard notation: indications of dynamics (abbreviated as *f* or *p* etc.), tempo or rhythmic feel (allegro, adagio, *alla marcia*, etc.), expression (*con forza*, tenderly, etc.). Somewhere in between, as far as specificity goes, are the notations for slurs, phrasing, attack (staccato, non-legato, etc.), that are visual, though sometimes also indicated verbally.

Making compositions (scores) only out of words can include quite specific prescriptions, especially if numbers are involved: e.g. make 3 simultaneous sounds every 2 seconds. But generally verbal instructions will be more indeterminate or open – or indeterminate and open in a different way – than standard notation, another reason for my using them. Of course standard notations are full of indeterminacies as well – compare various performers' understanding of a non-legato notation, or of 'allegro', etc.

One could also ask, what is the specificity that is notated? The notation tells you play c, f sharp and b at dynamic level 'pp'. That's clear and specific enough, but the musical sense? I tell you 'make sounds with stones'. No pitch, duration, rhythmic procedures, dynamics. But the piece is quite specific about the sound itself, the stones – that will be its identity. To be sure considerable stretching is possible. Usually when the piece is played, though its overall duration is not specified, it will run from 5 to 10 minutes. There is though a recorded performance of it that runs for an hour, including (because of an agreement among the performers that each would make no more than 15 sounds over the total time) vast spaces of silence. Very different versions of the same score, but always the specific identity of the performed sound of stones (only). This kind of variability has long interested me, and the verbal scores are a way of realizing it. Also realizing it very economically – the score consists entirely of just maybe five or so lines of prose.

My prose pieces generally involve instructions for particular tasks that result in performed sound, within a restricted set of conditions that define a given composition. Another kind of verbal composition is more purely suggestive – more like 'graphic' music, in the sense of providing the player with graphic images which must be interpreted subjectively and turned into sounds (Cornelius Cardew's *Treatise* is a classic example). I first encountered examples of this in La Monte Young then Cardew (*Sextet: The Tiger's Mind*). I do it rarely, but the last section of *Burdocks* consists of the words, 'Flying, and possibly crawling or sitting still', where the latter two actions are literal instructions but the first may be taken 'symbolically', that is, suggesting that one make sounds one imagines to represent some aspect of flying, or one represents flying by a theatrical action that may not involve much sound at all. My intent was, at the end of a longish and quite variously indeterminate piece, to open it up in a different way, ending with the beginning of something different.

Commentary: *Stones*

James Saunders

The pieces in Christian Wolff's *Prose Collection* were mostly written from 1968–71, with two pieces, *X for Peace Marches* (c. 1986) (see Fig. 36, page 54) and *Instrumentalist(s)–Singer(s)* (1997), being added later. While parts of other pieces by Wolff use verbal notation, such as *Burdocks* (1970–1), *Ordinary Matter* (2001), and some of the series of *Microexercises* (2006–), the 15 pieces in *Prose Collection* represent his most sustained use of the medium. Although by 1968 the use of contingency and indeterminacy was well developed in his work, drawing in part on his association with John Cage and David Tudor, Wolff points to another reason for making verbal scores:

> In the late 1960s, trying to find ways of providing new music for non-professional performers, including people with no previous musical experience, I made a set of pieces consisting only of brief prose instructions. There was no need to be able to read musical notation. The instructions were the scores, characterized by a combination of precise specifications and general, suggestive guidance, so as to enable the performers both to focus their playing and yet to play freely. I intended a kind of exploratory improvisation, free of specialized virtuosity and of the technical and psychological pressures associated with concert performance. I also hoped to bring about among the layers a feeling for self-imposed discipline as well as individual freedom, both in turn made possible, and given resonance, by their need to work together.[1]

This freedom is apparent in *Stones* (1968), where a range of options is suggested, temporal indications are largely absent, and the instrumentation is readily available. Wolff comments on the origin of the piece 'as an informal solo exploration, on a long afternoon on a stony beach, of some of the range of sounds, resonances, pitches and articulations possible through such an exploration using one specified kind of (percussive) material'.[2]

Stones demonstrates Wolff's characteristically ambiguous use of language to suggest options and openness of interpretation. With the exception of the first two clauses and the final sentence, which are marked for the imperative mood, everything else is optional. The opening phrase, 'Make sounds with stones, draw sounds out of stones' and the concluding, 'Do not break anything', state what should happen in the piece. The intervening text qualifies or modifies these statements. The choices the score provides suggest the kind of actions and material that might be employed, but are not exhaustive.

---

[1] Wolff, C., 'Using the Past to Serve the Present: On political texts and new music', in Wolff, 1998, pp. 128–30.

[2] Wolff, C., 'Revolutionary Noise: Floating rhythm and experimental percussion', in Wolff, 1998, p. 202.

This mix of constraint and freedom is explained by Wolff as, 'an extreme instance of combining maximum transparency, flexibility and freedom for the performers with at the same time an unmistakable, irreducible identity'.[3] *Stones* contains a lot of space for performer interpretation, but is not so open as to allow any possible use of stones. Wolff explains this in relation to his approach to testing the level of indeterminacy in a score:

> What I do is think of the worst case given the indeterminate conditions and the freedom which I give to the performers: what could somebody do given the restrictions I've set? What's the worst that they could do from my point of view? If I can accept that, if that's still okay, then the thing is all right.[4]

There are two approaches to using stones specified in the score. Sounds can be made with stones in either an active or passive way: stones cause sounds to occur, or sounds are drawn from stones. Wolff gives examples of the way in which these approaches might be realised. In the second sentence of the score, three specific categories of sound production are suggested, each of which opens up different types of instrumental possibilities. In the first category, 'striking stones with stones', stones are involved both actively and passively in sound production. Although striking implies a forceful action, there is no further qualification as to the manner in which stones might be struck. In the second category, 'stones on other surfaces', the stones are used only in an active way. The use of 'on' to define these actions is ambiguous however. There is an implication that surfaces are struck by stones, following on from the first clause (i.e. use stones to strike stones or other surfaces), but 'on' might also be taken to indicate friction sounds, or the placement and manipulation of stones on surfaces (he gives the example 'inside the open head of a drum').

The final category is the most open however. 'Other than struck' suggests that the stones are used in a passive way, as objects to be activated using other materials. It also denies the possibility of striking stones with other objects, requiring from the performer a careful consideration of the nature of striking as an action. So while the first example, 'bowing', permits friction-based sounds, other methods might be deemed percussive: consider blowing, spraying, or wrapping. However, the second example, 'amplified', is qualitatively different; amplification makes otherwise less obvious changes perceptible, for example very small movements or changes in temperature. This final category could, however, also allow for an active use of stones, depending on whether 'struck' is seen as referring to the stones or to the other objects or surfaces (bowing with stones, rather than bowing stones). Although Wolff clearly advocates 'striking stones with stones' as the main activity, there are therefore a variety of ways in which the remaining instructions might be interpreted.

---

[3] Wolff, C., 'Stones' in Wolff, 1998, p. 494.
[4] Wolff, C., 'I can't shake Webern's influence' in Wolff, 1998, p. 170.

The temporal aspects of the piece are also relatively open: the score is free of any imposed measurement with regard to time. At the end of the first sentence there are two comments about the distribution of sounds, suggesting that they should mostly be discrete, but 'sometimes in rapid sequences'. The first of these suggestions, that sounds are generally distinct and separated, is also a textural indication, which mitigates against dense and continuous sounds, privileging shorter isolated events. These might occasionally combine to produce constellations of sound, as indicated by the second comment, but the implication could be for performances to feature sequences of events. The score does not state whether this is an indication to be observed as a group, in the case of an ensemble performance, or individually.

This lack of specificity is found only in *Stones* and *Pit Music* within Wolff's *Prose Collection*. All the other pieces give more explicit indications as to the structure of a performance. The score for *Stones* gives no lead as to how sounds and performers might relate to one another, and there is no mention of elements such as pitch, duration and dynamics. Given the percussive nature of the piece, the absence of any instruction regarding rhythmic possibilities is telling. In general, Wolff's music uses a variety of approaches to organising this parameter, including cueing and contingency, free time, heterophony and conventionally barred music, but here the role of rhythm is simply not stated.

As Wolff observes: 'It could be patterned as the player decides or (and) simply emerge from the process of exploring the sound possibilities, the noise, of one's stones.'[5] This attitude may be noticed throughout the score, which leaves many decisions to the performer, and potentially to a group if there are more performers involved. This view is consistent with Wolff's general approach to the organisation of social groups, in which he promotes collective decision-making:

> The score's nature is such that it cannot assert absolute authority, and though this isn't explicit, the players (if there are more than one) have to come to an agreement about how they will set about doing the piece, deciding together or (and) delegating leadership and so forth.[6]

This is apparent in the individualised approach taken by the Wandelweiser Composers Ensemble when recording *Stones* in the atelier of Burkhard Schlothauer's apartment in Berlin in 1995,[7] epitomising a particular aesthetic to which Wolff is sympathetic.[8] Performer Michael Pisaro explains:

---

[5] Wolff, C., 'Revolutionary Noise: Floating rhythm and experimental percussion', in Wolff, 1998, p. 202.

[6] *Ibid*.

[7] Christian Wolff, *Stones*, wandelweiser komponisten ensemble, edition wandelweiser records EWR 9604, 1996.

[8] See Wolff's response to the 1991 composition seminar in Boswil, Switzerland, whose subject was quiet music, and at which Wandelweiser composers Antoine Beuger, Jürg Frey, Chico Mello and Manfred Werder were present. Wolff, C., 'Quiet Music' in Wolff, 1998, p. 232.

We had one rehearsal only: just enough to situate everyone to the recording environment and to see what people were doing. Each person made their own realization of the score, given minimal requirements from Antoine [Beuger] – I think ten sounds, however one wanted to understand that, to be made over the course of the 70 minutes duration of the recording. Naturally everyone had a different method of realizing the piece. Antoine had used chance procedures, and it had thrown up a need to make three sounds at once, quite a trick given the kinds of sounds he had chosen (involving balancing something and striking it in two different ways with stones simultaneously, if I remember correctly). This took some amusing acrobatics, but in the end came off successfully.

Thomas Stiegler made every stone sound using his violin, intertwining pebbles with bow hair in the strings, dropping tiny stones on the body – it was like a miniature symphony in a violin. Burkhard dragged a large stone very gently over the floor of the atelier for a long, long time. Kunsu Shim's sounds were all to occur within a period of about two minutes, 55 minutes into the recording. He sat without any visible motion (as far as we could tell, none whatsoever) for the first 55 minutes and then quietly, almost inaudibly, made ten extremely delicate sounds with a few very small pebbles and some cloth. Jürg Frey, as someone who had performed many pieces by Wolff, had determined, Wolff-style, to hinge a few of his sounds upon actions by others, unbeknownst to the people playing. By chance this had created a situation where the sign for the beginning of a sound and its end (i.e. the actions of two different performers) necessitated that he rub two good size stones over another gently for nearly half an hour. At the end of this Jürg was covered in white dust.[9]

This was a particularly long performance. According to Wolff, 'usually when the piece is played, though its overall duration is not specified, it will run from 5 to 10 minutes'.[10] Duration will inevitably be contingent on the preferences of the performers, and the resources (people, sound sources, environment) that shape the performance context. For example, the different interpretation of the variables 'a number of sizes and kinds' defines aspects of a particular performance: what if there are two stones, or 100; if you use gravel, or small rocks? This might produce, as Wolff suggests, 'very different versions of the same score, but always the specific identity of the performed sound of stones (only). This kind of variability has long interested me, and the verbal scores are a way of realizing it.'[11]

---

[9] Pisaro, 2009.
[10] Wolff, C., (2009) *On Verbal Notations*, see p. 412 of this book.
[11] *Ibid.*

Amnon Wolman

February 26, 2000

Statement

A new sound, a very nervous, taut and nerve-racking sound. You hear it and almost want to put your finger in your ear to dampen it, but you hold back, reasoning that it will mutate, it will turn into something else, but it doesn't. It is an annoying piercing shrill, similarly to a difference tone it is seemingly placed inside your ear. It persists and perseveres. It is not quite electronic, or not what we think of when we say an electronic sound. It clearly has a source, possibly it originates from a machine, a drill that someone controls with their finger and soon they will stop, but they don't. It just keeps on going. Every once in a while the volume seems to have a bearing and it is possible that perhaps it will disappear, but it doesn't. It just keeps on going. It continues and continues - intended on and on. When you (and I) spin our heads it seems to alter only slightly, but then you recognize that it didn't really change. It is not clear if that change was in my head, wishful-thinking or an actual transition. But it is very conspicuous that it is not a variation at all, it's the same. It may go down now, it may even end, but it doesn't. It just keeps on going. Suddenly we are aware that we have no power over it, we can not turn it off, we can not leave, it will stay until someone else will turn it off, until the composer (shall we call her/him that?) will decide to move to something else, another musical gesture. Thinking about such a notion, the prospect brings us some relief, but our focus is brought back to this annoying constant buzz. The thing about it, is that maybe it is not always the same. It is automated like a boring tool but it is not repeating, so when we succeed in thinking of something else it suddenly make these minute small changes and our attention is drawn back to it. It is still there all the time.

February 26, 2000

Statement

Amnon Wolman, 4 February 2009

The interest in text pieces came about from two directions. I started writing text scores for improvisation ensembles in 1988 when working on *Nautilus*, a collaboration of live dance/video/music at SF State University. This piece used texts to convey instructions to musicians, and was made of language taken from the traditional discourse of Western music. But the most useful aspect that came out of this piece/process/research was that I found out that I could specify time in the score in a non-linear way. For example, consider the instruction, 'Start by playing this melody and continue improvising on it, on and off, for the next few minutes. When you are not improvising you may whistle a tune or dance a jig' (this is not a quote from a specific piece but a useful example). In this example the discourse is one of Western music: 'melody', 'improvising', 'tune', and 'jig' are all words that have specific meaning in this discourse. But time, in this example, is not only flexible (i.e. the composer doesn't know how long this section of the piece would be: 'few minutes') but also non-linear. The text describes the action for the full length of the section ('on and off for a few minutes') and then goes back in time to fill the holes in time with new sounds or actions.

The second direction which led me to a different type of text piece is based on a response that John Cage made in one of our classes at Northwestern University to the question, 'what is music?' He responded: 'it must have something to do with sound.' It took me several years to ponder this statement and discover that what made me uncomfortable about it was my interpretation that sound is a literal physical entity, while the other aspect of 'sound', the imaginary one, the one we can recall in our mind without any physical sensation, I treated as a separate entity. This started a process of compositional activity which I grouped under the heading 'imaginary pieces'. These pieces are created by the listener in her/his mind without any physical sensation. The discourse here uses the English language in its normal day-to-day use and, importantly, within the bounds of Western culture. So I use images like 'the beeping sound of a life-support system' to evoke a sound which I feel is familiar to any TV-watching Western audience and is quite precise in its sound contents. Or when I use the image 'a flute-like pretty melody', I use it to evoke a less determined sound but one where I know a lot about its sound contour. Composing in the mind of the audience entails, I believe, describing the sounds in words, so the choice of language and the determination of its cultural context are imperative. And, obviously, this encourages the translations of the text to the language of the locale of the performance. Since I believe that most performances of the pieces happen online, English seemed to be the most appropriate and relevant choice. I use the term discourse rather then performance practice. The term 'discourse' within our academic/artistic discourse clearly identifies cultural context and social structures as components of the discussion. On the other hand, the term 'performance practice' is placed within musicians' discourse and seems to make these two distinctions blurry. 'Performance practice' refers to a body of knowledge that a musician performing a piece uses. 'Discourse' encompasses both that discussion and also the body of knowledge that the audience employs when it listens to a piece of music or is involved in the performance of music.

I found two very powerful tools in this discourse. The first is that it provided me with the ability to mix ugly sounds with beautiful ones without having the 'ugliness' become an issue of discussion between the composer and the audience. If asked to imagine 'ugly' sounds, an audience member will choose a sound that is appropriately ugly for her/him. The second is the ability to choose words according to how they sound and place them next to each other to create rhythmic patterns. This is obvious and elementary in the discourse of poets. 'This sound is tremendously slow, tremendously slow' attempts to convey the sound by using the sound of 's' and attempts to influence the rhythm by repeating the words. This, as in poetry, may get lost in a translation, so I try to limit my use of it.

In the imaginary pieces the audience is provided with a sheet of paper on which the text is printed, and given a certain time to read the text and play the sound in their heads. The notation and layout is important as it does imply certain musical elements. Size of words and the distance between them are, I assume, translated into accents and spaces in time in the imaginary music. There was a suggestion that I project the text one line at a time, gaining more control of time and the unfolding of the piece in the mind. I may do a piece like that in the future (perhaps very soon), but I found that idea problematic for the older pieces, mostly because the flexibility of non-linear time may be lost. For example a sentence such as 'earlier a melody sung by an old female Arab voice started but it just now became noticeable' may lose the power it has of moving backwards in time. If time is explicit, as it is when the line appears in the projection in a pre-specified moment, the conviction that we moved backwards in time may be lost. But, as I said, this new idea has my interest, and it does seem to solve one problem that the text pieces have: that descriptions of time of different durations are read at equal durations. For example, 'the low timbre becomes louder very slowly' and 'the high sound becomes softer very quickly' take the same amount of time to read, but should take different lengths of time to play in one's head.

As I am writing this I am reading Oliver Sachs' book *Musicophilia*. It's a wonderful, amazing book that summarizes the current research on how the brain processes music, sound, and the memory of music. There is abundant evidence that the ability to imagine music and sound is common to all of us, and the ability to create new music based on memories of music in the mind is also common. My imaginary pieces, in this context, seem very obvious, and not at all radical or unusual.

The imaginary pieces present an expression of another one of my interests, that of audience/performer/composer interactions. For many years I've struggled with the role of the audience and their placement in the world of music, and what it does to the music itself. There are many questions that arise. The first one that comes to mind is the placement of the audience as a trapped group of like-minded individuals. In any live music concert the audience is identified as a group of equal members, equal in that they are all there for one reason, that is to listen to the music. This can be, and is, sometimes translated to mean that they are also going through a similar experience, and that the music played was heard by all in the same way. This is the basis of, for example, music criticism, where the critic is responding to a performance which, it is assumed, all around heard the same thing. This is a notion that I reject. Many times I came out of a concert and while attempting to describe to my friends what it is I heard, I discovered that they heard something else altogether. In the classical music world there is an even more restrictive situation. The audience is placed in such a way (the lights are on) which makes leaving the hall in the middle of a piece close to impossible. In essence the audience is trapped in their seats for the duration of the piece. Obviously it is a choice that they made responsibly in advance, but can people not change their minds? Perhaps the most significant question that arises, for me, as an aspect of the traditional placement of the audience, is that the sound we hear as musicians is so much better, and richer than what the audience gets. When you are on stage, in the orchestra, the choir, or next to a pianist alone, what I hear, in terms of sound, is much richer and all-engulfing than any sound projected to the audience directly or through loudspeakers. How to get the audience to move among the performers, to feel free to move in and out of the space, and to get a sense that their experience is both individual and collective are questions that I tried to solve to varying success in different pieces (*The Andy Warhol Diaries*, *NU Piece*, *Cruising Prohibited When Lights Flashing*) in the installations (the *Speakers Suite*, *The Speakers Army Jacket*, *Attention Step*) and in the imaginary pieces. In the imaginary pieces the individual and private is expressed and emphasized. The audience member is the performer. The total experience and the sounds created to represent it are clearly individual, and it is the commonality of the experience which is uncertain and may be discussed. The freedom of the choice of involvement with the piece is held exclusively within the prerogative of the listener/performer.

La Monte Young

Composition 1960 #2

Build a fire in front of the audience. Preferably, use wood although other combustibles may be used as necessary for starting the fire or controlling the kind of smoke. The fire may be of any size, but it should not be the kind which is associated with another object, such as a candle or a cigarette lighter. The lights may be turned out.

After the fire is burning, the builder(s) may sit by and watch it for the duration of the composition; however, he (they) should not sit between the fire and the audience in order that its members will be able to see and enjoy the fire.

The composition may be of any duration.

In the event that the performance is broadcast, the microphone may be brought up close to the fire.

5 · 5 · 60

Composition 1960 #3

Announce to the audience when the piece will begin and end if there is a limit on duration. It may be of any duration.

Then announce that everyone may do whatever he wishes for the duration of the composition.

5 · 14 · 60

Composition 1960 #4

Announce to the audience that the lights will be turned off for the duration of the composition (it may be any length) and tell them when the composition will begin and end.

Turn off all the lights for the announced duration.

When the lights are turned back on, the announcer may tell the audience that their activities have been the composition, although this is not at all necessary.

6 · 3 · 60

Composition 1960 #5

Turn a butterfly (or any number of butterflies) loose in the performance area.

When the composition is over, be sure to allow the butterfly to fly away outside.

The composition may be any length but if an unlimited amount of time is available, the doors and windows may be opened before the butterfly is turned loose and the composition may be considered finished when the butterfly flies away.

6 · 8 · 60

Piano Piece for Terry Riley #1

Push the piano up to a wall and put the flat side flush against it. Then continue pushing into the wall. Push as hard as you can. If the piano goes through the wall, keep pushing in the same direction regardless of new obstacles and continue to push as hard as you can whether the piano is stopped against an obstacle or moving. The piece is over when you are too exhausted to push any longer.

2:10 A.M.
November 8, 1960

Composition 1960 #6

The performers (any number) sit on the stage watching and listening to the audience in the same way the audience usually looks at and listens to performers. If in an auditorium, the performers should be seated in rows on chairs or benches; but if in a bar, for instance, the performers might have tables on stage and be drinking as is the audience.

Optional: A poster in the vicinity of the stage reading: COMPOSITION 1960 #6
by
La Monte Young
admission

(price)

and tickets, sold at stairways leading to stage from audience, admitting members of the audience who wish to join the performers on stage and watch the remainder of the audience.

A performance may be of any duration.

July 2, 1960

Piano Piece for David Tudor #1

Bring a bale of hay and a bucket
of water onto the stage for the
piano to eat and drink. The
performer may then feed the piano
or leave it to eat by itself. If the
the former, the piece is over after
the piano has been fed. If the
latter, it is over after the piano
eats or decides not to.

October 1960

Piano Piece for David Tudor #2

Open the keyboard cover without
making, from the operation, any
sound that is audible to you.
Try as many times as you like.
The piece is over either when
you succeed or when you decide
to stop trying. It is not
necessary to explain to the
audience. Simply do what you
do and, when the piece is over,
indicate it in a customary way.

October 1960

Piano Piece for David Tudor #3

most of them
were very old grasshoppers

November 14, 1960

Composition 1960 #7

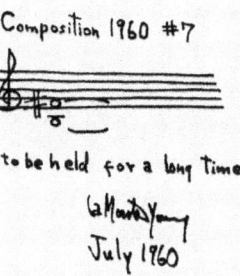

to be held for a long time

La Monte Young
July 1960

Composition 1960 #10
    to Bob Morris

Draw a straight line
and follow it.

October 1960

Composition 1960 #13
to Richard Huelsenbeck

The performer should
prepare any composition
and then perform it as
well as he can.

November 9, 1960

Composition 1960 #15
to Richard Huelsenbeck

This piece is little whirlpools
out in the middle of the ocean.

9:05 A.M.
December 25, 1960

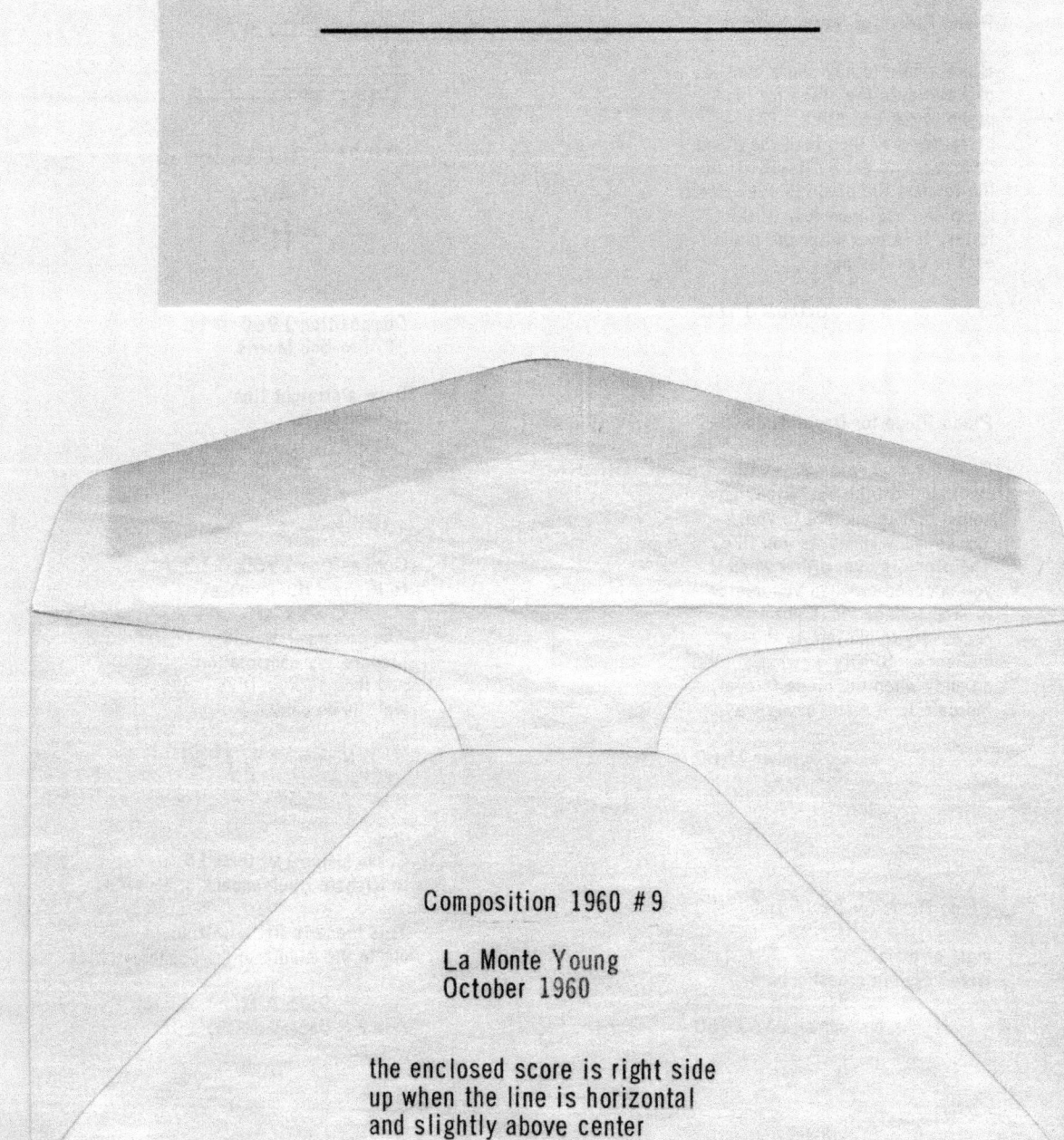

Composition 1960 #9

La Monte Young
October 1960

the enclosed score is right side
up when the line is horizontal
and slightly above center

◀ 153 *La Monte Young, Compositions 1960. La Monte Young: SCORES Reproduced from AN ANTHOLOGY.*

Composition 1960 # 2 (5.5.60)
Composition 1960 # 3 (5.14.60)
Composition 1960 # 4 (6.3.60)
Composition 1960 # 5 (6.8.60)
Piano Piece for Terry Riley # 1 (November 8, 1960)
Composition 1960 # 6 (July 2, 1960)
Piano Piece for David Tudor # 1 (October, 1960)
Piano Piece for David Tudor # 2 (October, 1960)
Piano Piece for David Tudor # 3 (November 14, 1960)
Composition 1960 # 7 (July, 1960)
Composition 1960 # 10 (October, 1960)
Composition 1960 # 13 (November 9, 1960)
Composition 1960 # 15 (9:05 a.m., December 25, 1960)
Composition 1960 # 9 (October, 1960) (envelope with card)

La Monte Young

11 II 07 Corrected Numbering System for 1960 Works

Some scholars have requested that I clarify the numbering system for my 1960 works. To begin with I will admit that the identification of both *Compositions 1960 #s 12* and *14* may be lost in the mists of time. There is a saying, "If you remember the '60s, you weren't there." I stand guilty as accused by some and as suggested by others that perhaps I used too many inspirational supplements. Nonetheless, *Compositions 1960 #s 1 - 11* are clear and listed below in sequence; *Compositions 1960 #s 13* and *15* are also clear. Only *Compositions 1960 #s 12* and *14* remain questions. Because I do not have exact dates for *Invisible Poem Sent to Terry Jennings* and *Target for Jasper Johns,* I may have considered one of these to be *Composition 1960 # 12* and one of these to be *Composition 1960 # 14.* Please note: Those compositions that are a definite part of the original numbering system have a double indent in this list. All others are treated differently.

[Untitled] (1959-60), live friction sounds: **Not counted in *Compositions 1960* numbering system.**

[Untitled] (1959-62), jazz-drone improvisations: **Not counted in *Compositions 1960* numbering system.**

> *Poem for Chairs, Tables, Benches, etc.* (January 21, 1960), chairs, tables, benches and unspecified sound sources: **Should be counted as # 1**

2 Sounds (April, 1960), pre-recorded friction sounds: **Not counted in *Compositions 1960* numbering system.**

Arabic Numeral (Any Integer) to H.F. (April, 1960), piano(s) or gong(s) or ensembles of at least 45 instruments of the same timbre, or combinations of the above, or orchestra: **Not counted in *Compositions 1960* numbering system.**

Compositions 1960 (1960), performance pieces, including

> *Composition 1960 # 2* (May 5, 1960),

> *Composition 1960 # 3* (May 14, 1960),

> *Composition 1960 # 4* (June 3, 1960),

> *Composition 1960 # 5* (June 8, 1960),

> *Composition 1960 # 6* (July 2, 1960),

> *Composition 1960 # 7* (July, 1960),

> *Electronic Composition 1960 # 8* (October, 1960); Bob Dunn recorded and performed the sounds, modeled on the piano sound from *Vision* on five mono tapes, and he also made a time structure based on a realization of *Poem,* all of which he gave to Richard Maxfield who realized the five tapes into a 3-channel version according to the score provided. This realization also included manipulation of the speed of the tapes. I first presented this work as the background music for *Lecture 1960,* which I delivered at Richard Maxfield's studio as a part of his class in Electronic Music at The New School.

> *Composition 1960 # 9* (October, 1960),

> *Composition 1960 # 10* (October, 1960),

> *Electronic Composition 1960 # 11* (c. October-early November, 1960)

Piano Pieces for David Tudor (1960): **Not counted in *Compositions 1960* numbering system.**

performance pieces, including

> *Piano Piece for David Tudor # 1* (October, 1960),
>
> *Piano Piece for David Tudor # 2* (October, 1960),
>
> *Piano Piece for David Tudor # 3* (November 14, 1960),

Invisible Poem Sent to Terry Jennings (October, November or December, 1960), performance piece: **Could have been intended to be counted as *Composition 1960 # 12*.**

Piano Piece for Terry Riley # 1 (2:10 AM, November 8, 1960), performance piece: **Not counted in *Compositions 1960* numbering system.**

> *Composition 1960 # 13* (November 9, 1960),

Piano Piece for Terry Riley # 2 (8:31 AM November 12, 1960, rejected by the composer 9:57 AM, November 12, 1960), performance piece: **Not counted in *Compositions 1960* numbering system.**

> *Composition 1960 # 15* (9:05 AM, December 25, 1960),

Target for Jasper Johns (1960), piano: **Could** have been intended to be counted as ***Composition 1960 # 14*. Although labeling *Target for Jasper Johns* as # 14 would place it before # 15 (above) in sequence, *Target* was several pages long and *could* have been begun before # 15 and finished after # 15. I cannot find any date for *Target* on the score or in any of my notes or files, but I had always remembered it to be the last piece of the year 1960. I tended to date my scores when they were finished rather than when they were begun. Nonetheless, *Target could* have been begun and numbered # 14 before I created # 15. Then, before *Target* was finished, I may have had the inspiration to create # 15, which was finished as soon as I thought of it and therefore was finalized as # 15. Meanwhile, I continued to work on *Target* but it is unclear exactly when and if I actually considered it finished. *Target* had been intended for David Tudor to demonstrate his extraordinary pianistic virtuosity. It was supposed to be ferociously fast and with the tempo indication "as fast as possible". At some point, Toshi Ichiyanagi and one of his students did a four hands read-through on the piano at Yoko's loft in order that I could get an idea of how fast it could be played. The work consisted of only four pitches based on one of what I eventually called my "Dream Chords" but these pitches were set in a widely spaced intervallic layout on the keyboard. By the time of the four hands reading, I had only notated a few pages and I had planned to notate more. At the read-through I became concerned at how obviously difficult the piece was for even two pianists because it was going rather slowly. Although, for the sake of accuracy they had not prepared their read-through to be presented at a concert tempo, I began to seriously reconsider whether or not David could ever play it as fast as I had intended it. At this point, the work was in a state of limbo and I went on to other things, without putting a date on it. Years later, probably not earlier than 1989, I told David about the work. He responded that I should have sent it to him and that he might have been able to have found a way to perform it. Of course, by the time I told him the story, he was no longer playing piano. Moreover, since 1974 I had performed a combined total of at least 65 public and invitational live concerts of *The Well-Tuned Piano* and in 1987 Gramavision had released the 5-CD set of the 1981 5-hour continuous concert. Although I was no longer interested in *Target,* it may have been one of the ideological precursors of the early '60s Clouds I played on the sopranino saxophone that evolved into the extended long sustained Clouds of *The Well-Tuned Piano.***

Commentary: 1960 Works

James Saunders

La Monte Young's works from 1960, as published in *An Anthology*, were composed from May to December 1960, encompassing the time he relocated from San Francisco to New York. Although Young now feels his subsequent work with frequency relationships surpasses these early pieces,[1] the set includes some of the first verbal scores to prescribe situations that explore the boundary between music and theatre. In an interview with Richard Kostelanetz in 1966, Young explains:

> Both categories apply. I divide my works into music pieces, and musical-theatre pieces. All my pieces, I feel, deal with music, even the butterflies and the fire. In every case, I was writing them as musical compositions to be played at musical performances. In fact, a certain amount of their impact relates to the fact that they are performed in a classical concert situation.[2]

He makes a link between these pieces and contemporaneous work by other New York artists working on the border of music and theatre, commenting that: 'Although my 1960 compositions are unique events, and in that sense related to Events and Happenings, they are most effective when performed in a conventional concert setting.'[3]

Young also sees his 1960 works as 'one of the beginnings of concept art',[4] and explains they were initiated by his response to two specific situations:

> One is my visit to Darmstadt in the summer of 1959 where I met David Tudor and heard him play live, heard him talk about John Cage, and just saw what a wonderful performer he was. [...] I met him that summer at Darmstadt when I was in Stockhausen's class. His ideas and John Cage's ideas had a big influence on me. But at the same time, being at Berkeley in this very stifling academic situation also had an influence on me. The *Compositions 1960* were a reaction to being at Berkeley. They were a sociological reaction. To some degree, they are a social statement.[5]

In many ways La Monte Young's 1960 works exemplify some core concepts in verbal notation, which have been sustained and explored in the work of many other scorers. In particular, they present a range of intriguing attitudes to duration. Young seems to employ two different methods to

---

[1] See Young, L. 'Why I Withdrew from Fluxus', in Hendricks *et al.*, 2008, p. 54, and pp. 436–7 of this book.

[2] Kostelanetz, R. 'Conversation: La Monte Young', in Kostelanetz, 1968, p. 194.

[3] Young, 2001.

[4] *Ibid.* He also states that: 'Henry Flynt has referred to my *Compositions 1960* as having special significance for him when he coined the term "concept art".' For an explanation of this term, see Flynt, 1961.

[5] Young and Zazeela, 2003.

determine duration in *Compositions 1960*: duration is determined by the performer, or it is determined by other circumstances. In some pieces in this set no durational constraint is specified. Several of the pieces deal with a singular event with a prescribed beginning and end, and Young states his desire to 'concentrate and delimit the work to be a single event or object in these less traditionally musical areas'.[6]

The principal method for determining duration that the scores adopt is a decision made by the performer. In *Composition 1960 #3*, this is the focus of the score, which instructs the performer to 'Announce to the audience when the piece will begin and end if there is a limit on duration', and then that 'everyone may do whatever he wishes for the duration of the composition'. In this respect, the composition is complemented by Christian Wolff's view that:

> Form in music could be taken as a length of programme time. [...] A piece as it starts and stops is indicated by the actions of its performers (even when no sounds are scored at all). Form is a theatrical event of a certain length, and the length itself may be unpredictable.[7]

In #3 the audience will know in advance when the piece will begin and end, although the score states that an end time needs to be given only if there is a limit on duration. This creates two very different situations for the audience, dependent on whether the performance duration is either known or unknown in advance of the event.

A different situation arises with *Composition 1960 #4*, which states that the audience must be told when the composition begins and ends. During this piece, the lights are turned out, and at the end it may be revealed that the audience's 'activities have been the composition'. It contrasts with #3, where this information is given in advance and the audience are explicitly given permission to do what they want. Young notes that in one performance of #4, 'Sure enough, plenty of people tore up their programs, and a few made other noises. Everybody thought I had programmed these events into the composition but I hadn't.'[8] In both pieces, the audience's actions for a specific duration become the composition, although the manner in which this situation is explained to the audience is not the same. Given the potential for no intentional audience sounds to occur, Kostelanetz compares #4 with Cage's *4'33"*, to which Young responds:

> They are related, except that in John's you have a classic setting in which one sits at the piano and turns the pages for each movement – going through the motions of a classical form. In my piece, I just announced a block of time, which may be of any length. In the original manuscript, I said that, "When the lights are turned back on, the announcer may tell

---

[6] Kostelanetz, 1968, p. 195. For more discussion of Young's work in relation to 'events', see Kotz, 2007, pp. 72–98.

[7] Wolff, C. 'Precise Actions under Variously Indeterminate Conditions: On Form', in Wolff, 1998, p. 38.

[8] Kostelanetz, 1968, p. 194.

the audience that their activities have been the composition." This is not at all necessary, and I have never done it in that form.[9]

Composition 1960 #6 also presents the actions of the audience as the content of the composition. Here the performers sit on the stage, which is set up to mirror the seating layout for the audience. As with *#3* and *#4*, a performance of *#6* 'may be of any duration' (*#4* uses the word 'length'). Although *#3* and *#4* require that the duration is either set by the person arranging the performance in advance or during the event, in *#6* this may also be the case or it might be determined by the audience. For example, in *#6* the piece might end when the members of the audience decide to leave.

The other piece to state that a performance may be of any duration is *Composition 1960 #2*. Here the score instructs the performer to 'Build a fire in front of the audience.' It is unusual that Young does not suggest that the piece ends when the fire burns out. This is perhaps implied by the instruction 'After the fire is burning, the builder(s) may sit by and watch it for the duration of the composition', and that the fire 'may be of any size', but duration is not explicitly stated. The score makes no mention of how the fire might be extinguished.

Composition 1960 #13 to Richard Huelsenbeck[10] also uses performer choice implicitly to determine the duration. It instructs the performer to 'prepare any composition and then perform it as well as he can'. The duration of the chosen source piece in performance will therefore determine the duration of Young's composition.

In contrast, two of the 1960 works use mental or physical factors to help determine duration. In *Piano Piece for Terry Riley #1*, the performer must 'Push the piano up to a wall and put the flat side flush against it' as the general condition of the composition. This activity continues, accepting the possibility of pushing the piano through the wall such that it might stop against other objects, with the piece being over 'when you are too exhausted to push any longer'. So while there is still performer input when determining the end of the piece, here it is based on an assessment of personal stamina and the will to continue.

In *Piano Piece for David Tudor #2*, the performer must 'Open the keyboard cover without making, from the operation, any sound that is audible to you [the performer]'.[11] This activity continues until 'you succeed or when you decide to stop trying'. Here the reference point is external – that of the piano lid movement making an audible sound – but the decision to stop still resides with the performer. It is possible to determine a successful completion of the action using an objective criterion: the lid is opened without a sound being audible to the performer. But if this activity continues

---

[9] *Ibid.*

[10] Richard Huelsenbeck was a founder member of Zurich's Cabaret Voltaire, and of the Dada movement.

[11] *Piano Piece for Terry Riley #1* and *Piano Piece for David Tudor #2* are the only two pieces from the 1960 works to use the second person ('you'). The others variously use the imperative mood, third person ('the performer'), and passive voice, or are not immediately suggestive of instructions.

unsuccessfully for sufficient time, it draws a parallel with *Piano Piece for Terry Riley #1* as the decision to stop rests with the performer, based on an assessment of the will to continue attempting the task.

Two of the works from 1960 use external factors to determine duration. *Piano Piece for David Tudor # 1* gives two options for determining the end of the piece. The score instructs the performer to: 'Bring a bale of hay and a bucket of water onto the stage for the piano to eat and drink. The performer may then feed the piano or leave it to eat by itself.' The score then specifies the end conditions for the piece. Either the piece is over 'after the piano has been fed' by the performer (performer choice), or 'after the piano eats or decides not to'. While the definition of 'eats' is subject to interpretation, it is likely that, however, the performer will again need to determine when the piano has been fed, or what its decision was. Young comments:

> To me the concept was extremely important. The humor is there. Nobody laughs harder than me when I see that piece performed. Some people have done hilarious realizations of it. It's very funny. George [Maciunas] got that, but he didn't so much get the deeper side of it.[12]

Composition 1960 #5 provides an empirical condition for the end of a piece, however. The score gives the instruction to: 'Turn a butterfly (or any number of butterflies) loose in the performance area.' The composition may conclude, where an unlimited amount of time is available, 'when the butterfly flies away' through the previously opened doors and windows. This is the only verifiable end-condition specified in the 1960 works. Even the audibility of opening and closing the piano lid in *Piano Piece for David Tudor #2* contains a subjective response from the performer, and it is impossible to determine the appetite of the piano definitively in *Piano Piece for David Tudor #1*. Although the flight of the butterfly provides an unpredictable way to measure performance time, for Young the piece is principally about the sounds made by the butterfly.[13] He observes in his 'Lecture 1960':

> I asked her [Diane Wakoski] if she thought the butterfly piece was music to any less degree than *Composition 1960 #2* which consists of simply building a fire in front of the audience. She said, 'Yes, because in the fire piece at least there are some sounds.' I said that I felt certain the butterfly made sounds, not only with the motion of its wings but also with the functioning of its body

---

[12] Young and Zazeela, 2003.

[13] Young explains his choice of a butterfly for this piece when reflecting on its composition 'on my way to Mount Tamalpais, the biggest mountain in the Marin County area, and I started thinking about the butterfly. Alone, it made a very beautiful piece. Being very young, I could still take something so highly poetic and use it without the fear I would have now – that it would be trampled on. Now, I would offer something quite a bit more substantial than a butterfly or a fire – something that can't be so easily walked on. After all, a butterfly is only a butterfly. No matter how much I write about the fact that a butterfly does make a sound – that it is potentially a composition – anyone that wants to can say, "Well, it's only a butterfly".' Kostelanetz, 1968, p. 192.

and that unless one was going to dictate how loud or soft the sounds had to be before they could be allowed into the realms of music that the butterfly piece was music as much as the fire piece. She said she thought that at least one ought to be able to hear the sounds. I said that this was the usual attitude of human beings that everything in the world should exist for them and that I disagreed. I said it didn't seem to me at all necessary that anyone or anything should have to hear sounds and that it is enough that they exist for themselves. When I wrote this story out for this lecture I added, 'If you think this attitude is too extreme, do you think sounds should be able to hear people?'[14]

Young notes elsewhere in his 'Lecture 1960' that Diane Wakoski suggested 'Maybe the butterfly piece should begin when a butterfly happens to fly into the auditorium.'[15]

Of the remaining five works, two do not give any explicit indication of duration. *Piano Piece for David Tudor #3* and *Composition 1960 #15 to Richard Huelsenbeck* use a poetic mode of expression to create a more abstract relationship with the potential actions to be carried out by performers, and make no overt reference to marking time.

The other three works focus on the line as a continuum. *Composition 1960 #7* is the only piece in the set to use a stave, with a fragment indicating the pitches B3 and F#4 placed above a text which reads: 'to be held for a long time'. The instruction in *Composition 1960 #10 to Bob Morris* is 'Draw a straight line and follow it', and *Composition 1960 #9* comprises a scorecard printed with a horizontal line. Young went on to make 29 realisations of *#10* in 1961. These were recorded as *Compositions 1961 #s 1–29*, with each being a separately-dated instance of the text of *#10*. Young performed all 29 pieces in March 1961, 'long before many of them had ever been written according to their dates of composition'.[16] He explains that *#10* 'can be performed in many ways. At that time, I employed a style in which we used plumb lines. I sighted with them, and then drew along the floor with chalk', and that in the versions realised as *Compositions 1961*, 'I drew over the same line each time, and each time it invariably came out differently. The technique I was using at the time was not good enough.'[17] Despite the continuity implied by a line which has no indicated end, Young links the instances of realising these pieces to the other 1960 works and their form as singular events:

As we have observed, I have been interested in the study of a singular event, in terms of both pitch and other kinds of sensory situations. I felt

[14] Young, 1965, p. 75. Reproduced with permission from 'Lecture 1960', Copyright © La Monte Young 1963, 1965, 1969, 1990, 1995, 2002.

[15] *Ibid.*, p. 74.

[16] Young explains that he determined the concept on 6 January 1961 then 'took a yearly average of the number of pieces I had completed over a given period of time, and spaced that number equally throughout 1961, with one composition on the first day of the year, and one on the last day. It came out to one every thirteen days, and that night I quite coldly wrote out the dates' (Kostelanetz, 1968, p. 204).

[17] Kostelanetz, 1968, p. 205.

that a line was one of the more sparse, singular expressions of oneness, although it is certainly not the final expression. Somebody might choose a point. However, the line was interesting because it was continuous – it existed in time. A line is a potential of existing time. In graphs and scores one designates time as one dimension. Nonetheless, the actual drawing of the line did involve time, and it did involve a singular event – 'Draw a straight line and follow it.'[18]

[18] *Ibid.*, p. 204.

Why I Withdrew from Fluxus

La Monte Young, May 2008

Through their early performances and publications, the *Compositions 1960* became a primary influence not only on 'concept art' but also on conceptual art, performance art and on the Fluxus movement generated after George Maciunas met me in New York in 1960–61. George Maciunas was influenced by associating with me, by attending the concerts I curated at Yoko Ono's loft in 1960–61, and by observing all of the work I had collected as the editor of *An Anthology* when I gave him the opportunity to create the graphic design for the book. At the time I introduced George to the New York avant-garde art scene, he was still interested in presenting the works of Luening and Ussachevsky and showing Socialist Realist art. As Henry Flynt has pointed out, 'George had to be dragged kicking and screaming into the avant-garde' (telephone conversation, June 17, 2002). George was a remarkable organizer with boundless energy. He was a great humanitarian and brought me loaves of bread and cans of food when I was starving. Nonetheless, in the hands of Maciunas, the influence of my ideas quickly degenerated into slapstick vaudeville. I always felt that George was the fifth Marx Brother and I loved his humor but it distorted the intention of my works.

Henry Flynt reminded me in a recent phone call (April 2008) that in the earliest appearances of the word 'Fluxus', George frequently supplied graphics of paraphernalia for the administration of enemas and/or patients receiving enemas. Through these graphic examples, George essentially expressed that, to him, art was excrement, which was in keeping with the socialist idea that all art except social realism was an excess of capitalist imperialism. Therefore, making a joke of abstract and conceptual art was an intentional part of the game.

For many artists whose work had no strong identity of its own, Fluxus provided the sense of unity in which there was strength and the sense of commonality and belonging, as to a church. In addition, George's generous offering of his skills as an entrepreneur and PR man were a boon that most could not resist.

On the door and programs for the concert series I presented at Yoko's loft in 1960–61, I placed the statement, 'The purpose of this series is not entertainment.' I took great care to select the artists I presented based on the originality of their contributions at that time, and I gave each artist two evenings devoted solely to his or her work. Maciunas, on the other hand, grouped anyone and everyone that he could under the banner of 'Fluxus' and jammed as many names onto one program as possible, creating humorous variety shows of sensory titillation. I withdrew from Fluxus as soon as I figured out what George's intentions were. He drafted every dog, cat and his brother into his Marx Brothers vaudeville shows, and I wanted no part of it. As a result, even though I was probably the primary influence on Maciunas (George coined the word Fluxus around May or June 1961 and I was there the first time he ever mentioned it), I have aggressively tried to disassociate myself and my work from the Fluxus movement.

It is to be noted regarding Fluxus vs. Stasis: Change, or flux is inevitable. Stasis, or remaining the same, is impossible. Therefore, to achieve the static state is the goal, while the state of flux, variation, or contrast, is unavoidable and thus unnecessary as a goal.

Some individuals have not been able to understand why I abandoned the 'word pieces' genre in order to devote my full time to music based on frequency relationships. Just as words are elements of languages, frequency relationships are elements of the language of music. Music, however, is an infinitely more complex language with infinitely more elements than languages comprised of words.

In the notes for *The Well-Tuned Piano* I have written: 'Since intervals from the system of rational numbers are the only intervals that can be repeatedly tuned *exactly*, they are the only intervals that have the potential to sound *exactly* the same on repeated hearing. It is for this reason that the feelings produced by rational intervals within a gradually expanding threshold of complexity have the potential to be recognized and remembered and, consequently, develop strong emotional impact. The inherent precision of the measurability and repeatability of intervals within the practical complexity threshold of the set of rational numbers provides the elements for a language/communications system with an ever increasing range of nuance and refinement of vocabulary. Any system of language is dependent on the fact that information is repeatable, and this is precisely what the system of just intonation provides. Through this system we can, first, catalogue each feeling with its corresponding rational number, and then actually create, store, retrieve and, finally and most importantly, repeat the feeling, relative to the musician's ability to tune the intervals.' For a psycholinguistic discussion of emotional response to music in relation to the development of language competence, see Juan G. Roederer, *Introduction to the Physics and Psychophysics of Music* (New York: Springer-Verlag, 1979), pp. 11–12.

While some feel that my 'word pieces' were exceptionally innovative and perhaps my most conceptual and imaginative artistic statements, I feel that my work with music based on frequency relationships is much more conceptual and imaginative and goes far beyond the word pieces.

There is an ancient Sanskrit saying:

Even if he be an expert in the revealed and the traditional scriptures, in literature and all sacred books, the man ignorant of music is but an animal on two feet.

(as quoted by Alain Danielou [without citation] in *Northern Indian Music*, p. 97, Frederic A. Praeger, Inc., New York, Washington, 1969.)

Sources

The verbal scores featured in this book represent only a small proportion of those collected in the course of the research. The sources listed below are starting points for finding other pieces to explore, and full references can be found in the bibliography.

Single-Composer Anthologies

Collections of scores by some of the composers mentioned in this book have been published in single-composer anthologies. These are often excellent resources as they generally provide a lot of additional context and documentation alongside the scores. Examples include: Hugh Davies, *Sounds Heard*; Kenneth Maue, *Water in the Lake*; Pauline Oliveros, *Software for People, Deep Listening: A Composer's Sound Practice*, and *Roots of the Moment*; and Yoko Ono, *Grapefruit*.

The series of single-composer books of collected writings and interviews published by MusikTexte (www.musiktexte.de) also contain a significant number of verbal scores by Robert Ashley, Alvin Lucier, Frederic Rzewski and Christian Wolff, supported by much contextual information.

Some of the Great Bear Pamphlets published by Dick Higgins' Something Else Press include verbal scores. Of particular note are the collections *by Alison Knowles,* Philip Corner's *Popular Entertainments*, and Bengt af Klintberg's *The Cursive Scandinavian Salve*. All the pamphlets are available for free download in new editions from www.ubu.com, and a printed facsimile edition has been published by Primary Information (www.primaryinformation.org).

Anthologies

La Monte Young's *An Anthology of Chance Operations* includes some verbal scores, alongside other work by New York artists.

Many of the books listed in the bibliography contain verbal scores. A broad selection can be found in Michael Nyman's seminal *Experimental Music: Cage and Beyond*, which includes scores by English and American composers made before the publication of the first edition in 1974.

The Experimental Music Catalogue was founded in 1969 by Christopher Hobbs and its series of themed anthologies present many of the pieces that appeared in Nyman's *Experimental Music*. The catalogue is still active and run by Hobbs and Virginia Anderson. They publish a facsimile of the *Verbal Anthology* (www.experimentalmusic.co.uk).

Roger Johnson's 1981 publication *Score: An Anthology of New Music* groups scores into different categories, such as 'Exercises, Rituals and Meditations', or 'Music for Voices'. It contains a wide range of scores using stave, graphic and verbal notation, mostly by American composers.

There are many publications on Fluxus that contain verbal scores. The principal sources are the *Fluxus Codex* and the more recent *Fluxus Scores and Instructions: The Transformative Years 'Make a Salad'*, which are both edited by Jon Hendricks. These publications include excellent reproductions of many Fluxus event scores, and many other examples can be found in the exhibition catalogues and critical studies cited in the bibliography.

The *Fluxus Performance Workbook*, published as part of the journal *Performance Research* (vol. 7, no. 3, 2002), includes a large selection of verbal scores by Fluxus artists. They have been reset using a standard font and layout so lose aspects of the original typography. It is available to download from www.thing.net/~grist/ld/fluxus.htm.

Publishers

German-based publisher Edition Wandelweiser (www.wandelweiser.de) publishes the work of some of the contributors to this book – Antoine Beuger, Michael Pisaro, Sam Sfirri, Craig Shepard and Manfred Werder – as well as others.

Composer collective and publisher Frog Peak Music (www.frogpeak.org) has many scores, including Philip Corner's gamelan works, and Christian Wolff's *Prose Collection* (which can be downloaded for free from its website). As well as publishing individual scores, there are some notable anthologies including *The Frog Peak Rock Music Book*, which features several verbal scores that use stones or rocks in some way.

Online

Many verbal scores can, of course, be found online at composers' and artists' websites, and elsewhere in isolation. There are also a number of excellent repositories, such as www.ubu.com, which contain examples.

The dedicated wiki-repository UDP (www.uploaddownloadperform.net) offers users the opportunity to 'share your scores, actions, rituals, movements, choreography, texts, instructions, suggestions, recipes, meditations' by uploading scores, downloading others, and performing them. Developed and maintained by Adam Overton, it includes scores by a wide range of composers and artists.

Bill Drummond's ongoing choir project The17 has produced a large number of scores by both Drummond and the many other members of the group (over 3,500 at the time of writing), including a high proportion of school children. All of these are available to download from www.the17.org.

Bibliography

Agamben, G. (1999) *Potentialities*, Stanford, California: Stanford University Press.

Alberro, A. and Norvell, P. (eds) (2001) *Recording Conceptual Art*, Berkeley, Los Angeles and London: University of California Press.

Alberro, A. and Stimson, B. (1999) *Conceptual Art: A Critical Anthology*, Cambridge, Massachusetts: MIT Press.

Alberro, A. and Zimmerman, A. (1998) 'NOT HOW IT SHOULD WERE IT TO BE BUILT BUT HOW IT COULD WERE IT TO BE BUILT', in A. Alberro, A. Zimmerman, B. H. D. Buchloh and D. Batchelor, *Lawrence Weiner*, London: Phaidon, p. 49.

Ashley, R. (2000) *Music with Roots in the Aether*, Cologne: MusikTexte.

—(2009) *Outside of Time: Ideas About Music*, Dietrich, R. (ed.) Cologne: MusikTexte.

Bailey, D. (1992) *Improvisation: Its Nature and Practice in Music*, London: The British Library National Sound Archive.

Barrett, G. D. (2009) 'Artist Statement, 2009', http://synthia.caset.buffalo.edu/~gbarrett/bio.html [accessed 8 December 2009].

Basho, M. (2008) *The Complete Haiku*, Tokyo: Kodansha International Ltd.

Beckett, S. (1953) *Watt*, London: Faber.

Biber, D., Johansson, S., Leech, G., Conrad, S. and Finegan, E. (2007) *Longman Grammar of Spoken and Written English*, Harlow: Pearson.

Boal, A. (2002) *Games for Actors and Non-Actors*, Abingdon: Routledge.

Brecht, G. (1966) *Chance-Imagery*, New York: Something Else Press.

—(1991a) *Notebook I: June 1958–September 1958*, Braun, H. (ed.), Cologne: Walther Koenig.

—(1991b) *Notebook II: October 1958–April 1959*, Braun, H. (ed.), Cologne: Walther Koenig.

—(1991c) *Notebook III: April 1959–August 1959*, Braun, H. (ed.), Cologne: Walther Koenig.

—(1998a) *Notebook IV: September 1959–March 1960*, Braun, H. (ed.), Cologne: Walther Koenig.

—(1998b) *Notebook V: March 1960–November 1960*, Braun, H. (ed.), Cologne: Walther Koenig.

—(2005a) *Notebook VI: March 1961–June 1961*, Braun, H. (ed.), Cologne: Walther Koenig.

—(2005b) *Notebook VII: June 1961–September 1962*, Braun, H. (ed.), Cologne: Walther Koenig.

Bryars, G. (1983) 'Vexations and its performers', in *Contact*, no. 26, Spring, 12–20.

—(2010) 'Notes for Huddersfield for performance of early works', http://www. gavinbryars.com/work/writing/occasional-writings/notes-huddersfield-performance-early-works [accessed 5 May 2010].

Bryars, G., Hobbs, C. and Nyman, M. (eds) (1972) *Verbal Anthology*, London: Experimental Music Catalogue.

Cage, J. (1969) *Notations,* New York: Something Else Press.

—(1978) *Silence*, London and New York: Marion Boyars Publishers.

—(1981) *For the Birds*, London and New York: Marion Boyars Publishers.

—(1985) *A Year from Monday*, London and New York: Marion Boyars Publishers.

Cardew, C. (ed.) (1972) *Scratch Music*, London: Latimer New Directions.

Carroll, L. (1992) *Through the Looking Glass*, London: Vintage.

Chapman, R. (1984) *The Treatment of Sounds in Language and Literature*, Oxford: Basil Blackwell.

Chase, S. and Thomas, P. (eds) (2010) *Changing the System: The Music of Christian Wolff*, Aldershot: Ashgate.

Chase, William G. (ed.) (1973) *Visual Information Processing*, New York and London: Academic Press.

Cianciusi, W. (2007) *Event Scores*, Morrisville, North Carolina: Lulu Enterprises.

Coffin, C., Donohue, J. and North, S. (2009) *Exploring English Grammar: From Formal to Functional*, London and New York: Routledge.

Collins, N. (ed.) (2001) 'Not Necessarily "English Music"', *Leonardo Music Journal*, vol. 11.

Concannon, K. (2008) 'Yoko Ono's Cut Piece From Text to Performance and Back Again', *A Journal of Performance and Art*, PAJ 90, vol. 30, no. 3, September, 81–93.

Cox, C., and Warner, D. (eds) (2006) *Audio Culture: Readings in Modern Music*, London and New York: Continuum.

Davies, H. (2002) *Sounds Heard*, Chelmsford: Soundworld Publishers.

Dennis, B. (1975) *Projects in Sound*, London: Universal Edition.

Delio, T. (1984) *Circumscribing the Open Universe*, Lanham, Maryland: University Press of America.

De Salvo, D. (ed.) (2005) *Open Systems: Rethinking Art c. 1970*, London: Tate.

Deutscher, G. (2006) *The Unfolding of Language*, London: Arrow Books.

Dewey, J. (2005) *Art as Experience*, New York: Penguin.

Diamond, J. (1986) 'Philip Corner: You Can Only Be Who You Are', in *Balungan*, vol. 2, no. 3, Spring, 23–32.

Drummond, B. (2008) *17,* London: Beautiful Books.

Empson, W. (2004) *Seven Types of Ambiguity*, London: Random House.

Evans, V. and Chilton, P. (eds) (2010) *Language, Cognition and Space*, London: Equinox.

Exner, A. and Goldmann, M. (1992) *Fluxus Da Capo*, Wiesbaden: Kulturamt der Landeshauptstadt Wiesbaden.

Fairclough, N. (2001) *Language and Power*, Harlow: Longman.

Fawcett, A., Guadarrama García, K. L. and Hyde Parker, R. (2010)

Translation: Theory and Practice in Dialogue, London and New York: Continuum.

Fetterman, W. (1996) *John Cage's Theatre Pieces: Notations and Performances*, Amsterdam: Harwood Academic Press.

Fietzek, G. and Stemmrich, G. (eds) (2004) *HAVING BEEN SAID: WRITINGS & INTERVIEWS OF LAWRENCE WEINER 1968–2003*, Ostfildern-Ruit: Hatje Cantz Verlag.

Flam, J. (1996) *Robert Smithson: The Collected Writings*, Berkeley, Los Angeles and London: University of California Press.

Flynt, H. (1961) 'Essay: Concept Art', http://www.henryflynt.org/aesthetics/conart.html [accessed 6 October 2010].

Fowler, H. W. (1965) *A Dictionary of Modern English Usage*, Oxford: Oxford University Press.

Friedman, K. (ed.) (1998) *The Fluxus Reader*, Chichester: Academy Editions.

—(2002) *52 Events*, Edinburgh: Show and Tell Editions.

Friedman, K., Smith, O. and Sawchyn, L. (2002) *The Fluxus Performance Workbook*, Performance Research e-Publications, http://www.thing.net/~grist/ld/fluxusworkbook.pdf [accessed 8 September 2010].

Gadsby, A. (2002) *Longman Language Activator*, Harlow: Pearson Education Limited.

Gale, P. (ed.) (2004) *Artists Talk 1969–1977*, Nova Scotia: The Press of the Nova Scotia College of Art and Design.

Garland, P. (ed.) (1984) *SOUNDINGS 13: The Music of James Tenney*, Santa Fe: Soundings Press.

Geeraerts, D. (ed.) (2006) *Cognitive Linguistics: Basic Readings*, Berlin: Mouton de Gruyter.

Goode, D. (ed.) (1995) *The Frog Peak Rock Music Book*, Lebanon, New Hampshire: Frog Peak Music.

Gowers, E. (1987) *Complete Plain Words*, London: Penguin.

Halliday, M. A. K. and Matthiessen, C. M. I. M. (2004) *An Introduction to Functional Grammar*, London: Hodder Education.

Halliday, M. A .K. and Webster, J. J. (2009) *Continuum Companion to Systemic Functional Linguistics*, London and New York: Continuum.

Halprin, L. (1969) *The RSVP Cycles: Creative Processes in the Human Environment*, New York: George Braziller.

Hapgood, S. (1994) *Neo-Dada: Redefining Art 1958–1962*, New York: American Federation of Arts.

Harder, H. and Nievers, K. (eds) (1995) *Chambers: Alvin Lucier, Sol LeWitt*, Kiel: Stadtgalerie Kiel and Gesellschaft für akustische Lebenshilfe.

Harley, T. (2008) *The Psychology of Language*, Hove and New York: Psychology Press.

Hartshorne, C. and Weiss, P. (eds) (1931–58) *Collected Papers of Charles Sanders Peirce*, vol. 2, Cambridge, Massachusetts: Harvard University Press.

Hasegawa, R. (ed.) (2008) 'The Music of James Tenney', *Contemporary Music Review*, vol. 27, part I.

Hendricks, G. (ed.) (2003) *Critical Mass: Happenings, Fluxus, Performance, Intermedia and Rutgers University, 1958–1972*, New Brunswick: Rutgers University Press.

Hendricks, J. (ed.) (1983) *Fluxus etc./Addenda I*, New York: Ink &.

—(1995) *Fluxus Codex*, New York: Harry N. Abrams.

—(2002) *What's Fluxus? What's Not! Why.* Detroit: G. and L. Silverman Fluxus Collection Foundation.

Hendricks, J., Bech, M. and Farzin, M. (2008) *Fluxus Scores and Instructions: The Transformative Years 'Make a Salad'*, Roskilde: Museum of Contemporary Art, Roskilde.

Hewings, A. and Hewings, M. (2005) *Grammar and Context*, London: Routledge.

Higgins, H. (2002) *Fluxus Experience*, Berkeley, Los Angeles and London: University of California Press.

Houben, E-M. and Schlothauer, B. (2007) *MusikDenken: Texte der Wandelweiser-Komponisten*, Zurich: Edition Howeg.

Houben, E-M. and Zelenka, I. (2009) *1 Milieu – ein Buch nicht nur zum Lesen*, Zurich: Edition Howeg.

Houser, N. and Kloesel, C. (eds) (1992) *The Essential Peirce. Selected Philosophical Writings. Vol. 1 (1867–1893)*, Bloomington and Indianapolis: Indiana University Press.

Hughes, P. and Brecht, G. (1976) *Vicious Circles and Infinity*, London: Jonathan Cape.

Huxley, M. and Witts, N. (eds) (2008) *The Twentieth-Century Performance Reader*, Abingdon: Routledge.

Jack, A. (1972) 'The Group Scene' in *Music and Musicians*, vol. 20 no. 7, March, 22–6.

Jackson, H. and Zé Amvela, E. (2007) *Words, Meaning and Vocabulary*, London and New York: Continuum.

Janssen, R. (2007) *Interview with Alison Knowles*, Breda: Fluxus Heidelberg Center, http://www.fluxusheidelberg.org/interviewwithalisonknowles_v1.3.pdf [accessed 8 September 2010].

Jarvie, G. (2007) *Bloomsbury Grammar Guide*, London: A & C Black.

Jenkins, J. (1993) *In the Spirit of Fluxus*, Minneapolis: Walker Art Gallery.

Johnson, R. (ed.) (1981) *Score: An Anthology of New Music*, New York: Schirmer.

Joseph, B.W. (2008) *Beyond the Dream Syndicate: Tony Conrad and the Arts After Cage*, New York: Zone Books.

Kahn, D. (1999) *Noise Water Meat*, Cambridge, Massachusetts: MIT Press.

Kim-Cohen, S. (2009) *In the Blink of an Ear*, New York: Continuum.

Klein, E. (2003) *A Comprehensive Etymological Dictionary of the English Language*, Bingley: Emerald.

Klintberg, B. af. (1993) 'Fluxus Games and Contemporary Folklore: On the Non-Individual Character of Fluxus Art', *Konsthistorisk Tidskrift*, vol. 62, no. 2, 115–25.

Knowles, A. (2000) *Footnotes*, New York: Granary Books.

—(2010) *American Mavericks*, http://musicmavericks.publicradio.org/features/index.html#interviews [accessed 8 September 2010].

Kostelanetz, R. (1968) *The Theatre of Mixed Means: An Introduction to Happenings, Kinetic Environments and Other Mixed-Means Performances*, New York: Dial Press.

Kotz, L. (2007) *Words to be Looked At: Language in 1960s Art*, Cambridge, Massachusetts: MIT Press.

Labelle, B. (2007) *Background Noise: Perspectives on Sound Art*, London and New York: Continuum.

Lane, C. (ed.) (2008) *Playing with Words*, London and Cromford: CRiSAP and RGAP.

Le Poidevin, R. and MacBeath, M. (eds) (1993) *The Philosophy of Time*, Oxford: Oxford University Press.

Lippard, L. (1997) *Six Years: The Dematerialization of the Art Object*, Berkeley, Los Angeles and London: University of California Press.

Long, R. (2009) *Heaven and Earth*, London: Tate Publishing.

Long, R. and Tufnell, B. (eds) (2007) *Selected Statements and Interviews*, London: Haunch of Venison.

Lucier, A. (1995) *Reflections: Interviews, Scores, Writings*, Oehlschlägel, R. and Gronemeyer, G. (eds) (1995) Cologne: MusikTexte.

Lucier, A. and Simon, D. (1980) *Chambers*, Connecticut: Wesleyan University Press.

Lukoszevieze, A. (1998) 'Different Strokes: Philip Corner talks to Anton Lukoszevieze', *Resonance*, vol. 7, no. 1, 13–17.

—(2003) 'Die Welt als Musik durchwandern', *Musiktexte*, no. 99, December, 65–74.

Lyons, M., Singer, D. and Waterman, A. (eds) (2008) *Between Thought and Sound*, New York: The Kitchen.

Macfarlane, K., Stone, R. and Watson, G. (eds) (2009) *Play for Today: Cornelius Cardew*, London: The Drawing Room.

Maconie, R. (2005) *Other Planets: The Music of Karlheinz Stockhausen*, Lanham: The Scarecrow Press.

Martin, H. (1978) *An Introduction to George Brecht's Book of the Tumbler on Fire*, Milan: multhipla edizioni.

Maue, K. (1979) *Water in the Lake: Real Events for the Imagination*, London: Harper and Row.

Miura, I. and Fuller Sasaki, R. (1965) *The Zen Koan*, San Diego: Harcourt Brace Jovanovich.

Möller, T., Shim, K. and Stäbler, G. (2005) *SoundVisions*, Saarbrücken: PFAU.

Neuhaus, M. (2004) 'LISTEN', http://www.maxneuhaus.info/soundworks/vectors/walks/LISTEN/ [accessed 7 September 2010].

Nevill, T. (ed.) (1989) *Towards a Cosmic Music: Texts by Karlheinz Stockhausen*, Longmead: Element Books.

Nicholls, D. (2002) *The Cambridge Companion to John Cage,* Cambridge: Cambridge University Press.

Nyman, M. (1971) 'Believe it or not melody rides again', *Music and Musicians*, vol. 20, no. 2, October, 26–8.

—(1976) 'George Brecht: Interview', *Studio International*, vol. 192, no. 984, November/December, 256–66.

—(1999) *Experimental Music: Cage and Beyond*, Cambridge: Cambridge University Press.

Oliva, A. B. (1990) *Ubu fluxus ibi motus 1990–1962*, Milan: Mazzotta.

Oliveros, P. (1984) *Software for People: Collected Writings 1963–80*, Baltimore: Smith Publications.

—(1998) *Roots of the Moment*, New York: Drogue Press.

—(2005) *Deep Listening: A Composer's Sound Practice*, Lincoln: iUniverse.

—(2010) 'Mission Statement', *Deep Listening Institute*, http://deeplistening. org/site/content/about [accessed 8 June 2010].

Ono, Y. (2000) *Grapefruit*, New York: Simon & Schuster.

Osborne, P. (2002) *Conceptual Art*, London and New York: Phaidon.

Palestine, C. (2003) *Sacred Bordello*, London: Black Dog Publishing.

Palmer, F. R. (1990) *Modality and the English Modals*, Harlow: Longman.

Parsons, M. (1976) 'Systems in Art and Music', *The Musical Times*, vol. 117, no. 1604, October, 815–18.

Partridge, E. (1975) Usage and Abusage, Harmondsworth: Penguin.

Peirce Edition Project (ed.) (1998) *The Essential Peirce: Selected Philosophical Writings.Vol. 2 (1893–1913)*, Bloomington and Indianapolis: Indiana University Press.

Pisaro, M. (2009) 'Wandelweiser', http://erstwords.blogspot.com/2009/09/ wandelweiser.html [accessed 28 October 2010].

Politi, G. (1992) 'George Brecht: sure, we had reasons, but we had no goals', in *Flash Art*, no. 167, November/December, 58.

Potter, K. (1981) 'Just the tip of the iceberg: Some aspects of Gavin Bryars' music', *Contact*, no. 22, Summer, 4–15.

—(2000) *Four Musical Minimalists*, Cambridge: Cambridge University Press.

Prévost, E. (ed.) (2006) *Cornelius Cardew: A Reader*, Harlow: Copula.

Reich, S. (1974) *Writings about Music*, Halifax, Canada: The Press of the Nova Scotia College of Art and Design/New York: New York University Press.

—(2002) *Writings on Music*, Oxford: Oxford University Press.

Ritzel, F. (1970) 'Musik für ein Haus', in *Darmstädter Beiträge zur Neuen Musik*, Mainz: Schott.

Robinson, J. (2009) 'From Abstraction to Model: George Brecht's Events and the Conceptual Turn in Art of the 1960s', in *October*, no. 127, Winter, 77–108.

Robinson, J. and Fischer, A. M. (eds) (2005) *George Brecht: A Heterospective*, Cologne: Walther Koenig.

Rzewski, F. (2007) *Nonsequiturs: Writings and Lectures on Improvisation, Composition and Interpretation*, Oehlschlägel, R. and Gronemeyer, G. (eds) Cologne: MusikTexte.

Satie, E. (1997) *A Mammal's Notebook: Collected Writings of Erik Satie*, Melville, A. and Volta, O. (eds) London: Atlas Press.

Saunders, J. (ed.) (2009) *The Ashgate Research Companion to Experimental Music*, Aldershot: Ashgate.

Scollon, R. and Scollon, S.W. (1995) *Intercultural Communication*, Oxford: Blackwell.

Simpson, P. (2004) *Stylistics: A Resource Book for Students*, London: Routledge.

Sinclair, J. (ed.) (2005) *Collins Cobuild English Grammar*, Glasgow: HarperCollins.

Smith, D. (1977), 'Following a Straight Line: La Monte Young', *Contact*, no. 18, Winter, 4–9.

Stevens, J. (2007) *Search and Reflect*, London: Rockschool.

Steward, H. (1997) *The Ontology of Mind*, Oxford: Oxford University Press.

Stiles, K. and Selz, P. (1996) *Theories and Documents of Contemporary Art: A Sourcebook of Artists' Writings*, Berkeley: University of California Press.

Stockhausen, K. (1969/1993) 'AUS DEN SIEBEN TAGEN (FROM THE SEVEN DAYS)', in *AUS DEN SIEBEN TAGEN/FROM THE SEVEN DAYS* Intuitive Music, Stockhausen Complete Edition CD14, pp. 10–17.

—(1971) 'Questions and Answers on Intuitive Music', in *AUS DEN SIEBEN TAGEN/FROM THE SEVEN DAYS* Intuitive Music, Stockhausen Complete Edition CD14, pp. 74–102. Also online at http://www.stock-hausen.org/intuitive_music.html [accessed 2 September 2010].

—(1973) 'RICHTIGE DAUERN (RIGHT DURATIONS)', in *AUS DEN SIEBEN TAGEN/FROM THE SEVEN DAYS* Intuitive Music, Stockhausen Complete Edition CD14, pp. 30–3.

—(1989) *Towards a Cosmic Music*, Longmead: Element Books.

—(2000) *Stockhausen on Music*, London and New York: Marion Boyars Publishers.

Tilbury, J. (2008) *Cornelius Cardew: A Life Unfinished*, Harlow: Copula.

Tiravanija, R. (2009) 'In Another Country: Yoko Ono in Conversation with Rirkrit Tiravanija', *Artforum*, Summer, 281–4.

Touchon, C. (ed.) (2008) *Natural Born Fluxus*, Fort Worth: Ontological Museum Publications.

Tufte, E. R. (1990) *Envisioning Information*, Cheshire, Connecticut: The Graphics Press.

—(2001) *The Visual Display of Quantitative Information*, Cheshire, Connecticut: The Graphics Press.

—(2006) *Beautiful Evidence*, Cheshire, Connecticut: The Graphics Press.

Ungerer, F. and Schmid, H-J. (2006) *An Introduction to Cognitive Linguistics*, Harlow: Pearson.

Ushenko, A. P. (1958) *The Field Theory of Meaning*, Ann Arbor: The University of Michigan Press.

Wales, K. (2001) *A Dictionary of Stylistics*, Harlow: Pearson.

Wittgenstein, L. (2001) *Tractatus Logico-Philosophicus*, London and New York: Routledge.

Wolff, C. (1998) *Cues: Writings & Conversations*, Oehlschlägel, R. and Gronemeyer, G. (eds), Cologne: MusikTexte.

Wydick, R. C. (2005) *Plain English for Lawyers*, Durham: Carolina Academic Press.

Yoshimoto, M. (2005) *Into Performance: Japanese Women Artists in New York*, New Brunswick: Rutgers University Press.

Young, L. (ed.) (1963) *An Anthology of Chance Operations*, New York: La Monte Young & Jackson MacLow.

—(1965) 'Lecture 1960', *Tulane Drama Review*, vol. 10, no. 2, Winter, MIT, 73–83.

—(2001) 'Compositions 1960', *Diapason*, http://www.diapasongallery.org/archive/01_06_20.html [accessed 5 October 2010].

Young, L. and Zazeela, M. (1969) *Selected Writings,* Munich: Heiner Friedrich.

—(2003) 'La Monte Young and Marian Zazeela at the Dream House', *New Music Box,* http://newmusicbox.org/page.nmbx?id=54fp19 [accessed 5 October 2010].

Zevi, A. (ed.) (1995) *Sol LeWitt: Critical Texts*, Rome: I Libri di AEIOU and Incontri Internazionali d'Arte.

Index

Numbers in bold represent main sections in text; numbers in italics represent illustrations.

Lightning Source UK Ltd.
Milton Keynes UK
UKOW07f0403250517
301979UK00007B/137/P